# DANGEROUS AQUATIC ANIMALS OF THE WORLD

## A COLOR ATLAS

Australian blue-ringed octopus, *Octopus maculosus* Hoyle.

# DANGEROUS AQUATIC ANIMALS OF THE WORLD

## A COLOR ATLAS

By

### BRUCE W. HALSTEAD, M.D.

Director
International Biotoxicological Centre
World Life Research Institute
Colton, California

**WITH PREVENTION, FIRST AID, AND EMERGENCY TREATMENT PROCEDURES**
(in collaboration with Paul S. Auerbach, M.D.)

THE DARWIN PRESS, INC.
PRINCETON, NEW JERSEY USA

 Mosby Year Book

MOSBY-YEAR BOOK, INC.
ST. LOUIS, MISSOURI

Copyright © 1992 by Bruce W. Halstead

**Library of Congress Cataloging-in-Publication Data:**

Halstead, Bruce W.
    Dangerous aquatic animals of the world: a color atlas: with prevention, first aid, and emergency treatment procedures / by Bruce W. Halstead, in collaboration with Paul S. Auerbach.
        p.        cm.
    Includes bibliographical references.
    ISBN 0–87850–045–6
  1. Dangerous aquatic animals.    2. Dangerous aquatic animals—
—Pictorial works.    I. Auerbach, Paul S.    II. Title.
QL100.H297     1991
591.6′5′0916—dc20
                                    91–13746
                                       CIP

*Front Cover:* Great white shark, *Carcharodon carcharias* (Courtesy R. and V. Taylor)
*Back Cover:* Nocturnal jellyfish, *Pelagia noctiluca* (Courtesy C. Arenson)

*Book and cover design:* John T. Westlake, Darwin Productions

The paper in this book is acid-free neutral pH stock and meets the guidelines for permanence and durability of the Committee on Production Guidelines for Book Longevity of the Council on Library Resources. ∞

Printed in Singapore through Palace Press, San Diego

Published by
The Darwin Press, Inc.
P.O. Box 2202
Princeton, NJ 08543 USA

Mosby
Year Book
Dedicated to Publishing Excellence

To my beloved
TERRI LEE,
my loving wife
and constant
source of inspiration

# CONTENTS

# FOREWORD

Jean-Michel Cousteau
The Cousteau Society

AS I REFLECT on the subject of dangerous marine animals, I remember those situations in which I felt most threatened in the sea. Was it on Maupiti Island, in the Society Islands, while drift-diving in a narrow channel, meeting more than twenty gray reef sharks, each over seven feet in length, notorious man-biters when they feel their space is invaded? Was it while diving in the Mediterranean in a region where deadly weaverfish have attacked divers with their dorsal spines? Was it in the waters of Papua New Guinea when a highly venomous sea snake fearlessly approached me? Was it in a Roatan Island cave in the Caribbean, when I rounded a corner and came face to face with the toothy grin of a large green moray? Was it on the wreck of the *Rhone*, in the British Virgin Islands, while feeding fish when a five-foot barracuda made a lightning-quick attack through the school of fish surrounding me to grab a morsel of food (which could just as easily been my hand)? Was it on the Island of Wuvulu, in Papua New Guinea, when I disturbed a large group of stingrays resting in a cave, causing them to stampede, and in the process risked being envenomated in the chaos of stirred up sediment and panicked fish? Was it during numerous other excursions to the South Pacific when I swam near a blue-ringed octopus and among stinging Portuguese Man-of-Wars, or when I was attacked by small biting isopods on a night dive, or bumped into fire coral?

Honestly, none of these seemingly dramatic encounters with marine animals has taken up much of my thoughts. There is one animal, however, more than all those mentioned previously, that has consumed my attention. I know my father shares my feelings on this subject. "What is it," you might ask, "that the Cousteaus

worry about most in the sea?" The answer is sea urchins, those long-spined urchins of the genus *Diadema*. They lurk in crevices, stand guard over coral heads, and form marauding battalions on sandy bottoms. At night they emerge en masse, making the reef a living porcupine. On night dives, I focus my attention on the position of each part of my body in relation to ledges above, surrounding coral heads, and the bottom below. A miscalculation brings instant, stabbing pain, which builds for a few minutes then maintains itself at a constant level for at least twenty minutes. During this time, I can think of little else, and want to leave the water, to get away from the ache. But I know I will feel no better aboard *Calypso*. There is no escape; I must simply wait and endure. Each such mistake makes me more apprehensive of the inevitable next one.

For me, the most commonly encountered dangerous marine animal is the sea urchin. However, if I included *all* animals, the *most dangerous* would be *humans*. No other single species has eliminated others as we have. No other species has contaminated the waters with its waste as we have. If any animal species deserves condemnation for being the most harmful to its neighbors, it is clearly *Homo sapiens*. What amazes me is that we have the power of conscious thought and rational decision-making, and, yet, as a species, we cannot see that we are dependent on our surroundings for our own survival and well-being. And since we have the ability to make choices, it is by now clear that we must choose to protect and wisely manage our seas, which are vital to our survival and the survival of all life on earth. *We* cannot afford to be the most dangerous animal in the sea.

In light of the "Jaws" hysteria, I am relieved to see the publication of this book, *Dangerous Aquatic Animals of the World: A Color Atlas*, and am pleased that Dr. Bruce W. Halstead has been able to bring together the many diverse aspects of this fascinating subject. The scope of the book reflects the breadth of his knowledge. I cannot think of a person who has more experience in the field or can speak with more authority on dangerous, poisonous, and venomous marine animals. It is refreshing to see that such an emotionally charged subject can be discussed in an interesting yet rational manner.

The marine animals under discussion here are not bad or evil. Their offensive and defensive teeth, stings, venoms, and other toxins are designed to be dangerous. With an understanding of this fact, we can proceed to observe, study, and even enjoy these ingenious adaptations. *Our ignorance is the greatest danger in the sea.* Dr. Halstead has made a major contribution toward eliminating ignorance about some of the most fascinating animals in the sea, and, by doing so, has enabled all of us who venture on and in the sea to have a safer and more enjoyable experience.

January 6, 1991

# ACKNOWLEDGEMENTS

THIS BOOK IS an outgrowth and in one sense an aquatic expansion of my previous monograph, *Poisonous and Venomous Marine Animals of the World*, the latest edition of which was published by the Darwin Press, 1988. Much of the work associated with this present volume has been previously and gratefully acknowledged in my 1988 edition of that monograph and will not be detailed in this present volume. However, an additional number of individuals have played a major role as contributors to this present work and they will be duly noted.

After having participated in the Cousteau Society's Project Ocean Search and other activities at sporadic intervals over the past 18 years in New Guinea, Wuvulu, the Bismarck Archipelago, Hermit Islands, Ningo Islands, French Polynesia, the Amazon jungle, and the British Virgin Islands, and having watched my comrades in misery under the most uninviting circumstances, I decided that it was about time we share some printer's ink; hence, the debut of Jean-Michel Cousteau and his able Vice President of Science and Education, Dr. Richard Murphy, who have enriched this book with some of their penmanship. Richard Murphy is also an excellent underwater photographer, and I am delighted to be able to share some of his artistic accomplishments in this book. Thanks are also due Jean-Michel's delightful wife, Anne-Marie, who is not only an excellent photographer but an accomplished explorer in her own right. She and the Cousteau Society at large have assisted me in ways too numerous to detail. It is without any hesitancy and a great deal of gratitude that I admit I am in their debt.

This book has been greatly enhanced with the photographic and artistic contributions of a number of individuals (listed in alphabetic order)—B. Allison, R. A. Ames, C. Arenson, S. Arita, P. S. Auerbach, H. R. Axelrod, H. Baerg, J. H. Barnes, A. J. Bass, E. Bavendam, S. H. Bayer, I. Bennet, L. Béress, S. S. Berry,* R. Boolootian, J. Booth, A. B. Bowker, T. W. Brown, W. Burgess, R. Catala, E. Christian, R. Church, E. Clark, G. Coates, H. Cogger, N. Coleman, P. L. Colin, B. Dale, W. E. Duellman, I. W. Flye, K. Fogassy, S. Frier, S. K. Galloway, P. Giacomelli, A. Giddings, K. Gillett, D. W. Gotshall, S. H. Gruber, H. Hall, G. M. Hallegraeff, P. A. Hansen, H. Heatwole, R. Hildebrand, H. Hobard, M. Holmes, L. Hood, P. Humann, D. Irons, T. Iwago, W. L. Klawe, R. H. Knabenbauer, R. Kreuzinger, T. Kumada,* R. Kuntz,* C. E. Lane, D. J. Lee, A. R. Loeblich III, L. A. Loeblich, G. Lower, D. Ludwig, B. Magrath, R. M. Mandojana, B. J. Marlow, D. Masry, E. J. Martin, J. McCosker, C. Micklin, C. W. Meyer, K. F. Meyer,* D. Miller, S. A. Minton, D. Mooney, G. Mote, P. Mote, M. Murray, J. F. Myers, R. F. Myers, D. Nelson, R. L. O'Neal, D. Ollis, D. Perrine, E. Pope,* A. Powers, J. E. Randall, H. A. Reid,* E. Robinson, C. Roessler, E. S. Ross, G. D. Ruggieri,* E. T. Rulison, F. E. Russell, R. Russo, P. Saunders, M. S. Schlatter, R. C. Schoening, M. Shirao,* J. B. Siebenaler, M. Snyderman, H. Sommer,* K. Steidinger, R. Straughan,* J. Tashjian, R. Taylor, V. Taylor, K. Tomita, J. E. Wapstra, H. Waterman, G. J. W. Webb, D. Wobber, D. Woodward, and

* Deceased

XI

J. Zwick—and to the following organizations: American Museum of Natural History, Aquarium de Noumea, Australian Museum, California Academy of Sciences, Conservation Commission of the North American Territory of Australia, CSIRO Marine Laboratories (Tasmania), Food and Agriculture Organization of the United Nations (FAO), George Williams Hooper Foundation (University of California—San Francisco), Gulfarium, Miami Seaquarium, National Aquarium, New York Zoological Society, Ocean Images, Oceanographic Research Institute of South Africa, Osborn Zoological Laboratory, Scripps Institution of Oceanography, Sea World, T. F. H. Publications, Underwater Photographic Society, Museum of Natural History, University of Kansas, University of Kiel, University of Miami, University of Sydney, Vancouver Public Aquarium, Woods Hole Oceanographic Institution, Yale University, and the Zoological Station of Naples. Special thanks are due the staff of Media Services, Loma Linda University, for their numerous professional services, which were graciously rendered; and my daughter Shari, for her assistance. To all I am most grateful for their contributions to this book.

I wish to take this opportunity to thank Jerry Block and his wife, Jeanne, and to Richard Marconi for their generous financial support, which helped to make this book possible.

Judd Iverson provided a unique set of circumstances that also assisted greatly in bringing this book into reality.

The difficult and time-consuming effort of typing and checking over much of the page proof was the hard work of my former secretary and a great lady, Jennine M. Vinci. Thanks Jennine.

Last, but not least, is my undying gratitude to Ed Breisacher and his excellent colleagues—John T. Westlake, Albert McGrigor, and Kathleen Waters—of the Darwin Press. I feel that I have been especially blessed in being able to work with a publishing company of such high caliber.

BRUCE W. HALSTEAD
Colton, California    1991

# INTRODUCTION

THE MERE TITLE of "Dangerous Aquatic Animals of the World" tends to excite one's imagination. The reader is led to believe that dangerous biting, stinging, or electrifying beasts are to be found lurking in every dark hole or crevice in the aquatic world, waiting to attack a human. But after having spent over 40 years in quest of these often elusive and frequently magnificent creatures, I would be the first to witness that such is not the case.

After writing five heavily-documented large books of more than 1,000 pages per volume on *Poisonous and Venomous Marine Animals of the World* (1965, 1967, 1970, 1978, 1988) and three on *Dangerous Marine Animals* (1958, 1980, 1990), I came to realize that these creatures are not only magnificent to behold in their native environment but possess some amazing characteristics that should be appreciated by professionals and laymen alike. Thus, this *Color Atlas* was born.

One objective of this book is to depict the environment in which these remarkable creatures live. No attempt has been made in this book to provide a documented account of these creatures, but rather to present a pictorial guide to their identifying features and environmental niches. Extensive documentation can be found elsewhere.

The quest for dangerous aquatic organisms has literally taken me to every corner of the globe, to more than 150 countries and the islands of the seas of the world. This quest has been challenging, frustrating, exhilarating, depressing, and at times more stimulating than I had bargained for, but always rewarding.

An examination of a world map reveals that the center of the world of dangerous aquatic animals is to be found within the great Indo-Pacific faunal belt. Vast tropical reefs offer a submarine panorama that seems to vibrate and sparkle with a never-ending array of colors, at times in conflict with each other, but yet with an overall pervading harmony. In multiplied instances, beauty of form, gracefulness of carriage, lavishness of color, all seem to go hand in hand with disease and death. This is indeed one of the great paradoxes of the aquatic world.

The subject of sharks always conjures up fearsome, giant, toothy creatures ready to devour some hapless victim. Although some of these elements have a basis in fact, there is another aspect to these fishes that is deserving of greater attention. One has merely to observe a shark in movement to become awed by its power and almost effortless ability to glide through the water. If one examines their food-detection ability and sonic apparatus, sharks become very impressive creatures indeed and are certainly worthy of our respect and admiration. The shark immune system is even more astonishing. Sharks play an important ecological role in the aquatic environment and are deserving of conservation.

Stories about sharks and shark attacks date back to antiquity, but authoritative data on the subject have appeared in technical journals only within the recent past. Much of our knowledge of sharks and their behavior is a by-product of military interest in this subject. Through the combined efforts of the U.S. Office of Scientific Research and Development, the U.S. Navy, Army, and Air Force, the National Research Council, the Smithsonian Institution, and various civilian organizations, a fair amount of information is now available on sharks.

An international committee known as the Shark Research

Panel was first assembled in April 1958 in New Orleans, Louisiana, by the American Institute of Biological Sciences. The purpose of this committee was to formulate tentative recommendations for a broad scientific program dealing with the shark hazard problem, under the capable chairmanship of Perry A. Gilbert. The committee originally consisted of Lester R. Aronson, Bruce W. Halstead, Carl L. Hubbs, Arthur W. Martin, Leonard P. Schultz, J. L. B. Smith, Stewart Springer, Tohru Uchida, F. G. Wood, Jr., and Gilbert P. Whitley. A group of thirty-four scientists internationally recognized for their knowledge of sharks participated in the original conference.

One of the significant outgrowths of this conference was the ultimate establishment of the Worldwide Shark Attack File. Initially the Shark Attack File was housed at the Smithsonian Institution under the direct supervision of Leonard P. Schultz. Later it was moved to the Mote Marine Laboratory in Sarasota, Florida. Gilbert served as chairman of the Shark Research Panel during the almost twelve years of its existence. The Shark Attack File contained data on a series of 1,165 case histories covering the years 1941 through 1968, and was ultimately expanded to include 1,652 cases. Final analysis of the Shark Attack File was done by a group of statisticians and programmers of the U.S. Navy's Bureau of Medicine and Surgery, and the final publication appeared as a Special Technical Report (Contract No. N00014-73-C-0252), dated October 31, 1973, under the authorship of H. David Baldridge, entitled *Shark Attack Against Man*. A popularized paperback version of Baldridge's work, entitled *Shark Attack*, was published later in 1974.

Much of our knowledge of sharks and their attacks on humans are based on data from this file. In recent years, there has been a renewed interest in the study of shark repellents. Some of these repellents are the products of research in behavioral toxicity and employ various natural products derived from the sea itself (see *Shark Repellents From the Sea*, AAAS Selected Symposium 83, 1983). Interestingly enough, one of the substances being investigated is a crinotoxic secretion produced by the Moses sole, *Pardachirus marmoratus*, which lives in the Red Sea. (Further details on sharks and other biting creatures are discussed in Chapter II.)

In a very real sense, tropical reefs are areas in a state of constant biological and chemical warfare. Territorial rights among sponges, corals, echinoderms, and other organisms are often established by means of repugnatorial or defensive chemical substances known as allelochemicals, which in many ways exert an antibiotic effect on a grand scale, repelling and limiting the growth and expansion of other organisms. This is a facet of organic chemistry that promises to open up whole new horizons of knowledge. There are numerous substances having direct application to human medicine and offering new approaches to antimicrobial and antitumor therapies—an area of chemistry yet only poorly explored.

The world of aquatic chemistry, although only barely scratched, has nevertheless spawned what might be considered subsciences: *aquatic biotoxicology*, the science that deals with aquatic biological poisons, and *marine pharmacognosy*, the science that deals with crude substances in their natural state, derived from marine plants and animals.

*Aquatic Biotoxicology.* Since much of this *Color Atlas* deals with the subject of poisonous and venomous aquatic creatures, perhaps it would be best at this juncture to present an outline of the various types of toxic aquatic organisms. This classification takes into account some of the phylogenetic relationships of the organisms involved and the nature of the poisons that they purvey. In order to provide a better understanding of the nature of these poisons, a few basic definitions will also be given. A more complete glossary of these technical terms appears at the end of this book.

## CLASSIFICATION OF TOXIC AQUATIC ANIMALS
### INVERTEBRATES

This classification includes all of the toxic animals without a backbone. Toxic aquatic invertebrates can be conveniently divided into the following groups or phyla:

I. PROTISTA (PROTOZOA)—Planktonic plant animals
   This includes the planktonic one-celled organisms encountered by humans as a result of eating mollusks or fish that have fed on toxic dinoflagellates.

II. PORIFERA
   Some sponges produce chemical substances that are highly irritating to the skin, causing a severe dermatitis.

III. CNIDARIA (COELENTERATA)

There are a few species of coelenterates that are poisonous to eat (sea anemones and zoanthids), but the majority of them are venomous.

Class HYDROZOA—the hydroids
Class SCYPHOZOA—the jellyfishes
Class ANTHOZOA—the sea anemones, zoanthids, corals

IV. ECHINODERMATA—Starfishes, sea urchins, sea cucumbers

Poisonous echinoderms are limited to certain species of sea urchins having toxic eggs and to sea cucumbers. Venomous species include the spiny Crown-O-Thorns starfish and a large number of sea urchins equipped with venomous spines and pedicellariae.

V. MOLLUSCA

Although numerous bivalve mollusks are known as transvectors of paralytic shellfish poisoning and other types of intoxicants, some of the toxic species are also of public health concern because of their venom organs. Included in this latter group are the venomous cone shells and octopuses.

VI. PLATYHELMINTHES—Flatworms

Some species of flatworms (turbellarians) are believed to be poisonous to eat.

VII. RHYNCHOCOELA—Ribbon worms

Some nemertean or ribbon worms are known to possess a fully developed venom apparatus.

VIII. ANNELIDA

Some of the polychaete worms possess numerous bristle-like setae or spines and can inflict an intense dermatitis. Certain polychaete worms possess powerful chitinous jaws which, in *Glycera*, are associated with venom glands.

IX. ARTHROPODA—Joint-legged animals, Asiatic horseshoe crabs, tropical reef crabs, and freshwater true bugs (Hemiptera).

Some species of Asiatic horseshoe crabs and tropical reef crabs may be poisonous to eat. There are only a few toxic aquatic insect species, and these are found largely in five families of true bugs that inhabit freshwater.

*VERTEBRATES*

This group includes all of the animals having a backbone. The largest single category of toxic aquatic animals are the fishes, which can be classified as follows:

I. POISONOUS FISHES

Fishes when ingested cause human biotoxication due to a toxic substance present in the fish. This group does not include fishes that may become accidentally contaminated by bacterial food pathogens.

A. ICHTHYOSARCOTOXIC FISHES. These contain a poison within the flesh (i.e., in the broadest sense), musculature, viscera, skin, or slime, which when ingested by humans will produce biotoxication. The toxins are oral poisons believed to be small molecular structures not usually destroyed by heat or gastric juices. These can be divided into three classes:

Class AGNATHA: Lampreys and hagfishes—causing cyclostome poisoning.

Class CHONDRICHTHYES: Sharks rays, chimaeras—causing elasmobranch poisoning as a result of eating their flesh or viscera.

Class OSTEICHTHYES: The true bony fishes.

*Ciguatoxic fishes.* About 400 species of marine tropical reef fishes have been incriminated in human intoxications. Only a few representative species are shown in this *Color Atlas.* The poisons are complex nerve poisons.

*Clupeotoxic fishes.* This group includes some of the herrings, anchovies, and possibly other related species. Apparently the poison is obtained from eating planktonic organisms and resembles paralytic shellfish poison.

*Gempylotoxic fishes.* This group includes the gemphylid fishes, otherwise known as the escolars, or pelagic mackerels. They contain an oil that has a very pronounced purgative effect.

*Scombrotoxic fishes.* This group involves intoxications resulting from the eating of inadequately preserved scombroid fishes, i.e., tunas, skipjack, mackerels, albacore, and related species. The poison develops in the flesh of the fish due to bacterial activity in the musculature.

*Hallucinogenic fishes.* This form of poisoning is caused by eating certain types of tropical reef fishes and produces hallucinations. No fatalities have been reported.

*Tetrodotoxic fishes.* This group includes the puffer fish and is commonly known as puffer poisoning. This is one of the most violent forms of fish poisoning and carries a high mortality rate.

*Ichthyootoxic fishes.* Many fish, mostly freshwater species and a few marine species, develop a poison within their gonads, particularly during the reproductive period of the year, just before spawning. This is sometimes referred to as fish roe poisoning. There is a definite relationship between gonadal activity and toxin production.

*Ichthyohemotoxic fishes.* This group includes fishes having poisonous blood. Intoxications are quite rare because the poison is destroyed by gastric juices and heat.

B. ICHTHYOCRINOTOXIC FISHES. This second major category of toxic fishes includes species that release a poison through their skin by means of specialized secretory organs. This includes the soapfish, trunkfishes, and others.

C. VENOMOUS FISHES. This third category includes a wide range of fish species having specialized secretory organs and a wound-producing device such as a spine or tooth.

## II.   POISONOUS AMPHIBIANS

Some amphibians produce extremely violent poisons:
1. Toxic toads and tree frogs
2. Toxic salamanders

## III.   POISONOUS REPTILES

Some marine turtles and aquatic snakes are toxic:

1. Poisonous marine turtles. Some species of marine turtles are believed to become poisonous because of feeding on toxic marine plants. The exact source of the poison is unknown.

2. Venomous aquatic snakes. The sea snakes are the most abundant of reptiles, and some species contain very potent venoms. There are also the freshwater moccasin, jararacussu, and water cobra.

## IV.   POISONOUS MARINE MAMMALS

The livers of some whales, polar bears, walruses, seals, and sea lions may be toxic to eat.

This brief classification of poisonous aquatic animals reveals a vast range of animal species living in a great diversity of geographical areas and habitats. A brief clarification of the language of biological poisons follows, since the terminology used in dealing with toxic organisms is sometimes confusing.

*Biotoxicology,* the science of plant and animal poisons, is concerned with a vast number of toxic chemical substances, many of which remain to be characterized. Biotoxins are of two major types: *phytotoxins,* or plant poisons, and *zootoxins,* or animal poisons. Biotoxins can be classified in a variety of ways according to one's approach to the subject. This *Color Atlas* does not deal with poisonous plants.

*Zootoxins,* or animal poisons, can be further subdivided into the *oral poisons* and those that are administered by means of a venom apparatus, known as the *parenteral poisons.* The administration of venoms entails mechanical trauma, whereas other types of poisoning do not. The term "poisonous" may be used in the generic sense, referring to both oral and parenteral poisons; however, it is more commonly used in the specific sense to designate oral poisons. Thus, *all venoms are poisons, but not all poisons are venoms.* Oral aquatic biotoxins are generally thought to be small molecular substances, whereas most venoms are believed to be large molecular substances, a protein, or in close association with one. A third general type of marine biotoxin, referred to as *crinotoxins*, are poisons produced by specialized glands, but they are not accompanied by a venom-purveying structure. Crinotoxins are found in flatworms, nemerteans, and fishes. The crinotoxin is generally released into the adjacent environment by means of pores, in a manner somewhat comparable to the action of sweat glands. For the most part, little is known about the nature of these poisons. Additional definitions appear in the glossary at the end of the book.

Little is known of the biological significance of biotoxins. However, biotoxins appear to serve as defensive or offensive mechanisms to ward off enemies, in food procurement, or they may be accidentally contracted in the food chain of the organism. This is an area of ecological research that only now is beginning to receive attention.

Even a cursory view of these toxic creatures is bound to raise the question, what is the nature of these poisons? How and why did they come about? And, of what practical value are they?

The amazing thing about some of these oral intoxicants is how a microscopic animal (sometimes classified as a plant by botanists) can take simple atoms of carbon, hydrogen, oxygen, and nitrogen and produce a complex of some of the world's most violent poisons. Some of these poisons are so complex in structure that they have exhausted the capabilities of our best chemical minds and challenged the mettle of our finest analytical instruments. The how and why are questions that are difficult to answer. Perhaps scientists will never know for a certainty. From a speculative viewpoint, it is believed that some of these poisons are used as defensive weapons, whereas, in other instances, some of the enemies of these toxic organisms do not appear to be affected. The biogenesis of these poisons, how they are produced by the organism, is unknown and continues to frustrate the biotoxicologist.

One exciting aspect of the subject of aquatic poisons is their potential for therapeutic application in human disease. The science that deals with this subject is known as marine pharmacognosy.

*Marine pharmacognosy* is that science that deals with the knowledge of crude drug substances, in their natural states, derived from marine plants and animals. Natural products derived from these organisms comprise a great variety of chemical substances having useful properties with potential therapeutic application. These substances include such classical materials as carrageenan, alginates, ichthamol, agar, cod liver oil, protamine sulfate, spermaceti, and many others. However, more recent investigations have uncovered infinitely more complex and unique biodynamic molecules having antimicrobial, antiviral, antihelminthic, anticoagulant, antispasmodic, antitumor, anti-inflamatory, immunomodulator, antihypertensive, antidepressant, antiedema, antianaphylaxis, necrotic, hemolytic, radioprotective, muscle relaxant, bronchodilator, aspirin-like effects, and so on. Despite this enormous assemblage of valuable pharmacological information, it is estimated that less than one percent of the drugs currently in use in medicine are of marine origin.

The therapeutic potential of the sea can best be appreciated by examining the marine environment. The earth's total water supply is about 326 million cubic miles, 97 percent of which is sea water. The oceans of the world cover 71 percent of the earth's surface. Much of the solar energy received by the ocean is utilized by minute plants living in the upper twenty-five fathoms that manufacture a host of organic chemical agents. About seventy biochemical steps are required to convert light into energy usable by the organism by means of the process of photosynthesis. Atoms of carbon, hydrogen, oxygen, nitrogen, and a variety of metals are biosynthesized into a remarkable array of extremely complex substances, most of which possess biological activity. These "seaweeds" take many forms and serve as the primary food source of the sea. It is estimated that this vegetable matter annually amounts to 4,000 tons per square mile. Marine plants produce about 85 percent of the food produced by all plants on earth. Feeding upon this vegetable matter, either directly or indirectly, are myriads of marine animals. In the study of marine biotoxins it has been shown that potent biochemical agents may originate at lower trophic levels (e.g., algae) within the food web and eventually make their way through a sequence of organisms involving plants, invertebrates, fishes, and even mammals.

In some instances, these biochemicals may be modified, whereas in others they appear to be stored within the tissues of the organism apparently without undergoing any change. Thus, carnivorous fishes feeding at the upper trophic levels are literally a biochemical product of their predecessors. An interesting example of this biochemical succession is found in the case of ciguatoxin, which appears to be capable of passing from plant to invertebrate and on to a variety of fishes. This phenomenon presents certain opportunities for those searching for biodynamic substances because organisms at one level may serve as concentrators of substances derived from a lower trophic level.

Marine drugs have been of commercial importance since the days of Emperor Fu Hsi (2953-2858 B.C.) of ancient China. (Incidentally, in China, the fish is a symbol of regeneration.) Drugs of marine origin are listed in the *Great Herbal of China,* or the *Shen Nung Pen Ts'ao Ching* (ca. A.D. 200), and the *Chinese Materia Medica of Fish Drugs* of the Tang Dynasty (ca. A.D. 618). A more modern rendition of the *Chinese Materia Medica of Fish Drugs* was translated into English in 1936 by Bernard E. Read of the Henry Lester Institute of Medical Research in Shanghai. At the present time, the People's Republic of China publishes the only scientific journal in the world dealing with the subject of marine pharmacognosy, appropriately entitled *Journal of Marine Drugs,* published by the Shangdong Institute of Marine Materia

Medica, Qingdao. Crude marine drugs continue to be sold in modern times throughout the Orient; most of these products are based on these ancient writings. China is said to have more than 1,000 marine therapeutic products.

In Russia, there is currently active exploration in the field of marine pharmaceuticals taking place at the institute of Marine Biology, Far-East Scientific Centre, and the Institute of Biologically Active Substances, The Academy of Sciences in Vladivostok.

American pharmaceutical companies (Groton Bio Industries, Abbott Laboratories, SmithKline and French, Schering, Upjohn, Pfizer, Merck, Hazelton Laboratories, Lederle, and others) have demonstrated short bursts of pharmaceutical energy and sporadic sorties in the field of marine pharmacognosy, but not much of a sustained effort.

Considerable interest in marine pharmaceuticals has been generated in the United States largely by means of the stimulus supplied by the "Drugs From the Sea" symposia sponsored by the Marine Technology Society. Four such symposia have been conducted thus far: in 1967, 1969, 1972, and 1974. All have been well attended by scientists from governments, industry, universities, and research institutions. Unfortunately, most American marine pharmacognostic efforts have died, along with many other oceanographic efforts, in the committees of the White House and the United States Congress.

The most intensive single effort by a commercial pharmaceutical company in marine pharmacology was once made by Hofman-LaRoche Company in Australia, where it established the Roche Research Institute of Marine Pharmacology at Dee Why, N.S.W., Australia. The Institute operated for only seven years (1974–81). During this period, an extensive investigation was launched by a highly-skilled, multidisciplinary group of scientists. The result was a variety of new and exciting products, including a muscle relaxant from the sponge *Tedania digitata,* a bronchodilator from a new species of sponge, a potential antidepressant from the sponge *Aplysinopsis reticulata*, an anti-inflammatory from the blue-green alga *Rivularia firma*, and prostaglandins from the red alga *Gracilaria edulis*. The active principle from *Tedania* proved to be a novel nucleoside, 1-methylisoguanocine. This substance was found to be not only a muscle relaxant, but also had antihypertensive and anti-inflammatory properties as well. The wide-spectrum activities of this compound led to the idea that it might be a chemical modulator in the body. This finding drew attention to other novel and important molecules with potential application to the treatment of leukemia, respiratory disease, and behavior modification. Unfortunately, at the very peak of these exciting discoveries, the entire project was scrapped and the research team dissolved because of a lack of funding.

On a national scale, probably some of the most intensive and widespread research is presently going on in a large number of universities and research institutions in Japan. Perhaps one of the more significant products from this research is that of fugu or puffer poison, chemically known as tetrodotoxin. This is one of nature's most potent poisons. The poison is not only used in Japan as an analgesic and in the treatment of a number of disorders including arthritis, headaches, and pain control in terminal cancer, but is used also as a muscle relaxant in disorders where convulsions are dominant. Tetrodotoxin has been studied extensively as a neurophysiological probe in order to better understand the workings of the human nervous system.

Few fields offer greater scientific and economic potential than that of marine pharmacognosy, and few offer greater promise in providing solutions to a greater array of mankind's most serious diseases. However, few fields are faced with greater technical, economic, and bureaucratic hurdles. What is the ultimate answer? Probably Japan offers the greatest hope because of its integrated approach in dealing with matters of national import. Japan has already given priority to research in the fields of health and pharmaceuticals. Moreover, the government, banking industry, commercial companies, and the academic community have learned to work together as a single force. In view of its historical position as a progressive, research-oriented maritime nation, it is anticipated that Japan will ultimately produce a greater economic harvest from marine pharmacognosy than any other nation on earth, with the single possible exception of China.

* * *

Why study poisonous aquatic organisms? Part of the question has been answered—as a source of new therapeutic agents. Another answer deals with the role of aquatic animal poisons as they constitute a public health hazard. Aquatic products play a significant role in man and animal food products. Studies indicate that most economically important fisheries are not in northern or southern latitudes, but rather are in tropical seas infested by toxic creatures. Poisonous fishes and shellfish are becoming recognized as significant public health problems. Aquatic biotoxins must not be taken lightly since these compounds are some of the most lethal poisons known to mankind. Moreover, certain biotoxications are on the increase, both geographically and in the numbers of organisms involved. Recent studies on paralytic shellfish poisonings have shown a definite increase in incidence. Outbreaks of paralytic shellfish poisonings can result in severe financial losses to all those involved in the shellfish industry. In some regions, certain species of shellfish remain toxic for prolonged periods of time, during which time no harvesting is possible. (*See* Chapter V for further information on this subject.)

Another important aspect of aquatic intoxications is the possible relationship of industrial pollutants to naturally occurring biotoxins. For example, the sinking of a ship reputedly caused outbreaks of ciguatera fish poisoning. According to all available public health reports, before 1965 poisonous fishes were never known to occur at Washington Island in the Line Islands, even though they were found elsewhere in the tropical Pacific islands. The cause of the outbreak was attributed to the sinking of the freighter *MS Southbank* on December 26, 1964. The freighter was heavily loaded with metals and other substances that may have contributed to the triggering of the outbreak. Many of the common reef fishes of this area had always been eaten daily by the native population without ill effects. Salvage crews had caught and eaten fishes with impunity in the immediate vicinity of the wreck up to the time that the portion of the ship containing the main cargo had been completely sunk. Then in August 1965, the fishes previously edible in the vicinity of the ship suddenly and without warning became ciguatoxic, and the crew members who ate them became violently ill. Similar occurrences elsewhere have been reported many times over the past 100 years.

Marine organisms concentrate within their bodies chemical substances that they obtain from the sea water or by feeding on other organisms. An example of this is shellfish poisoning. Shellfish feed on plankton that, in turn, feed on microorganisms and extract chemical nutrients from seawater. Shellfish that feed on quantities of toxic dinoflagellates (e.g., *Gonyaulax*) become poisonous, and people become poisoned by eating the toxic shellfish. A similar process apparently takes place in ciguatoxic fishes, clupeotoxic fishes, poisonous crabs, and probably other types of poisonous marine animals in which the organism merely serves as a transvector of the poison. The food chain or web does not always begin with dinoflagellates, but may include any of a number of marine plants, invertebrates, bacteria, or even herbivorous fishes. In the case of ciguatera, the sequence is believed to start with benthic marine algae, or dinoflagellates (*Gambierdiscus*), which are ingested by herbivorous fishes, which in turn are eaten by carnivorous fishes. Each trophic level ingests the poisons that occur in the organisms they eat. When a person eats a large, toxic, carnivorous reef fish, he receives poisons accumulated as a result of a long nutritional chain that begins at the lower trophic levels, down to the initial algae, or bacteria.

The field evidence (and this is all that is available at present) strongly suggests that under certain environmental conditions in tropical insular areas pollutants may provide the necessary chemical stimulus to trigger "naturally occurring" biotoxicity cycles such as ciguatera fish poisoning. There is abundant evidence that when the proper mix of chemical constituents are present in the environment of some types of marine organisms, biotoxins are produced. In their absence, these poisons are not produced. Under normal circumstances, most of the marine organisms involved are nontoxic and may actually be valuable food resources.

Electric fishes constitute a relatively minor health hazard, but are significant because of their contributions to our knowledge of metabolism and the phenomenon of electrogenesis. Electric fishes are unique among vertebrates. Interestingly, about 250 fish species have been found to possess electric organs capable of emitting an electrical discharge. These fishes include the South American electric eels, *Electrophorus* and *Gymnotus* (which are not actually eels), an electric catfish, and marine stargazers. The drug acetylcholine, which is extracted from the electric organs of *Electrophorus*, has been used as an antidote in the treatment of war gas injuries. The electrical discharge was used, in antiquity, in the treatment of a variety of diseases. The study of electrical discharge has also proved helpful in sonic research. (*See* Chapter VII.)

Finally, the candirú parastic catfish of the Amazon undoubtedly holds the all-time title for uniqueness as the only vertebrate that attempts to parasitize humans. (*See* Chapter VIII.)

Why study dangerous aquatic animals? Perhaps because there are few subjects that invite one to view such a gamut of carriage, such complexity of molecular structures, such therapeutic potential, and such great diving adventure and overall excitement.

Welcome to the world of the dangerous!

Long-spined sea urchin *Diadema setosum* (Leske). Photograph taken at Wuvulu Island, Bismarck Archipelago.     (Courtesy Richard C. Murphy, The Cousteau Society, Inc.)

# CHAPTER I

# The Fragile Hydrosphere: Water—The Medium of Life

by Richard C. Murphy
The Cousteau Society

DANGEROUS AQUATIC ANIMALS inhabit a fragile environment, the delicacy of which we are just beginning to appreciate. We can attribute the habitability of our planet to one substance: water. Our planet is truly an oasis in space, thanks to appreciable quantities of liquid water. Life as we know it cannot exist without water, and, in a sense, life itself is water *alive*.

Historically, our species has clearly appreciated the value of water by locating civilizations according to the availability of water and by depending upon water as a link and a barrier to social interactions. Until recently, though, we have not appreciated the fact that water is highly mobile, continuously cycling and recycling through the biosphere. Some cycles are rapid; for example, water fixed in photosynthesis along with carbon dioxide creates organic matter and then is catabolized by plants and animals back to water and carbon dioxide. These cycles may occur in a matter of seconds or minutes. Larger cycles involve evaporation from the sea, atmospheric transport, precipitation, movement through aquifers, and eventual river runoff back to the sea. Ocean circulation may involve surface currents or a 1000-year deep sea cycling before returning it to the surface for evaporation again. Water involved in the production of fossil fuels or glaciers may cycle on the order of tens of thousands to hundreds of thousands of years. But the fact remains that water does constantly move through our biosphere. Consequently, how we use or misuse water at one locale cannot be considered an isolated event. In the most literal sense, the mobility of water demonstrates the ecological concept that everything is connected.

To gain a better appreciation for what this life-giving substance really is, let's consider the water molecule, with its fascinating oxygen atom and its valence of $-2$, meaning that it has two electrons available for covalent bonding. Of particular interest is the fact that these electrons are not positioned at opposite sides of the oxygen nucleus, but rather they are approximately on the same side of the atom. Consequently, when two hydrogen atoms attach to share these electrons, they are likewise positioned close to each other at an angle of $105°$. As a result, the water molecule has a positively charged side and a negatively charged side. It is said to be polarized.

This feature accounts for many of water's wonderful properties. For example, water likes itself. As positive sides of water molecules attach to negative sides of others, like a magnet, they become tightly bound together, making water a very stable substance. A surprisingly great amount of heat must be added to water to convert it to a gas, to vaporize it, thus giving water great heat storage capacity. Because of this, water and ocean currents regulate the climate of the earth. The Gulf Stream acts as a great thermostat, carrying tropical heat from the Caribbean to the shores of England. Likewise, the ocean acts as a thermostat along the coast of Southern California through its contribution of water vapor to the air. Average coastal temperatures range from 40°F (4.4°C) to 90°F (32.2°C). A mere hundred miles inland, away from the oceanic influence, temperatures extend generally 10°F lower or higher than those on the coast, depending on the season. On the moon, however, temperatures extend from about 275°F (+135°C) at noon to about −311° (−155°C) at night. These extremes are primarily due to the absence of water vapor surrounding the moon.

All of the heat absorbed in vaporization is released as water condenses. One can appreciate how much energy that is by considering the typical thunderheads one sees on a hot summer afternoon: they can release as much heat as a large atomic bomb.

Because of water's polarity, water molecules pack themselves very closely in the liquid form, making water very dense. This gives rise to another curious and vital property. When water freezes (solid phase), it becomes less dense and floats on the liquid base. In nearly all other substances, the solid phase is more dense. The fact that ice floats is vital to life and the cycles of water. Were ice to sink, it would cover the bottom of all deep seas and upper latitude lakes and remain there, insulating the water above. Many forms of deep sea life would be nonexistent; ocean circulation would be profoundly different, and the entire climate of the earth might be altered because of this simple property.

The fact that water is less dense as a solid means that it expands upon freezing when the molecules realign themselves from the condensed liquid form to the expanded crystalline form. Because of this, water is an important force in the weathering and erosion of rocks. As water percolates down through cracks in rocks and then freezes, it expands and fractures them, breaking them into smaller pieces as the first step in the formation of soil.

Water, because of its polarity, also is attracted to other molecules. This is what makes water such an efficient solvent. More substances dissolve in water than in any other fluid: water is the universal solvent. As Jacques Cousteau has said, "Life is water alive."

The mobility of water and its solvent capabilities make water particularly vulnerable to pollution. We live on a water planet, and ours is a closed system. We use and reuse the same resources. We are totally dependent on the water we have. We can neither get rid of it nor can we get more. This in turn makes us vulnerable to the pollutants that it carries. As Thor Heyerdahl, the great ocean explorer, eloquently expressed, "The ocean is as round as the earth, landlocked in every direction, with thousands of inlets, but not a single outlet . . . a spaceship without exhaust pipe. We have begun to realize that no chimney is tall enough to pierce the atmosphere and send fumes into space, nor is any sewer long enough to pipe our pollutants beyond the borders of our common sea." Contrasting this global perspective, some sanitary engineers point out that because water is so abundant and the relative quantities of pollutants are so small, the dilution effect renders these potentially toxic substances harmless. Consider the facts. Of the total amount of water on earth (326,000,000 cubic miles) only 0.017 percent (55,300 cubic miles) is available as surface water in lakes and streams. Fresh water is obviously a precious commodity and the scale of dilution is very different depending on the limits of the system considered. But, even this point has been rendered moot when ecologists discovered the process of biomagnification. This phenomenon occurs when diluted substances in water become incorporated into the bodies of lower trophic level organisms (diatoms, algae) and are consumed by the organisms of the next higher trophic level (zooplankton, grazers) along with their load of pollutants; and these animals are then consumed by small predators, which are in turn consumed by others, and so on. At each step, the sum of the pollutants in the prey organisms becomes incorporated into its predator, giving each level of the food chain a more and more concentrated dose of pollutant.

Through this process the pollutant burden is biologically magnified. This process is well documented and has resulted in some birds and fish having pollutant concentrations in their bodies one hundred thousand to one million times the concentration of pollutants in their surroundings. The effects of these magnified doses of pollutants may affect the biochemistry and health of the organism as well as ours when we ingest them. These effects are not necessarily immediately observable, but rather may affect the resistance of organisms, have latent effects, or may even affect subsequent generations. The toxicity and persistence of such substances as heavy metals, radioactive particles, and exotic organic chemicals, including PCBs and pesticides, indicate that once released into the water system they will remain to haunt us for some time into the future, even if we were to stop releasing them.

It must be emphasized that because of the universality of water and its endless cycling in the biosphere, water problems become human problems. As water flows cyclically in nature, so must it flow in human systems. Our linear approach to water, wherein we use it, contaminate it, then throw it away, must be replaced by circular usage. Water taken from the biosphere should be retained within the human system; the water material should be extracted and reused as a resource; and, likewise, the water should be retained for another cycle in the human system.

Our coastal zones receive by far the greatest volume and diversity of pollutants through dumping and land runoff, but it is these same zones where the seas are most productive. Salt marshes and sea grass communities convert as much solar energy into living matter as coral reefs and rain forests. In addition, these ecosystems provide habitats and food for other organisms in higher trophic levels. But massive reductions of sea grass beds have recently been documented in the Chesapeake, with the primary cause being attributed to anthropogenic increases in nutrients and toxic chemicals. As habitats are lost and as populations succumb to the effects of pollutants, we are doing ourselves a great disservice through the elimination of food sources. More than fifty percent of fish and shellfish caught in the United States live or are dependent on the shallow waters of our coastal zones. Considering the amounts

of substances entering our coastal waters from the pathogenic microorganisms to heavy metals to exotic and highly toxic organic substances (1983 EPA estimate: 1,500 tons of chemical waste per person per year), it is not surprising that health advisories are frequently issued for fish and shellfish obtained in these coastal zones.

But the impact of pollutants on marine organisms goes beyond the domain of food. These pollutants affect the health of marine organisms, and they can alter biochemical systems that may have great potential value to us. The presence of biologically active chemicals in marine species provides us with a fantastic potential for useful substances, including but not limited to pharmaceuticals. For example, research conducted by Sister M. R. Schmeer on the edible quahog clam, *Mercenaria mercenaria*, revealed a substance called "mercenene" that could reduce tumor growth. Experiments with mice having malignant tumors showed that mercenene caused complete tumor regression in 70 percent of the treated animals. All of the untreated mice died. She also found to her chagrin that clams from polluted water did not produce mercenene. Just about every major group of marine organisms has some chemical substances that are potentially useful to humans. The mechanism of these chemical actions can provide us with insights into the functioning of our own bodies—and has already been very useful in understanding the action and functioning of nerves and muscles. Ultimately, some of mankind's most important cures may come from the sea. But the marine medicine chest is being contaminated and lost as the diversity of stressed ecosystems is reduced to only the most hardy of species. As we produce and dump in the sea some of the most toxic substances known, we are eliminating some of the best potential cures. The solution is clear: do not produce highly toxic and persistent substances. If such chemicals are created, reuse them or completely detoxify them before releasing them into the environment.

Another aspect of environmental pollutants involves their possible relationship to the buildup of biotoxicity cycles in marine organisms. Field evidence suggests that under certain environmental conditions, pollutants may provide the necessary chemical constituents to trigger "naturally occurring" biotoxicity cycles, involving such problems as ciguatera fish poison or dinoflagellate poisons.

All this points up to the fragility of the sea and the consequences to its inhabitants if environmental pollution continues unabated. It is not unrealistic to say that the fate of the sea will ultimately be our fate too.

# CHAPTER II

# Wound-Producing Aquatic Animals

INCLUDED WITHIN the traumatogenic or biting category of aquatic animals are the following:

SHARKS
GIANT MANTA RAY
BARRACUDA
MORAY EELS
BLUEFISH
NEEDLEFISH
GIANT GROUPER
SAWFISH
MARLIN
CHARACINS
TRIGGERFISHES
CROCODILES, ALLIGATORS, GAVIALS
SEALS, SEA LIONS, WALRUSES, POLAR BEARS
KILLER WHALE
GIANT TRIDACNA CLAMS
GIANT SQUID

In reviewing this list of culprits, it becomes obvious that not all of these organisms bite—the manta ray can be quite abrasive, the needlefish punctures, and the giant tridacna clam is capable of crushing—but all of them possess the common denominator of being able to inflict a wound.

## SHARKS

Few animals in the aquatic environment have a greater ability to intimidate humans than sharks. In pursuit of their noxious characteristics, man has all too often overlooked some of their unique qualities, for the sharks are among the most magnificent of creatures.

### Species, Distribution, Size, and Characteristics

Sharks are members of the vertebrate class Chondrichthyes, formerly known as Elasmobranchs. They differ greatly from the common bony fishes. The skeleton of sharks is composed of cartilage rather than bone; their external covering is of special placoid scales; they lack a swimbladder; they possess an asymmetrical or heteroceral tail and a liver that may comprise as much as twenty percent of their body weight; they have an immune system that is without equal; and they are

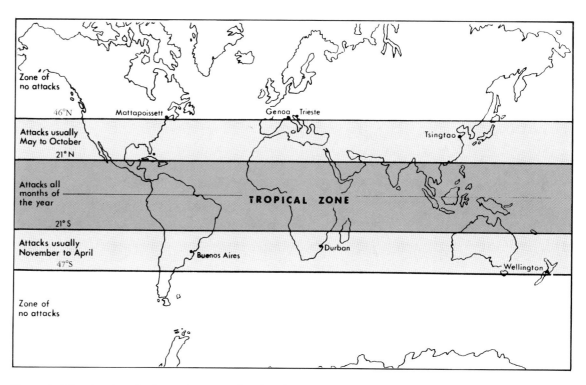

Figure 1. Map showing shark attack zones (after Coppleson).

5

equipped with a superb sensory system. Many sharks are powerful, fast swimmers.

It is estimated that there are about 250 species of sharks, of which about twenty-seven have been incriminated in attacks on humans. Our knowledge of these attacks is based largely on data compiled by the Worldwide Shark Attack File, under sponsorship of the U.S. Navy. From these we learn that attacks have occurred between latitudes 47° south and 46° north, or as far north as the upper Adriatic Sea, and as far south as South Island, New Zealand. (*See* Figure 1). Shark attacks have been most common in waters where the water temperature is above 20°C (68°F), although some attacks by the great white shark have occurred in cooler waters. Shark attacks tend to be seasonal, during warm weather periods, when both sharks and humans are likely to encounter each other. The greater danger is during the late afternoon and night when the sharks are most actively feeding.

The size of the shark is a matter of practical concern. Of the 250 species, about eighty percent of them achieve lengths of over 2 meters (6 feet).* But *not all* large sharks are dangerous. Fortunately, the largest shark, the giant whale shark, *Rhiniodon typus* Smith (1),† which may exceed a length of 13 meters (45 feet) and may appear to be dangerous, is a plankton feeder and has no interest in humans.

The potentially dangerous species of sharks are generally the larger sharks that possess suitable dentition. Most of the shark biters are those that feed on large fish, other sharks, seals, and larger organisms. If the shark is more than 1.2 meters (4 feet) and is equipped with adequate teeth, the animal should be treated with respect.

Shark reproduction varies according to the species:

---

* Weights and measurements are in general given in metric units, followed in parenthesis with approximate English equivalents.

† The boldface numbers (in parenthesis) in the text identify the species under discussion and refer the reader to the number in the plate sections following the respective chapters.

some species are hatched from eggs (oviparous) and some are born alive (viviparous) or from eggs within the uterus and then born alive (ovoviviparous). Fertilization in all sharks, however, is internal. The pelvic fins of the male are modified to form intromittent organs, known as claspers, which the male uses to convey the sperm to the female.

SENSORY SYSTEM

Sharks have long been considered to be of a low order of intelligence, but if this is true they certainly make up for it by possessing a superb sensory system, which could easily make them the envy of the animal world. The means employed by sharks to detect their prey is a subject of prime interest to anyone studying shark attacks on humans.

Sharks are equipped with the usual sensory organs of eyes, an auditory apparatus, and an olfactory mechanism. It was previously believed that sharks had poor eyesight, but it is now known that they have excellent visual sensitivity for color and for distinguishing an object moving past a dark background. Vision is believed to be the prime sensory organ employed at close range, especially in clear water. Shark eyes are equipped with a *tapetum lucidum*, a mirror-like reflecting layer under the retina that increases the amount of light to the eye. Some shark species can close or open the tapetum according to the amount of light received. The musculature of the eyeball enables the shark to maintain continual eye contact or to track an object even when the shark is twisting, turning, or moving ahead. Thus, the eyes of a shark are well adapted to its predatory activities.

Sharks have an exquisite sense of smell. It has been estimated that as much as seventy percent of the brain in some shark species is devoted to olfactory receptors. Olfaction enables a shark to detect blood and food in the water, possibly in dilutions as low as in parts per billion.

Although sharks appear to emit no sounds, they

have an extremely sensitive sonic system and are able to detect low-frequency vibrations at great distances. The ear is only one of several organs that is used for sound reception. The human ear can perceive sounds in the range of 20 to 20,000 Hz (cycles per second), but the shark's sensitivity is largely in the range of 10 to 600 Hz. The only external evidence of the shark ear is a small duct that leads to a three-chambered inner ear.

The shark has another sound receptor system known as the lateral line system. The lateral line system is comprised of numerous fine canals filled with a watery solution just under the skin, extending from the back along the side to the tail. By means of this system sharks are able to detect sound movements in the water, and even objects. The sonic system of a shark is always on and listening, and any movement that resembles that of a wounded fish struggling is bound to excite a shark. Sharks appear to be more responsive to sounds in the 25 Hz to 50 Hz range.

Another telereceptor present in sharks is a series of sensory pores, called the Ampullae of Lorenzini, or flask cells, which cover the head. The function of these cells has been a matter of conjecture, but it is now believed that they are electromagnetic sensors. With these organs they can detect prey buried in the sand. These electromagnetic sensors may also be used by sharks to detect the earth's magnetic fields and the changing polarity of water, providing pelagic sharks with a navigational aid. Sharks probably have the greatest electromagnetic sensitivity of any organisms in the animal kingdom.

Sharks are also equipped with free neuromasts or pit organs that are distributed in distinct patterns in conjunction with modified placoid scales. One line is situated below the lower jaw, another at the forward basal of the pectoral fins, and others are scattered along the dorsum in varying patterns depending upon the species. These organs appear to be chemoreceptors and are sometimes referred to as the "common chemical sense" of the shark. They may function to detect various chemical substances in the water.

Thus, the shark is a highly "computerized" sensory marvel without a peer either in water or on land.

## DENTITION

The teeth are the one characteristic that serves as the hallmark of sharks. The morphology of the teeth varies from one species to the next, and are specific for each species. In general, there are two main types of shark teeth: (1) sharp, triangular-shaped teeth used for cutting, as exemplified in the great white shark and all of the members of the family Carcharhinidae. Triangular cutting teeth may have smooth cutting edges or fine serrations (Figure 2a, b). (2) Long, pointed, oval-shaped teeth, which are round or semicircular in cross section, acting like a spike but incapable of cutting, as exemplified in the mako shark. The triangular, plate-like tooth is the most common form in sharks. The second type of tooth is used only for seizing prey.

Shark teeth, unlike those in mammals, for example, are not implanted in sockets, but are attached on their base to a sheath of connective tissue that serves as the tooth bed. Most sharks have five or six reserve or replacement rows of teeth behind the functional teeth, arranged one on top of the other under a cover or thin sheath of mucous membrane. The number of teeth that are in actual use at any given time varies with the species of shark and with the different parts of the jaw. When functional teeth are lost, they are replaced by the reserve teeth. In the case of the lemon shark (*Negaprion brevirostris*), for example, this replacement has been found to take place over a period of seven to fourteen days and is believed to take a similar length of time in other shark species. The cause of the replacement may be by accident or by the normal, orderly migration to the outer anterior margin of the jaw. The progression of tooth replacement continues throughout the life of the shark and also provides for the increase in the size of the teeth as the shark grows older.

## FEEDING PATTERNS

The feeding patterns and swimming habits of

a

b
Figure 2a, b. Jaws taken from a great white shark, about 2.4 meters (8 feet) in length.

a. Note the fully developed teeth behind the first row. These are the replacement teeth. One or more series of teeth may be functional at any one time, and a continuous pavement of less-developed teeth is also present behind the functional teeth. Teeth are usually lost from mechanical damage or normal attrition, but are replaced within seven to fourteen days.

b. Rear view. The fully developed replacement teeth are best seen in the lower jaw.

(Courtesy, Oceanographic Research Institute, Durban, South Africa)

Figure 3. Sharks in a feeding frenzy. During a frenzy, sharks become extremely aggressive and unpredictable. Three common reef shark species can be seen in this photograph: whitetip, blacktip, and gray reef shark. Photo taken at Marion Reef, Coral Sea. (R. and V. Taylor)

**Aggressive** | **Non-aggressive**

Figure 4. Drawing showing aggressive and normal behavior patterns in the gray reef shark (*Carcharhinus amblyrhyncus*). When the shark strikes the aggressive pose, it is time for the diver to take cover or to get out of the water. (L. Hood, after D. Nelson)

sharks vary from one species to the next, but for the purposes of the present discussion, they can be grouped into three general types:

*(1) Normal Feeding Pattern:*
This pattern can best be described as a situation in which one or several sharks are seen moving about with purposeful movements either in quest of food or actually feeding. In some instances the movements may be slow and determined; in others, erratic and swift. The swimming pattern, approach, and final attack may vary with the species and circumstances.

*(2) Frenzied Feeding Pattern:*
The frenzied feeding pattern most frequently develops after an explosion, sinking of a vessel, crash of a plane, the sudden availability of food, or blood in the water. The frenzied behavior is further enhanced by the proximity of other sharks in large numbers. Under these circumstances, the swimming behavior becomes exceedingly erratic. During these periods, sharks may become cannibalistic and turn on each other. (*See* Figure 3).

ATTACK PATTERNS
    The studies conducted on attacks on humans have shown that in most instances the attacking shark was never seen prior to contact. There is no single behavior performance that is seen in all shark species, but in the case of the gray reef shark (*Carcharhinus amblyrhyncus*), it will usually go into an agonistic or combative behavior pattern (Figure 4). In this instance the shark swims very erratically just prior to attacking the victim. At this time the back of the shark is bowed into a hunched position and the pectoral fins are extended forward. The shark then swims stiffly, with its head moving back and forth almost as much as the tail. This is then followed by a swift rush at the victim. Almost every conceivable type of activity has been observed under the heading of aggressive behavior. Shark attacks on man are sometimes preceded by one or more contacts, which range from gentle bumping to violent collisions (22, 23, 24). At times impacts can be severe enough to knock the victim completely out of the water.

    Sharks have been known to single out an individual in a crowd and continue to attack the victim to the total exclusion of all other persons, including those who attempt to rescue the victim. However, because of the unpredictability of sharks, it is difficult to anticipate any particular course of action.

PROVOKED AND UNPROVOKED ATTACKS
    A large number of attacks occur as a direct result of *provoking* the shark to a response, such as spearing, poking, grabbing the shark by the tail, tantalizing the shark with dead fish, blocking off an escape passageway, or some other activity that annoys the shark. Encounters of this type should be avoided. Nevertheless, the shark may also attack without provocation. An evaluation of the Shark Attack File reveals that there have been about twenty-eight documented shark attacks each year, with a case fatality rate of about thirty-five percent.

## Sharks Dangerous to Humans

    Only a few of the more dangerous shark species have been selected for inclusion here:
    GREAT WHITE SHARK, *Carcharodon carcharias* (Linnaeus) (2, 3, 4). This shark is reputed to be the most dangerous of all and has the largest number of

attacks on humans credited to it. Despite its fearsome reputation, some shark experts believe that this shark is not primarily a "man eater," but rather a "man biter." From the viewpoint of the victim, this is a distinction that is more philosophical than pragmatic. This shark attains a length of 6 meters (20 feet) or more, and a weight of more than 1,818 kilograms (4,000 pounds). Despite its size, it is a good example of grace and power in motion, and is awesome to behold. A relatively slow swimmer, it is nevertheless a powerhouse of brute strength—a king among the finny creatures of the ocean. The great white shark is characterized by its obtusely conical head, heavy body, strongly lunate caudal fin, and large triangular serrate teeth. The outer tips of the pectoral fins are blackish. This shark ranges throughout the tropical and temperate oceans of the world. Although generally oceanic, it may come into shallow water, and tends to be solitary.

TIGER SHARK, *Galeocerdo cuvier* (Peron & LeSueur) (5). This shark is listed as having the second highest number of attacks on humans. The tiger shark attains a length of at least 5.2 meters (17 feet), and possibly longer. Younger specimens have very distinctive markings of oblique or transverse dark blotches on the back and fins, hence the term "tiger." Large specimens tend to be gray or grayish brown, darker above than on the sides and belly. Other distinctive characteristics of the tiger shark are its teeth, a short snout, and sharply pointed tail. Although the tiger shark *may appear* to be sluggish, it can be, when stimulated, a vigorous and powerful swimmer and at times quite aggressive. The tiger shark is found throughout tropical and subtropical regions inshore and offshore, and may enter river mouths. It is said to be the most common of the large sharks in the tropics.

MAKO SHARK, *Isurus oxyrinchus* (Rafinesque) (6). The mako shark is a potentially dangerous shark and has been incriminated in attacks on humans. The mako is one of the handsomest of the sharks, having a graceful, well-proportioned body. The shark is blue to blue-gray above, white below, with a dorsoventrally flattened and greatly expanded, or keel-like, caudal peduncle. It is an aggressive and savage biter with a fearsome-looking set of jaws. The teeth are large, long, flexous in outline, and bladelike in appearance. It is one of the most active and swiftest swimming of all the sharks, noted for leaping out of the water when hooked— a characteristic that has caused it to be listed officially as a great game fish. The mako has also been involved in more attacks on boats than any other shark species. The mako attains a length of 3.6 meters (12 feet) and inhabits all tropical and temperate oceans.

NURSE SHARK, *Ginglymostoma cirratum* (Bonnaterre) (7). The nurse shark is generally a harmless species, found lying sluggishly on the bottom. It is usually found in schools. Human beings come into contact with it by inadvertently swimming near the shark or by stepping on it, at which time it has been known to bite. The nurse shark attains a length of about 4.2 meters (14 feet). Its color is a rich yellowish- to grayish-brown, darker above than below, and is characterized by the presence of a long barbel on the anterior margin of each nostril and a deep groove connecting the nostril with the mouth. Several attacks have occurred from one of its Australian relatives, known as the wobbegong, *Orectolobus ornatus* (DeVis) (19).

BULL SHARK, *Carcharhinus leucas* (Valenciennes) (8). This species is believed to be identical to the Lake Nicaragua shark *(C. nicaraguensis)*, Zambezi shark *(C. zambezensis)*, and the Ganges River shark *(C. gangeticus)*, all of which have been involved in attacks on humans. It inhabits the warm waters of the Atlantic, Pacific, and Indian oceans. These sharks are also found in freshwater in Lake Nicaragua and Lake Izabel, Guatemala, and Lake Jamoer, New Guinea, and extend into the upper reaches of the Amazon and the rivers of Australia, Iraq, Asia, and Southeast Africa; it is seldom found far from land. This is a heavy, slow swimming species, but can move rapidly when stimulated. It is gray above and white below, with fins dark-tipped in the young. It attains a length of 3.6 meters (12 feet).

OCEANIC WHITETIP SHARK, *Carcharhinus*

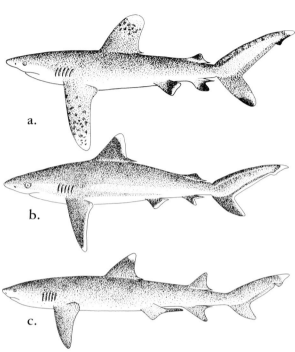

Figure 5. Comparative drawings of three "whitetip" sharks:

a. Oceanic whitetip shark, *Carcharhinus longimanus*. Note the rounded dorsal fin and somewhat speckled appearance of the tip of the fin.

b. Silvertip shark, *Carcharhinus albimarginatus*, showing the white tip of the dorsal fin, which extends on down the posterior margin of the fin and the white tips of the caudal fin, both upper and lower lobes, and white tip of the pectoral fins.

c. Whitetip reef shark, *Triaenodon obesus*, showing the white tips of the dorsal and caudal fins.    (From Bass)

*longimanus* (Poey) (9). This is a very active, deep water oceanic shark, which seldom if ever comes close to shore. The whitetip is an active, fearless swimmer, and has been involved in attacks on humans. It is found in the warm waters of the Atlantic, Pacific, and Indian oceans. It attains a length of 3.6 meters (12 feet).

This shark is distinguished by the broadly rounded apex of the first dorsal fin, the convexity of the posterior outline of the lower caudal lobe, long pectoral fins, and a very short snout in front of the nostrils. Little is known of the habits of this shark, but it is considered to be one of the most dangerous and aggressive sharks.

The oceanic whitetip shark should not be confused with its smaller relative, the silvertip shark, *Carcharhinus albimarginatus* Rüppell, and the more common whitetip reef shark, *Triaenodon obesus* (Rüppell).

There is a distinct difference in the proportions of the first dorsal fin, which is longer than its base in *C. longimanus*, but shorter in *C. albimarginatus*. The latter species is also smaller in size (up to about 2.4 meters [8 feet]) and tends to inhabit more frequently inshore areas near coral reefs, but not to the extent that *T. obesus* does; the tips of all the fins have conspicuous white markings (Figure 5). *C. albimarginatus* has not been known to attack humans, but is considered potentially dangerous.

The whitetip reef shark, *T. obesus*, is a smaller reef shark, distinguished by a blunt snout, and a large second dorsal fin almost equal in height to the first dorsal. (See 15). *T. obesus* is a common species of shallow, tropical reef areas of the Indian and Pacific oceans and has been incriminated in attacks on humans; generally, however, it is not considered to be an aggressive species. It has white tips on the first dorsal and upper caudal fins and attains a length of 2 meters (7 feet).

BRONZE WHALER, *Carcharhinus brachyurus* (Günther) (10). This shark ranges along the southeast coast of Australia. It is an active, aggressive, open-water shark and has been involved in attacks on humans off the coast of Australia. It attains a length of 2.7 meters (9 feet). Its color is bronze above to a creamy white below.

COMMON or BLACK WHALER, *Carcharhinus obscurus* LeSueur) (11). This is a large and dangerous shark, growing to a length of 3.6 meters (12 feet) and a weight of 440 kilograms (968 pounds). It is found both offshore and in shallow waters along the east coast of Australia and is frequently found in rivers and harbors. Its color is dark gray to sandy above, and whitish below, with the tips of its fins often dusky. The whalers received their names because they are often found in the vicinity of whales.

LEMON SHARK, *Negaprion brevirostris* (Poey) (12). Attacks on humans by lemon sharks have been documented. The distinctive features of the lemon shark are a second dorsal fin almost as large as the first, a broadly rounded snout, and its unique teeth. It attains a length of 3.3 meters (11 feet). Its color is usually yellowish brown, brown, or dark bluish gray, above, with lower sides tinged with yellow or greenish olive, and a pale yellow or greenish olive underside. This shark is primarily an inshore species found in bays, creeks, ponds, and around docks. It ranges from New Jersey south to Brazil. A related species, *N. acutidens* (Rüppell), is found in the warm shallow waters of all major oceans.

GRAY REEF SHARK, *Carcharhinus amblyrhyncos* (Bleeker) (13a, b). This shark has been frequently designated in the literature as *C. menisorrah* and has been repeatedly incriminated in attacks on humans. The species is frequently found in large schools and when aggravated can become quite dangerous despite its comparatively small size. When stimulated by food, gray reef sharks can rapidly enter into a frenzied feeding pattern at which time their swimming becomes very erratic and swift (Figure 4). They attain a length of 2.1 meters (7 feet) or more. The gray reef shark is abundant in the lagoons of coral islands and close to shore in the Indo-Pacific and Indian Ocean. Its color is grayish above, paler to whitish below, with the fins grayish to blackish, but not black-tipped.

BLACKTIP REEF SHARK, *Carcharhinus melanopterus* (Quoy and Gaimard) (14). This shark is common along the margins of reefs throughout the Indo-Pacific region and extending into the Red Sea. Although usually solitary, the shark is sometimes found in the company of the gray and whitetip reef shark. This shark is generally docile, but has been involved in attacks on humans. It attains a length of 1.8 meters (6 feet), and its color is brownish to blackish above, paler to white below, with strikingly black fin tips. The shark can usually be frightened away by making overt movements toward it.

WHITETIP REEF SHARK, *Triaenodon obesus* (Rüppell) (15). This shark is seldom incriminated in attacks on humans; nevertheless, it is potentially dangerous. A common solitary shark of the reefs of the Pacific and Indian oceans, and the Red Sea, it is distinguished by the white tips of the first dorsal, pectoral, and upper caudal fins. Its color is gray above and white below.

SAND SHARK, *Eugomphodus taurus* (Rafinesque) (16, 17). This shark has been involved in attacks on humans. Generally a somewhat sluggish species that feeds at night, it can be swift and savage at times. It is usually found inshore, near the bottom, and attains a length of 3 meters (10 feet). It inhabits the Mediterranean and Atlantic oceans and the coasts of Japan, China, Australia, and Africa. Its color is gray or brown above, pale or dirty white below, and sparsely flecked with brown spots on the back and sides, with fins covered with brown spots.

MACKEREL SHARK, *Lamna nasus* (Bonnaterre) (18). This shark is generally regarded as a dangerous species. It tends to be a sluggish swimmer, but can become active and aggressive when stimulated. It attains a length of 3 meters (10 feet) or more. It inhabits warm temperature regions of all oceans. Its color is bluish gray, or gray above and white below.

WOBBEGONG SHARK, *Orectolobus ornatus* (DeVis) (19). The wobbegong and several related species of the carpet sharks have been incriminated in attacks on humans. It attains a length of 2.1 meters (7 feet). Wobbegongs are usually found in shallow water amongst seaweeds and rocks. The shark has a carpet-like pattern of color, with blotches, spots, and marblings, and the body has fleshy lobes; its appearance tends to camouflage it with its surroundings, a background color that may be gray or brown. It is found off the coast of eastern Australia.

HAMMERHEAD SHARK, *Sphyrna zygaena* (Linnaeus) (20, 21). This shark is characterized by the peculiar flat, wide, hammer- or bonnet-shaped head. Hammerheads tend to be leisurely swimmers, frequently observed swimming slowly as if basking in the sun. It attains a length of 4.2 meters (14 feet). Hammerheads are found in warm and tropical waters of all oceans. Its color is dark olive or brownish gray above, paler to white below, with tips of the fins dusky to black. There are as many as nine species of hammerheads, and possibly more.

BLUE SHARK, *Prionace glauca* (Linnaeus) (22). This pelagic species lives in the open sea, but may be found along coastal areas. Generally a slow swimmer, it may become active and aggressive when in pursuit of food. The species is widely distributed throughout tropical and warm temperate oceans. It may attain a length of 3.3 meters (11 feet).

## GIANT MANTA RAY

GIANT MANTA RAY, *Manta birostris* (Donndorff) (25–28). The manta ray is truly a majestic creature This species has a fin spread of more than 6 meters (20 feet) and a weight of 1,590 kilograms (3,500 pounds). The manta is not aggressive and is dangerous only because of its sheer bulk. Moreover, it possesses coarse dermal denticles that can cause severe abrasions of the skin if one were to brush against them. Helmet divers have been killed when their airlines became entangled in the cephalic fins of a curious manta investigating the divers' bubbles. Mantas are generally seen swimming or basking near the surface of the water with the tips of their long pectoral fins curling above the surface.

Swimming or diving in the midst of a school of mantas is a delightful, never-to-be-forgotten experience. Mantas are sometimes seen leaping out and falling back into the water with a tremendous splash. They are generally plankton feeders but may eat crustaceans and small fish at times. Their color varies from reddish to olivaceous brown to black above, sometimes with large, dark irregular markings, and a light color beneath. They are found in subtropical and tropical seas of both hemispheres.

## BARRACUDA

GREAT BARRACUDA, *Sphyraena barracuda* (Walbaum) (29–32). There are about twenty species of barracuda, some of which are schooling in their habits (31). All species are voracious carnivores and differ somewhat in their aggressiveness. The great barracuda has a reputation for being aggressive and pugnacious, but it seldom attacks divers. It tends to be solitary in its habits and has a great curiosity for any bright shiny object. The great barracuda attains a length of 2.4 meters (8 feet) and a weight of 48 kilograms (106 pounds). The mouth is large, V-shaped, and filled with enormous knife-like canine teeth (32). At times the fish may appear motionless in the water, but it can accelerate with tremendous speed and attack fiercely. Barracudas are widely distributed throughout all subtropical and tropical areas of the world.

## MORAY EELS

About twenty species of moray eels are found throughout the temperate and warm seas of the world. One example is the tropical moray eel, *Gymnothorax marginatus* (Rüppel) (33), which inhabits the Indo-Pacific region. Although moray eels are notoriously powerful and vicious biters, they rarely attack a person unless provoked. Humans encounter moray eels as the result of sticking a hand in a hole inhabited by an eel. The eels have strong knife-like teeth and powerful jaws

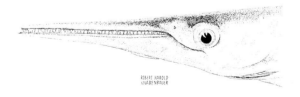

Figure 6. Needlefish, *Strongylura gigantea*. Enlarged view of the needle-like beak, which is capable of inflicting a fatal wound.    (R. H. Knabenbauer)

capable of inflicting serious lacerating wounds (34), and their tough, slimy skin makes them difficult to grasp and to penetrate with a knife. Despite their apparent viciousness, they can be readily tamed with food and can make good pets. Some of the larger species attain a length of 3 meters (10 feet) and are more than 35 centimeters (about one foot) in diameter.

## BLUEFISH

BLUEFISH, *Pomatomus saltatrix* (Linnaeus) (35a, b). The bluefish is a carnivorous, ferocious, powerful, and fast-swimming fish. It has a voracious appetite and kills far more than it needs for food. It travels in large schools and wreaks havoc with schools of anchovy, sardines, shad, and other fishes upon which it feeds. It is considered a valuable game fish. The bluefish is equipped with sharp, conical canine teeth in both the upper and lower jaws that are quite capable of inflicting a nasty bite. It attains a length of 1.2 meters (4 feet) and a weight of 12.3 kilograms (27 pounds), and is widely distributed throughout the temperate and tropical seas of the world, with the exception of the eastern Pacific.

## NEEDLEFISH

NEEDLEFISH, *Tylosaurus crocodilus* (LeSueur) (36a, b). The needlefish is sometimes referred to as a saltwater garfish because it has a long slender body and possesses two elongate jaws that are filled with sharp, unequal conical teeth (Figure 6). Large needlefish may attain a length of 1.8 meters (6 feet). Needlefish are attracted to light, and several fatalities have been reported where persons fishing or wading at night with lanterns have been accidentally impaled when the needlefish, attracted by the light, jumped out of the water and speared the victim. Indo-Pacific region.

## GIANT GROUPER

GIANT GROUPER, *Promicrops lanceolatus* (Bloch) (37). There are several species of grouper, such as the example listed, which attain a large size. Some of the larger species may attain a length of 3.6 meters (12 feet) and a weight of more than 227 kilograms (500 pounds). Groupers are a potential hazard because of their large size and huge cavernous jaws, which are filled with multiple rows of cardiform teeth. Groupers tend to be curious and fearless. They are usually found lurking in underwater caverns, old wrecks, and around rocks, and have attacked divers who accidentally bumped into them in underwater caves. They are found throughout temperate and tropical seas.

## SAWFISH

**LARGE-TOOTH SAWFISH,** *Pristis perotteti* Müller and Henle (38). There are about six species of sawfishes throughout the world and all of them are characterized by having a calcified rostral blade margined with sharp rostral teeth. Sawfishes are among the largest of elasmobranchs, commonly achieving a length of 6 meters (20 feet) or more, and a weight of 585 kilograms (1,287 pounds) or more. Sawfishes are found in most warm seas of the world. They live chiefly in shallow water bottom areas, usually muddy or sandy, not far from shore, and are most commonly found in sheltered bays or in estuaries, in brackish water, and may ascend into the tidal zone, and above, of large rivers. They are also found landlocked in Lake Nicaragua. They use the rostral saw to slash back and forth in schools of fish, thereby killing or stunning their victims, much as swordfish, sailfish, and marlins use their swords. Sawfishes do not aggressively attack humans, but accidental contact with their rostral saws can inflict serious injuries. The number of rostral teeth varies from species to species.

## MARLIN

**PACIFIC STRIPED MARLIN,** *Makaira mitsukuri* (Jordan and Snyder) (39). The marlin is a very active game fish. Although seldom considered as a dangerous species, when aggravated it can deliver considerable damage with its well-developed bill. It has been known to attack small boats. Little is known about the life history of this well-known fish and some confusion continues as to its speciation. It is found along the Pacific coast of North America, Hawaii, and Japan, preferring water temperatures of 22°C (70°F) or above. It attains a length of 2.4 meters (8 feet) and a weight of 228 kilograms (500 pounds).

## CHARACINS

**PIRAÑHA,** *Serrasalmus nattereri* (Kner) (40a, b). There are several species of South American characins that are equipped with formidable sets of razor-sharp teeth (Figure 7). Pirañha probably have one of the worst reputations as a dangerous fish. A significant component of their attack pattern is that they always work in schools, never attacking singly, but in schools of several hundred fish at a time. Pirañhas seldom attack uninjured animals or human beings invading their habitat. However, once attracted by a commotion and blood in the water, they can reduce an animal or human to a skeleton within a very short time. When pirañha are placed in aquaria they transform into shy and easily frightened fish. Nonetheless, they are biters and at times become cannibalistic. *S. nattereri* attains a length of about 30 centimeters (12 inches), but some of the larger pirañha such as *S. piraya* attain a length of 60 centimeters (24 inches) or more. *S. nattereri* is a very handsome fish—colored slate gray above, with a blackish silver shine and numerous shimmering dots, and brilliant red below. They are found in eastern South America, from Guyana south to La Plata.

**SABRE-TOOTH CHARACIN,** *Rhaphiodon gibbus* Agassiz (41). This freshwater characin is equipped with large jaws armed with sharp, powerful teeth and a compressed herring-like body. The appearance of the body is somewhat grotesque, almost as if it had a vertebral column malformation. It is predatory in its habits and capable of inflicting a painful bite. It inhabits the Ama-

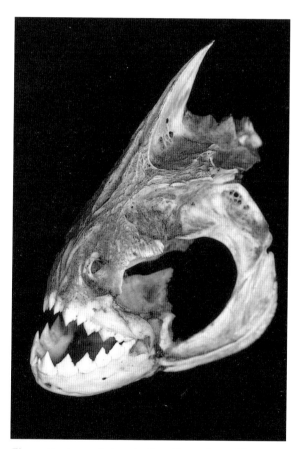

Figure 7. Jaws of the pirañha, *Serrasalmus*. The razor-sharp teeth of pirañhas are constructed for biting and tearing off chunks of flesh. A school of these fish can provide a lot of action. They tend to be cannibalistic.
(Courtesy B. Allison, WLRI photo)

zon, north to the Guyana rivers and the Rio de la Plata, and attains a length of 33 centimeters (13 inches).

## TRIGGERFISHES

Triggerfishes constitute a little-known marine hazard. They are generally shy and not very fast swimmers, cruising about with an undulating movement of their second dorsal and anal fins. Under usual circumstances it is difficult to make contact with most triggerfishes since they tend to scurry into crevices or holes in the reef where they peek out unobtrusively. However, during mating season the females of at least two species may become quite aggressive and are capable of inflicting painful bites. Triggerfishes are equipped with strong jaws, each with eight long, protruding, and chisel-like teeth in an outer row, backed by an inner row of six teeth. The two species that have been documented as biters are:

YELLOW-SPOTTED or BLUE TRIGGERFISH, *Pseudobalistes fuscus* (Bloch and Schneider) **(42)**. *P. fuscus* attains a length of about 55 centimeters (21 inches).

TITAN TRIGGERFISH, *Balistoides viridescens* (Bloch and Schneider) **(43)**. *B. viridescens* attains a length of 75 centimeters (29 inches). Both species inhabit the Indo-Pacific region.

## CROCODILES, ALLIGATORS, GAVIALS

All of the members of this group belong to the single reptile order *Crocodylia* **(44–51)**. These are the largest and most ferocious of the living reptiles. The crocodilians are divided into three families and are distinguished from each other as follows: (1) *Crocodylidae*, or crocodiles, in which the fourth tooth of the lower jaw is the best developed and fits into an open notch in the upper jaw, so that the tooth is visible when the mouth is closed; the fifth tooth is the largest in the upper jaw; (2) *Alligatoridae*, or alligators, in which the fourth tooth of the lower jaw fits into a laterally closed pit in the upper jaw and the fourth tooth is the largest tooth of the upper

jaw; (3) *Gavialidae*, or gavials, in which the snout is greatly lengthened and all of the teeth are the same size (Figure 8).

Crocodiles are found in freshwater streams and lakes, and saltwater areas, of the tropical regions of the world, and in the waters of the Indo-Pacific. Some of them can attain a large size (7.2 meters [24 feet]).

SALTWATER CROCODILE, *Crocodylus porosus* (Schneider) **(44)**. This crocodile has an extensive range that includes India, Sri Lanka, South China, the Malay Archipelago, Palau, Solomon Islands, northern Australia, and New Guinea. The saltwater crocodile has been observed swimming at sea out of sight of any land. It attains a length of more than 6 meters (20 feet).

JOHNSTON'S RIVER CROCODILE, *Crocodylus johnstoni* Krefft **(50)**.

NILE CROCODILE, *Crocodylus niloticus* Laurenti **(51)**.

At night crocodiles enter rice paddy fields and marshy lands in search of prey. The ferociousness of crocodiles is well-documented. In areas where they are endemic, they take numerous lives. Crocodiles frequently attack with a loud hissing sound, grasp the victim with a powerful bite, and in the process of dismembering the victim, drown it with a quick twirling movement of the body. They may sweep an animal off its feet by a swift blow of the tail.

Alligators are New World animals, with the exception of the Chinese alligator, *Alligator sinensis* (Fauve), which is found in the lower portion of the Yangtze River. *A. sinensis* attains a length of about 2 meters (6 feet). The best known of the alligators is the American alligator, *A. mississipiensis* (Daudin), which attains a length of about 4.5 meters (15 feet). The American alligator ranges from North Carolina south to Florida and to the Rio Grande, Texas. Caiman are members of the alligatorid genera—*Caiman, Melanosuchus,* and *Paleosuchus*—and range from Central America to the central part of South America. They live in the backwaters of rivers or in slow flowing waters with muddy bottoms and soft sand banks. Included in this group

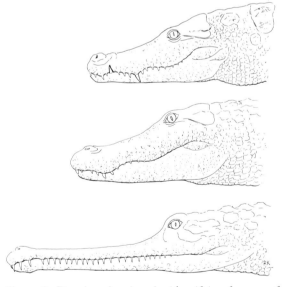

Figure 8. Drawing showing the identifying features of: *Crocodiles*—fourth tooth of the lower jaw fits into an open notch in the upper jaw; *Alligators*—fourth tooth of the lower jaw fits into a laterally closed pit in the upper jaw; *Gavials*—all teeth are the same size and the jaw is greatly elongated.          (R. H. Knabenbauer)

are two species, *Caiman crocodilus* (Linnaeus) and *C. latirostris* (Daudin), both of which attain a length of about 2.5 meters (8 feet). The largest of the caimans is the black caiman, *Mesanosuchus niger* (Spix). It attains a length of 4.7 meters (15 feet) and inhabits central South America. The smallest of the caimans are members of the genus *Paleosuchus*, which attain a length of only 1.45 meters (under 5 feet) and live in rapid flowing waters of northern and central South America, particularly in jungle streams with rocky bottoms and banks.

The gavials consist of a single genus and species, the Indian gavial, *Gavialis gangeticus* (Gmelin), which can attain a length of 7 meters (23 feet). The most striking feature of the gavial is its long narrow snout. The gavial rarely leaves the water since its legs are weak, but it is equipped with a strong tail. The gavial lives in the deep flowing rivers in the region of the Ganges, Mahanadi, and Brahmaputra rivers of India.

The habits of most crocodilians are somewhat similar. Usually they spend the night in the water and during the day lie in the sun, except when it gets too warm, in which case they will find a shady place or enter the water for a brief period of time. Crocodilians are seldom encountered in the open waters of large lakes. They feed on a wide range of organisms, including beetles, fish, turtles, and large mammals. Crocodilian teeth are situated in deep sockets and are not suited for tearing apart or chewing. The teeth are used only for seizing and grasping prey. Consequently, crocodilians will frequently hide the carcass of the animal underwater until it begins to rot, which makes it easier for them to swallow. Crocodilians remove pieces of flesh by firmly grasping a part of the body and then suddenly twisting in the water about the long axis of their body. This rolling process may take place several times. Crocodilians have the strange habit of swallowing large numbers of stones, the purpose of which is not known. Their digestive processes are quite rapid. Crocodilians have been ruthlessly slaughtered by humans and, despite their ferocity, deserve protection.

## SEALS, SEA LIONS, WALRUSES, POLAR BEARS

CALIFORNIA SEA LION, *Zalophus californianus* (Lesson) (52, 53, 54). Seals and sea lions are generally rather docile, but during the breeding season they can become quite aggressive. Large bulls may be quite irritable during this mating period and should be approached only with considerable caution. A large bull can inflict a very painful bite.

WALRUS, *Odobenus rosmarus* (Linnaeus) (55). Walruses are generally docile, but, when on land and cut off from an exit to the sea, they may become aggressive and can inflict dangerous wounds with their tusks. Their livers may be toxic and should not be eaten. These mammals inhabit the Arctic Ocean. The bulls attain a length of 3.7 meters (12 feet) and a weight of 1,260 kilograms (2,772 pounds).

POLAR BEAR, *Thalarctos maritimus* (Phipps) (56). Unprovoked aggression toward humans is rare, but, when provoked, the polar bear can become a formidable and fearless foe. They have been known to stalk their victims in a relentless manner. Female polar bears with cubs are particularly dangerous. The liver and kidneys of polar bears may be extremely toxic and can cause death if eaten. Polar bears inhabit the circumpolar Arctic and are excellent swimmers. The males attain a length of 3.3 meters (11 feet) and a weight of more than 450 kilograms (990 pounds).

## KILLER WHALE

KILLER WHALE, *Orcinus orca* (Linnaeus) (57). The killer whale has turned out to be somewhat of a controversial subject, since it has long been accorded the reputation as a killer of the sea, which the name so clearly indicates.

The killer whale is the largest and one of the most intelligent of all dolphins. It ranges throughout all oceans, from tropical to polar latitudes. A fast-swimming predator, with powerful jaws capable of dispatching a seal or porpoise with a single bite, the killer whale is equipped with a formidable array of cone-shaped teeth, which are directed toward its throat for grasping and holding. Killer whales feed on a variety of marine organisms, including invertebrates, fish, birds, seals, walruses, and even some of the larger whales. *Orcinus* can attain a length of 9 meters (30 feet). It has allegedly attacked humans, but this has not been fully documented. Despite their playful antics in an oceanarium, they deserve respect in their ocean home. Above all, the killer whale deserves to be protected.

## GIANT TRIDACNA CLAMS

GIANT TRIDACNA CLAM, *Tridacna gigas* (Linnaeus) (58). These clams are found throughout many tropical waters, but the largest species are found in the western Indo-Pacific. Some of them attain a huge size, weighing more than 200 kilograms (440 pounds). Accidents from tridacna clams are rare, because the valves close rather slowly, but drownings have occurred from divers accidentally stepping into an open clam and having the large valves clamp down on a foot or a hand.

## GIANT SQUID

GIANT SQUID, *Architeuthis princeps* Verrill (59a, b). The giant squid has a reputation for attacking anything in sight, including large whales. It is reputed to be the largest, swiftest, and most terrifying invertebrate in the sea, and its maximum size has never actually been accurately determined; however, two tentacles measuring 14 meters (46 feet) were once vomited by a captive whale in an oceanarium, and it was estimated that these came from a squid measuring at least 20 meters (66 feet) and probably weighing 38,250 kilograms (84,150 pounds). A giant squid measuring 15 meters (49 feet) has chitinous teeth-ringed suckers measuring about 10 centimeters (4 inches) in diameter. Sperm whales have been examined having sucker wounds measuring 46 centimeters (18 inches) in diameter, and this would mean that the scars on the whale were probably inflicted by a monstrous squid measuring at least 61 meters (200 feet) in length.

Giant squid are equipped with strong chitinous rings equipped with teeth on each of the suckers; they are arranged in two regularly alternating rows on the distal half of each of the ten arms. When these horny sucker-equipped arms come in contact with their prey, they can inflict serious wounds. Giant squid are also equipped with large chitinous biting jaws surrounded by powerful jaw muscles, which comprise the buccal mass. The shape of the jaws resembles that of an inverted parrot's beak, but the arrangement of the jaws differs from the parrot in that the ventral half bites outside the dorsal half and is wider and longer. The buccal mass is also equipped with venom glands that secrete a poison. The same anatomical arrangement is generally present in all cephalopods.

**PLATE 1.** Giant whale shark, *Rhiniodon typus* Smith. This is the largest of the living sharks. Despite its massive size, upwards of 13 meters (43 feet), the creature has small teeth, feeds on plankton, and is gentle in nature, permitting divers to swim around it unharmed. Photo taken in the Sea of Cortez.
(H. Hall)

2

3  4

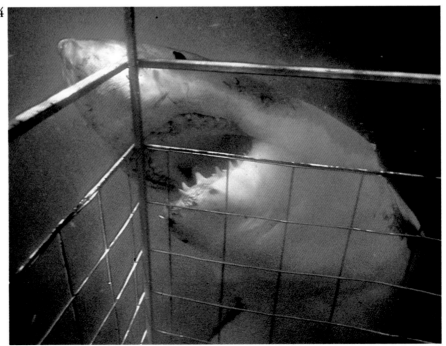

PLATE 2. Great white shark, *Carcharodon carcharias* (Linnaeus). A large specimen can exert an estimated biting force of twenty tons per square inch of tooth surface. Attains a length of about 6 meters (20 feet).

(R. and V. Taylor)

PLATE 3. A great white shark takes the bait with bulldog ferocity. With a tearing and shaking motion, the shark can easily chop a large fish in half or remove large masses of flesh from a seal or human. Note that one tooth is missing; within a short time it will be replaced by one of the fully developed reserve teeth.

(Courtesy A. Giddings, Ocean Images, Inc.)

PLATE 4. A great white shark charges the cage protecting the photographer. When food, blood, or low-frequency vibrations are present in the water, sharks quickly shift from a normal swimming pattern to an excited state, at which time they become unpredictable and may attack anything in sight.

(Courtesy A. Giddings, Ocean Images, Inc.)

PLATE 5. Tiger shark, *Galeocerdo cuvier* (Peron & LeSueur). The common name, tiger shark, comes from the striped markings of the juvenile, which tend to fade in the adults. Attains a length of about 5.2 meters (17 feet). (R. and V. Taylor)

PLATE 6. Mako shark, *Isurus oxyrinchus* (Rafinesque). This is one of the most aggressive and fastest swimming sharks. Note the rasp-like teeth, which are capable of inflicting a very nasty bite. Attains a length of about 3.6 meters (12 feet). (M. Snyderman)

PLATE 7. Nurse shark, *Ginglymostoma cirratum* (Bonnaterre). This is a sluggish, relatively harmless species, but attacks have occurred as a result of a diver bumping into the shark. Attains a length of 4.2 meters (14 feet).

(R. and V. Taylor)

PLATE 8. Bull shark, *Carcharhinus leucas* (Valenciennes). This shark belongs to a complex of species found in both fresh- and saltwater. They all have been incriminated in attacks on humans. Attains a length of 3.6 meters (12 feet). (WLRI photo)

PLATE 9. Oceanic whitetip shark, *Carcharhinus longimanus* (Poey). This large, active shark is found mostly in deep water. It is distinguished by its size (3.6 meters [12 feet]), rounded fins, mottled white fin tips, and relatively blunt snout.

(Courtesy A. Giddings, Ocean Images, Inc.)

PLATE 10. Bronze whaler, *Carcharhinus brachyurus* (Günther). This shark attains a length of 2.7 meters (9 feet) and is an active and aggressive open-water shark that has been responsible for a number of fatalities in Australia. Photo taken in the Coral Sea area. (Courtesy C. Roessler)

5

8

6

9

7

10

11

15

12

13a

13b

14

16

PLATE 11. Black whaler, *Carcharhinus obscurus* (LeSueur). This heavy-bodied shark has been involved in attacks on humans along the east coast of Australia. Attains a length of 3.6 meters (12 feet).

(R. and V. Taylor)

PLATE 12. Lemon shark, *Negaprion brevirostris* (Poey). This shark has been incriminated in attacks on humans. The lemon shark is one of the few species of large sharks that does well in captivity; consequently, it has been used a great deal as an experimental animal in shark biology. Attains a length of 3.3 meters (11 feet).

(D. Perrine)

PLATE 13. Gray reef shark, *Carcharhinus amblyrhynchos* (Bleeker):

a. Often found swimming in very large schools, these sharks are curious, aggressive, and tenacious. When disturbed, they may arch their backs, drop their pectoral fins, and then attack. This agonistic, or aggressive stance, is a warning signal to anyone intruding in their territory. Attains a length of 2.1 meters (7 feet). Great Barrier Reef, Australia. (H. Hall)

b. When attracted by food, gray reef sharks may venture into shallow water near the beach, their backs out of water, thrashing wildly about. On more than one occasion, they have driven divers out of the water and onto the beach. Jaluit, Marshall Islands.

(D. Ollis, WLRI photo)

PLATE 14. Blacktip reef shark, *Carcharhinus melanopterus* (Quoy and Gaimard). One of the common sharks seen in shallow reef areas, it seldom attacks humans, and can easily be frightened away. Attains a length of 1.8 meters (6 feet). Hermit Island, Bismarck Archipelago. (R. and V. Taylor)

PLATE 15. Whitetip reef shark, *Triaenodon obesus* (Rüppell). A very common small reef shark, it is usually quite timid, but capable of attacking. Valerie Taylor is seen here photographing the shark in the Coral Sea. Attains a length of 2.4 meters (8 feet).

(R. and V. Taylor)

PLATE 16. Sand shark, *Eugomphodus taurus* (Rafinesque). Generally sluggish, this shark has a voracious appetite; it feeds actively at night and lives mostly near the bottom as an inshore species. Attains a length of 3 meters (10 feet).

(Courtesy Sea World, San Diego)

17

19

18

20

PLATE 17. Sand shark, *Eugomphodus taurus* (Rafinesque). When attacking, this shark can be swift and savage. Taken in the Coral Sea. (R. and V. Taylor)

PLATE 18. Mackerel shark, *Lamna nasus* (Bonnaterre). A potentially dangerous species, this shark tends to be a sluggish swimmer, but may become active and aggressive when in pursuit of food. Attains a length of 3 meters (10 feet) or more. (R. H. Knabenbauer)

PLATE 19. Wobbegong shark, *Orectolobus ornatus* (DeVis). This is one of the carpet sharks, so-called because of their protective coloration. Usually found in shallow water on the bottom, they may attack waders and swimmers. Attains a length of 2.1 meters (7 feet). Photo taken off New South Wales, Australia. (R. and V. Taylor)

PLATE 20. Hammerhead shark, *Sphyrna zygaena* (Linnaeus). Hammerhead sharks are usually seen singly or in small aggregations (two to five), but at times may be observed in large numbers in such places as the Sea of Cortez. During these schooling periods, the sharks appear to be oblivious to outside intruders; thus, divers can swim among them without harm.

(Courtesy E. T. Rulison)

PLATE 21. In the midst of a large school of hammerheads. Sea of Cortez, Baja California.

(Courtesy R. Murphy, The Cousteau Society, Inc.)

PLATE 22. Valerie Taylor tests the protective value of a chain-link coat of mail from the bite of a blue shark, *Prionace glauca* (Linnaeus). Photo taken near San Diego, California. (R. and V. Taylor)

PLATE 23. Victim bitten in the wrist by an unidentified shark, near Guam, Mariana Islands.

(R. C. Schoening)

PLATE 24. Victim bitten by a large shark, believed to be a whaler. The victim managed to escape by beating the shark on the head and eyes with his hands. Near Ninegou Island, Bismarck Archipelago.

    a. Back view.

    b. Front view. Note teeth marks from the bite.

(Courtesy A.-M. Cousteau,
The Cousteau Society, Inc.)

21

22

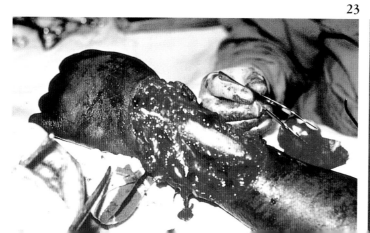

23

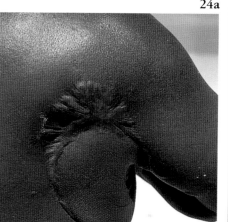

24a

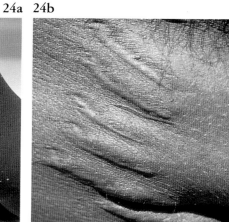

24b

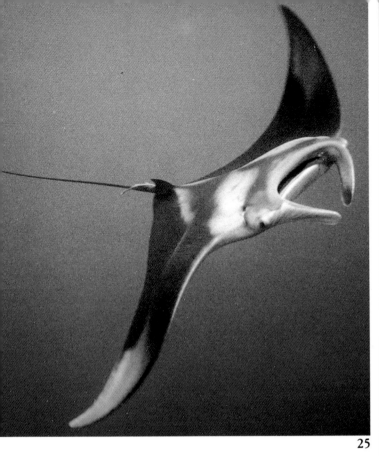

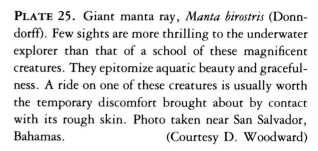

**PLATE 25.** Giant manta ray, *Manta birostris* (Donndorff). Few sights are more thrilling to the underwater explorer than that of a school of these magnificent creatures. They epitomize aquatic beauty and gracefulness. A ride on one of these creatures is usually worth the temporary discomfort brought about by contact with its rough skin. Photo taken near San Salvador, Bahamas. (Courtesy D. Woodward)

**PLATE 26.** Giant manta ray, *Manta birostris* (Donndorff). Note the two remoras clinging to the back of the manta ray. (Courtesy E. T. Rulison)

**PLATE 27.** Giant manta ray, *Manta birostris* (Donndorff). Larry, the author's son, tries to catch a ride on the back of a manta ray. Sea of Cortez.
(Courtesy R. Murphy, The Cousteau Society, Inc.)

**PLATE 28.** Giant manta ray, *Manta birostris* (Donndorff).
(Courtesy R. Murphy, The Cousteau Society, Inc.)

**PLATE 29.** Great barracuda, *Sphyraena barracuda* (Walbaum). Despite its ferocious appearance and an impressive set of canine teeth, barracuda tend to be more curious than aggressive and are sometimes surprisingly timid. Few attacks on humans have been recorded. Key Biscayne, Florida. (P. S. Auerbach)

**PLATE 30.** The photographer caught this great barracuda by surprise in a rocky crevice. Belize, Gulf of Honduras. (Courtesy E. T. Rulison)

**PLATE 31.** Mexican barracuda, *Sphyraena ensis* Jordan and Gilbert. This is one of a number of smaller species of barracuda that are frequently encountered swimming in large schools. Although equipped with large teeth, they are harmless, and there is usually no danger in swimming among them. Sea of Cortez, Baja California. (Courtesy E. T. Rulison)

25

28

29

26

27

30

31

**PLATE 32.** The mouth of the great barracuda is well equipped for grasping and tearing. Photo taken at the Marine Biological Station, Al Ghardaqa, Red Sea, Egypt. (D. Ollis, WLRI photo)

PLATE 33. Moray eel, *Gymnothorax marginatus* (Rüppel). Valerie Taylor looks into the face of a large moray eel. Generally, morays are not aggressive, but attacks on humans are known. Interestingly, they make excellent pets, responding to food and kindness. They have sharp, conical teeth, and, when they bite, they hold on with bulldog tenacity. Most encounters are the result of sticking one's hand into the mouth of a moray hiding in a hole in a coral reef. Great Barrier Reef, Australia. (R. and V. Taylor)

PLATE 34. A moray bite consists of puncture wounds and lacerations. Guam, Marianas Islands.
(R. C. Schoening)

PLATE 35. Bluefish, *Pomatomus saltatrix* (Linnaeus):
a. These voracious feeders are extremely destructive to a school of fish. Their "meat-grinder jaws" slash at anything in sight. Capable of inflicting serious wounds, they must be handled with care, even when taken on board a boat. They are usually found in large schools. Attains a length of 1.2 meters (4 feet).
(National Fisheries Service,
U.S. Department of the Interior)
b. Close-up of the head of *P. saltatrix* displaying a set of sharp teeth. (R. H. Knabenbauer)

PLATE 36. Needlefish, *Tylosaurus crocodilus* (LeSueur):
a. There are several closely related species, and all have been involved in attacks on humans. In most instances, the victim was impaled by the javelin-like jaws. Several persons have died from chest wounds in which the jaws penetrated the victim's heart. Large specimens may attain a length of 1.8 meters (6 feet).
(R. F. Myers, Coral Graphics)
b. Note close-up of needle-like jaws of an unidentified species of *Strongylura*, a closely related species of *Tylosaurus*, taken at Eniwetok, Marshall Islands.
(R. F. Myers, Coral Graphics)

PLATE 37. Giant grouper, *Promicrops lanceolatus* (Bloch). This large specimen was encountered by a diver under a large coral head in the lagoon of Jaluit Island, Marshall Islands. It weighed 240 kilograms (528 pounds). Groupers tend to be curious and fearless and have attacked divers who accidentally bumped into them in underwater caves.
(D. Ollis, WLRI photo)

PLATE 38. Sawfish, *Pristis perotteti* Müller and Henle. Injuries to humans from contact with the saw-like beak of these fishes have been reported but not documented. The "saw" is used for digging in the sand; by flailing it from side to side, the sawfish can impale or injure its prey. Sawfish are usually encountered in muddy waters, and they may enter river mouths. Attains a length of 6 meters (20 feet).
(Miami Seaquarium)

33

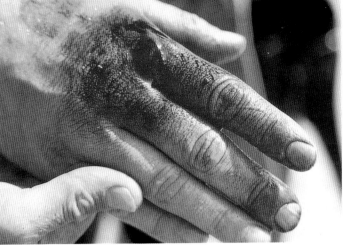
34

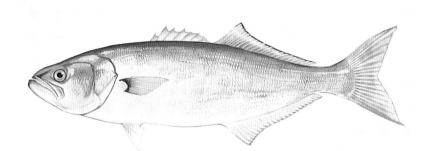

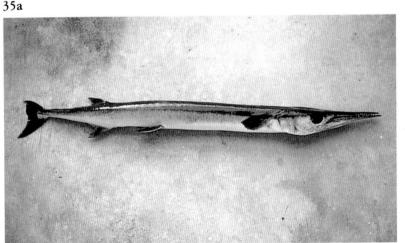
35a

35b

36a

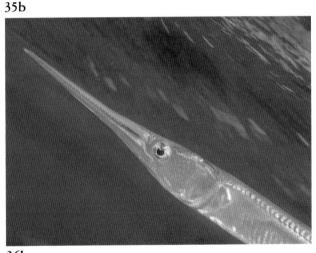
36b

37 38

39

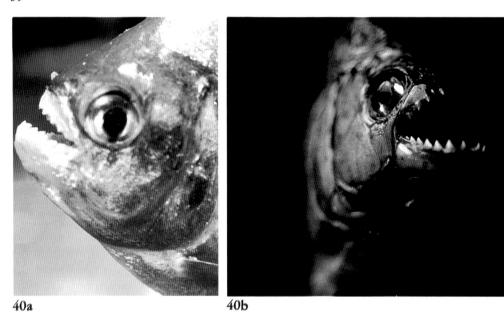

40a        40b

42

43

**PLATE 39.** Pacific striped marlin, *Makaira mitsukuri* (Jordan and Snyder). A rare underwater photo of the striped marlin. Marlin and swordfish have been known to attack boats. The head spear is capable of inflicting a nasty puncture, but direct attacks on humans have not been documented. Sea of Cortez, Baja California.

(Courtesy E. T. Rulison)

**PLATE 40 a, b.** Piraña, *Serrasalmus nattereri* (Kner). The piraña has a bad reputation, but there are surprisingly few documented attacks on humans. They are attracted by blood in the water, are well equipped for biting (as can be seen in these two photos), and are capable of reducing an animal to a skeleton within a short period of time. Singly, they are timid, but in schools they tend to become quite aggressive.

(Courtesy T. F. H. Publications)

**PLATE 41.** Sabre-tooth characin, *Rhaphiodon gibbus* Agassiz. This freshwater characin is equipped with large jaws armed with sharp, powerful teeth, capable of inflicting a painful bite. It inhabits the Amazon, north to the Guyana rivers and the Rio de la Plata, and attains a length of 33 centimeters (13 inches).

(Courtesy R. Murphy, The Cousteau Society, Inc.)

**PLATE 42.** Yellow-spotted or blue triggerfish, *Pseudobalistes fuscus* (Bloch and Schneider). Length 55 centimeters (21 inches). (From Gunther)

**PLATE 43.** Titan triggerfish, *Balistoides viridescens* (Bloch and Schneider). The triggerfishes can be aggressive and may inflict painful bites. Length 75 centimeters (29 inches). (R. F. Myers)

44

45

46

47

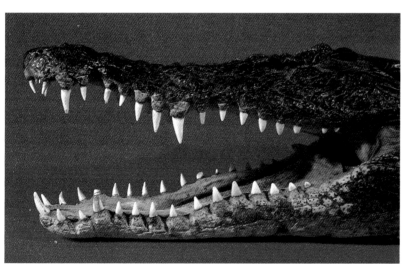

48

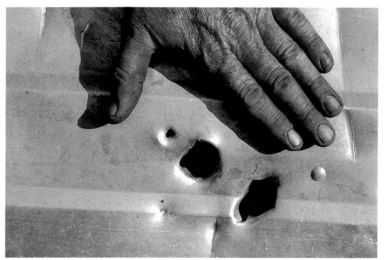

49

**PLATE 44.** Saltwater crocodile, *Crocodylus porosus* (Schneider). Few creatures are better equipped for grasping and tearing flesh than the crocodiles. This species has been responsible for many human deaths. They are capable of moving with surprising speed on land. The saltwater crocodile is usually found in mangrove swamps in shallow waters. Attains a length of 6 meters (20 feet) or more. Palau, Micronesia.

(D. Ludwig)

**PLATE 45.** Lair of the saltwater crocodile at the base of a mangrove tree. The lair is constructed of a loose mound of leaves not far from the water's edge. Palau, Micronesia. (D. Ludwig)

**PLATE 46.** A newly hatched saltwater crocodile. Even at this tender age, it is snapping and vicious and will draw blood with its sharp little teeth. The female lays about 30 to 50 eggs, usually during June through September. Incubation requires about 1½ months. The egg shell is a mosaic of numerous small, rough platelets cemented together by calcium salts and adhering to an inner membrane. Wyndham, West Australia. (Courtesy G. J. W. Webb)

**PLATE 47.** The saltwater crocodile is sometimes found swimming far out at sea. Photo taken off the coast of Palau, Micronesia. (D. Ludwig)

**PLATE 48.** The jaws of the crocodile are well constructed for dismembering a victim. (WLRI photo)

**PLATE 49.** Holes inflicted in an aluminum boat by a 5.6 meter (18 foot) saltwater crocodile. Wyndham, West Australia. (Courtesy G. J. W. Webb)

50

51

52

53

**PLATE 50.** Johnston's River crocodile, *Crocodylus johnstoni* Krefft. This crocodile is found in northern Australia in inland freshwater billibongs, lagoons, and rivers. Although injuries to humans have been reported, this crocodile is usually shy and seldom encountered. Attains a length of 3 meters (10 feet). Wyndham, West Australia.

(Courtesy G. J. W. Webb)

**PLATE 51.** Nile crocodile, *Crocodylus niloticus* Laurenti. In Africa, this crocodile has been incriminated in numerous attacks on humans. Crocodiles spend many hours basking in the sun; during the heat of day they seek shady areas. Photo taken on the Zam-
bia River near Victoria Falls, Zimbabwe.

(Courtesy S. Frier, The Cousteau Society, Inc.)

**PLATE 52.** California sea lion, *Zalophus californianus* (Lesson). Sea lions are usually not aggressive, but during the mating season the bulls can become quite pugnacious. The bulls attain a length of 2.3 meters (8 feet). The bulls attain a length of 2.3 meters (8 feet). Divers can usually swim among a herd of seal lions without harm. Sea of Cortez, Baja California.

(Courtesy E. T. Rulison)

**PLATE 53.** A spectacular view of the California sea lion caught in a moment of reflection. Sea of Cortez, Baja California. (Courtesy H. Hall)

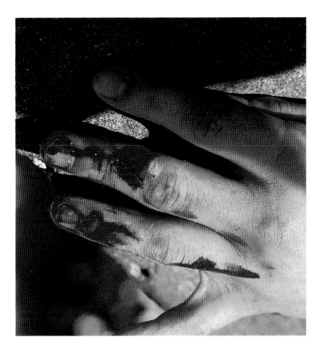

**PLATE 54.** Sea lions do bite, as shown in this photo. The diver provoked a male sea lion, which inflicted a bite. Fortunately, sea lions make a quick lunge and then retreat. (R. C. Schoening)

55

56

**PLATE 55.** Walrus, *Odobenus rosmarus* (Linnaeus). A small herd of walrus swimming off Diomede Islands, Alaska. Walrus are generally frightened by humans, but, when cut off from an escape route, they can become dangerous and can inflict a deadly wound with their ivory tusks. Attains a length of about 3.7 meters (12 feet) and a weight of 1,260 kilograms (2,770 pounds). (Courtesy U.S. Fish and Wildlife Service, (D. Irons)

**PLATE 56.** Polar bear, *Thalarctos maritimus* (Phipps). The polar bear can be extremely dangerous, particularly when a female is encountered with her cub. In adverse conditions, when trying to survive, they have been known to track down humans. Attains a length of 3.3 meters (11 feet) and a weight of 450 kilograms (990 pounds). (R. H. Knabenbauer)

57          58

59a

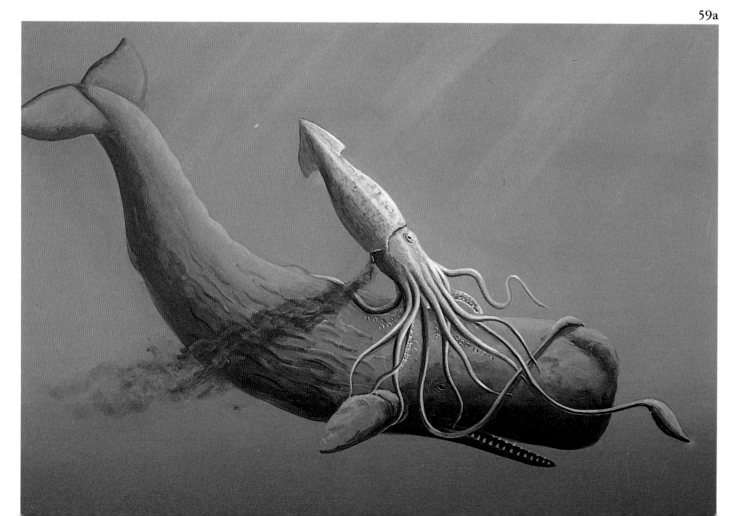

**PLATE 57.** Killer whale, *Orcinus orca* (Linnaeus). This magnificent mammal has long been maligned as a "killer"; however, in captivity it has proved to be intelligent and docile. Nevertheless, killer whales are equipped with a powerful set of jaws containing large, conical teeth. These animals are potentially dangerous and should be treated with respect. There are records of attacks on humans in the arctic, but these have not been adequately documented. The killer whale is also a beautiful and imposing marine mammal. Attains a length of 9 meters (30 feet).   (R. H. Knabenbauer)

**PLATE 58.** Giant tridacna clam, *Tridacna gigas* (Linnaeus). These clams can weigh more than 200 kilograms (440 pounds) and reach a length of 1.5 meters (5 feet). The closure of the clam shell is a very slow process, and in order to become entrapped in the giant tridacna clam, the victim would need to be very slow moving or unwary, to say the least. Great Barrier Reef, Australia.       (Courtesy A. Smith)

**PLATE 59a, b.** Giant squid, *Architeuthis princeps* Verrill. The number of species of giant squid has never been fully determined. Most of the giant squid are credited to the genus *Architeuthis*, which is found worldwide. The "giant squid" of the Humboldt Current (off the coast of Peru) is *Ommastrephes gigas* (D'Orbigny), which is said to attain a length of 3.6 meters (12 feet) and a weight of 135 kilograms (297 pounds), a diminutive "giant squid" in comparison with some of the larger specimens of *Architeuthis*.

  a. A giant squid attacking a sperm whale.

                    (D. Mooney)

  b. Mouth, beak, and suckers of the giant squid.

              (R. H. Knabenbauer)

59b

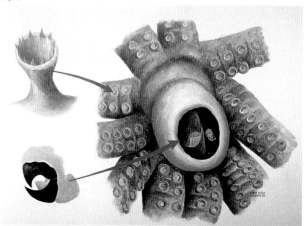

# CHAPTER III

# Aquatic Animals that Sting—Invertebrates

PERHAPS IT IS appropriate to begin by describing those features of an organism that constitute its venomousness. All venomous creatures share two characteristics: 1) they possess a *wound-producing traumatogenic instrument* of some type, i.e., a tooth, fang, spine, or a similar structure that is capable of injecting the poison into the victim; and 2) the traumatogenic device is associated with some sort of a *specialized poison gland* that secretes the venom. The traumatogenic device and the venom gland together comprise the *venom apparatus*. In many instances, the complexity of anatomical design and poison mechanism challenges one's imagination, e.g., the nematocysts, or stinging organs, of coelenterates. Sponges, however, possess only a simple mechanism consisting of sharp spicules, or needle-like structures, that are irritating upon contact.

Included within the category of venomous aquatic animals, that is, those that sting, are:

PORIFERA: Sponges
CNIDARIA (COELENTERATES): Hydroids, Jellyfishes, Sea Anemones, Corals
MOLLUSKS: Cone Shells, Cephalopods
ECHINODERMS: Starfishes, Sea Urchins
ANNELID WORMS: Polychaete Worms
ARTHROPODS : Aquatic Bugs

Venomous aquatic invertebrates are remarkably varied and often of great beauty.

## PORIFERA
### Sponges

To many people, the thought of a sponge brings to mind something one uses in bathing. The bath sponge, for example, is but the dead skeleton of the animal. Living sponges, however, are somewhat different and quite interesting organisms; some may grow to large sizes and have beautiful coloring. Nearly all produce chemical compounds that offer great promise as future therapeutic agents; but they can also inflict some nasty skin rashes.

For many centuries, sponges were considered to be plants, but they are, in fact, multicellular animals. Their animal nature was established in 1857. It is now estimated that there are more than 5,000 species of sponges, but their taxonomic classification is in a state of flux.

Sponges not only have an enormous geographical range but also a great vertical range within the sea. They exist from the intertidal zone to a depth of more than 2,800 meters (9,200 feet). Except for a single freshwater family, all sponges are marine.

Sponges range in size from pin-head proportions to species that attain a diameter of about 1 meter (39.37 inches), with a thickness of the body wall of about 30 centimeters (12 inches). Some of the tubular sponges *(Verongia)* can attain a length of 2 meters (6.6 feet). Encrusting sponges, such as members of the sponge

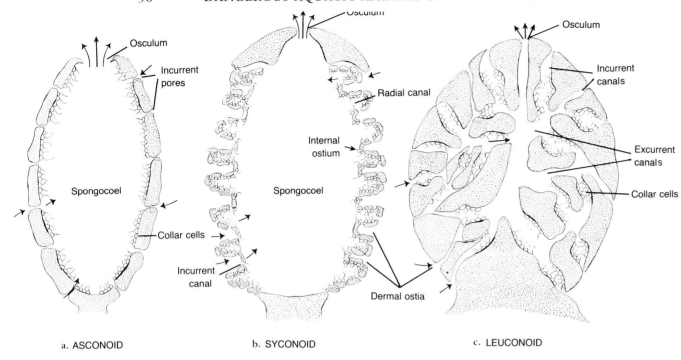

Figure 1. Three basic types of sponge structures and their canal systems; a. Asconoid; b. Syconoid; c. Leuconoid.
(L. Hood, after Buchsbaum)
Buchsbaum)

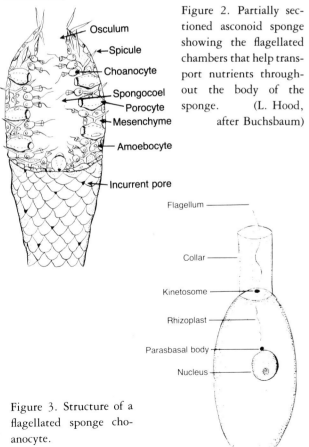

Figure 2. Partially sectioned asconoid sponge showing the flagellated chambers that help transport nutrients throughout the body of the sponge. (L. Hood, after Buchsbaum)

Figure 3. Structure of a flagellated sponge choanocyte.
(L. Hood, after Hegner)

stage. Their distribution in the aquatic environment is brought about largely by the actively swimming ciliated larvae or by a current of water carrying the young forms from place to place before they become attached.

Sponges feed on minute organic particles, living or dead, which are suspended in water, and enter the sponge through the pores and are then carried into the flagellated chambers (Figure 2). They function by means of an elaborate canal system, which serves in much the same manner as the circulatory system in higher animals. This system provides for the exchange of nutrients through the body and for the excretion of wastes.

Choanocytes, which are flagellated cells found within the canal system, beat continuously and create a current of water. In this manner, food particles are kept circulating within the body cavity (Figure 3). Choanocytes ingest food particles and form a food vacuole in which digestion takes place; the undigested residue is then discharged. Nutrients are passed from cell to cell and circulated to a limited extent by the amoeboid wandering cells of the mesenchyme, a loosely organized form of connective tissue.

Despite the obvious structural simplicity of sponges, they produce an impressive array of very complex chemical compounds having antimicrobial, antiinflammatory, and anticancer activity. These compounds are potential therapeutic agents. However, sponges also have a noxious side to the chemical agents they produce. Skin contact with some of these agents can produce severe rashes, which can be irritating, painful, and slow to heal.

family Spongillidae (60), at times become quite massive, reaching a size over 2 meters (6.6 feet) in diameter.

Sponges are among the most attractive of aquatic organisms because of their spectacular array of colors. Some are white, black, or gray, but others are yellow, orange, red, green, purple, violet, or a variety of pastel shades.

Although sponges lack organs, they do have groups of cells organized into specialized tissues. Sponges are equipped with a crude type of skeleton, which may consist of lime carbonate or silicon in the form of spicules and spongin, a substance that appears as intertwining fibers. The spicules are of a variety of types and serve to identify the various kinds of sponges into taxonomic groups (Figure 1). In some instances, the spicules may irritate the skin, but they are generally of minor medical concern.

Sponges are usually attached to some object and are therefore stationary, or sessile, animals in the adult

### Sponges Dangerous to Humans

BUCKLE SPONGE, *Fibulia nolitangere* (Duchassaing and Michelotti) (61). This sponge produces a stinging sensation, redness, and swelling of the hands when touched. The size is variable. It is found in the West Indies and Australia.

RED MOSS SPONGE, *Microciona prolifera* (Ellis and Solander) (62). This sponge is a member of the same family (Desmacidonidae) as *Fibulia* and causes a contact dermatitis, or skin irritation, that is common among fishermen in the northeastern United States. Symptoms consist of redness, stiffness of the finger joints, and swelling of the hands. If not properly treated, the dermatitis may spread and can become serious. This sponge forms a cluster having a height of about 15 centimeters (6 inches) and is found along the east coast of the United States, from Cape Cod south to South Carolina.

FIRE SPONGE, *Tedania ignis* (Duchassaing and Michelotti) (63). Contact with these sponges can result in an almost instantaneous stinging sensation and a severe dermatitis. The actual shape and size of the sponges vary greatly. It inhabits the West Indies.

# COELENTERATES (CNIDARIA)
## Hydroids, Jellyfishes, Sea Anemones, Corals

There is such a diversity of body structure in this group of organisms that at first sight they appear to be a conglomeration of unrelated animals. It is difficult to visualize such diverse creatures as a lace-like hydroid (81) dangling from a rock in an underwater cave, a jellyfish swimming through the water enveloping a juvenile fish (64), and a large blob with tentacles attached to a rock at the bottom of a bay (such as the Hell's Fire sea anemone [112]), all sharing certain morphological characteristics that bind them together.

All coelenterates have a body wall consisting of two layers, between which is the mesoglia, a jelly-like substance. The body contains a single gastrovascular cavity known as the coelenteron. The walls of the coelenteron are made of layers of simple tissue; hence coelenterates are said to have a tissue-level organization. Although coelenterates do not possess a coelom, or body cavity, they do possess a stinging apparatus comprised of thousands of stinging capsules known as nematocysts.

## Classification of Cnidarians

Coelenterates are grouped into three classes as follows:

**Hydrozoa:** This class includes the freshwater polyps (hydra), plumelike hydroids, small medusae, stony fire corals (*Millepora*), and the Portuguese Man-O-War (*Physalia*). There are about 2,700 species of hydroids, most of which are marine. The fire corals and numerous species of plumelike hydroids can inflict painful stings.

**Scyphozoa:** This class includes the jellyfishes. These are larger medusa, or free-floating forms, with eight notches in the margin of the bell. The deadly sea wasps (*Chironex, Chiropsalmus*) and the giant sea blubber (*Cyanea*), which may attain a diameter of more than 1.5 meters (5 feet) across the bell, are examples of this group. There are about 200 species of jellyfishes throughout the world.

**Anthozoa:** Included within this group are the sea anemones and the stony corals. The corals are notable for their precipitation of calcium, with the formation of calcareous structures that are known as reefs, or coral reefs. Some of the sea anemones (*Sagartia, Actinia, Anemonia, Triactis, Actinodendron*) are capable of inflicting very painful stings. Also included in this group is the extremely poisonous zoanthid *Palythoa*. There are about 6,100 species of anthozoans.

### Biology of Cnidarians

HYDROZOA: HYDROIDS

The hydroids are generally found attached to a substratum in shallow waters, from low tide down to depths of 1,000 meters (3,400 feet) or more. The ecological conditions in which hydroids are found are extremely variable and fluctuate according to species. Some species have a wide distribution, whereas others are restricted to definite latitudes. Generally speaking, hydroids are more abundant in temperate and cold zones. The form of the colony may be radically altered by such environmental factors as wave shocks, currents, and temperatures. Colonies usually are small or moderate in size, but some species may attain a length of 2 meters (6.6 feet). Because of the sessile habits of hydroids, commensalism—a relationship in which hy-

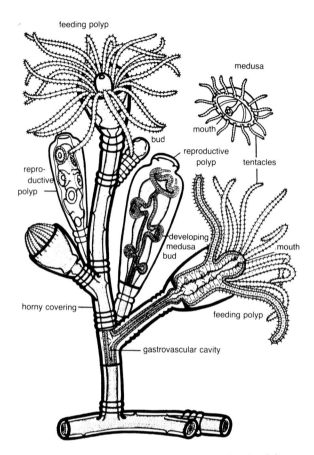

Figure 4. The basic structure of a colonial hydroid (*Obelia*).

(L. Hood, after Hegner)

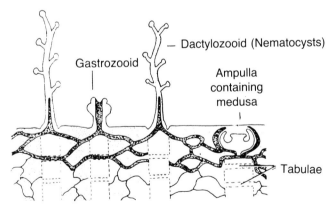

Figure 5. Cross section of the fire coral, *Millepora*, showing the structure of the canal system and the stinging dactylozooids, which contain the stinging nematocysts.

(L. Hood, after Hegner)

droids may attach themselves to other organisms and obtain their food without damaging the other—is a frequent occurrence. Since hydroids attach themselves to pilings, rafts, shells, rocks, or algae, and display their fine moss-like growth, they are sometimes mistaken for seaweed. Colonial hydroids are comprised of two kinds of polyps (individual organisms in the colony) or zooids: (1) *the feeding hydranth*, or *polyp*, that takes in food for the colony and (2) *the reproductive polyp*, or *gonangium* (Figure 4). The feeding polyps have a crown of tentacles and a central mouth that leads into the stomach cavity, to which all the other polyps are connected by the coenosarc, or common body cavity. The coenosarc encloses the common enteron, or gastric cavity. The nematocysts (nettle or stinging cells) are restricted to the tentacles. Food is procured by the use of the nematocysts.

Hydroids reproduce by budding. The free-swimming, solitary medusae, or larvae, that separate from the reproductive polyp produce ova that result in attached hydroids. Medusae are more difficult to obtain than are the plant-like hydroids, but they may be taken in fine-meshed plankton nets. The medusae may be likened to a tiny umbrella with a short handle, the manubrium, which contains the mouth. Tentacles provided with stinging cells hang from the velum, or margin, of the umbrella. Medusae swim in a jerky fashion, by means of spasmodic contractions of the umbrella. In the medusae, the sexes are separate.

The order Hydrocorallina, or hydroid corals, of which *Millepora* is the best-known genus, is widely distributed throughout tropical seas, mostly in shallow waters. Hydroid corals are important in the development of reefs, for they form upright, clavate, bladelike, or branching calcareous growths, or encrustations over other corals and objects. They vary in color from white to yellow-green and, because of their variable appearance, are sometimes difficult to recognize. The order is characterized by a massive exoskeleton of lime carbonate, the surface of which is covered with numerous minute pores. Millepores have two or three types of powerful nematocysts located on the polyps, polyp bases, and in the general coenosarc (Figure 5).

The Portuguese Man-O-War (*Physalia*) consists of floating colonies composed of several types of polypoid or medusoid individuals attached to a floating stem. They are pelagic animals, that is, they inhabit the surface of the open seas. They depend largely upon currents, wind, and tides for their movement. They are widely distributed as a group but are most abundant in warm waters. The float, or pneumatophore, of *Physalia* is greatly enlarged and is represented by an inverted, modified, medusan bell, whereas the remainder of the coenosarc is correspondingly reduced. *Physalia* may attain a large size, with a float 10 to 30 centimeters in length. From the underside of the float hang specialized zooids, such as gastrozooids, dactylozooids, and the reproductive gonodendra, with their gonophores or budding medusoids. The female gonophores are medusoid and may swim free, but the male reproductive zooid remains attached to the float. The gastrozooids or feeding polyps are without tentacles. Some of the tentacled dactylozooids are small. Several of the large dactylozooids, however, are equipped with very elongated fishing tentacles.

The number of fishing tentacles varies with the species of *Physalia*. In the Pacific form, *P. utriculus*, there is usually a single fishing tentacle; but in the Atlantic species, *P. physalis*, there are multiple fishing tentacles. Extending along the entire length of the large dactylozooid, a band of specialized tissue covers diverticulae of the gastrovascular cavity of the tentacle. These fishing tentacles or large dactylozooids may be found in the water to a depth of more than 30 meters (100 feet) and because of their transparent appearance, constitute a definite hazard to the unsuspecting swimmer. Upon contraction, the remainder of the tentacle shortens more completely than does the superficial band, and this causes the band to be thrown into the loops and folds that are known as "stinging batteries." The nematocysts are contained in cnidoblasts located in the superficial epithelium of the battery.

Scores of these fishing filaments may extend down into the water from a single *Physalia*. Each fishing filament contains about 750,000 nematocysts. When one considers the large number of fishing filaments on each *Physalia*, one finds a formidable venom apparatus.

When the animal is moving through the water, the fishing tentacles undergo a continuous rhythmic movement, alternately contracting and relaxing. Thus, there is a constant sampling of the water beneath the pneumatophore. If the tentacle brushes against prey, the nematocysts are stimulated, and they trigger the immediate release of the coiled nematocyst thread (Figure 6). The fully uncoiled thread may be several hundred times as long as the diameter of the parent capsule. The extreme length of the tubule, together with its hard chitinous barbs and spines, constitutes a highly effective trap. If the tip of the cnidal thread penetrates the victim, the toxin is conveyed directly into the body of the prey through the hollow thread. The thread can even penetrate a surgical glove.

The magnitude of the response to contact with the victim is proportional to the area of contact between tentacle and prey. A small animal, such as a copepod shrimp, may elicit the discharge of twenty to fifty adjacent nematocysts, whereas contact with a larger animal might evoke a discharge of several hundred thousand nematocysts. Gentle stimulation of the nematocysts results in a rapid release of the nematocyst thread, but does not dislodge the parent capsule from its position in the epithelium. Vigorous resistance by the prey results not only in greatly increasing the numbers of cnidae, but also in dislodging many of them from the epithelium. Dislodged nematocysts are replaced by cnidoblasts that differentiate outside the stinging battery but subsequently come to occupy a definitive position in the battery epithelium.

It is interesting that the loggerhead turtle (*Caretta caretta*) has been reported to feed on *Physalia*. The potency of the toxin and the ability of the *Physalia* nematocysts to penetrate even a surgical glove make this a gastronomic feat of no small accomplishment.

Also, certain nudibranchs such as *Glaucus, Claucilla, Pteraeolidia,* and *Janolus* (74, 75, 76a, b) may feed on *Physalia*, consuming and storing the nematocysts. The digestive system of the nudibranch does not destroy the nematocysts, which migrate through the body of the nudibranch to its tentacles. Once the nematocysts are in place in the tentacles, they can be employed as an effective defensive weapon by the nudibranch.

## Scyphozoa: Jellyfishes

All Scyphozoans, or jellyfishes, are marine and the majority are pelagic. A few species are known to inhabit depths of 2,000 fathoms or more. In the adult stage, most jellyfishes are free swimming. Because the swimming ability of most jellyfishes is relatively weak, their ocean journeys are greatly influenced by currents, tides, and wind. Scyphozoans are widely distributed throughout all seas. Many medusae reveal that they are affected by light intensity in that they surface during the morning and late afternoons and descend during midday and in darkness, whereas others react in just the opposite manner. A descent is usually made during periods of stormy weather. Swimming is accomplished by rhythmic pulsations of the bell, and this action determines the vertical rather than the horizontal progress of the animal. Jellyfishes display a remarkable ability to withstand considerable temperature and salinity changes. They are carnivorous; some of the larger species are capable of capturing and devouring large crustaceans and fish. Jellyfishes display a wide variety of sizes, shapes, and colors; many of them are semitransparent or glassy in appearance and often have brilliantly colored gonads, tentacles, or radial canals. Jellyfishes may vary in size from a few millimeters to more than 2 meters (6.6 feet) across the bell, with tentacles more than 50 meters (165 feet) in length, as in *Cyanea capillata*.

*Cyanea* has been aptly described as "a mop hiding under a dinner plate." It is a large, slimy jellyfish. The upper surface of the disc is circular, almost flat, roughened, and varied in coloration, usually bluish or

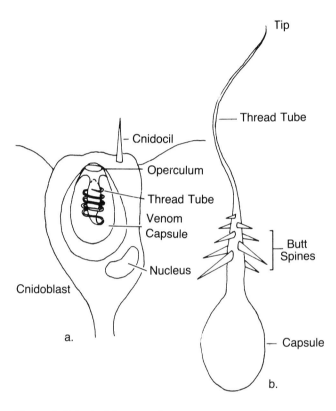

Figure 6. Principal features of nematocysts: (a) undischarged and (b) discharged        (R. Kreuzinger)

yellow-tinged. A multitude of threads several meters in length hangs from the undersurface of the disc. *Cyania* secretes a thick mucoid material that has a strong fishy odor.

Regardless of their size, jellyfishes are very fragile; many of them contain less than five percent of solid organic matter. Scyphomedusae have an eight-notch marginal bell, but lack a velum; the gonads are connected with the endoderm. Reproduction is by an alternation of generations, as in the hydroids, although the polyp stage is reduced. Jellyfishes have a complex system of branched radial canals, and numerous oral and marginal tentacles.

The cubomedusae are among the most venomous marine creatures known. The genera *Catostylus, Chirodropus, Chironex,* and *Chiropsalmus* contain some of the more dangerous species of the group. They range in size from a small grape to that of a grapefruit or larger.

Cubomedusae are widely distributed throughout all the warmer seas. Generally, they seem to prefer the quiet shallow waters of protected bays and estuaries, and sandy bottoms, although some species have been found in the open ocean. During the summer months, the immature forms, which usually stay on the bottom, reach maturity. The adults may then be found swimming at the surface. Light-sensitive cubomedusae, however, descend to deeper water during the bright sun of the middle of the day and come to the surface during early morning, late afternoon, and evening. Millions of cubomedusae have been observed hovering about 30 centimeters above the sandy bottom of some of the bays between Adelaide and Cape Jervis, Australia. Most of the specimens within the half-meter thick layer are found lying at an oblique angle, which is the customary position for the cubomedusae during such periods of inactivity. During the day the jellyfish ascend and gradually disperse in a zone ranging from the surface to a depth of 6 meters (20 feet) or more.

Cubomedusae are strong and graceful swimmers, capable of moving along at a steady two knots, and are believed to feed mainly on fish. They are very sensitive to water turbulence. During a flat, calm period they may appear in large numbers close to the beach in very shallow water. They are most abundant during the warm summer months, but have been recorded at other times of the year.

Little is known regarding the developmental stages and life histories of the members of this group, but apparently they spend their early life in brackish water estuaries. Cubomedusae have a box-like bell, an annular diaphragm that constricts the aperature of the bell-cavity, and four periradial stomach-pouches. One interesting feature of the cubomedusae is the presence of a highly developed eye, which has been well described in *Chironex* and in other species. On either side of the bell, a sense organ or rhopalium is set in a small niche containing both a position-sense organ and an optic apparatus of six eye-spots, the largest (the distal median eye-spot) having a biconvex lens.

The tentacles of the cubomedusae are interradial and arise just above the bell-margin. Their four proximal parts, or pedalia, which are tough and gelatinous, have a characteristic wing or spatula-like shape. A strong, outstanding pedalium containing a single tentacle of a cluster of four or more tentacles arises from each corner of the box-like medusa. In the case of *Chironex* and *Chiropsalmus*, the pedalia are claw-like and may have as many as 12 tentacles attached to a single pedalium. The hollow tentacles, generally thick and strong, taper distally to a blunt point. The outer surface is covered with rings of nematocysts. The tentacles are highly contractile and during life may extend down into the water for a distance of more than a meter. There is also an interesting symbiotic relationship between small juvenile fish and jellyfish (64).

## ANTHOZOA: SEA ANEMONES, CORALS

The class Anthozoa is comprised of two subclasses: (1) the Zoantharia, which includes the sea anemones, true corals, and zoanthids such as the extremely poisonous *Palythoa*, and (2) the Alcyonaria, which includes the soft corals, sea fans, sea pens, and sea pansies.

Sea anemones, or Actinarians, are one of the most abundant of seashore animals. There are approximately

1,000 species. Their bathymetric range extends from the tidal zone to depths of more than 2,900 fathoms. While they abound in warm tropical waters, some species inhabit arctic seas. Anemones vary in size from a few millimeters to a half meter or more in diameter. Most species are sessile and live attached to objects of various kinds, but are nevertheless able to creep about to some extent. When they are covered by water and undisturbed, the body and tentacles are expanded; and because of their variety of colors they frequently have a flowerlike appearance. If the animal is irritated or the water recedes, the tentacles may be invaginated rapidly and the body contracted. The food of anemones consists of mollusks, crustaceans, other invertebrates, and fishes. Most anemones have a short cylindrical body and flat oral disc margined with a variable number of tentacles around a slit-like mouth. The base or pedal disc of the anemone serves for attachment to objects. The mouth is connected to the enteron by a tube-like gullet. The body is internally divided into radial compartments by septa that are in multiples of six. The free inner margins of the septa within the enteron may bear convoluted septa filaments, which are continued as threadlike acontia bearing nematocysts. Occasionally, the acontia may be extended through pores in the body wall or through the mouth to aid in subduing prey. Nematocysts are also situated on the marginal tentacles. Reproduction may be either sexual or asexual by fission. There is no alteration of generations and no medusal stage.

True corals, or Madreporarians, require water temperatures of 20°C or higher and are confined largely to the torrid zone, although a few species do inhabit more temperate waters. The vertical distribution of corals ranges from the low tide zone to depths of about twenty fathoms. A few of the solitary corals are known to occur at 1,500 fathoms or more. Corals are a major constituent of living reefs. Along with calcareous algae, they dominate the reef in numbers and volume and provide the ecological niches essential to the existence of all other reef-dwelling animals and plants. Assuming that the oxygen supply and temperatures are favorable, the number of species of reef corals is controlled largely by

light intensity and radiant energy. This situation appears to be the result of the restrictive effect of the symbiotic zooxanthellae microorganisms in the tissues of corals. Temperature variation is a significant factor in determining the distribution of corals over reef flats, inasmuch as corals do not flourish where the water circulation does not maintain stable temperatures and provide fresh supplies of nutrients. Since carbonate ($CaCO_3$) is generally present in supersaturated quantities in seawater of normal salinity, it is not a significant factor in the distribution of corals. The average coral colony contains three times as much plant as animal tissue, and most of the plant tissue is comprised of filamentous green algae in the skeleton.

The stony hexacorals, which include *Acropora, Astreopora,* and *Goniopora,* tend to dominate reef communities as a result of their wide range of ecological adaptability, their growth habits, and their near immunity to predators. With the exception of certain fishes, living coral polyps are not a direct food supply for most marine organisms. This might suggest the presence of certain noxious chemical constituents within the tissues of the coral polyps. Corals are constantly hampered in their growth by such destructive forces as perforating, boring, and dissolving algae, sponges, mollusks, worms, and echinoids, and by fishes that nibble on them. Wave shock and the abrasive action of dislodged coral debris and sand exert further destructive effects.

Corals, small anemone-like polyps that have a reduced musculature, short tentacles, and no pedal disc, live in a stony cup having basal radial ridges (Figure 7). The individual polyps connect with each other through the coenosarc.

Corals are carnivores with highly specialized feeding mechanisms. With the use of tentacles and cilia, they are able to capture and consume living zooplankton. The primary function of the cilia is to remove debris and wastes from the polyps' surface. Because of their sedentary habits and limited tentacular range, corals are largely dependent upon good water circulation to bring food within range of contact. The nematocysts,

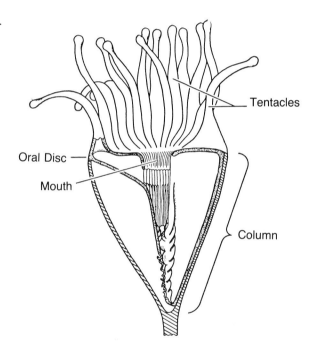

Figure 7. Structure of a coral polyp, diagrammatic, sagittal, or midline, section.

(R. Kreuzinger, after Vaugh and Wells)

frequently of a complex type, are present in the tentacles, body wall, gullet, and septal filaments. Madrepores may be white, pink, yellow, green, brown, or purple in color. There are about 2,500 species, most of which are colonial.

### Nematocyst: The Stinging Apparatus

The stinging apparatus of coelenterates is one of the most remarkable anatomical structures in the entire arsenal of venomous creatures. The apparatus consists of specialized stinging capsules located on the tentacles and other portions of the body of the organism (Figures 8, 9a, b, c).

Each of the double-walled capsular nematocysts is situated within specialized epidermal cells known as cnidoblasts (cnidocytes). Some species of coelenterates have a triggerlike device known as the cnidocil; other species lack a cnidocil, but are equipped with special chemoreceptors capable of detecting food and activating the nematocysts. Contained within the fluid-filled capsular nematocyst is a hollow, coiled, open-ended thread tube. The thread tube is everted through the opening at one end of the nematocyst, which is closed prior to discharge by apical flaps or a lid-like device called the operculum. The fluid within the nematocysts is the venom.

Undischarged nematocysts are usually spherical and rod-like in shape. They vary greatly in length, from about 3 to 100 μm. Twenty-seven different types of nematocysts are now recognized. Whereas several distinct size classes of the same type of nematocyst may be found in the tissue of a single coelenterate species, the functional significance of this is unknown.

The discharge thread varies in length, diameter, and morphology, and usually bears a formidable array of spinules. The structure of these nematocysts is of importance in their identification and have been found to be clinically useful in providing leads as to the species of coelenterate that may have caused the envenomation (Figure 9). The ability of a particular coelenterate to sting the victim depends to a large extent on the ability of the thread tube to penetrate the skin.

The mechanism of nematocyst discharge is the subject of much research and conjecture. A basic question in the nematocyst discharge issue concerns the propulsion mechanism of the thread tube once the operculum, or apical flaps, is released. When the nematocyst is discharged, the thread tube turns inside out (everts completely). There is usually a triple helix of spinules that bore in and firmly anchor the shaft of the tube in the flesh of the victim. One striking feature that has been observed in the discharge of the nematocyst is the great increase in the length and the diameter of the thread following discharge. Discharge time is only about 1/1000 of a second.

The explanation of the energy source producing the nematocyst discharge continues to be theoretical. There are several theories, but few confirmed facts. The control of the nematocyst discharge is not known.

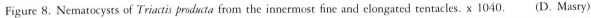

Figure 8. Nematocysts of *Triactis producta* from the innermost fine and elongated tentacles. x 1040.          (D. Masry)

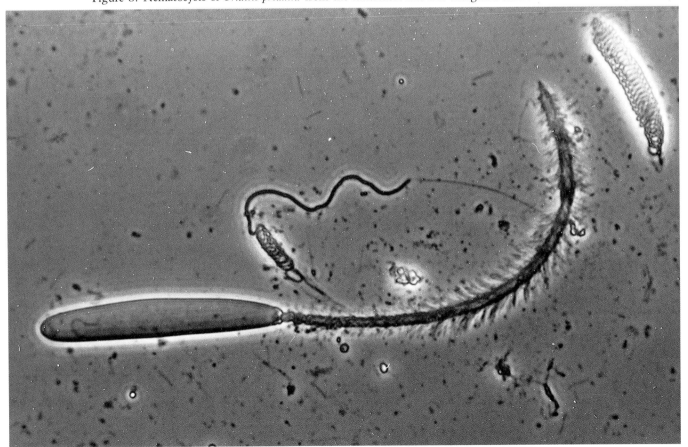

VENOM. Chemical studies have shown that most nematocyst venoms consist mainly of a complex mixture of peptides (or amides) or proteins. The toxic effects of nematocyst venoms vary greatly from one coelenterate species to the next and include hemolytic, dermatonecrotic, paralytic, and lethal cardiotoxic properties.

## Coelenterates Dangerous to Humans

The following is only a small sampling of a large number of coelenterate species capable of inflicting stings. They are arranged according to the foregoing classification and only a few examples of the more common dangerous species are presented. These stings vary in severity from mild skin irritations to severe lacerations, ulcers, and even death.

HYDROZOA: HYDROIDS

STINGING or FIRE CORAL, *Millepora complanata* Lamarck (66, 67).

STINGING or FIRE CORAL, *Millepora dichotoma* Forskål (65, 69).

STINGING or FIRE CORAL, *Millepora alcicornis* (Linnaeus) (68).

The fire corals are sometimes referred to as false corals. They are generally found living among true corals on reefs in warm tropical waters throughout the world. As previously noted, their form and size vary greatly from specimen to specimen. There are a number of closely-related species that are difficult for even the experts to identify accurately. Contact with their tiny polyps can produce an intense and immediate burning reaction.

ATLANTIC PORTUGUESE MAN-O-WAR or BLUE BOTTLE, *Physalia physalis* (Linnaeus) (70, 71). The appearance of this hydroid closely resembles that of a true jellyfish, and is frequently mistaken for one. *Physalia* is a colonial hydroid. It is usually found floating at the surface of the water. The stinging tentacles are suspended from a balloon-like float. The tentacles may trail down into the water for a depth of 30 meters (100 feet), which presents a real danger to an unsuspecting swimmer or a poorly-clad scuba diver. The Atlantic

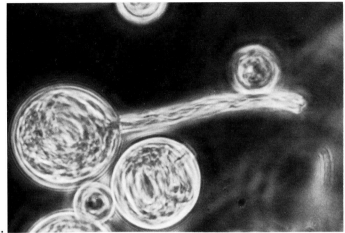

a.

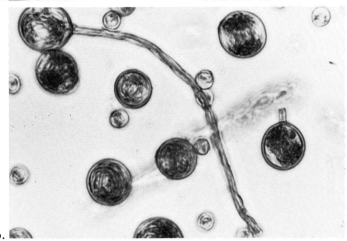

b.

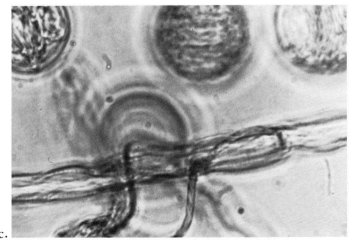

c.

Figure 9a–c. Photomicrographs of the nematocysts of *Physalia physalis*.

a. Phase-contrast photomicrograph of discharging nematocysts. Note opercular area of large nematocyst about to discharge (lower left). x 800.

b. Later state of discharging nematocyst. Note that the thread tube length is already many times the diameter of the parent capsule but is far from completely extended. Again note the two size groups of nematocysts. x 500.

c. Photomicrograph showing portions of two intertwined thread tubes—one from a large capsule and the more tortuous from a small capsule. x 1,280.

(Courtesy C. E. Lane)

*Physalia* ranges throughout the tropical Atlantic, from the Bay of Fundy, Hebrides, south to the West Indies, and the Mediterranean. The stings may be lethal. It attains a length of 35 centimeters (13 inches).

PACIFIC PORTUGUESE MAN-O-WAR or BLUE BOTTLE, *Physalia utriculus* La Martinière (72, 73) is found in the Indo-Pacific region. *Physalia* can pack a real wallop, producing intense pain, respiratory distress, and muscular paralysis; death from drowning is a potential danger.

STINGING HYDROID, *Aglaophenia cupressina* (Lamouroux) (77). The appearance of soft plume-like organisms dangling harmlessly from rocks or pilings can be a dangerous attraction. Contact with their stinging polyps can produce an intense stinging reaction, redness, and in some instances a severe rash. Closely related species include *Sertularella* sp. (78), *Lytocarpus nuttingi* Hargitt (79), *Lytocarpus philippinus* (Kirchenpauer) (80), *Pennaria tiarella* (Ayres) (81), and related species (82), all of which are found in the tropical Atlantic and Indian oceans. The size of these plumed hydroids varies greatly from a few centimeters (inches) to 30 centimeters (12 inches) or more in length.

SCYPHOZOA: JELLYFISHES

BROWN BLUBBER JELLYFISH, *Catostylus mosaicus* (Quoy and Gaimard) (83a, b). This is the most common species found along the coast of eastern Australia. Occurring mostly in estuaries, this jellyfish has a unique feature in that its stinging ability seems to vary with the season of the year. At times, it can be handled with impunity; but during the reproductive season (warmer months), it can inflict an intensely painful sting causing respiratory distress. There is a typical cross mark on top of the bell. The bell is about 30 centimeters (12 inches) in diameter.

MILKY JELLYFISH, *Chrysaora lactae* Eschscholtz (84). This jellyfish is so named because of its milky appearance, and is reputed to be a comparatively mild stinger. The bell is about 7 centimeters (2.7 inches) in diameter, but thought to attain a much greater size. It is found from the West Indies south to Brazil.

SEA NETTLE, *Chrysaora quinquecirrha* (Desor) (85). This one of the most beautiful of the jellyfishes. The sea nettle is rated as a moderate to severe stinger.

The diameter of the bell is about 25 centimeters (10 inches). It is found in most tropical seas of the world.

SEA BLUBBER or LION'S MANE, *Cyanea capillata* (Linnaeus) (86, 87). This jellyfish provided the basis for one of Sherlock Holmes' mysteries. It is one of the largest of all of the jellyfishes, measuring up to 2 meters (6.6 feet) across the bell, with tentacles hanging down in the water more than 50 meters (165 feet). *Cyanea* can inflict painful wounds (88). It is found in the North Atlantic and North Pacific oceans.

NOCTURNAL JELLYFISH, *Pelagia noctiluca* (Forskål) (89). This delightful little jellyfish is usually discovered at night, as its Latin name implies. Rated a mild stinger, *Pelagia* is found in warm waters throughout the world. The diameter of the bell is about 6 centimeters (2.3 inches).

The sea wasps, cubomedusae, or box jellies that follow include some of the most dangerous stingers known:

AUSTRALIAN SEA WASP, *Chironex fleckeri* Southcott (90). Undoubtedly the most deadly jellyfish inhabiting the marine environment, the sea wasp is found along the coast of North Queensland and the Northern Territory, Australia. A number of deaths have been caused by this creature, particularly in the vicinity of Cairns, Australia. Death can result within a few minutes after envenomation. The most dangerous season is during November through March. Warning signs are generally posted on the beaches, with first-aid instructions. Whatever first-aid action is to be taken must be done promptly, because the venom is capable of producing instant heart block. The sting from *Chironex* (91–95) can be severe, resulting in dramatic skin burns. The bell is about 7.5 centimeters (3 inches) in diameter or more.

SEA WASP, *Chiropsalmus quadrigatus* (Haekel) (96), is a species closely related to *Chironex*. It inhabits the Philippines, northern Australia, and the Indian Ocean. It can produce painful stings, but no deaths have been reported.

WEST INDIAN SEA WASP, *Chiropsalmus quadrumanus* (Müller) (97), is a similar species reported from the West Indies. The bell is about 14 centimeters (5.5 inches) in diameter.

SEA WASP, *Carybdea alata* (Reynaud) (98), a second West Indian species, is also referred to as a sea wasp. The bell is about 5 centimeters (2 inches) in diameter. Both *C. quadrumanus* and *C. alata* are capable of inflicting painful stings, but no deaths have been reported. They are usually encountered at night, where they are found near the surface. It should be noted when discussing sea wasps that the deadly *Chironex* does not occur in the West Indies or in North or South American waters.

STINGING MEDUSA, *Olindias tenuis* Fewkes (99). The family Olindiadidae, which includes *Olindias* and *Gonionemus,* is a group of shallow-water, bottom-living jellyfishes. *Olindias* are all tropical forms, frequently inhabiting the polluted waters of harbors, or over mud flats. Some species of *Gonionemus* are found in cold temperature waters.

STINGING MEDUSA, *Gonionemus vertens* Agassiz (100), has been incriminated in six deaths near Vladivostock (formerly U.S.S.R.), but is generally considered innocuous elsewhere. The diameter of the bell is about 15 millimeters (.6 inches).

JELLYFISH, *Nausithoë punctata* Kölliker (101–104), is one of the most interesting jellyfishes. The adult stage is relatively innocuous and small in size, about 15 millimeters (.6 inches) in diameter. However, the larval stage does not resemble the adult in size or appearance and was originally described as an entirely different species, namely *Stephanoscyphus racemosus* Komai (103). At this point in life, the juvenile form resembles more closely a cluster of sessile seaweed. Later studies revealed this "seaweed" to be not only an animal, but the juvenile stage of a free-swimming jellyfish! Contact with the adult is usually a minor encounter, but it is an entirely different matter with the juvenile, which can inflict painful wounds (102).

ANTHOZOA: SEA ANEMONES

WAX ROSE SEA ANEMONE, *Anemonia sulcata* (Pennant) (105b, 106). This attractive western European sea anemone ranges from Scotland and Norway, south into the Mediterranean Sea. Its nematocysts are quite potent, and it is capable of inflicting a powerful sting. *A. sulcata* has been the subject of a great deal of venomological research in Europe. The diameter is 20 centimeters (8 inches).

STRAWBERRY SEA ANEMONE, *Actinia equina* Linnaeus (105a, 107). This anemone inhabits the eastern Atlantic, ranging from the Arctic to the Mediterranean Sea and is reputed to be a moderate stinger. The diameter is about 7 centimeters (2.7 inches).

SEA ANEMONE, *Telmatactis rufa* (Verrill) (108, 109a-f), packs a powerful punch. Contact with the skin results in immediate intense pain, lymph adenopathy, numbness, nausea, constriction of the throat, respiratory distress, blistering, and ulceration of the skin that is slow to heal.

PARASITIC SEA ANEMONE, *Adamsia palliata* (Bohadsch) (105c). This interesting sea anemone is found attached to the shell of hermit crabs in what seems to be a mutually beneficial relationship. The species ranges from Norway south into the Mediterranean Sea. A moderate stinger, it has a diameter of about 4 centimeters (1.5 inches).

ROSY SEA ANEMONE, *Sagartia elegans* (Dalyell) (105d). This sea anemone ranges from Iceland, south into the Mediterranean Sea and is a moderate stinger. The diameter is about 8 centimeters (3.4 inches). The sponge fisherman's disease (*maladie des plongeurs*) is believed to be due to stings received from small sea anemones such as *Actinia* or *Sagartia,* which are attached to the base of sponges. In the process of removing the sponges, the fishermen are stung. Repeated stinging may produce severe hypersensitivity reactions.

RED SEA ANEMONE, *Triactis producta* Klunzinger (110a, b). This is a small sea anemone that is most active at night. It can produce a severe skin reaction; the wheal later becomes an ulcer, which is slow to heal. It inhabits the Red Sea region. The diameter is about 4 centimeters (1.4 inches).

HELL'S FIRE SEA ANEMONE, *Actinodendron plumosum* Haddon (112–115). When this anemone is in a contracted state on the bottom, it appears as a large blob of mud or a rock. It attaches to rocks, corals, or the underside of ledges, but is never found in the sand. When extended, it has an attractive flowerlike appearance. This sea anemone is one of the most dangerous kinds and is capable of inflicting a very painful wound. The wound later becomes a chronic sore and may take several months to heal. The victim may also evidence fever, prostration, and gastric upset. The diameter is about 15 centimeters (6 inches) to 30 centimeters (13 inches).

BURROWING SEA ANEMONES: Some of the most dangerous stingers among the anemones are those found burrowing in the sand or mud of tropical bays. Several species of the genus *Cerianthus,* for instance, can inflict very painful stings. This group of anemones is found in shallow waters throughout tropical seas. Representative of this genus are:

CYLINDER SEA ANEMONE, *Cerianthus filiformis* Carlgren (116,117), a powerful stinger.

GRIFFITH'S SEA ANEMONE, *Megalactis griffithsi,* Saville Kent (118), also a powerful stinger.

Another very attractive burrowing anemone is:

ARMED SEA ANEMONE, *Dofleini armata* Wasilieff (119), which also packs a potent sting. All of the foregoing burrowing anemones are Indo-Pacific species. An example of their stinging ability is seen in (109).

RIBBED SEA ANEMONE, *Alicia costae* (Panceri) (120) is from the Mediterranean Sea. It has a West Indian counterpart:

MARVELOUS SEA ANEMONE, *Alicia mirabilis* (Johnson) (121). This anemone is indeed impressive to behold and even more impressive to touch. Contact with its multiple stinging batteries may result in serious stings that will long be remembered.

TORCH SEA ANEMONE, *Lebrunea danae* (Duchassaing and Michelotti) (122). This attractive sea anemone can inflict a painful sting. It inhabits the Caribbean region. The diameter is about 5 centimeters (2 inches).

ANTHOZOA: CORALS

ORANGE TUBE CORAL, *Tubastrea tenuilamellosa* (Milne-Edwards and Haime) (123). When the polyps are expanded at night, they are a strikingly beautiful yellow-orange and can be mistaken for small sea anemones. This is one of the few known stinging true corals. The sting is similar to that inflicted by some hydroids. The diameter of the oval disc is about 1 centimeter (.5 inch).

STINGING BUBBLE CORAL, *Physogyra lichtensteini* Milne-Edwards and Haime (124a, b). The tentacles of this sea anemone appear as bubbles, which contain batteries of powerful stinging nematocysts. An interesting feature, observed by photographer Douglas Faulkner, is that these "bubbles" appear to expand and contract with the ebb and flow of the tidal cycle. In the Indo-Pacific region several closely-related species are found. The colonies are about 1 meter (39 inches) or more in diameter and have a height of 50 centimeters (20 inches) or more.

## Coral Cuts

Corals can inflict severe cuts and are one of the most frequent causes of underwater injuries. Despite their delicate appearance, stony corals, such as the *Acropora* species (125–128), have calcareous outer skeletons with razor sharp edges. These injuries start as small minute cuts or scratches and rapidly escalate into painful sores; if they are not treated promptly and properly, they turn into a full-blown cellulitis in a matter of hours. The severity of coral cuts is probably due to a combination of factors: mechanical laceration of the skin; limited envenomation by nematocysts if such takes place; introduction of foreign matter into the wound (calcium carbonate, sand, debris, slime, microorganisms); secondary bacterial infections; and climatic conditions (high temperature and humidity) suitable for bacterial growth. Coral cuts are superficial, but slow to heal, and may cause temporary disability. Minor cuts can become major medical problems and should never be ignored.

## MOLLUSKS
### Cone Shells, Cephalopods

The mollusks comprise a very large group of about 45,000 species. They inhabit a wide range of habitats and have a wealth of forms. Mollusks are among the most drab and the most spectacular in terms of their coloration. The nudibranch gastropods, for example, parade a beauty of form and coloration seldom exceeded by any other group of organisms in the aquatic environment.

Mollusks are unsegmented invertebrates having a soft body and usually secreting a calcareous shell. A muscular foot is present, which may be modified to serve various functions. Covering at least a portion of the body is a soft skin, the mantle, the outer surface of which secretes the shell. Respiration is by means of gills or a modified primitive pulmonary sac. Jaws are present in some species. In four of five classes, food is obtained by the use of a rasp-like device called a radula. In the cone shells and a few others, the radular ribbon is lost and the teeth are modified into hollow, harpoon-like structures. In the bivalves, such as the clams, the radula is absent.

The phylum Mollusca is generally divided into five classes:

1) *Amphineura:* Chitons (nonvenomous).
2) *Scaphopoda:* Tooth or Tusk Shells (non-venomous).
3) *Gastropoda:* snails and slugs. The *Gastropoda* include land, freshwater and marine snails, and slugs. Members of this class are characterized by a univalve, or single, shell. The body is asymmetrical in a spirally-coiled shell (the slugs are an exception to this arrangement). Typically there is a distinct head, with one or two pairs of tentacles, two eyes, and a large, flattened, fleshy foot. Gastropods may be either monoecious or dioecious, and are mostly oviparous.

In the suborder Toxoglossa, there are three families—Conidae, Turridae, and Terebridae—believed to be provided with venom organs. However, of the toxoglossids, only the family Conidae has been incriminated in human envenomations. It is estimated that there are 33,000 living species of gastropods.

4) *Pelecypoda:* Bivalves (scallops, oysters, clams, mussels, etc.). The members of this class are characterized as having a shell of two lateral valves, usually symmetrical with a dorsal hinge, a ligament, and closed by one or two adductor muscles. There are no venomous species in this group. It is estimated that there are 11,000 living species of pelecypods.

5) *Cephalopoda:* Squid, octopus, nautilus, and cuttlefish. The shell is external, internal, or absent. The head is large and contains conspicuous and well-developed eyes. The mouth, armed with horny jaws and a radula, is surrounded by eight or ten tentacles equipped with numerous suckers. Rapid movements can be produced by expelling water from the mantle cavity through the siphon. The sexes are separate. The toxicity of the salivary secretions of *Octopus* has been of principal interest to venomologists. There are about 650 species, all of which are marine.

Research on molluskan venomology is still in its infancy and much remains to be learned about the phylogenetic distribution of venom organs among mollusks. This is indeed an area for much productive research in the future, for there is increasing evidence that venom organs are present in a far greater number of mollusks than was formerly suspected.

Only two groups of venomous mollusks will be discussed here; namely the cone shells and the octopuses.

### Cone Shells
#### Biology of Cone Shells

The families Conidae, Turridae, and Terebridae constitute the suborder Toxoglossa. The members of

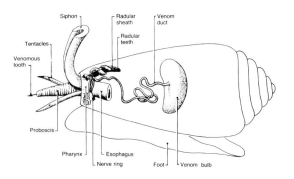

Figure 10. Venom apparatus of the cone shell (*Conus*).
(R. H. Knabenbauer)

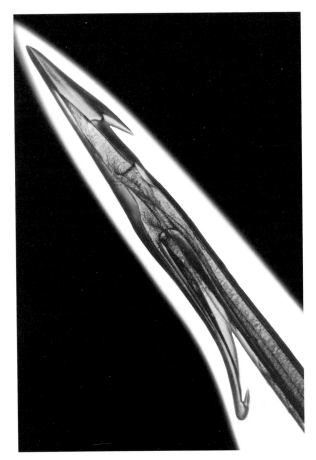

Figure 11. The harpoon-like tip of a radular tooth of *Conus striatus*—a truly magnificent but deadly work of art. The radular tooth is a flat sheet of chitin rolled into a hollow tube-like structure. The shaft of this tooth is filled with a lethal venom immediately prior to discharge and entry into the flesh of the victim. The venom is injected into the base and along the open shaft of the tooth under pressure from the venom bulb and duct. Length of tooth about 7 millimeters (.25 inches). (R. Kreuzinger)

Toxoglossa are characterized by the possession of a venom apparatus, but only the family Conidae has been incriminated in human intoxications. There are about 400 species in the family Conidae, all of them members of the single genus *Conus*, and with few exceptions these are confined to tropical and subtropical seas. The species *C. aulicus, C. geographus, C. gloria-maris, C. marmoreus, C. omaria, C. striatus, C. textile*, and *C. tulipa* have a well-developed venom apparatus and are capable of inflicting death in humans. Because of their size and the nature of their venom apparatus, numerous other species of cones are of potential danger to humans.

Cone shells are for the most part shallow-water inhabitants, since they range from tidal reef areas down to depths of several hundred meters. They are found in a variety of microhabitats. Some species are associated with the attached algae of coral reefs; others crawl about under coral heads; still others prefer a sandy or coral rubble substrate. Those species of cones most dangerous to humans are found chiefly in the sand or rubble habitat. Although not all sand dwellers have a bad reputation, they must be handled with caution.

The cone shells are chiefly nocturnal in habit, burrowing in sand or under coral or rocks in the daytime and becoming active at night to feed. The food of cones, varying somewhat with the species, consists of polychaete worms, other gastropods, pelecypods, octopuses, and small fishes.

Cones are predacious and kill by injecting a venom into the prey by means of a detachable, dartlike radular tooth. Food detection is believed to be largely through the use of a special chemoreceptory organ; this organ is more highly developed in the Conidae than in any other group of mollusks. Vision is believed to play a minor role in food procurement. Water is taken in through the siphon and directed over the gill, the osphradium, and the anus before leaving the mantle cavity. When food is detected, the cone becomes active and extends the proboscis about until contact is made with the prey. A single radular tooth is held within the lumen of the proboscis with its point slightly posterior to the aperture. Stimulation for release of the

radular tooth has been observed to be tactile. Upon contact with the prey, the radular tooth is ejected and penetrates the body of the victim. The effects of the venom are immediate and the victim is soon paralyzed. The mouth of the cone expands from a few millimeters in diameter to about two centimeters in some species. The impaled paralyzed victim, if small enough, is drawn into the mouth by rapid contraction of the proboscis. Finally, engulfment is completed by expansion of the buccal cavity around the victim. The buccal cavity remains distended for several hours after the ingestion of the prey, during which time the prey must be partially digested before it can pass on through the alimentary tract of the cone.

The activity of cones and their reactions to being handled vary greatly from one species to another. Some species tend to be timid and sluggish, and withdraw rapidly into their shell when disturbed. Several of the more tropical Indo-Pacific species, however, are quite active, and when they are picked up may extend their proboscis with their venom dart in place. *C. textile* may on occasion be very aggressive.

## Venom Apparatus of Cone Shells

The venom apparatus consists of the venom bulb, venom duct, radular sheath, and radular teeth (Figures 10, 11). The pharynx and proboscis, which are a part of the digestive system, also play an important role as accessory organs. The venom apparatus lies in a cavity within the animal. It is believed that preparatory to stinging, the radular teeth, which are housed in the radular sheath, are released to the pharynx, and thence to the proboscis, where they are grasped for thrusting into the flesh of the victim. The venom, believed to be produced in the venom duct, is probably forced under pressure by contraction of the venom bulb and duct into the radular sheath, and thereby forced into the coiled radular teeth.

## Cone Shells Dangerous to Humans

Although there are more than 400 species of cone

shells, there are only a few species that have been incriminated in human envenomations. The stings produced by cones are of the puncture wound variety. A stinging or burning sensation is usually the initial symptom. The numbness and tingling, which begins at the wound site, may spread, rapidly involving the entire body, but most pronounced around the lips and mouth. Other resulting symptoms are similar for most of the species, consisting of localized ischemia, cyanosis, and numbness in the area of the wound. In severe cases, muscular paralysis may be present. Respiratory distress is usually absent. Coma may ensue, and death is said to be due to cardiac failure. The clinical condition of the patient may get worse during the first six hours after being stung. If the victim survives, recovery usually occurs within a period of 24 hours, but the localized skin reaction may persist for several weeks.

Some of the more dangerous species are as follows:

COURT CONE, *Conus aulicus* Linnaeus (129a, b). This is one of the more dangerous species and believed to be capable of causing death. It ranges from Polynesia westward to the Indian Ocean and attains a length of 15 centimeters (5 inches) or more.

GEOGRAPHIC CONE, *Conus geographus* Linnaeus (130a, b). This is the most dangerous species of the cones and capable of delivering large quantities of venom. Ranging from the Indo-Pacific, Polynesia westward to the Indian Ocean, it attains a length of 13 centimeters (5 inches) or more.

MARBLED CONE, *Conus marmoreus* Linnaeus (131a, b; 132). This cone has been involved in human envenomations, but there are no documented deaths. The venom apparatus is large and well developed. It ranges from Polynesia westward to the Indian Ocean and attains a length of 10 centimeters (4 inches).

STRIATED CONE, *Conus striatus* Linnaeus (133). This is a dangerous and aggressive species and has caused human fatalities. It ranges from Australia to the Indian Ocean and attains a length of 10 centimeters (14 inches).

TEXTILE CONE, *Conus textile* Linnaeus (134a,

b; 135a, b, c). This is one of the more dangerous cone shells and has caused human fatalities. It ranges from Polynesia to the Red Sea and attains a length of 10 centimeters (4 inches).

TULIP CONE, *Conus tulipa* Linnaeus (136a, b). This species is believed to be potentially one of the more dangerous cone shells, but no human fatalities have been reported. It attains a length of 7.5 centimeters (3 inches).

## Cephalopods

### Biology of Cephalopods (Octopuses and Squids)

Cephalopods are distributed widely in all temperate and tropical seas, but in the Arctic and Antarctic circles they are restricted to a few species. True octopuses are primarily inhabitants of warmer waters. All cephalopods are marine and seem to have relatively little tolerance of extremes in salinity. *O. vulgaris* is one of the few members of this group to inhabit estuaries, but does this only when the salinity approaches that of open seawater. They live best in water with a density exceeding that of normal seawater. Most cephalopods inhabit depths of less than 100 fathoms, but a few species live at great depths. Many octopuses are found in rock pools in the intertidal zone. On the whole, adult octopuses prefer rocky bottoms, but some are found in muddy and sandy areas. Cuttlefish and squid seem to have an affinity for the open sea, although some are found in shallow water.

Cephalopods are largely predatory and carnivorous, feeding on crustacea, bivalves, and occasionally fish. From observations of octopuses feeding in aquariums, we have a good idea of some of their feeding habits. For example, an octopus will spread its tentacles and hover over the victim in a tent-like fashion. When a crab is first seized, it will struggle vigorously, with one claw grasping the edge of the web. However, within a few seconds the claw will open wide in the manner assumed during a defensive attitude and then slowly close. Within a short time the abdomen of the crab

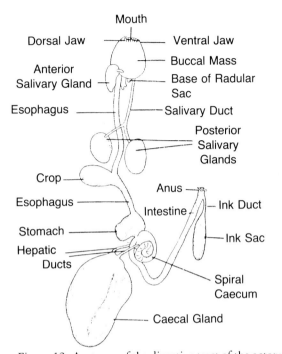

Figure 12. Anatomy of the digestive tract of the octopus. The poison is produced by the salivary glands.
(R. Kreuzinger, after Isgrove)

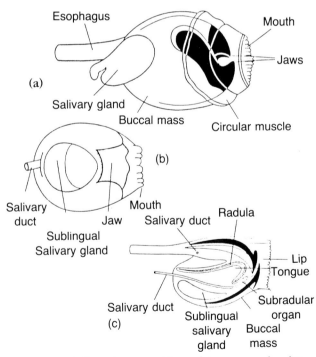

Figure 13. Buccal mass and jaws of the octopus showing (a) the sublingual salivary gland and (b) openings of the salivary ducts, which convey the poison (c).
(R. Kreuzinger, after Isgrove)

will unbend in the manner characteristic of death, the appendage will quiver, and a slight brownish-colored fluid will issue from the branchial canals. Within another 45 seconds the crab will appear to be dead. During this time the octopus will not attack the crab with its beak. Instead, the crab is being killed by a secretion from the salivary glands, of which there are two pairs, one pair being fairly large. In order to eat the crab, the octopus, with the use of its tentacle suckers and jaws, opens it at the dorsal juncture between carapace and abdomen, the place where the break comes when the crab molts. The octopus then pulls off the back of the crab, eats the viscera first, drops the back, pulls off the legs (which it cleans out), eats the contents, and drops the empty leg shells when it is finished.

Apart from the simpler reflexes involved in procuring food and mating, complex processes indicating memory and remarkable manipulative performances have been observed in cephalopods. When alarmed, cephalopods are able to move backward rapidly by ejecting powerful jets of water forward from the anterior opening in the funnel. The arms are stretched out horizontally in a straight line, with the visceral dome, or head, pointing forward. Octopuses also move about by gliding or creeping over the bottom. Usually, this latter method is used when the creature is in pursuit of food. Cephalopods will eject a dark cloud of "ink" when suddenly disturbed, which offers them excellent concealment and an opportunity to escape. Octopods, or octopuses, tend to be solitary, irritable, and pugnacious, whereas decapods, or squids, are more gregarious. On occasion, octopuses are known to display the interesting habit of autophagy, or the ability to eat their arms. Octopuses may reach 9 meters (29 feet) in length. Giant squids (see Chapter II, [59]), reputed to attain a length of 19 meters (63 feet) or more, are very pugnacious and can inflict a serious wound with their horny beaks. Octopuses and squids are considered to be an edible delicacy by many people.

## Venom Apparatus of the Octopus

The venom apparatus of the octopus is comprised of the so-called anterior and posterior salivary glands, the salivary ducts, the buccal mass, and the mandibles, or beak (Figures 12, 13). The mouth of the octopus is situated in the center of the oral and anterior surface of the arms, surrounded by a circular lip, fringed with fingerlike papillae. The mouth leads into a pharyngeal cavity having thick muscular walls. This entire muscular complex is known as the buccal mass, which is surrounded and concealed by the muscular bases of the arms. The buccal mass is furnished with two powerful dorsal and ventral chitinous jaws whose shape resembles that of a parrot's beak. The arrangement of the jaws differs from the parrot in that the ventral one bites outside the dorsal and is wider and larger. These jaws are able to bite vertically with great force, tearing the captured food, which is held by the suckers before it is passed on to the rasping action of the radula. The duct from the posterior salivary glands opens on the tip of the subradular organ, which appears as an outgrowth in front of the tongue. The paired ducts from the anterior salivary glands open into the pharynx laterally and posteriorly. The venom is discharged from these ducts into the pharynx.

## Cephalopods Dangerous to Humans

Many species of cephalopods are capable of inflicting wounds on humans. Some of the larger squid have a large buccal mass and sizable jaws that can easily remove a chunk of flesh and produce a painful wound. Only the small Australian blue-ringed octopus, *Octopus maculosus* (or *O. lunulatus* or *O. fasciatus*), inflicts lethal bites, but other species of *Octopus* (such as *Octopus apollyon* Berry) can also produce venomous bites.

Octopus bites usually consist of two small puncture wounds, which are produced by the sharp parrot-like chitinous jaws. A burning or tingling sensation is the usual initial symptom. At first, the discomfort is localized, but may later radiate to include the entire area. Bleeding is frequently profuse for the size of the bite, which may indicate that the clotting process of the blood is retarded. Swelling, redness, and heat commonly develop in the area around the wound. Recovery is generally uneventful. However, bites from the Australian blue-ringed octopus can be fatal. Initially, the bite may be painless. Within a few minutes the area around the bite appears blanched and soon becomes swollen and hemorrhagic. A stinging sensation may develop shortly thereafter. The injected venom, maculotoxin (which is chemically identical to tetrodotoxin, the poison found in pufferfish), is a potent neurotoxin causing a sensation of numbness and tingling around the mouth, neck, and head. This may be followed by nausea and vomiting. In severe envenomations, respiratory distress soon develops, followed by visual disturbances, ocular paralysis, dizziness, difficulty in speech and swallowing, lack of motor coordination, muscular weakness, and, possibly, complete paralysis. In fatal cases, the patient loses consciousness; death is due to respiratory paralysis. If the patient survives, the paralysis lasts from 4 to 12 hours.

Several fatalities have been reported from octopus bites. The following report is one such example—an incident that took place near East Point, Darwin, Australia. According to the account, a diver captured a small blue-ringed octopus (probably *Octopus lunulatus*), which had a span of about twenty centimeters. The diver permitted the octopus to crawl over his arms and shoulders, and finally to the back of his neck, where the animal remained for a few moments. During the period that the octopus was on his neck, a small bite was inflicted, producing a trickle of blood. A few minutes after the bite, the victim complained of a sensation of dryness in his mouth and of difficulty in swallowing. After walking a short distance up the beach from the scene of the bite, the victim began to vomit, developed a loss of muscular control, and finally suffered from respiratory distress and was unable to speak. Even though he had been rushed to hospital and placed in a respirator, the victim expired about two hours after being bitten.

OCTOPUS, *Octopus apollyon* Berry (137, 138). The color and pattern of this octopus are subject to considerable fluctuation depending upon the background in which the octopus is found.

AUSTRALIAN BLUE-RINGED or SPOTTED OCTOPUS, *Octopus maculosus* Hoyle (139a, b). This is an Indo-Pacific species, ranging from Australia, Japan, and into the Indian Ocean. It is believed that the death of the Australian diver, recounted above, may have been caused by a closely-related species, *O. lunulatus* Quoy and Gaimard, since it is believed to have a more northerly distribution. It is thought that there is a third species of Australian blue-ringed octopus, *O. fasciatus* Hoyle; the validity of three separate species, however, remains a question of debate among mollusk experts.

## ECHINODERMS
### Starfishes, Sea Urchins

Echinoderms, characterized by radial symmetry, have a body with usually five arms, or radii, around an oral-aboral axis comprised of calcareous plates forming a more or less rigid skeleton or of plates and spicules embedded in the body wall. Spines and pedicellariae are present in the starfishes and sea urchins, but are absent in some of the others. The coelom is complex and includes a water vascular system with tube feet. The digestive tract may or may not include an anus. The sexes are usually separate. Echinoderms, with the exception of a few planktonic holothurians, are mostly bottom dwellers. It is estimated that there are about 5,300 species.

The echinoderms are divided into four classes:

1) *Asteroidea:* Starfishes (only two species of which are known to be venomous).

2) *Ophiuroidea:* Brittle stars (nonvenomous).

3) *Echinoidea:* Sea urchins (several species are venomous).

4) *Holothuriodea:* Sea cucumbers (nonvenomous, but some are poisonous to eat).

Only two groups are of importance as venomous species, namely, starfishes and sea urchins.

### Starfishes
#### Biology of Venomous Starfishes

Starfishes are free-living echinoderms that have a

flat, star-shaped or pentagonal body, usually with a continuous disc that has five or more ray-like extensions called arms. Tube feet are located in open furrows along the underside of the arms. These arms contain the digestive glands and genital organs. Located on the upper, or aboral, surface are many blunt, calcareous spines. The stomach is large and sac-shaped, the intestines minute, and the mouth turned downwards. With the use of their tube feet, starfishes move about over the floor of the sea by slow, gliding movements. Usually the sucking disks are not used when walking over a smooth bottom, but only when the starfish is climbing. Starfishes are voracious, and they eat other echinoderms, mollusks, and worms.

Because of their remarkably extensible mouth, starfishes are able to swallow relatively large animals. If the animal is too large to swallow, the starfish extrudes its stomach and digests the food outside its body. By exerting steady pressure with the use of its tube feet, it is able to pry open mollusks. Thus, starfishes are of economic significance to the oyster industry. Since starfishes are not generally used for food, their commercial value is negligible.

During early summer, eggs and sperm are released into the water where the fertilization of starfishes takes place. It is believed the starfishes usually take about four years to attain full size. Their ability to regenerate damaged parts of their body is phenomenal.

Starfishes are among the most common of shore animals, and they range from the intertidal zone to great depths. They inhabit a wide variety of biotopes, rocks, sand, mud, coral, etc. Starfishes usually dislike light and therefore seek shaded areas.

## Venomous Apparatus of Starfishes

Only two species of venomous starfishes are known: *Acanthaster planci*, an Indo-Pacific species, and a close relative, *Acanthaster elissi* (Gray), of the eastern Pacific region.

*Acanthaster* possesses 13 to 16 arms or rays. The outer surface of the body is covered by a series of large, sharp spines that are completely enveloped by a thin layer of skin. Contact with these spines can be a painful experience, since the spines are soft calcareous structures that may break off in the wound and are difficult to remove. Moreover, glands in the skin secrete a venom that can produce a severe inflammatory response in the victim, consisting of redness, swelling, vomiting, numbness, and in rare instances, paralysis.

## Starfishes Dangerous to Humans

CROWN-O-THORNS STARFISH, *Acanthaster planci* (Linnaeus) (140–143). This starfish has become infamous because of its devastating effects in denuding the coral reefs of the western Pacific. A voracious feeder on corals, it leaves a destructive path of dead corals wherever it goes. It ranges throughout the Indo-Pacific region, from Polynesia to the Red Sea, and attains a length of 60 centimeters (23 inches).

## Sea Urchins

### Biology of Venomous Sea Urchins

Sea urchins are free-living echinoderms having a globular, egg-shaped, or flattened body. The viscera are enclosed within a hard shell, or test, formed by regularly-arranged plates carrying spines articulating with tubercules on the test. Between the spines are situated three-jawed pedicellariae, which are of interest to the venomologist and will be subsequently described in detail. In some species of sea urchins, the spines are also venomous. Tube feet are arranged in ten meridian series rather than in furrows. A double pore in the test corresponds to each tube foot. The intestine is long and coiled, and an anus is always present. The gonads are attached by mesenteries to the inner aboral surface of the test. The mouth, situated on the lower surface, turns downward, and is surrounded by five strong teeth incorporated in a complex termed "Aristotle's lantern." Their power of regeneration is great; but autotomy, or the ability to sever a body segment as an escape measure, as observed in the asteroids, does not occur. By means of spines on the oral side of the test, sea urchins move slowly in the water. The tube feet are utilized to climb vertical surfaces. Some forms have the ability to burrow into crevices in rocks, while others cover themselves with shells, sand, and bits of debris.

Some urchins are nocturnal, hiding under rocks during the day and coming out to feed at night. Echinoids tend to be omnivorous in their feeding habits, ingesting algae, mollusks, foraminifera, and various other types of benthic organisms.

Sea urchins are dioecious, that is, they have separate sexes, hermaphroditism occurring only as a rare anomaly. Sexual dimorphism is generally absent. Spawning usually takes place during the spring and summer in the Northern Hemisphere, but somewhat earlier in the more southern latitudes. Several species of European and tropical echinoids serve as important sources of food to man. Only the gonads are eaten, either raw or cooked, but in some tropical regions they are poisonous to eat. The bathymetric range of echinoids is great, extending from the intertidal zone to great depths.

## Venom Apparatus of Sea Urchins

SPINES:

The spines of sea urchins vary greatly from group to group. In most instances the spines are solid, have blunt, rounded tips, and do not constitute a venom organ. However, some species have long, slender, hollow, sharp spines that are extremely dangerous to handle. The acute tips and the spinules permit ready entrance of the spines deep into the flesh, but because of their extreme brittleness, the spinules break off readily in the wound and are difficult to withdraw. The spines in *Diadema* may attain a length of a third of a meter (one foot) or more. It is believed that the spines of some of these species secrete a venom, but this has not been experimentally demonstrated. The aboral spines of *Asthenosoma* are developed into special venom organs carrying a single large gland. The point is sharp and serves as a means of introducing the venom (Figures 14, 15).

PEDICELLARIAE:

Pedicellariae are small, delicate, seizing organs, which are found scattered among the spines of the shell. There are several different types of pedicellariae. One of these is called the globiferous pedicellariae because of its globe-shaped head, and serves as a venom organ. The pedicellariae are comprised of two parts—a terminal swollen, conical head, which is armed with a set of calcareous pincer-like valves or jaws, and a supporting stalk (Figure 16). The head is attached to the stalk either directly by the muscles or by a long, flexible neck. On the inner side of each valve, a small elevation provided with fine sensory hairs is found. Contact with these sensory hairs causes the valves to close instantly. The outer surface of each valve is covered by a large gland, which in *Toxopneustes* has two ducts that empty into the vicinity of a small, toothlike projection of the terminal fang of the valve. A sensory bristle is located on the inside of each valve. Contact with these bristles causes the small muscles at the base of the valve to contract, thus closing the valves and injecting the venom into the skin of the victim.

One of the primary functions of pedicellariae is that of defense. When the sea urchin is at rest in calm waters, the valves are generally extended, moving slowly about, awaiting prey. When a foreign body comes in contact with them, it is immediately seized. The pedicellariae do not release their hold as long as the object moves, and if it is too strong to be held, the pedicellariae are torn from the test, or shell, but continue to bite the object. Detached pedicellariae may remain alive for several hours after being removed from the sea urchin and may continue to secrete venom into the victim.

### Method of Envenomation: Spines

Penetration of the needle-sharp sea urchin spines may produce an immediate and intense burning sensation. The pain is soon followed by redness, swelling, and an aching sensation. Numbness and muscular paralysis have been reported and secondary infections are not uncommon.

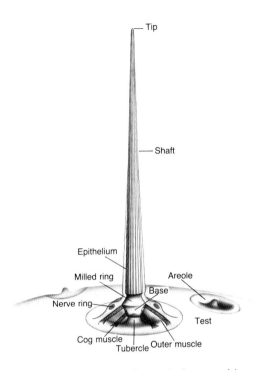

Figure 14. Structure of a typical sea urchin spine. (R. Kreuzinger)

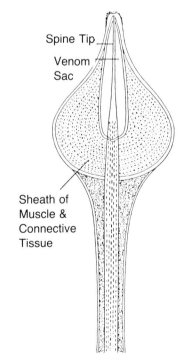

Figure 15. Aboral venomous spine of the sea urchin *Asthenosoma*.
(R. Kreuzinger, after Mortensen)

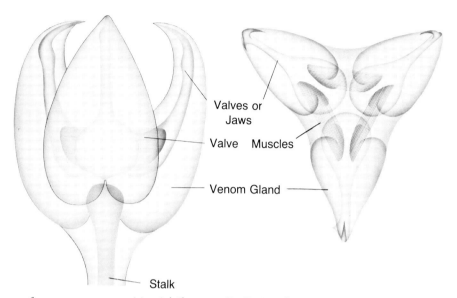

Figure 16. Structure of a venomous sea urchin globiferous pedicellarium from the test, or shell. Each calcareous jaw is tipped with a sharp fang and surrounded by a large venom gland.    (R. Kreuzinger, after Mortensen)

*Method of Envenomation: Pedicellariae*
The sting from pedicellariae may produce an immediate, intense radiating pain, faintness, numbness, generalized muscular paralysis, loss of speech, respiratory distress, and, in severe cases, death.

## Sea Urchins Dangerous to Humans

There are a number of species of sea urchins potentially dangerous to humans, but only a few representative species will be listed. The symptoms produced by these sea urchins are generally similar.

FELT CAP SEA URCHIN, *Toxopneustes pileolus* (Lamarck) (144a, b). The spines of this sea urchin are quite short. However, when the pedicellariae are extended, the sea urchin may appear in life as a brilliantly colored dense bed of small flowers. Be not deceived! Hidden beneath this beauty are the venom-clad spiny jaws of the globiferous pedicellariae, and, in this species, potential death. The pedicellariae may vary in color, being purple, yellow, red, green, or white, and sometimes in varying combinations. The diameter of the test is 13 centimeters (5 inches). It ranges throughout the Indo-Pacific region, from Malaysia to East Africa, and Japan.

ELEGANT SEA URCHIN, *Toxopneustes elegans* Doderlein (145), a close relative of *T. pileolus,* is found in the waters of Japan. The diameter of the test is 7.5 centimeters (3 inches) or larger.

ROSY SEA URCHIN, *Toxopneustes roseus* (Agassiz) (146a, b, c), is a less toxic species found in the eastern Pacific; it can produce painful stings. A close-up photograph of the globiferous pedicellariae of *Sphraechinus granularis,* a related species, can be seen in (147a, b).

LONG-SPINED or HAIRY SEA URCHIN, *Diadema setosum* (Leske) (148a, b; 149; 150), and *Diadema antillarum* Phillipi (151) are among the most commonly encountered hazards of the marine environment of the Indo-Pacific and West Indies, respectively. The spines of these urchins are found sticking out of every conceivable crevice, under rocks, amongst corals, and in the most unexpected places. The spines may extend outward from the test for a length of 30 centimeters (12 inches).

The following sea urchins contain venomous spines:

PURSE SEA URCHIN *Phormosoma bursarium* Agassiz (152, 157), which is found in the Indo-Pacific.

IJIMAI SEA URCHIN *Asthenosoma ijimai* Yoshiwara (153), also found in the Indo-Pacific.

VARIABLE SEA URCHIN *Asthenosoma varium* Grube (154), found in the Indo-Pacific.

TAM O'SHANTER SEA URCHIN, *Araeosoma thetidis* (Clark) (155, 156), found off the coast of Australia.

Impalement by the spines of these sea urchins provides an experience long to be remembered (158a, b).

# ANNELID WORMS
## Polychaete Worms

The phylum Annelida, or segmented worms, are organisms having an elongated, usually segmented body with paired setae. The outer covering of the body consists of a thin, nonchitinous cuticle. The digestive system is tubular, the coelom is large, and the vascular system is closed. Some species have well-developed chitinous jaws. Cosmopolitan in distribution, annelids are found in marine, freshwater, and terrestrial environments. Marine annelids also have a wide distribution bathymetrically and are for the most part bottom dwellers, either creeping or burrowing in mud, pilings, corals, or under rocks. Some are sedentary in their habits, building calcareous or fibrous tubes, whereas a few are pelagic. It is estimated that there are more than 6,200 species of annelids.

The phylum Annelida is comprised of three classes:

(1) *Polychaeta:* Marine sandworms, tube worms, etc.

(2) *Oligochaeta:* Freshwater annelids and terrestrial earthworms.

(3) *Hirudinea:* Leeches.

Very little is known regarding the toxicity of annelids. Several species of marine annelids have been reported as noxious to humans because of their pungent, bristlelike setae; and at least one species, *Glycera dibranchiata,* is capable of inflicting venomous wounds with its jaws (Figures 17a-c). A toxic substance has also been isolated from the tissues of certain polychaete worms, which is the only class that will be discussed here.

## Polychaete Worms

### Biology of Polychaete Worms

The polychaetes are divided into two major groups: the Errantia, which includes most of the free-moving kinds, and the Sedentaria, or tube-dwelling and burrow-inhabiting species. The polychaetes that have been incriminated as toxic are largely errant species.

Polychaetes have cylindrical bodies and are metameric, or segmented, having numerous somites, or body units—each bearing a fleshy paddle-like appendage, or parapodia, that bears many setae. The head region has tentacles. There is no clitellum, a kind of accessory reproductive organ, and there are no permanent gonads. Fertilization is commonly external, and the sexes are usually separate. Polychaetes have a trocophore larval stage, and there is asexual budding in some species.

Most polychaetes are free-living; a few live as parasites attached to the outer body of other organisms. They have a bathymetric range from the tide line to depths of more than 5,000 meters (16,404 feet). A few species are pelagic, living in the open sea. Some of the burrowing worms feed on bottom detritus, whereas the tube dwellers subsist on plankton. Polychaetes generally spend their existence·crawling under rocks, burrowing in the sand or mud in and around the base of algal growths; or they construct tubes, which they leave at periodic intervals in search of food. The majority of polychaetes range in size from 5 to 10 centimeters; however, some of the syllids are only 2 millimeters in length, whereas the giant Australian species *Onuphis terres* and *Eunice aphroditois* may attain a length of a meter or more.

The most renowned members of the polychaete group are the palolo worms, members of the genus *Palolo* of tropical Pacific Islands such as Samoa and Fiji. There is also a European species of *Palolo* whose reproductive swarmings are similar to the Pacific variety. Palolo worms live in holes and crevices among rocks and coral growth on the ocean bottom. Each year on a certain day the worms come to the surface of the ocean in vast swarms in order to reproduce (159). In certain parts of the world, the natives insist that there is a definite relationship between the toxicity of some species of marine fishes and the swarming of palolo worms.

The giant Australian polychaetes *E. aphroditois* and *O. teres* have powerful chitinous jaws with which they are able to inflict a nasty bite. The blood worm *Glycera dibranchiata* has venom glands associated with its jaws and can inflict a painful bite (162).

Many polychaetes are very beautiful—colored red, pink, or green, or with a combination of colors—and are iridescent.

## Venom Apparatus of Polychaete Worms

SETAE:

The members of the polychaete genera *Chloeia, Eurythoë, Hermodice,* and others, possess elongate pungent chitinous bristles, or setae, which project from the parapodia. The parapodia are a pair of lateral appendages extending from each of the body segments. The structure appears as a more or less laterally compressed fleshy projection of the body wall. Each parapodium is biramous, or split; it consists of a dorsal portion, the notopodium, and a ventral part, the neuropodium. Each division of the parapodium is supported internally by one or more chitinous rods, termed acicula, to which are attached some of the parapodial muscles. Each of the distal ends of the two parapodial divisions turn inward to form a setal sac or pocket in which the projecting setae are situated. Each seta is secreted by a single cell at the base of the setal sac. Generally, the setae or polychaetes project some distance beyond the end of the parapodium. However, *Eurythoë* and *Hermodice* have the ability to retract or extend their setae to a remarkable degree. When the living worm is at rest, the setae appear to be quite short and barely in evidence; but when irritated, the setae are rapidly extended and the worm appears to be a mass of bristle.

The severity of symptoms reported in some of the clinical accounts lends credence to the belief that both *Eurythoë* and *Hermodice* possess venomous setae. The setae of both *Eurythoë complanata* and *Hermodice carunculata* appear to be hollow and at times seem to be filled with fluid. A setae of *E. complanata* has a series of hook-like spinules along the shaft, whereas the setae of *H. carunculata* is without spinules and has a needle-like appearance. The setae of *Chloeia* are said to be nonvenomous, but are listed as "stinging" by some accounts. The nature of the venom glands of these worms has not been fully explained.

JAWS:

*Glycera* possesses a long, tubular proboscis (Figure 17a) that can be extended to about one-fifth the length of the body. When the proboscis is retracted, it occupies approximately the first twenty body segments. The pharynx is located behind the proboscis and bears four jaws or fangs, which are arranged equidistant around the pharyngeal wall. Attached to and immediately following the pharynx is an S-shaped esophagus. The proboscis and associated portions of the digestive tract lie free, unattached, in the coelom. An explosive extension of the pharynx results from the sudden contraction of the longitudinal muscles, which slide from the pharynx forward, and straighten out the esophagus. The four fangs appear at the tip of the proboscis when the pharynx is in the extended position.

Each jaw appears as a curved fang, to which is attached the venom gland. The duct and body of the gland lie within the pharyngeal wall and can be observed only by dissection. The gland empties its contents through the long slender duct, which has its opening at the base of the fang.

Bristle worm *(Chloeia, Eurythoë, Hermodice)* stings may result in an intense inflammatory reaction of the skin, consisting of redness, swelling, a burning sensation, numbness, and itching. *Hermodice carunculata* is able to inflict a "paralyzing effect" with its setae. Contacts with the setae of bristle worms have been likened to handling the spines of prickly pear cactus or nettle stings. Severe complications may cause secondary infections, gangrene, and loss of the affected part.

*Eunice aphroditois, Onuphis teres, Glycera dibran-*

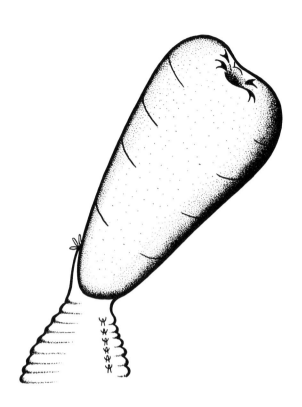

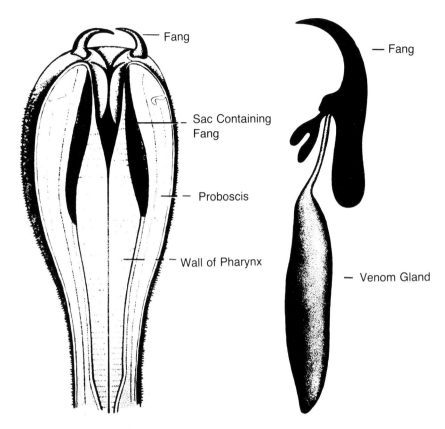

Figure 17a–c. Proboscis of *Glycera*

a. Enlargement of proboscis of *Glycera* showing the fangs at the opening of the mouth.

b. Longitudinal section of the extended proboscis of *Glycera*, showing fangs and related structures.

c. Fang and venom gland removed from the proboscis. (R. Kreuzinger, after Ehlers)

*chiata, G. alba,* and *G. ovigera* are able to inflict painful bites. Whether *Eunice* and *Onuphis* have venom glands associated with their jaws is not known, but the glycerids are believed to secrete a venom at the time of biting. The bite has been compared to a bee sting and results in swelling, redness, and pain. Two to four minute oval lesions are present at the site where the jaws pierce the skin. There may be blanching of the skin immediately surrounding the lesions due to the effects of the venom. With the exception of severe itching, recovery is generally uneventful within a period of several days.

## Polychaete Worms Dangerous to Humans

There are many species of annelid worms that could be used as examples, but the following species are representative of the two types: 1) those having biting jaws (*Glycera, Eunice*), and 2) those having stinging setae (*Eurythoë, Hermodice*).

BLOODWORM, *Glycera dibranchiata* Ehlers (160, 161, 162). Blood worms live in mud burrows in the intertidal zone and below low water areas. They are used extensively in the United States and Canada as bait worms. Found along the coast from North Carolina to northeastern Canada, they attain a length of up to 37 centimeters (14 inches).

BRISTLE WORM, *Eurythoë complanata* (Pallas) (163a, b). This is a very beautiful worm, soft and fluffy in appearance. But be not deceived: the fluffy appearance is comprised of hundreds of sharp bristles. Found in the Gulf of Mexico and throughout the tropical Pacific, it attains a length of 10 centimeters (3 inches) or more.

FLESHY BRISTLE WORM, *Hermodice carunculata* (Pallas) (164a, b), a closely related species, is found in the Gulf of California, and attains a length of 30 centimeters (11 inches) or more.

BITING REEF WORM, *Eunice aphroditois* (Pallas) (165a, b, c). The *"aphroditois"* refers to "exciting sexual pleasure," but one would need to be a masochist to reach a high from the biting jaws of this wormy beast. Circumtropical in distribution, it attains a length of 150 centimeters (58 inches).

# ARTHROPODS
## Aquatic Bugs

The insect order Hemiptera, or true bugs, are a large group of insects with representative species in abundance throughout the world. There are more than 55,000 species of bugs, but only a few of them are aquatic and venomous to humans. Since there appears to be some confusion about which bugs are equipped with a true venom apparatus and which ones merely release their poisons through openings in the cuticle and into the environment, aquatic bugs will be discussed in Chapter V under "Poisonous Aquatic Bugs" (p. 131).

**PLATE 60.** Sponges may attain a large size, such as this Spongillidae. The diver is examining the opening of a large unidentified barrel sponge about 90 centimeters (3 feet) in diameter. Wuvulu, Bismarck Archipelago.

(Courtesy R. Murphy, The Cousteau Society, Inc.)

61

62

63

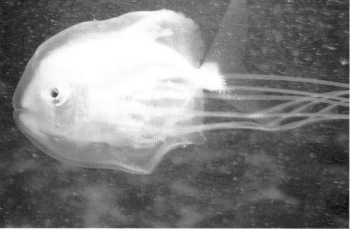

64

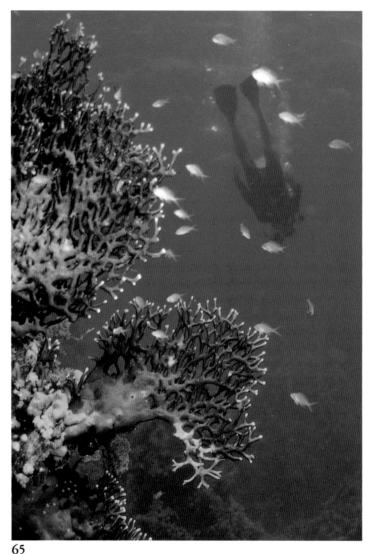

65

66

**PLATE 61.** Buckle sponge, *Fibulia nolitangere* (Duchassaing and Michelotti). Contact with this sponge produces a stinging sensation, redness, and swelling. The size is variable. Found in the West Indies and Australia.          (Photo by E. H. Hergstrom, courtesy of R. V. Southcott)

**PLATE 62.** Red moss sponge, *Microciona prolifera* (Ellis and Solander). This sponge causes a chemical dermatitis among fishermen in the northeastern United States. Symptoms consist of redness, joint stiffness, and swelling of the hands. The sponge forms a cluster having a height of 15 centimeters (6 inches), and is found along the eastern coast of the United States.          (G. Lower)

**PLATE 63.** Fire sponge, *Tedania ignis* (Duchassaing and Michelotti). Skin contact with this sponge produces an instantaneous, intense stinging sensation and a severe dermatitis. The shape and size vary greatly. It inhabits the West Indies.          (R. Straughan)

**PLATE 64.** An unidentified juvenile fish was found swimming inside this little jellyfish. When the two were separated, the fish immediately swam back into the protection of the jellyfish "security blanket." The length of the jellyfish bell is 4 centimeters (1.5 inches).
(Courtesy R. Murphy, The Cousteau Society, Inc.)

**PLATE 65.** Diver working in the vicinity of large clusters of fire coral, *Millepora dichotoma* Forskål, Sharm-Al-Sheikh, Sinai Peninsula, Red Sea. The size is variable.          (Courtesy R. Mandojana)

**PLATE 66.** Cluster of fire coral *Millepora complanata* Lamarck. The growing margin of the fire coral is usually light in color, whitish, yellow, or greenish. Contact with this coral results in an instantaneous, powerful burning or stinging sensation and red welts. The size is variable. Bonaire, Netherlands Antilles.
(Courtesy A. B. Bowker)

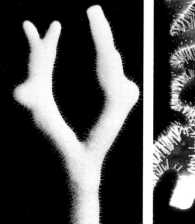
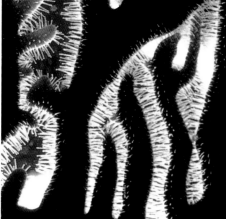

67  68

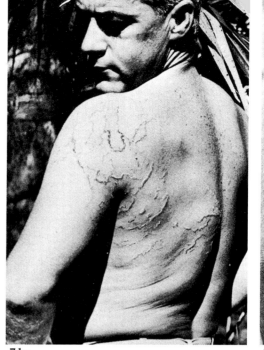
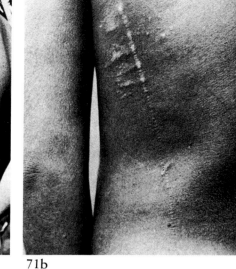

71a                                    71b

69  70

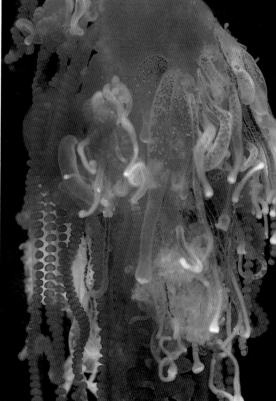

72                                    73
74

**PLATE 67.** Fire coral, *Millepora complanata* Lamarck, in a close-up photo.          (R. and V. Taylor)

**PLATE 68.** Close-up enlargement of *Millepora alcicornis* Linnaeus with back lighting showing the stinging dactylozooids. Taken at Antigua, West Indies.

(Courtesy R. Murphy, The Cousteau Society, Inc.)

**PLATE 69.** Sting inflicted by *Millepora dichotoma*. The lesion consisted of a mildly painful reddened urticaria-like rash that gradually subsided after about six hours. Taken at the Marine Biological Station, University of Cairo, at Al Ghardaqa, Red Sea.          (D. Ollis)

**PLATE 70.** Atlantic Portuguese Man-O-War, *Physalia physalis* (Linnaeus). This "jellyfish" is actually a colonial hydroid. The gas-filled float provides support for the cluster of stinging tentacles suspended beneath. A small fish known as *Nomeus gronovi* can swim freely amongst the tentacles without harm. If any other fish attempts this trick it is instantly stung and killed. The float attains a length of 35 centimeters (13 inches) or more and the tentacles may hang down to a depth of 30 meters (98 feet) or more.

(Courtesy C. Arenson)

**PLATE 71a, b.** Sting by *P. physalis*. The instantaneous sting was described as "intense beyond descrip-

tion." Scars lasted over a year and were very sensitive to sunburn. Deaths have been reported.

(Courtesy R. Straughan)

**PLATE 72.** Pacific Portuguese Man-O-War, *Physalia utriculus* (La Martinière). This is a smaller species than *P. physalis* but packs an equally potent wallop. The float attains a length of 13 centimeters (5 inches) and the tentacles may hang down to a depth of 12 meters (40 feet).          (K. Gillett)

**PLATE 73.** Close-up view of stinging tentacles and smaller polyps of *Physalia utriculus*. The tentacles contain large concentrations of batteries of stinging nematocysts. Contact with these tentacles can produce a severe and painful dermatitis, leaving the victim gasping for breath because of respiratory distress. Photo taken at Sydney, New South Wales, Australia.

(J. F. Myers)

**PLATE 74.** Nudibranch, *Glaucus marinus* (Dupont), feeding on nematocysts of a small jellyfish, *Porpita umbella* Müller. The diameter of the jellyfish is 4 centimeters (1.5 inches). *Glaucus* will use the nematocysts for its own defense. Florida.

(Courtesy R. Murphy, The Cousteau Society, Inc.)

75

76a  76b

77  78

79

80

81

PLATE 75. Stinging nudibranch, *Pteraeolidia ixanthina* (Angas). This nudibranch feeds on a variety of hydroids and stores their untriggered nematocysts in the tips of the cerata, which are marked with yellow. When alarmed, the cerata flare out, and skin contact results in an immediate release of the nematocysts and a very painful sting. Port Jackson, Australia.

(Courtesy R. Russo)

PLATE 76a, b. Bearded nudibranch, *Janolus barbarensis* (Cooper):

a. This nudibranch also feeds on stinging hydroids. Found in tidal pools, southern California.

b. Close-up of *J. barbarensis* showing the alimentary canals through which the nematocysts are conveyed to the orange tips of the cerata.    (Courtesy R. Russo)

PLATE 77. Stinging hydroid, *Aglaophenia cupressina* (Lamouroux). This hydroid grows in large clumps. The specimen in this photo is only a single branch and can inflict a painful sting. The height of the colony is about 12 centimeters (4.7 inches). Taken at Heron Island, Australia.    (K. Gillett)

PLATE 78. Stinging hydroids come in a beautiful array of shapes and sizes; they are capable of delivering a painful sting. Most species do not have common names. This unidentified hydroid is possibly a *Sertularella* species. The tiny cotton ball-like tufts contain batteries of stinging cells. The size is variable, about 10 centimeters (4 inches) or less in height. Taken at Bonaire, Netherlands Antilles.

(Courtesy A. B. Bowker)

PLATE 79. Stinging hydroid, *Lytocarpus nuttingi* Hargitt. A collection of stinging feathers! The height of the colony is about 10 centimeters (4 inches). Sea of Cortez, Baja California.

(Courtesy R. Murphy, The Cousteau Society, Inc.)

PLATE 80. Stinging hydroid, *Lytocarpus philippinus* (Kirchenpauer). Stings from this hydroid are similar to *Pennaria* and *Aglaophenia*, but are generally more painful and may be serious. Note that this large colony is growing from a single main stalk. The height is about 20 centimeters (8 inches). Heron Island, Great Barrier Reef, Australia.    (K. Gillett)

PLATE 81. Stinging hydroid, *Pennaria tiarella* (Ayers). This hydroid is sometimes referred to as the "stinging weed." The height of the colony is about 10 centimeters (4 inches). Sea of Cortez, Baja California.    (D. Wobber)

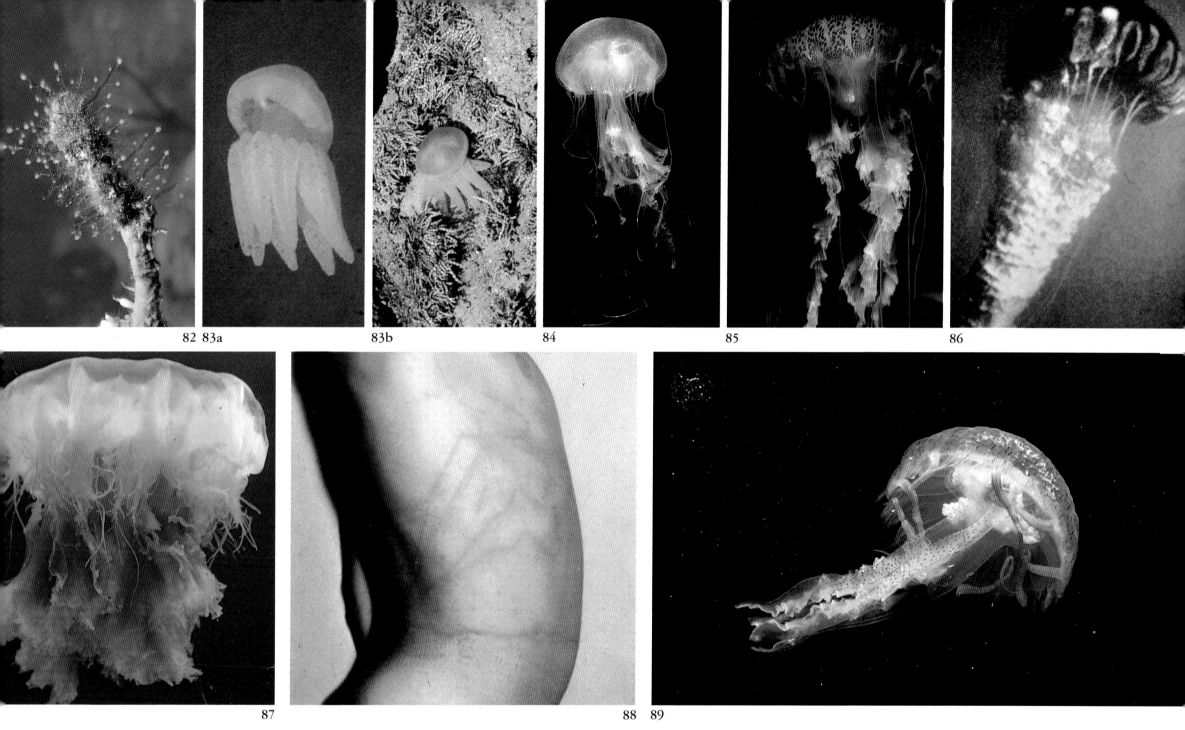

82 83a 83b 84 85 86

87 88 89

PLATE 82. A beautiful, unidentified hydroid, but a nasty stinger. San Salvador, Bahamas. (D. Woodward)

PLATE 83a, b. Brown blubber jellyfish, *Catostylus mosaicus* (Quoy and Gaimard). A unique feature of this jellyfish is that its stinging ability seems to be seasonal. At times it appears to be harmless, but during the reproductive season (warmer months) it can inflict a painful sting and cause respiratory distress. The most common jellyfish along the eastern coast of Australia, it is usually found in estuaries and bays. The bell is about 30 centimeters (12 inches) in diameter.

(Courtesy E. Pope)

PLATE 84. Milky jellyfish, *Chrysaora lactae* Eschscholtz, rated as a mild stinger. The diameter of the

bell is about 8 centimeters (2.7 inches). Found from the West Indies south to Brazil. Taken at Mayaguez, Puerto Rico. (Courtesy C. Arenson)

PLATE 85. Sea nettle, *Chrysaora quinquecirrha* (Desor). One of the most beautiful of the small jellyfishes, it is said to be a moderate to severe stinger. The diameter of the bell is about 25 centimeters (10 inches). Photo taken at Virgin Gorda, British Virgin Islands.

(Courtesy S. Frier, The Cousteau Society, Inc.)

PLATE 86. *Cyanea capillata* (Linnaeus). This is one of the largest jellyfishes, measuring up to 1.5 meters (5 feet) across the bell, with tentacles hanging down to a depth of 15 meters (50 feet). Taken from movie footage. (P. Saunders)

PLATE 87. Smaller specimen of *C. capillata*. The diameter of the bell measures 20 centimeters (8 inches). Photo taken at Woods Hole Biological Laboratory, Massachusetts. (G. Lower)

PLATE 88. Stings inflicted by *Cyanea capillata* on a small boy, one hour after stinging. The red marks outline the areas of contact by the jellyfish tentacles. The pain is described as a burning sensation. Cairns, Australia. (Courtesy J. H. Barnes)

PLATE 89. Nocturnal jellyfish, *Pelagia noctiluca* (Forskål). This jellyfish is generally found at night and is rated as a mild stinger. Salivar, Puerto Rico.

(Courtesy C. Arenson)

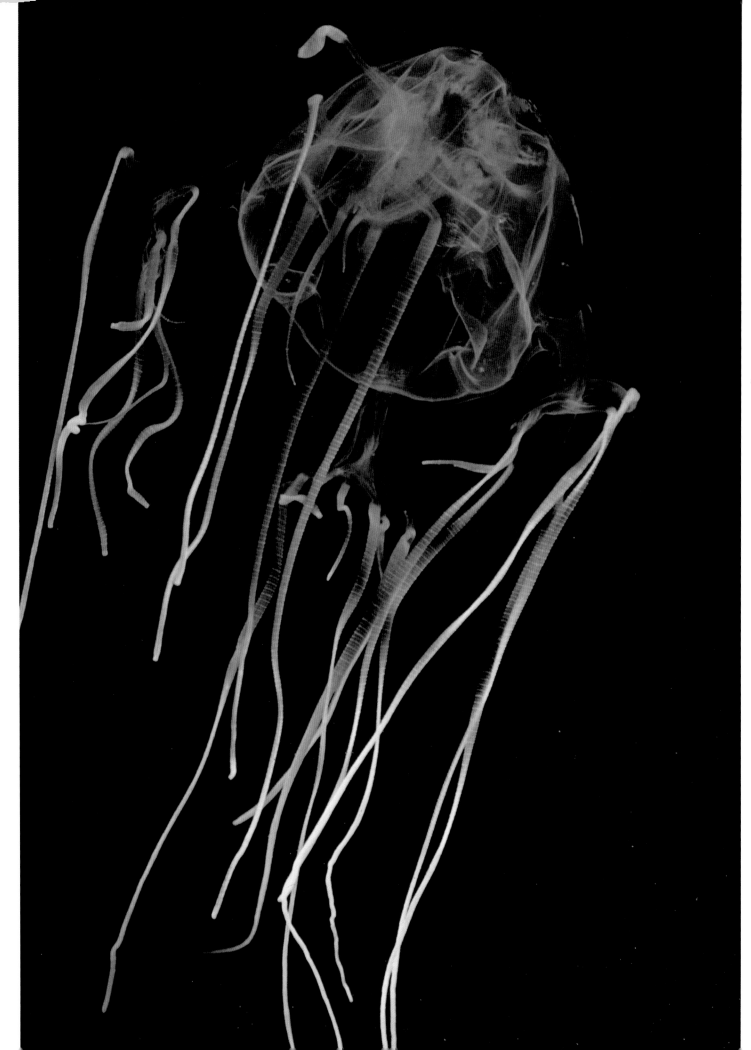

PLATE 90. Australian sea wasp, *Chironex fleckeri* (Southcott). This cubomedusa, the most dangerous of all marine organisms, ranges along the coast of North Queensland and the Northern Territory. *C. fleckeri* seems to have a high IQ for a jellyfish. It can swim over to an object, examine it, and decide whether to sting it or swim away from the object. If it decides to sting, the victim may die within minutes or hours. The sting is very painful. This photograph of a living specimen was taken near Cairns, Queensland, Australia, and is believed to be the finest ever taken of the living organism. The specimen measured 7.5 centimeters (3 inches) across the bell. The tentacles of *C. fleckeri* may hang down to a depth of 3 meters (10 feet) or more. The animal is translucent and difficult to see in the water. (K. Gillett)

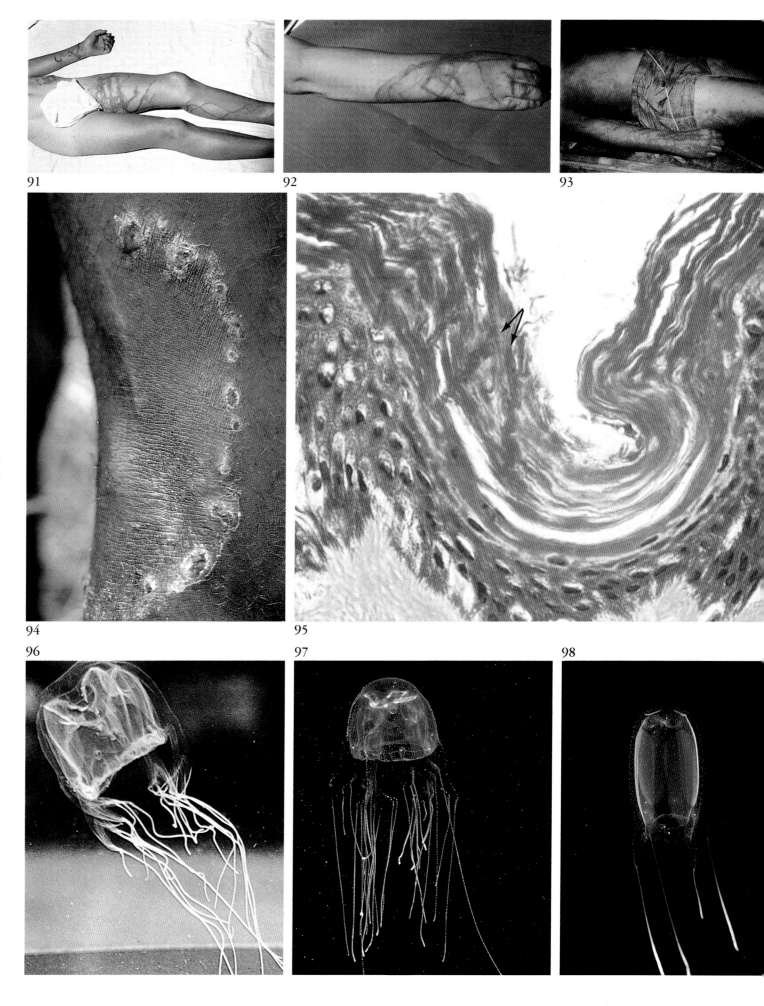

PLATE 91. Near fatal sting by *C. fleckeri* on a 13-year-old boy at Cairns, Australia. The boy's life was saved by flooding his skin immediately with rubbing alcohol. Vinegar is said to be even more effective.
(Courtesy J. H. Barnes)

PLATE 92. Photograph of the arm of a 4-year-old male fatally stung by *C. fleckeri*. The child was being taught to swim by his father in one meter of water near shore. Adequate first aid (alcohol or vinegar) was not administered, and the child died in about 35 minutes. Cairns, Australia.     (Courtesy J. H. Barnes)

PLATE 93. Photograph of a ten-year-old boy fatally stung by *C. fleckeri* near Mackay, Queensland, Australia. The boy died in less than 10 minutes.
(Courtesy G. J. W. Webb)

PLATE 94. Right side of a native stung by *Chironex* showing the outline of contact by one of the tentacles. Maningrida, Arnhem Land, Australia.
(Courtesy G. J. W. Webb)

PLATE 95. Human skin section from a fatal case of stinging by *C. fleckeri*. Arrows point to the path of penetration by nematocysts. Masson's stain. x 1600.
(Courtesy D. J. Lee)

PLATE 96. Sea wasp, *Chiropsalmus quadrigatus* Haekel. This species is sometimes confused with *Chironex*, which is a more dangerous species. A closely related species, *C. quadrumanus* occurs in the Atlantic, from North Carolina south to Brazil, and in the Indian Ocean and off the coast of northern Australia. The bell is about 10 centimeters (4 inches) in diameter.
(Courtesy J. H. Barnes)

PLATE 97. West Indian sea wasp, *Chiropsalmus quadrumanus* (Müller). This sea wasp is seen mainly at night. Fortunately the sting is not fatal, even though painful. The bell is about 14 centimeters (5.5 inches) in diameter. El Tongo Beach, Puerto Rico.
(Courtesy C. Arenson)

PLATE 98. Sea wasp, *Carybdea alata* (Reynaud) is also referred to as a sea wasp and is found in the West Indies. This is a strikingly handsome species, but can inflict a painful sting. It is nocturnal in its habits. The bell is about 5 centimeters (2 inches) in diameter. Cayman Islands.     (P. Humann)

**PLATE 99.** Stinging medusa, *Olindias tenuis* Fewkes. This jellyfish can inflict a painful sting. The diameter of the bell is 3.5 centimeters (1.3 inches). Phosphorus Bay, Puerto Rico. (Courtesy C. Arenson)

**PLATE 100.** Stinging medusa, *Gonionemus vertens* Agassiz. This little medusa is generally considered to be a mild stinger, but it has been reported as causing six deaths near Vladivostock, Russia. This photo of a living specimen was taken in the aquarium, Friday Harbor, Puget Sound, Washington.

(R. Boolootian, courtesy P. Saunders)

**PLATE 101.** Few organisms have been more perplexing to zoologists than the jellyfish *Nausithoë punctata* Kölliker. In the adult stage, it appears as a free-swimming medusa, but in the larval stage (**Plates 103, 104**) it resembles a cluster of seaweed. The adult medusa is about 15 millimeters (0.5 inches) in diameter. (R. Kreuzinger, after Mayer)

**PLATE 102.** Sting inflicted by larval stage of *N. punctata*. Contact with the skin results in an immediate and intense stinging sensation, accompanied by swelling, blistering, and ulceration, lasting several weeks. (D. Ludwig)

**PLATE 103.** "Stinging alga." The larval stage of *N. punctata* was once considered to be a separate organism and was scientifically named *Stephanoscyphus racemosus*, a name that has since been discontinued. The seaweed appearance of this organism is quite confusing to those not familiar with its biology. The size of the cluster is quite variable. This cluster is about 20 centimeters (8 inches) in diameter. Koror, Palau, Western Caroline Islands. (G. Mote)

**PLATE 104.** Close up of cluster of larval stage of *N. punctata*. (G. Mote)

**PLATE 105.** Drawing showing some of the more important stinging sea anemones of Europe and the Mediterranean region:

  a. Strawberry sea snemone, *Actinia equina* Linnaeus. Diameter about 7 centimeters (2.7 inches).

  b. Wax rose sea anemone, *Anemonia sulcata* (Pennant). Diameter about 20 centimeters (8 inches).

  c. Parasitic sea anemone, *Adamsia palliata* (Bohadsch). Diameter about 4 centimeters (1.5 inches).

  d. Rosy sea anemone, *Sagartia elegans* (Dalyell). Diameter about 8 centimeters (3 inches).

(H. Baerg, after Stephenson)

**PLATE 106.** Wax rose sea anemone, *Anemonia sulcata*, in its natural habitat. It is clearly evident from this photograph why this is called the "wax rose sea anemone." (J. Zwick, courtesy L. Béress)

**PLATE 107.** Strawberry sea anemone, *Actinia equina*, taken in an aquarium at the zoological station, Naples, Italy. Stings may result in swelling, redness, itching, and ulceration of the affected area. This is one of the causes of "sponge fishermen's disease." This anemone is frequently attached to sponges, and divers harvesting commercial sponges encounter stings from this anemone when handling the sponges.

(Courtesy P. Giacomelli)

**PLATE 108.** Sea anemone, *Telmatactis rufa* (Verrill). Contact with the skin produces an instant stinging sensation similar to that produced by fire coral. Later the pain may radiate up to the arm pit, and numbness may develop over the entire arm. Other symptoms include nausea, dizziness, constriction of the throat, respiratory distress, shortness of breath, and a progressing intensification of pain at the wound site with a gradual swelling of the affected area.

(Courtesy S. H. Bayer)

**PLATE 109.** The progression of a sea anemone sting (*T. rufa*), showing the right forearm of a woman stung while diving near Treasure Cay, Great Abaco, Bahamas. (a) Third day—severe blistering of the skin. (b) Third week—slow healing. (c) Sixth week—scab formation with ulceration. (d) Eighth week—crater-like ulceration. (e) Seventh month—ulcer has not completely healed. (f) One year later—the healing process in some of the sea anemone stings is amazingly slow. Apparently the integrity of the envenomed tissues has been greatly reduced. (Courtesy S. H. Bayer)

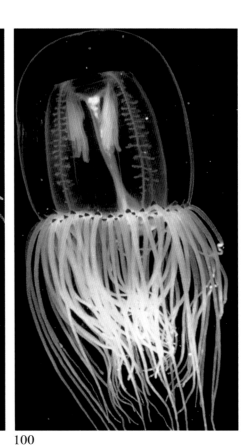

99

100

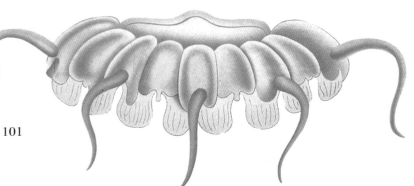

101

102

103

104

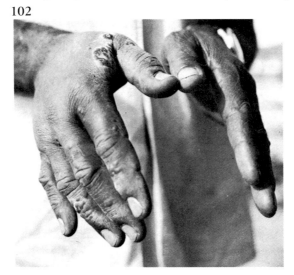

A

B

C

D

105

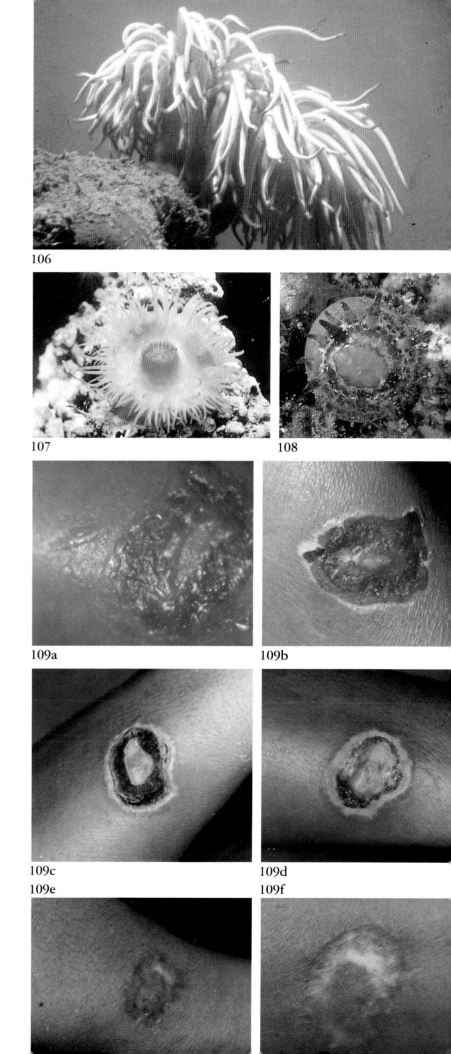

106

107

108

109a

109b

109c

109d

109e

109f

110a 110b 111

112 113 114

115 116 117

118 119 120

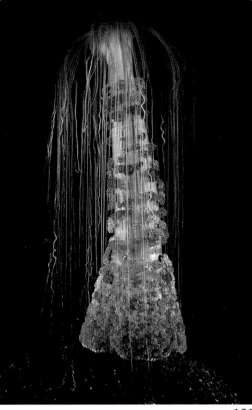

121

122

123

PLATE 110. Red sea anemone, *Triactis producta* Klunzinger. Despite its small size (diameter 4 centimeters [1.4 inches]), this little beast can deliver a painful punch. Like other sea anemone stings, the reddened, swollen skin soon breaks down into a painful ulcer, which may last for weeks or months. Taken near the Marine Biological Laboratory, Eilat, Israel.

a. Taken during the day, when the tentacles were contracted. (Courtesy D. Masry)

b. Taken at night, when the tentacles were extended. (Courtesy D. Masry)

PLATE 111. Wound on left wrist produced by *T. producta*. Initial contact caused a burning or stinging sensation, followed by swelling at the sting site and then of the entire arm. The pain became increasingly intense, followed by numbness. There was no ulceration (although ulceration may occur), and the lesion gradually healed in about six weeks.

(Courtesy D. Masry)

PLATE 112. Hell's Fire sea anemone, *Actinodendron plumosum* Haddon. This photograph, taken in Guam, shows one of the most dangerous of the stinging sea anemones. Its sting is similar to that of a nettle, but the pain becomes progressively more intense. Note that the tentacles are extended, usually a nighttime occurrence. (R. F. Myers)

PLATE 113. *Actinodendron* in its natural habitat at Cam-Ranh Bay, South Vietnam. The photograph was taken during the day, when the anemone's tentacles were withdrawn; nevertheless, the creature is capable

of stinging. This anemone is sometimes mistaken for a blob of mud or a rock. (Courtesy P.A. Hansen)

PLATE 114. Undischarged nematocysts of *Actinodendron,* which appear spherical or rod-like in shape. x 1200. (Courtesy P. A. Hansen)

PLATE 115. Upper right leg of U.S. Air Force airman who was stung by *Actinodendron* while swimming in Cam-Ranh Bay, South Vietnam. Initial symptoms consisted of a mild stinging sensation, which became progressively worse; later the area became swollen and the skin broke down into numerous small ulcerations, which healed slowly over a period of several weeks.

(Courtesy P. A. Hansen)

PLATE 116. Cylinder sea anemone, *Cerianthus filiformis* Carlgren. Some sea anemones burrow in the mud or sand of tropical bays. Several species in this group can inflict extremely painful stings. The length of the tentacles varies, but in this specimen are about 20 centimeters (8 inches). Taken in the Coral Sea, Solomon Islands. (R. and V. Taylor)

PLATE 117. Blistering of the fingers produced by a burrowing sea anemone, believed to be *Cerianthus*. Ponape, Micronesia. (Courtesy E. T. Rulison)

PLATE 118. Griffith's sea anemone, *Megalactis griffithsi* Saville Kent. Reputed to be a bad stinger, the size varies. Taken at Fremantle, West Australia.

(N. Coleman)

PLATE 119. Armed sea anemone, *Dofleinia armata* Wasilieff. This handsome burrowing anemone is heav-

ily armed with potent stinging nematocysts. The size is variable, about 20 centimeters (8 inches) in length. Taken at Fremantle, West Australia. (N. Coleman)

PLATE 120. Ribbed sea anemone, *Alicia costae* (Panceri). All the members of this genus of sea anemones are very attractive and can inflict painful wounds. The tubercules on the sides of these anemones are armed with powerful batteries of stinging nematocysts. The diameter is about 7 centimeters (2.7 inches).

(Courtesy P. Giacomelli)

PLATE 121. Marvelous sea anemone, *Alicia mirabilis* (Johnson). This anemone is impressive to behold, and painful to touch. The diameter is about 5 centimeters (2 inches), but is variable in size. Taken at Aguadilla, Puerto Rico. (Courtesy C. Arenson)

PLATE 122. Torch sea anemone, *Lebrunia danae* (Duchassaing and Michelotti). This anemone produces a mild rash, itching, and swelling. Taken near La Parguera, Puerto Rico. (Courtesy C. Cutress)

PLATE 123. Orange tube coral, *Tubastrea tenuilamellosa* (Milne-Edwards and Haime). This is one of the few species of stinging corals, and a beautiful species it is! Contact with these gorgeous tentacles, which are extended mainly at night, results in a painful sting. The diameter of the oral disc is about 1 centimeter (.5 inches). These anemones are frequently found in underwater caves. Photo taken at Isla Santa Cruz, Gulf of California.

(Courtesy R. Murphy, The Cousteau Society, Inc.)

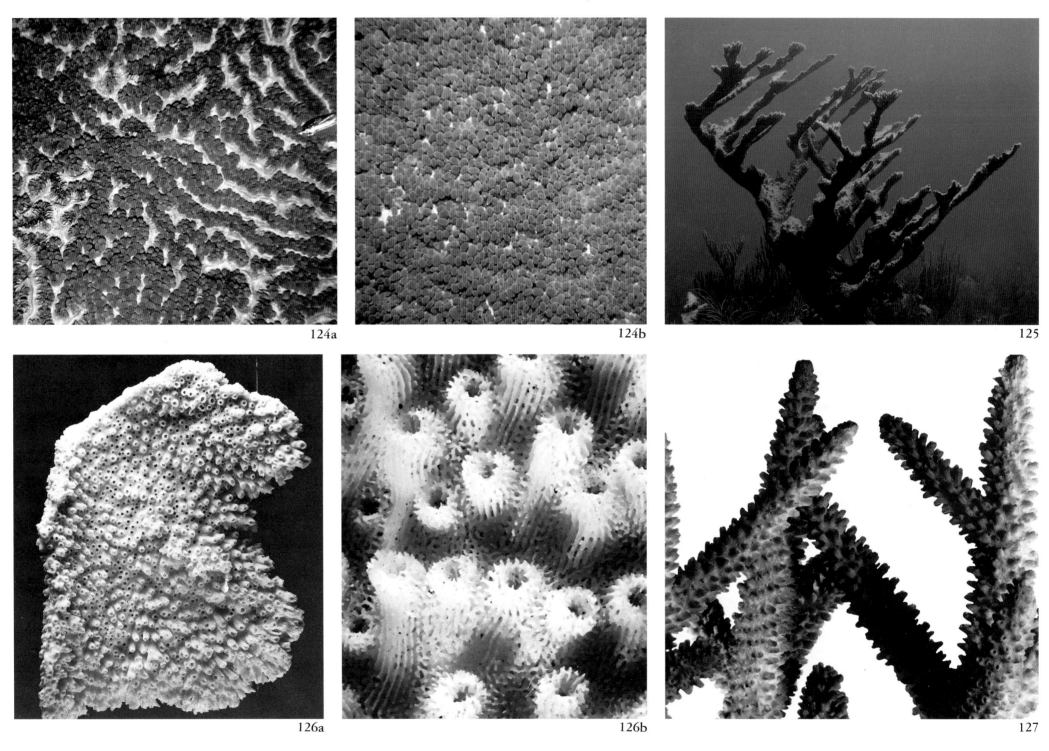

124a

124b

125

126a

126b

127

PLATE 124a, b. Stinging bubble coral, *Physogyra lichtensteini* Milne-Edwards and Haime. The bubbles, shown here in a partially expanded state, contract and expand with tidal cycles. Contact with these bubbles, equipped with powerful nematocysts, results in an immediate skin rash. The colonies grow to about 1 meter (39 inches) in diameter. Taken at Palau, Western Caroline Islands. (D. Ludwig)

PLATE 125. Staghorn coral, *Acropora palmata* (Lamarck), silhouetted in a clear reef area off Virgin Gorda, British Virgin Islands, possesses a razor-sharp skeleton that readily slices through the skin, producing painful lacerations, which may take weeks to heal in the tropics. Coral cuts are one of the most frequent causes of disability to divers working around coral reefs. (WLRI photo)

PLATE 126a, b. Close up showing the beautiful but cutting edge of *A. palmata*.

(Courtesy Smithsonian Institution)

PLATE 127. The branching corals, *Acropora* species, cannot only cut, but may also inflict serious puncture wounds. Swimming in a reef inhabited by them requires care and dexterity. Their multicolored hues provide a spectacular display long to be remembered. Taken at Heron Island, Australia. (K. Gillett)

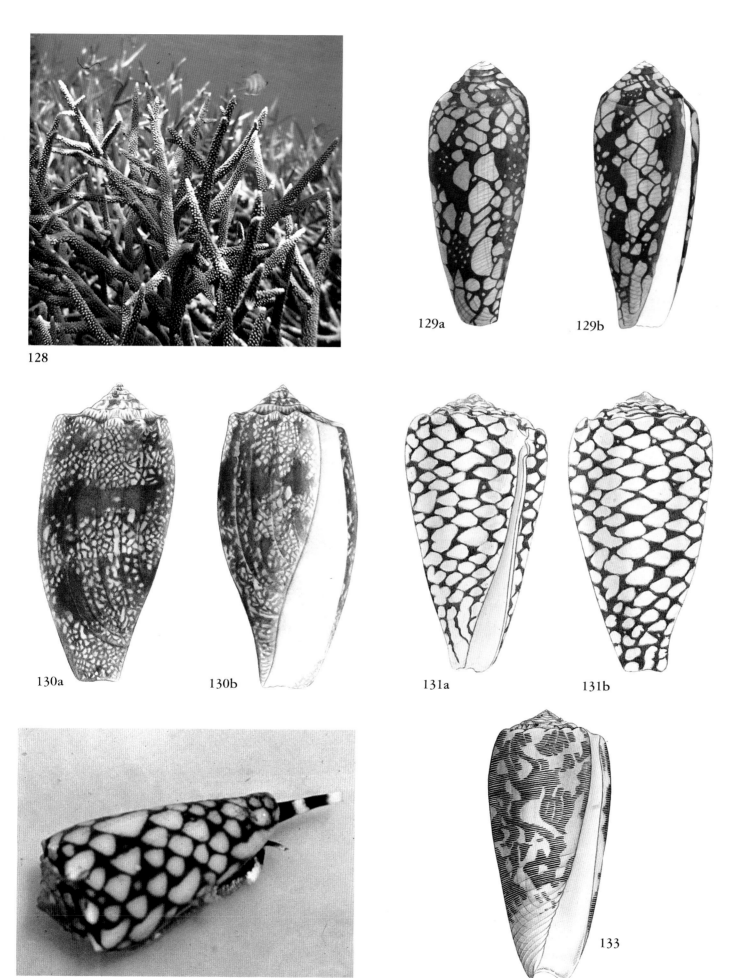

128

129a 129b

130a 130b

131a 131b

132

133

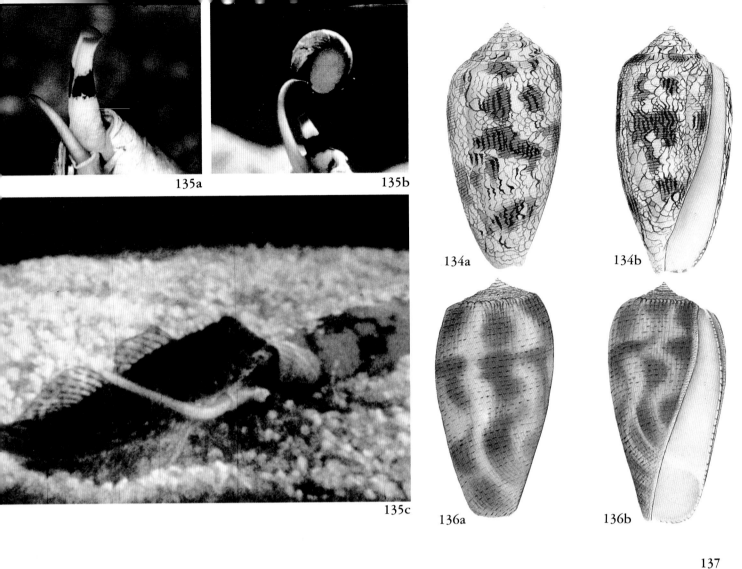

135a    135b

134a    134b

135c    136a    136b

137

PLATE 134a, b. Textile cone, *Conus textile* Linnaeus. This is a dangerous species that has caused human fatalities. It ranges from Polynesia to the Red Sea and attains a length of 10 centimeters (4 inches).

(K. Tomita)

PLATE 135. Textile cone, *C. textile* Linnaeus.

a. Close up showing extended siphon and tubular proboscis in the foreground. Extending from either side at the base of the proboscis are the tentacles. The process of stinging is accomplished with the use of the muscular proboscis.

b. Close up showing the cone shell in the act of striking a top shell, *Tegula*. The radular teeth originate in the radular sheath, are passed through the pharynx (a single tooth at a time), and then into the proboscis. A radular tooth is used as a harpoon-like device, which is grasped by the proboscis until the victim has been impaled. In this photograph, which was taken from a movie sequence of the stinging process, one can see the radular tooth extending from the extreme tip of the tubular proboscis and penetrating into the body of the mollusk.

c. *C. textile* in the process of stinging a blenny fish. The proboscis is also used to grasp the victim. Taken at Guam, Mariana Islands.

(Photographs by E. Pankow, courtesy P. Saunders)

PLATE 136a, b. Tulip cone, *Conus tulipa* Linnaeus. Although no human fatalities have been reported, this cone is an aggressive stinger. It is found from Polynesia to the Red Sea and attains a length of 7.5 centimeters (3 inches). (K. Tomita)

PLATE 137. *Octopus apollyon* Berry, named after the Greek god Apollo. This octopus may attain a length of more than 9 meters (29 feet). Despite its large size, it tends to be docile; on occasions, however, it bites. This is a very intelligent animal and at times outsmarts its would-be captors. Its color pattern and form vary greatly depending upon the background and circumstances in which the animal is found. Taken off the coast of British Columbia. (© F. Bavendam)

**PLATE 138.** Octopus bites believed to have been inflicted by *O. apollyon*. The bites took place while removing the animal from an aquarium at the Marine Science Center, Oregon State University, Newport, Oregon. The bite is similar to that of a bee sting, with profuse bleeding from the wound, redness, and swelling, and healing in about 10 days.

(Courtesy R. Hildebrand)

**PLATE 139.** Australian blue-ringed or spotted Octopus, *Octopus maculosus* Hoyle.

a. This living specimen was taken at Port Lincoln, Hopkins Island, Western Australia. This is believed to be the only species of octopus that has been incriminated in a human fatality. The specimen that caused the death of an Australian skindiver was small, about 20 centimeters (8 inches) in total spread. The victim had placed the octopus on his shoulder and was bitten on the upper back near the spinal column.

Symptoms consisted of dryness of mouth, difficulty in swallowing, vomiting, ataxia, loss of consciousness, and death within a period of two hours, even after having been given artificial respiration and treated in an iron lung. The episode occurred at East Point, about five kilometers from Darwin, Northern Territory, Australia. (Courtesy The Cousteau Society, Inc.)

b. Close-up of a tentacle of another specimen of *O. maculosus*. (K. Gillett)

**PLATE 140.** Crown-O-Thorns starfish, *Acanthaster planci* (Linnaeus). This starfish is covered with large spines, about 6 centimeters (2.5 inches) in length. Contact with these spines can be a very painful experience, causing a severe inflammatory reaction in the skin. Found in the Indo-Pacific, it attains a diameter of 60 centimeters (2 feet) or more. The number of arms varies from 13 to 16. This photograph was taken at Saipan, Marianas Islands. (Courtesy E. T. Rulison)

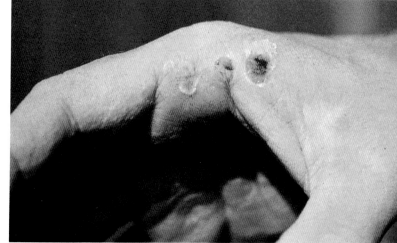

138

139a

139b

140

141

142

143

144a 144b

PLATE 141. *Acanthaster* is most notorious for the devastating effects of its eating living corals and destroying reefs in the Indo-Pacific. Note the manner in which this venomous starfish has denuded the adjacent coral. Taken at Heron Island, Great Barrier Reef.

(K. Gillett)

PLATE 142. Close up of *Acanthaster* spines, which cover the entire surface of this animal. The spines are venomous. (K. Gillett)

PLATE 143. *Acanthaster* is sometimes found carpeting the reef and destroying all living corals unfortunate enough to be in their pathway. This photograph shows a heavy infestation of *Acanthaster* on Slasher's Reef, Great Barrier Reef, Australia.

(Courtesy T. W. Brown)

PLATE 144a, b. Felt cap sea urchin, *Toxopneustes pileolus* (Lamarck).

a. The flower-like rosettes covering the test (shell) of this urchin are venomous pedicellariae, which are fully extended with the jaws wide open and waiting to grasp an object. This species can inflict a fatal wound.

b. Close up showing the venomous pedicellariae with the jaws wide open. Taken in Sydney Harbor, New South Wales, Australia.

(Photographs by C.V. Turner, courtesy E. Pope)

145

PLATE 145. Elegant sea urchin, *Toxopneustes elegans* Doderlein. The venomous pedicellariae of this species can inflict a painful sting, which may be lethal. The diameter of the test is 7.5 centimeters (3 inches). From Tokyo Bay, Japan.                    (T. Iwago)

PLATE 146. Rosy sea urchin, *Toxopneustes roseus* (Agassiz).

a. This sea urchin is somewhat temperamental in its biting habits, but capable of inflicting painful stings with its venomous pedicellarial jaws. The diameter of the test is 10 centimeters (4 inches). Taken near Caldivia, Bahia de Santa Elena, Ecuador.

(Courtesy S. Earle)

b. Close up showing the venomous pedicellariae of *T. roseus*. The jaws are open. Taken at night.

c. Same sea urchin as above. The jaws are closed. Taken during the day. Sea of Cortez, California.

(D. Wobber)

PLATE 147a-d. The structure of the venomous pedicellariae is clearly observed in these photographs.

a. Living pedicellariae on the test (shell) of the sea urchin *Sphaerechinus granularis* (Lamarck), from the Mediterranean Sea.

b. Live globiferous pedicellarium removed from the test. The jaws are closed. Note the large bulbous venom glands surrounding the jaws, which are completely hidden from view. The length of the pedicellarium is .5 centimeters (.2 inches).

c. Same pedicellarium with jaws open. The fang tips of the jaws can barely be seen at each point of the triangle.

d. Enlarged view of the open jaws of the pedicellarium. The specimens were taken at the aquarium, Zoological Station, Naples, Italy.

(Courtesy P. Giacomelli)

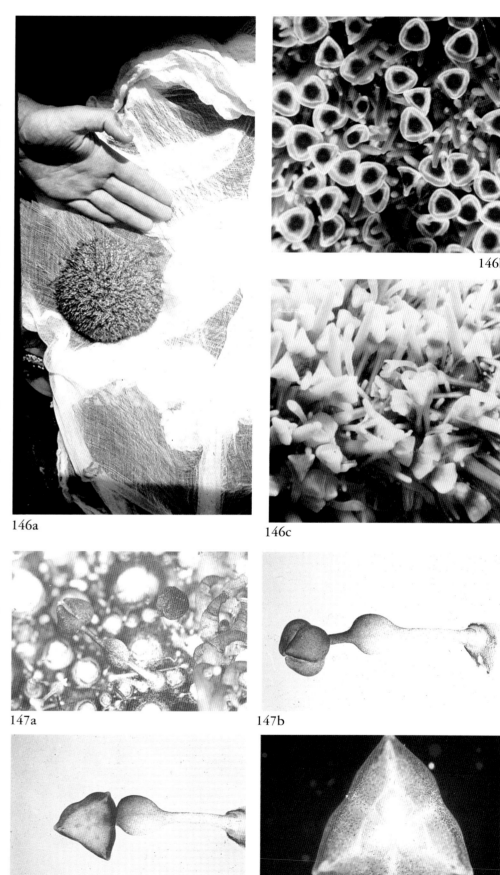

146a

146b

146c

147a

147b

147c

147d

148a

149

148b

150

151

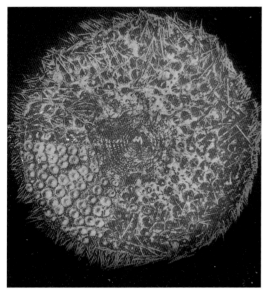
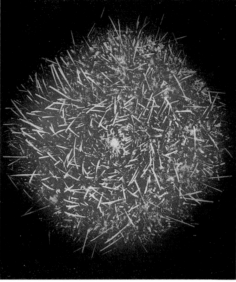
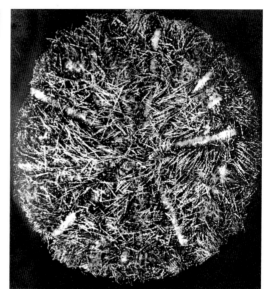

152           153           154 155

**PLATE 148a, b.** Long-spined or hairy sea urchin, *Diadema setosum* (Leske).

    **a.** A characteristic feature of this Pacific species is the isolated blue spots on the upper surface of the test, which has the appearance of a crown, hence the term diadem. Those long spines are a real hazard to anyone swimming near these urchins. The diameter of the test is about 10 centimeters (4 inches).

    **b.** The jewel-like spots are clearly visible here. Taken along the North Coast, New South Wales, Australia.           (A. Healy)

**PLATE 149.** *D. setosum*, taken at Wuvulu Island, Bismarck Archipelago.

    (Courtesy R. Murphy, The Cousteau Society, Inc.)

**PLATE 150.** Long-spined sea urchins can be a serious menace when they are hidden in a cluster of seaweed. These shrimpfish, *Aeoliscus strigatus* (Günther), take advantage of the protection of the spiny urchins, whose spines they resemble, and also take on the coloration of the surrounding eel grass. Palau, Western Caroline Islands.           (D. Ludwig)

**PLATE 151.** This is the West Indian edition of the long-spined sea urchin, *Diadema antillarum* Phillipi. Some parts of the Caribbean Sea are carpeted with thousands of these spiny creatures. The spines of *Diadema* are hollow and thought to contain a poison. Taken near Miami, Florida.           (R. Straughan)

**PLATE 152.** Purse sea urchin, *Phormosoma bursarium* Agassiz. This innocent looking Indo-Pacific sea urchin possesses oral spines that are ensheathed in venom sacs and is a dangerous species to handle. The diameter of the test is 16 centimeters (6.2 inches). Ventral (oral) view of a preserved specimen.           (From Mortensen)

**PLATE 153.** Ijimai sea urchin, *Asthenosoma ijimai* Yoshiwara, possesses spines ensheathed in a venom sac. This species is dangerous to handle and is feared by fishermen. The diameter of the test is 15 centimeters (6 inches). Preserved specimen is from Tolo, Sulu Archipelago.           (From Mortensen)

**PLATE 154.** Variable sea urchin, *Asthenosoma varium* Grube. Some of the spines of this sea urchin are ensheathed in a venom sac. The diameter of the test is 17 centimeters (6.7 inches). Found in the Indo-Pacific.           (From Mortensen)

**PLATE 155.** Tam O'Shanter sea urchin, *Araeosoma thetidis* (Clark). This Australian sea urchin possesses sharp secondary aboral spines that are encased in a venom sac and are capable of inflicting painful stings. They are generally captured in deep water trawls. When first captured, they may appear melon-shaped and bristling with spines, but soon deflate themselves by losing a large amount of water, at which time they assume a flattened appearance such as is generally seen in preserved specimens. The spines are very fragile and break off readily in the wound. This specimen was taken in 70 fathoms of water off Coogee, New South Wales, Australia. The diameter of the test is up to 20 centimeters (8 inches).

    (Photograph by J.F. Myers, courtesy E. Pope)

156

157

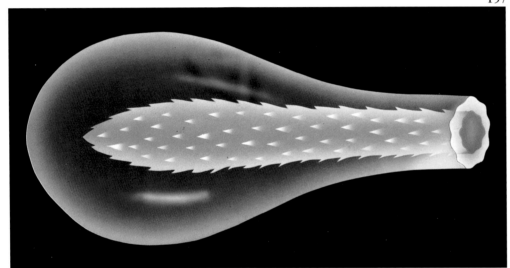

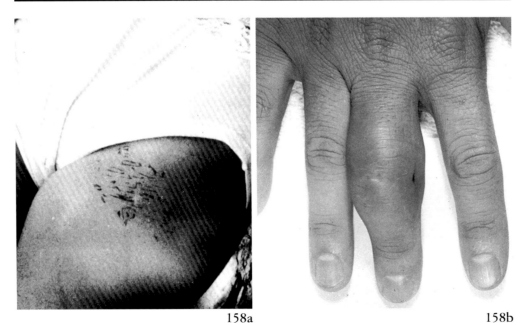

158a                              158b

PLATE 156. Tip of a secondary aboral spine of *Araeosoma thetidis* (Clark) ensheathed in a venom sac. When the spine penetrates the flesh, the venom sac is ruptured and the venom released into the wound. The spines may attain a length of 35 centimeters (13.7 inches), but are generally shorter.

(R. Kreuzinger, after Mortensen)

PLATE 157. Tip of a primary oral spine of *Phormosoma bursarium* Agassiz ensheathed in a venom sac.

(R. Kreuzinger, after Mortensen)

PLATE 158a, b. Sea urchin wounds.

a. Photograph of a six-year-old girl stung by the Mediterranean sea urchin, *Arbacia lixula* (Linnaeus). There were no spines embedded in the skin. Wounds were caused by the spines and bites of the pedicellariae. The wound area became reddened and swollen, and the child developed chills and a fever. Taken near Pula, Yugoslavia.          (Courtesy G. Maretić)

b. A severe chronic soft tissue reaction resulting from a puncture wound produced by a spine from the purple sea urchin *Strongylocentrotus purpuratus*. The swelling continued for a period of several months, eventually resulting in bone destruction. It required surgical repair. The wound healed in about one year.

(Courtesy R. L. O'Neal)

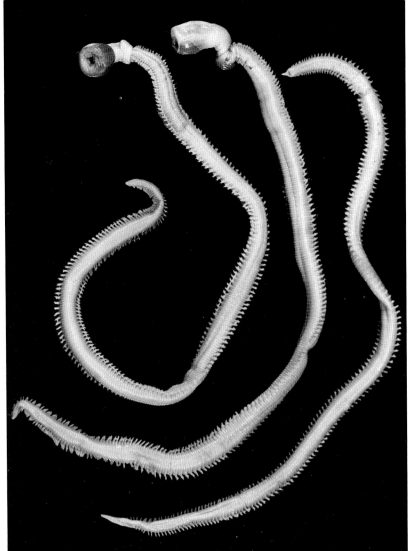

159 160

**PLATE 159.** The swarming of palolo worms is a festive occasion in Fiji and elsewhere in the South Pacific. This takes place at dawn for two days in each of the months of October and November, the day prior to the day on which the moon is in its last quarter. The worms are present in greatest number on the second day. The posterior portion of the worm becomes modified to carry the sex cells or gonads. The sex cells are formed only in the posterior part of the worm. After a period of development, the worm backs out of the burrow, and, when the modified portion is fully protruded, it breaks off and wiggles to the surface, swimming about and shedding eggs or sperm. The sea takes on the appearance of vermicelli soup, as can be seen in this photograph taken near Makonagai, Fiji. The anterior portion of the worm remains in coral crevices and eventually regenerates a new posterior segment. The males are light brownish in color while the females tend to be greenish.

The natives relish palolo worms as food, which they eat in a variety of ways—raw, boiled, fried in batter, scrambled with eggs, and in soup. And they consider palolo eggs a great delicacy. Photo taken at Makonga, Fiji.          (WLRI photo)

**PLATE 160.** Bloodworm, *Glycera dibranchiata* Ehlers. These worms are used extensively in the United States and Canada as bait worms. They burrow in the mud, and when handled will sometimes bite. They attain a length of 37 centimeters (14 inches).   (R. Kreuzinger)

**PLATE 161.** *G. dibranchiata:*
   a. showing the anterior end of the worm with the proboscis extended. From a film clip.
                          (Courtesy P. Saunders)
   b. looking into the jaws. The four dark lines are the fangs. From movie footage.
                          (Courtesy P. Saunders)

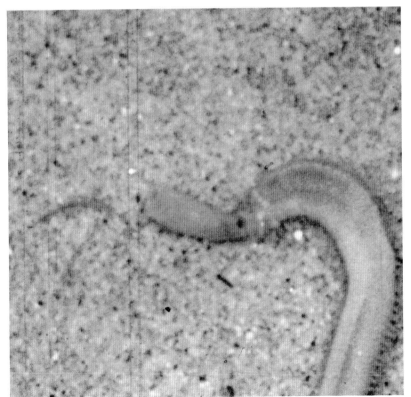

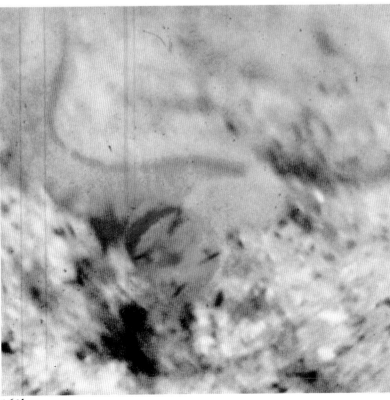

161a  161b

163a
163b

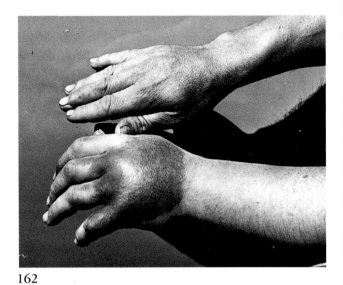

162

PLATE 162. The result of a bite on the hand from *Glycera*. The hand was swollen and very painful. The wounds consist of two to four small puncture wounds. Wegeport, Yarmouth County, Nova Scotia.

(I.W. Flye, courtesy W.L. Klawe)

PLATE 163. Bristle worm, *Eurythoë complanata* (Pallas).

a. This beautiful fluffy little worm is quite deceiving. The fluff is comprised of a mass of sharp bristles that can produce a painful envenomation. Don't touch! It attains a length of 10 centimeters (4 inches). Photograph taken at Bonaire, Netherlands Antilles.

b. Close up showing the "fluffy" stinging bristles, which are very sharp and easily penetrate gloves.

(A.B. Bowker)

PLATE 164a, b. Fleshy bristle worm, *Hermodice carunculata* (Pallas). This species is said to be one of the most dangerous of the bristle worms. Reputedly capable of delivering a "paralyzing effect" with its hollow, venom-filled bristles or setae, it is found in the West Indies. Its length is 30 centimeters (11.7 inches).

(WLRI photo)

PLATE 165a. Biting reef worm, *Eunice aphroditois* (Pallas). The bite of this reef worm can be quite painful. It attains a length of 150 centimeters (58 inches). Taken near Sydney, Australia.

b. A portion of the mouth of *Eunice* has been removed from a preserved specimen to reveal the biting jaws. (K. Gillett)

c. Close up of the head of *Eunice*. The jaws appear as a black dot in the center of the mouth. (K. Gillett)

164a

164b

165a 165b

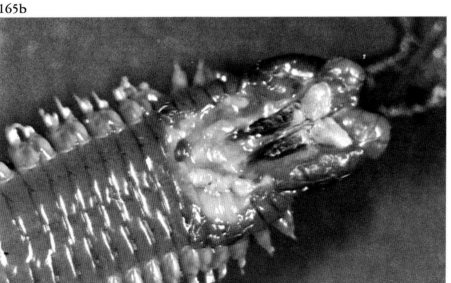

165c

# CHAPTER IV

# Aquatic Animals that Sting—Vertebrates

THIS CHAPTER INCLUDES a remarkable group of venomous or stinging animals with backbones. They fall into three categories: fishes, reptiles, and a single mammalian species. The stinging fishes are a very diversified group, as one can see from their varied relationships, appearance, color, and habitat. They display an interesting variety of venom organs. Venomous aquatic snakes are primarily marine, but a few species inhabit freshwater swamps and streams. The following vertebrate groups are discussed in this chapter:

*Venomous Fishes*
    HORN or SPINY SHARKS (Dogfish)
    STINGRAYS
    CHIMAERAS: Elephantfishes, Ratfishes
    CATFISHES
    MORAY EELS
    WEEVERFISHES
    SCORPIONFISHES
    TOADFISHES
    SURGEONFISHES
    FLYING GURNARDS
    DRAGONETS
    RABBITFISHES
    SCATS
    STARGAZERS
    LEATHERBACKS (Leatherjackets)

*Venomous Snakes*
    SEA SNAKES
    FRESHWATER SNAKES

*Freshwater Venomous Mammal*
    DUCKBILLED PLATYPUS

## *VENOMOUS FISHES*

### HORN OR SPINY SHARKS (Dogfish)

The spiny dogfish is referred to in the *Halieutica* (A.D. 200), a fishing poem of Grecian antiquity, thus: "Dogfish, from their prickly mail, well-named the spinous. These in punctures sharp, a fatal poison from their spines inject." However, it was not until 1921 that the English surgeon H. Muir Evans discovered that the dorsal spines of the dogfish are true venom organs producing a mildly toxic substance. The spiny dogfish is found on both sides of the North Pacific and North Atlantic oceans and is widely distributed throughout temperate and tropical seas.

There are three different families of horn or spiny sharks, or dogfish. One species, in particular, has been incriminated in human envenomations, namely,

SPINY DOGFISH, *Squalus acanthias* Linnaeus (166), which inhabits the more northerly regions of the Pacific and Atlantic oceans.

A close relative of *S. acanthias* is:

HORNSHARK, *Heterodontus francisci* (Girard) (167, 168), found along the California coast, from Point Conception to Lower California and into the Gulf of California. The venomous spines are too blunt to be dangerous.

Dogfish are somewhat sluggish in their movements and erratic in their migrations, traveling singly or in schools. Dogfish extend in their bathymetric range from the surface to a depth of 100 fathoms or more. They have voracious appetites and consume a variety of fishes, coelenterates, mollusks, crustaceans, and worms. Dog-

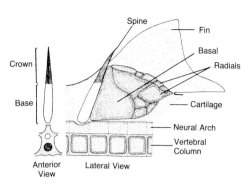

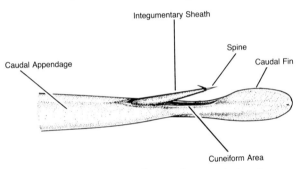

Figure 1. Venom apparatus of the spiny dogfish, *Squalus acanthias*. This drawing is of the first dorsal fin and spine. The second spine is similar in arrangement.    (D. Goe)

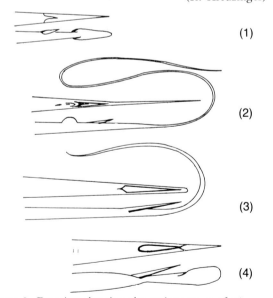

Figure 2. Caudal appendage of a typical stingray (*Urolophus*), showing the general anatomy of the sting.
(R. Kreuzinger)

Figure 3. Drawing showing the various types of stingray caudal appendages.    (Mrs. R. Kreuzinger)

fish are economically important because of the damage they do to fishing gear.

## Venom Apparatus of Spiny Dogfish

Wounds of the spiny dogfish are inflicted by the dorsal stings (spines), a single spine located adjacent to the anterior margin of each of the two dorsal fins. The venom gland appears as a glistening, whitish substance situated in a shallow groove on the back of the upper portion of each spine. When the spine enters the skin, the venom gland is damaged and the venom enters the flesh of the victim (Figure 1).

# STINGRAYS

Stingrays constitute one of the largest and most important groups of venomous marine organisms. They are second only to the coelenterates in the number of envenomations they inflict in humans. It has been estimated that there are upwards of 1,500 stingray attacks in the United States each year. Most stingrays inhabit marine waters, but one family, the Potamotrygonidae, are found in the streams and rivers of South America, equatorial Africa, and Laos, and some of them are encountered in coastal brackish water in the vicinity of river mouths. The saltwater stingray species are divided into six families. Although there are numerous species of stingrays, most of them are found in a somewhat similar environment.

Rays are common inhabitants of tropical, subtropical, and warm temperate seas. With the exception of the family Potamotrygonidae, which is confined to freshwater, rays are essentially marine forms, some of which may freely enter brackish waters or freshwater. Although most common in shallow water, rays swim in moderate depths as well. A deep-sea species has been reported from the central Pacific Ocean. Sheltered bays, shoal lagoons, river mouths, and sandy areas between patch reefs are favorite habitats of rays. They may be observed lying on top of the sand, or partially sub-

merged, with only their eyes, spiracles, and a portion of the tail exposed (169). Rays burrow into the sand or mud, and with their pectoral fins they excavate worms, mollusks, and crustaceans upon which they feed.

## Venom Apparatus of Stingrays

The venom apparatus, or sting, of stingrays is an integral part of the caudal, or tail, appendage (Figure 2). A study of stingrays reveals that there are four general anatomical types of venom organs, which vary somewhat in their effectiveness as a defensive weapon. The types, shown in Figure 3, are:

(1) *Gymnurid:* This type is found in the butterfly rays (*Gymnura*). The sting is small, poorly developed, and situated close to the base of the tail, making it a relatively feeble striking organ.

(2) *Myliobatid:* This type is found in the bat, or eagle, rays (*Myliobatis, Aetobatis, Rhinoptera*). Their tails terminate in a long, whip-like appendage. The stings in these rays are frequently large and well developed, but situated near the base of the tail. Under the proper circumstances these rays can use their venom organs to good advantage.

(3) *Dasyatid:* This type is found in the stingrays proper (*Dasyatis* and *Potamotrygon*). The sting is well developed as in the previous type, but is located farther out from the base of the tail, making it a more effective striking organ. Stingrays possessing this type of venom apparatus are among the most dangerous kinds known. Their tails terminate in a long whip-like appendage.

(4) *Urolophid:* This type is found among the round stingrays (*Urolophus*). The caudal appendage to which the sting is attached is short, muscular, and well developed. Urolophid rays are also dangerous to humans, and can inflict a well-directed sting resulting in an envenomation.

In general, the venom apparatus of stingrays consists of the serrate spine and an enveloping sheath of skin. Together they are termed the sting. Stingrays usually possess only a single spine at a time, but it is not unusual to find specimens with two or more (Figure 4). Apparently, the spine remains until it is removed by injury. There is no evidence to support the idea that the spines are shed each year. As the young spine grows out from the tail, it takes with it a layer of skin, the so-called integumentary sheath, which continues to ensheathe the spine until it is removed by injury or wear.

The spine is composed of a hard, bone-like material, called vaodentine. Along both sides of the spine are a series of sharp recurved teeth. The spine is marked by a number of irregular, shallow furrows that run almost the length of the spine. Along either edge, on the underside of the spine, there are deep grooves; these grooves are termed the ventrolateral-glandular grooves. If they are carefully examined, it will be observed that they contain a strip of soft, spongy, grayish tissue extending throughout their length. The bulk of the venom is produced by this tissue in the grooves, although lesser amounts are believed to be produced by other portions of the integumentary sheath and in certain specialized areas of the skin on the tail adjacent to the spine. These grooves serve to protect the soft delicate glandular tissue that lies within them, and, even though all of the integumentary sheath may be worn away, the venom-producing tissue continues to remain within these grooves. Thus, a perfectly clean-looking spine can still be venomous. Figure 5 shows the structure of a stingray's sting.

Stingray wounds are either of the laceration or puncture type (Figures 6, 7). Penetration of the skin and underlying tissue is usually accomplished without serious damage to the surrounding structures, but withdrawal of the sting may result in extensive tissue damage due to the recurved spines and retrorse teeth. Swelling in the vicinity of the wound is a constant finding. The area around the wound at first has an ashy appearance, later beomces bluish, and then reddens.

Although stingray injuries occur most frequently in the area of the ankle joint and foot as a result of

Figure 4. Caudal appendage of the spotted eagle ray, *Aetobatus narinari*, showing an example of multiple stings. It is not unusual to find more than one sting or spine on the tail of many stingrays. There is no evidence that the spines are replaced each year, but, when they are replaced, it is probably due to accidental removal.

(From Gudger)

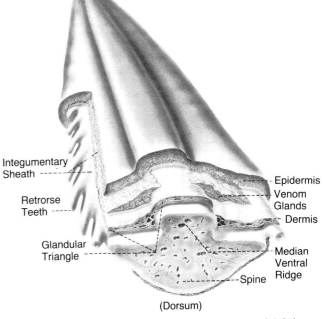

Figure 5. Drawing showing the cross section of a typical intact stingray sting in an upside down position.

(L. Barlow)

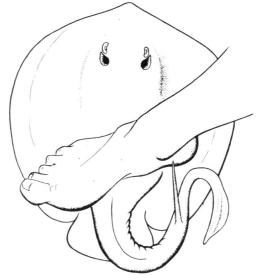

Figure 6. Drawing showing how a stingray inflicts its sting. (R. Kreuzinger)

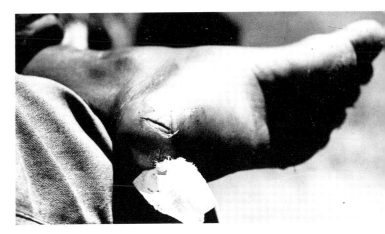

Figure 7. Stingray wounds start out as puncture wounds, but, when the sting is removed, it generally results in a nasty, jagged laceration because of the tearing action of the sharp retrorse teeth. The tearing process increases the exposure of the tissues to the venom produced in the integumentary sheath. Wound inflicted by *Aetobatus narinari*, Veracruz, Mexico. (M. Murray)

stepping on the ray, instances have been reported in which the wounds were in the chest. Chest wounds may result in death.

Pain is the predominant symptom and usually develops immediately or within a period of ten minutes following the attack. The pain has been variously described as sharp, shooting, spasmodic, or throbbing. Freshwater stingrays are reputed to cause extremely painful wounds. More generalized symptoms are a fall in blood pressure, vomiting, diarrhea, sweating, rapid heartbeat, and muscular paralysis; deaths have also been reported.

### Stingrays Dangerous to Humans

Because of the large number of venomous stingray species, only a few representative examples will be depicted here. All of the species included are equipped with a well-developed venom apparatus and are capable of inflicting painful lacerations. Their ability to hide undetected makes them especially dangerous.

DASYATIDAE: STINGRAYS or WHIPRAYS

AUSTRALIAN GIANT STINGRAY, *Dasyatis brevicaudata* (Hutton) (170, 171). This species is reputed to be the largest stingray in the world. It may attain a length of 4.5 meters (15 feet) or more, a width of 2.2 meters (7 feet), and a weight of more than 325 kilograms (715 pounds). The sting from one such ray measured 37 centimeters (14.5 inches)—an imposing brute to say the least. There is a case report in which a giant 3-meter (10 feet) Australian stingray drove its sting through the lower third of a man's leg between the tibia and fibula, leaving a 17.7 centimeter (7 inches) laceration. Several fatal cases are on record from stingray wounds in the chest, heart, and liver. *D. brevicaudata* inhabits the Indo-Pacific region.

DIAMOND STINGRAY, *Dasyatis dipterurus* (Jordan and Gilbert) (172). This is a fairly common species that ranges from British Columbia to Central America. It attains a length of about 2 meters (6.5 feet).

EUROPEAN STINGRAY, *Dasyatis pastinaca* (Linnaeus) (173). This is the famous "Pastinaca marina" of antiquity. Pliny, the great naturalist of ancient Rome, claimed that so great was the prowess of this piscine that it was able to kill a tree by stinging it. On the other hand, he also recommended grinding up its sting and using it as a toothache potion. This creature inhabits the northeastern Atlantic Ocean, Mediterranean Sea, and Indian Ocean, and attains a length of about 2.5 meters (8 feet).

SOUTHERN STINGRAY, *Dasyatis americana* Hildebrand and Schroeder (174, 175). This is a common West Indian species that inhabits the western Atlantic from New Jersey to southern Brazil. It attains a length of 2 meters (6.5 feet).

GYMNURIDAE: BUTTERFLY RAYS

BUTTERFLY RAY, *Gymnura marmorata* (Cooper) (176). The butterfly ray possesses such a small venom organ that it is almost useless as a defensive organ. The ray ranges from Point Conception, California, south to Mazatlan, Mexico. This ray is wider than it is long, having a wing span of 2.2 meters (7 feet).

MYLIOBATIDAE: EAGLE RAYS

SPOTTED EAGLE RAY, *Aetobatis narinari* (Euphrasen) (177). This is a handsome ray and presents a thrilling sight when flapping its fins majestically through the water. This species is an example of a multispined stingray; it ranges throughout tropical and warm-temperate regions of the Atlantic Ocean, Indo-Pacific, and Red Sea.

CALIFORNIA BAT RAY, *Myliobatis californicus* (Gill) (178, 179). This ray ranges from Oregon to Magdalena Bay, Baja California. It attains a width of 1.2 meters (47 inches). A fairly common species, it can be frequently observed in open, sandy areas near kelp forests.

RHINOPTERA: COW-NOSED RAYS

COW-NOSED RAY, *Rhinoptera bonasus* (Mitchill) (180). Cow-nosed rays are frequently observed swimming in small schools just above the ocean floor. Their width is about 2 meters (6.5 feet); they are found along the coastal western Atlantic, from New England to Brazil.

### UROLOPHIDAE: ROUND STINGRAYS

The round stingrays are noted for their ability to strike an object with their powerful muscular tails with unerring accuracy. This stingray family accounts for a major percentage of stingray envenomations.

ROUND STINGRAY, *Urolophus halleri* Cooper **(181, 182)**. This ray ranges from Point Conception, California, south to Panama Bay, and attains a length of 50 centimeters (19 inches) or more.

SPOTTED ROUND STINGRAY, *Urolophus maculosus* (Garman) **(183)**, is believed to be a color variant of *Urolophus halleri*.

YELLOW STINGRAY, *Urolophus jamaicensis* (Cuvier) **(184)**, is found in the western tropical Atlantic, from Florida southward into the Caribbean. It attains a length of 67 centimeters (2.2 feet).

### POTAMOTRYGONIDAE: Freshwater Stingrays

The freshwater stingrays are an interesting group that inhabits South America, equatorial Africa, and Laotian streams and brackish-water river mouths. They most closely resemble the dasyatid rays in their habits since they are usually found buried in the mud or sand. Because they are found in turbid water, they are difficult to detect and thus constitute a serious hazard to anyone wading in streams inhabited by them. They are sometimes found 1,000 kilometers (620 miles) inland from the sea. Freshwater stingrays feed on small fish and crustaceans. They tend to be small in size, less than 1 meter (39 inches) in length, and resemble the round rays *(Urolophus)* in appearance. Despite their small size and short, pointed tails, they can inflict extremely painful wounds, which are slow to heal and may result in chronic ulcers and nasty scars (Figure 8a, b). Our knowledge of these rays is still quite meager.

SOUTH AMERICAN FRESHWATER STINGRAY, *Potamotrygon motoro* (Müller and Henle) **(185)**.

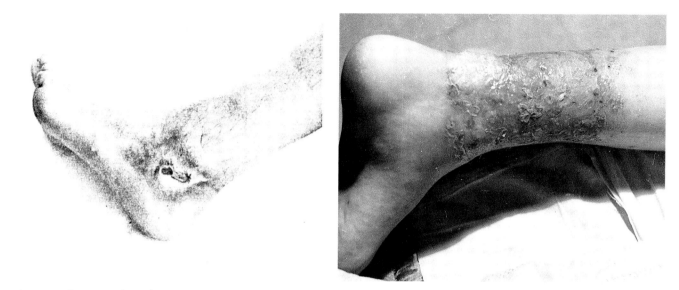

Figure 8a, b. Stings from freshwater stingrays can be extememly painful. The initial laceration or puncture wound soon breaks down into a nasty ulcer that may take months to heal; or a gangrenous wound that, if improperly treated, may require amputation. Anterior and posterior view of a gangrenous wound.
(Courtesy M. M. Castex)

Found in the freshwater rivers of Paraguay and the Amazon River, south to Rio de Janeiro, Brazil, it has a disc width of 54 centimeters (21 inches). This species has a bad reputation and has caused many envenomations.

PAUCKE'S FRESHWATER STINGRAY, *Potamotrygon pauckei* Castex **(186)**. This ray is said to produce one of the most potent venoms of any of the freshwater rays studied. It is found in the freshwater rivers of Argentina, Paraguay, and Uruguay. The width of the disc is 43 centimeters (17 inches).

## CHIMAERAS
### Elephantfishes, Ratfishes

Chimaeras, elephantfishes, or ratfishes, as they are variously called, are a group of cartilaginous fishes having a single external gill opening on either side, covered by a skin fold that leads off the gill chamber. Externally, ratfishes are more or less compressed laterally, tapering posteriorly to a slender tail. The snout is rounded, or cone-shaped, extended as a long, pointed beak, or bears a curious hoe-shaped proboscis. There are two dorsal fins. The first fin is triangular, usually higher than the

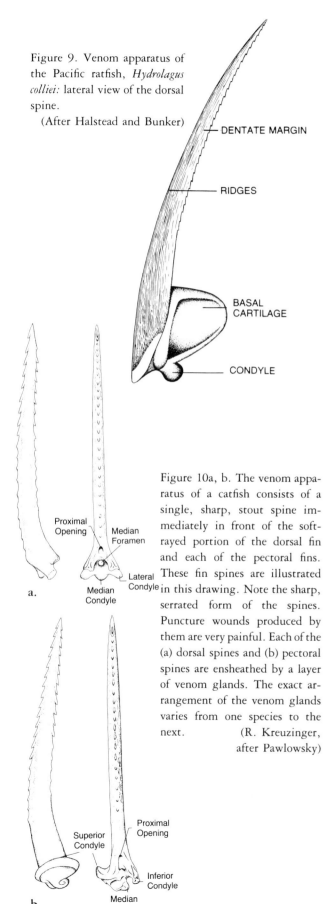

Figure 9. Venom apparatus of the Pacific ratfish, *Hydrolagus colliei:* lateral view of the dorsal spine.

(After Halstead and Bunker)

— DENTATE MARGIN

— RIDGES

BASAL CARTILAGE

CONDYLE

Figure 10a, b. The venom apparatus of a catfish consists of a single, sharp, stout spine immediately in front of the soft-rayed portion of the dorsal fin and each of the pectoral fins. These fin spines are illustrated in this drawing. Note the sharp, serrated form of the spines. Puncture wounds produced by them are very painful. Each of the (a) dorsal spines and (b) pectoral spines are ensheathed by a layer of venom glands. The exact arrangement of the venom glands varies from one species to the next.        (R. Kreuzinger, after Pawlowsky)

Proximal Opening
Median Foramen
Lateral Condyle
Median Condyle
a.

Superior Condyle
Proximal Opening
Inferior Condyle
Median Condyle
b.

second, and edged anteriorly by a strong, sharp-pointed bony spine that serves as a venom organ. Ratfishes have a preference for cooler waters, and have a depth range from the surface down to 1,400 fathoms. They are weak swimmers and die soon after being removed from the water. They have well-developed dental plates and can inflict a nasty bite.

### Venom Apparatus of Ratfishes

The venom apparatus of ratfishes consists of a single dorsal sting, which is situated along the anterior margin of the first dorsal fin (Figure 9). Along the back of the spine is a shallow depression that contains a strip of soft, grayish tissue—the venom gland.

### Ratfishes Dangerous to Humans

EUROPEAN RATFISH, *Chimaera monstrosa* Linnaeus (187). These fish inhabit the north Atlantic Ocean from Norway and Iceland to Cuba, the Azores, Morocco, the Mediterranean Sea, and South Africa. They attain a length of 1 meter (39 inches).

PACIFIC RATFISH, *Hydrolagus colliei* (Lay and Bennett) (188a, b). Found along the Pacific coast of North America, it attains a length up to 1 meter (39 inches).

Ratfishes inflict a very painful puncture wound with their sharp dorsal stings. The pain is immediate and tends to increase in severity for a few minutes, and may continue to be severe for several hours, gradually lessening in intensity. A dull ache may continue for days. The area around the wound may become numb and may develop a cyanotic or a blackish appearance. The outer area may be pale, swollen, and similar in appearance to a severe inflammatory reaction. Joint aches and swollen lymph nodes may be present. It is assumed that wounds from this fish are largely accidental since the fish is not reputed to be aggressive. However, they are also equipped with powerful jaws and are capable of inflicting nasty bites. The viscera of these fish have been found to be toxic to laboratory animals.

## CATFISHES

Catfishes come in a wide variety of sizes and body shapes, varying from short to greatly elongated, or even eel-like. The head is sometimes very large, wide or depressed, or may be very small. The lips are usually equipped with long barbels. The skins of these fishes are thick and slimy, or may be covered with bony plates. No true scales are ever present. Included within this group are about 1,000 species, most of which are found in the freshwater streams of the tropics. There are also a few marine species. However, only a few representative species have been selected here. Some catfish species have been designated as "parasitic" because of their ability to penetrate the urethra, vagina, and anus of humans. (*See* Chapter VIII).

### Venom Apparatus of Catfishes

Venomous catfishes have a single sharp, stout spine immediately in front of the soft-rayed portion of the dorsal and pectoral fins. This spine is enveloped by a thin layer of skin, the integumentary sheath, which is continuous with that of the soft-rayed portion of the fin. There is no external evidence of the venom glands, which are located as a series of glandular cells within the outer, or epidermal, layer of the integumentary sheath. The venom, or glandular, cells are most concentrated at the anterolateral and posterolateral margins of the sting where they are sometimes clumped two or three cells deep within the epidermal layer. The spines of some species are also equipped with a series of sharp, recurved teeth (Figure 10a, b) that are capable of producing a severe laceration of the victim's flesh, thus facilitating absorption of the venom and subsequent secondary infection. Catfish spines are also particularly dangerous because they can be locked into the extended position at the will of the fish. The spines of doradid catfishes are highly developed and indeed formidable (Figure 11).

AXILLARY GLANDS:

Some catfishes are also equipped with axillary glands. The outlet of the axillary appears as a small orifice in the shoulder region just behind the gill opening and above the pectoral fin, as seen in the drawing of *Galeichthys felis* (Figure 12). There is no external evidence of the gland, other than this small pore. The actual gland is quite small; in a catfish measuring 75 centimeters in length, the gland is only 2 x 2.8 mm and somewhat chestnut shaped.

The axillary gland of the Australian estuary catfish, *Cnidoglanis macrocephalus* (Cuvier and Valenciennes) was tested and found to produce a muscular paralysis in test animals. The axillary glands in *C. macrocephalus* are well developed; however, the manner in which they function is not known. It is believed that the glands serve as a crinotoxin, releasing the poison into the environment without the assistance of a traumatogenic device. (*See also* Chapter V.)

## Catfishes Dangerous to Humans

CATFISH, *Galeichthys felis* (Linnaeus) (189). Ranges from Cape Cod to the Gulf of Mexico. Length 40 centimeters (15.7 inches).

LABRYNTHIC CATFISH, *Clarias batrachus* (Linnaeus) (190). Ranges from the coasts of India to those of Java, Borneo, Sumatra, and the Philippine Islands. Length 30 centimeters (11.7 inches).

EAST INDIAN CATFISH, *Heteropneustes fossilis* (Bloch) (191). Found along the coasts of India, Ceylon, and Vietnam. Length 25 centimeters (9.7 inches).

ORIENTAL CATFISH, *Plotosus lineatus* (Thunberg) (192). Occurs in the vicinity of river mouths throughout much of the Indo-Pacific area. Length 30 centimeters (11.7 inches).

SEA CATFISH, *Bagre marinus* (Mitchill) (193). Inhabits the east coast of North America from Cape Cod to Rio de Janeiro, Brazil. Length 35 centimeters (13.7 inches).

CAROLINA MADTOM, *Noturus furiosus* Jordan and Meek (194). Length 12 centimeters (4.7 inches). Inhabits freshwater streams of eastern North Carolina.

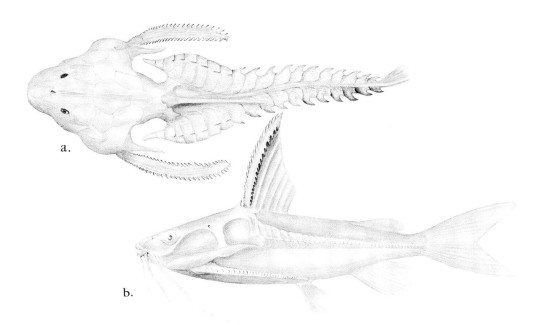

Figure 11a, b. Doradid catfishes are noted for their heavy armor and highly-developed dorsal and pectoral spines. (a) Dorsal view of *Platydoras costatus* (Linnaeus) showing heavy-armored skin consisting of spiny scutes, or plates, and the heavily-armed pectoral spines. (b) Side view of *Centrochir crocodili* (Humboldt) showing dorsal spine. Note the large retrorse teeth along the margins of the dorsal spine. The spines depicted in these drawings are representative of this group of catfishes. In some species of doradid catfishes the osseous spines are said to be accompanied by venom glands, and together they present a formidable traumatogenic device capable of inflicting painful wounds.

(K. Fogassy, after Eigenmann)

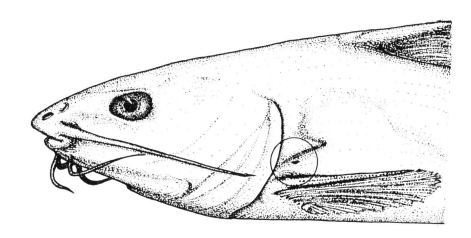

Figure 12. Lateral view of head and shoulder region of *Galeichthys felis*. A circle is drawn around the posthumeral region to designate the small axillary pore that opens to the axillary gland.

(From Halstead, Kuninobu, and Hebard)

BRINDLED MADTOM, *Noturus miurus* (Jordan) (195). Illinois to Lake Erie, Lake St. Clair drainage, Allegheny drainage, and Mississippi River drainage. Length 10 centimeters (4 inches).

TADPOLE MADTOM, *Noturus mollis* (Mitchill) (196). Eastern and central North American river drainages. Length 10 centimeters (4 inches).

The pain of catfish stings is generally described as an instantaneous stinging, throbbing, or scalding sensation, which may be localized or may radiate up the affected limb. Some of the tropical species, such as *Plotosus*, are capable of producing violent pain, which may last for 48 hours or more. Immediately after being stung, the area around the wound becomes pale. The pallor is soon followed by a cyanotic appearance, and then by redness and swelling. In some cases, swelling may be very severe, accompanied by numbness and gangrene of the area around the wound. Shock may be present. Improperly treated cases frequently result in secondary bacterial infections of the wound. Because of recurved teeth along the margin of their spines, some species of catfishes may produce wounds that may take weeks to heal. Catfishes are common in the aquarium trade, are constantly handled, and some people are stung. Deaths have been reported from stings of some tropical catfishes.

## MORAY EELS

Moray eels are members of the family Muraenidae. The bodies of these fishes are scaleless, elongated, and rounded, or more or less compressed. The dorsal and anal fins are continuous with the caudal and are generally covered by thick skin. The pectoral and pelvic fins are absent.

The meager amount of research that has been conducted on so-called venomous eels is concerned with one single species:

EUROPEAN MORAY EEL, *Muraena helena* Linnaeus (197), is distributed along coastal areas of the eastern Atlantic Ocean and Mediterranean Sea. Other species have been listed as venomous by modern authors, but this has not been proven.

From earliest times, the teeth of *Muraena helena* have been considered as constituting a venom apparatus (198). However, anatomical studies fail to show any evidence of venom glands. It has been suggested that the palatine mucosa may secrete a toxic substance. The bite of a moray eel can be very painful and may become infected.

## WEEVERFISHES

Weevers are small, attractive marine fishes that attain a maximum length of 46 centimeters (18 inches). They are members of the family Trachinidae and are among the most dangerous venomous fishes of the temperate zone. Primarily dwellers of flat, sandy, or muddy bays, weevers are commonly seen burying themselves in the soft sand or mud with only their heads partially exposed. They may dart out rapidly and strike an object with their cheek spines—with unerring accuracy. When a weever is provoked, the dorsal fin is instantly erected and the gill covers expanded. Because of their habit of concealment, aggressive attitude, and highly developed venom apparatus, they constitute a real danger to any diver working in their habitat.

### Venom Apparatus of Weeverfishes

The venom apparatus of the weeverfish consists of the dorsal and opercular spines and their associated glands. The dorsal spines vary from five to seven in number. Each of the spines is enclosed within a thin-walled sheath of skin from which protrudes a needle-sharp tip (Figure 13). Removal of the sheath reveals a thin, elongated, tapering strip of whitish spongy tissue lying within the grooves near the tip. Attached to the upper and lower margins of the spine are the pear-shaped venom glands. Weever venom has been found to act as both a neurotoxin and hemotoxin, similar to some snake venoms.

### Weeverfishes Dangerous to Humans

Four species of weeverfishes are generally recognized, but only two of the more common species are represented here:

GREATER WEEVERFISH, *Trachinus draco* Linnaeus (199, 200, 201). Occurs from Norway and the British Isles southward to the Mediterranean Sea and along the coast of North Africa. Length 45 centimeters (17.7 inches).

LESSER WEEVERFISH, *Trachinus vipera* Cuvier (202). Inhabits the North Sea, southward along the coast of Europe, and the Mediterranean Sea. Length 15 centimeters (6 inches).

Weever wounds usually produce an instant pain described as a burning, stabbing, or "crushing" sensation, initially confined to the immediate area of the wound, then gradually spreading through the affected limb. The pain gets progressively worse until it reaches an excruciating peak, generally within thirty minutes. The severity is such that the victim may scream, thrash wildly about, and lose consciousness. In most instances, morphine fails to give relief. Untreated, the pain commonly subsides within twenty-four hours. Tingling, followed by numbness, develops around the wound. The skin around the wound at first is blanched, but soon becomes reddened, hot, and swollen. The swelling may be quite extensive and continue for ten days or longer. Other symptoms consist of headache, fever, chills, delirium, nausea, vomiting, dizziness, sweating, cyanosis, joint aches, loss of speech, slow heartbeat, palpitation, mental depression, convulsions, difficulty in breathing, and death. Secondary infections are common in cases improperly treated. Gangrene has been known to develop as a complication. Recovery may take from several days to several months (Figure 14).

## SCORPIONFISHES

Members of the family Scorpaenidae, the scorpionfishes, are widely distributed throughout all tropical and temperate seas. A few species are also found in arctic waters. Many scorpaenids attain a large size and are valuable food fishes, whereas others are relatively small and of no commercial value. Some species are extremely venomous.

Venomous scorpionfishes have been divided into

Figure 13. Venom apparatus of *Trachinus draco* showing the venomous dorsal spines, inset, which are situated in lateral glandular grooves of the dorsal spine, and venom apparatus of the opercular spines, which are situated on the dorsal and ventral aspects of the opercular spines. The weeverfish is frequently buried in the sand and when aggravated can dart out of the sand and inflict an extremely painful wound using either the dorsal or opercular spines.
(R. H. Knabenbauer)

three main groups on the basis of the structure of their venom organs, namely:

(1) Zebrafish (*Pterois*);
(2) Scorpionfish (*Scorpaena*); and
(3) Stonefish (*Synanceja*).

### ZEBRAFISH

Zebrafish are among the most beautiful and ornate of coral reef fishes. They are generally found in shallow water, hovering about in a crevice, or at times swimming unconcernedly in the open. They are also called turkeyfish because of their interesting habit of swimming around slowly and spreading their fan-like pectorals and lacy dorsal fins like a turkey displaying its plumes. These fish are frequently observed swimming in pairs and are apparently fearless in their movements. Acceptance of an invitation to reach out and grab one of these fish results in an extremely painful experience, because hidden under the "lace" are needlesharp fin stings. The fearlessness of *Pterois* makes it a particular menace to anyone working in its habitat, the shallow water coral reefs, and home aquariums.

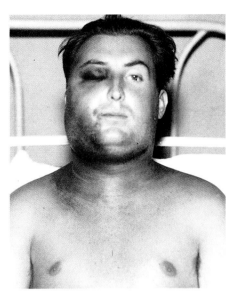

Figure 14. Austrian diver stung by *Trachinus vipera* near Ischia Island, Naples, Italy. The diver was diving near a sand bank and came upon a lesser weever, which permitted the diver to touch it. Suddenly, the weever started moving in a snake-like fashion and quickly turned, facing the diver with fins vibrating in a most aggressive manner. Before the diver was able to withdraw, the weeverfish darted at him and struck him twice, first striking his mask and then his right jaw. The pain was intense and soon followed by respiratory distress. The right side of his face became severely swollen and cyanotic. The victim begged for someone to shoot him and put him out of his misery. The patient was taken to a hospital where he was given symptomatic treatment. Later he developed a massive hematoma on the right side of his face and neck as seen in these photographs. Gradually the patient's condition improved. The patient was discharged 10 days after hospitalization.
(From Halstead)

## SCORPIONFISH

Members of the genus *Scorpaena* are for the most part shallow-water bottom dwellers, found in bays, along sandy beaches, rocky coastlines, or coral reefs, from the intertidal zone to depths of 50 fathoms or more. Their habit of concealing themselves in crevices, among debris, under rocks, or in seaweed, together with their protective coloration, which blends them almost perfectly into their surrounding environment, makes them difficult to see. When challenged, they have the defensive habit of erecting their spinous dorsal fin and flaring out their armed gill covers, pectoral, pelvic, and anal fins. The pectoral fins, although dangerous in appearance, are unarmed.

## STONEFISH

Stonefishes are largely shallow-water dwellers, commonly found in tidepools and shoal reef areas. *Synanceja* has a habit of lying motionless in coral crevices, under rocks, in holes, or buried in sand or mud. They appear to be fearless and completely disinterested in the careless intruder.

### Venom Apparatus of Scorpionfishes

The venom organs of scorpionfishes vary markedly from one group to the next. A comparison of some of the more important differences appears in the comparative drawing (Figure 15) and chart below:

| Structure | Zebrafish (*Pterois*) | Scorpionfish (*Scorpaena*) | Stonefish (*Synanceja*) |
|---|---|---|---|
| Fin spines | Elongated, slender | Moderately long, heavy | Short, stout |
| Integumentary sheath | Thin | Moderately thick | Very thick |
| Venom glands | Small-sized, well-developed | Moderate-sized, very well developed | Very large, highly developed |
| Venom duct | Not evident | Not evident | Well developed |

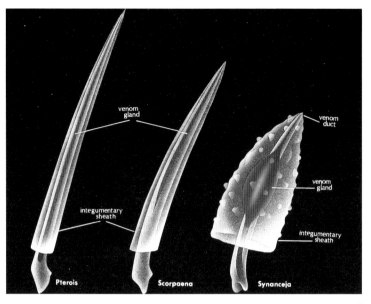

Figure 15. A comparison of the structure of the three basic types of venom organs found in scorpionfishes, namely, *Pterois, Scorpaena,* and *Synanceja.*                    (R. Kreuzinger)

### ZEBRAFISH TYPE

The zebrafish, or *Pterois*, type has a venom apparatus consisting of 13 dorsal spines, 3 anal spines, 2 pelvic spines, and their associated venom glands. The spines are for the most part long, straight, slender, and camouflaged in delicate, lacy-appearing fins. Located on the front side of each spine are the glandular grooves, open on either side, which appear as deep channels extending the entire length of the shaft. Situated within these grooves are the venom glands. The glands are enveloped in a thin covering of skin, the integumentary sheath.

### SCORPIONFISH TYPE

The scorpionfish, or *Scorpaena*, type have a variable number (frequently 13) of dorsal spines, as well as 3 anal, and 2 pelvic spines, and their associated venom glands. The spines are shorter and heavier than those found in *Pterois*. The glandular grooves are restricted to about the distal two-thirds of the spine. The venom glands lie along the glandular grooves, but are limited to about the distal half of the spine. The enveloping integumentary sheath is moderately thick.

## STONEFISH TYPE

The stonefish, or *Synanceja*, type usually have 13 dorsal spines, 3 anal spines, 2 pelvic spines, and their associated venom glands. The venom organs of this fish differ from the others by the short, heavy spines and greatly enlarged venom glands, which are covered by a very thick layer of warty skin.

During the act of stinging, the spines penetrate the flesh of the victim and in so doing the integumentary sheaths are compressed toward the base of each spine. Pressure is exerted on the integumentary sheaths and thus on the venom glands that are attached to the sides of the spines. The venom glands are covered with a dense, collagenous connective tissue; consequently, pressure exerted on the venom gland forces the venom to be expelled through the venom ducts that open at the distal tip of the spine. It is necessary for a spine to penetrate the flesh to a depth of 0.6 to 1.0 centimeters before sufficient pressure is exerted on the venom glands to expel the venom. The dorsal spines of *Synanceja* are sharp, stout, and can readily pass through a rubber sneaker or sandal. Stings from these fish may be extremely painful, and fatalities have been reported.

This fish is particularly dangerous because of its camouflaged appearance, frequently resembling a large clump of mud or debris. The spines of *Synanceja* are difficult to detect because they are almost completely hidden (Figure 16).

### Scorpionfishes Dangerous to Humans

#### ZEBRAFISH

SHORT-FINNED ZEBRAFISH, *Brachirus zebra* (Quoy and Gaimard) (203). This species inhabits the Indo-Pacific region, from Polynesia to East Africa. Length 12 centimeters (4.7 inches).

LIONFISH, *Pterois antennata* (Bloch) (204). This species also inhabits the Indo-Pacific. Length 30 centimeters (12 inches).

TURKEYFISH, ZEBRAFISH, or LIONFISH, *Pterois volitans* (Linnaeus) (205), a species closely related to *P. antennata*, is one of the most attractive and spec-tacular of the reef fishes, but its spines are laced with poison. Look, but don't touch! It also inhabits the Indo-Pacific region.

LIONFISH, *Pterois radiata* (206, 207). This fish is truly one of the most magnificent of all the zebra- or lionfish.

#### SCORPIONFISH

This group is sometimes referred to as the true scorpionfishes. There are a large number of species in this complex, which inhabits primarily marine tropical and warm temperate waters of the world. It is a difficult group to identify. The following have been selected because of their noxious reputations and intimidating appearance. All of the members included in this section have well-developed venom organs.

BULLROUT or SULKY, *Apistus carinatus* (Bloch and Schneider) (208). This species inhabits the coast of India, Indonesia, the Philippine Islands, China, Japan, and Australia. Length 16 centimeters (6.2 inches).

WASPFISH or FORTESQUE, *Centropogon australis* (White) (209). This fish inhabits New South Wales and Queensland, Australia. Length 15 centimeters (6 inches).

BULLROUT, *Notesthes robusta* (Günther) (210). Inhabits New South Wales and Queensland, Australia. Length 25 centimeters (9.7 inches).

CALIFORNIA SCORPIONFISH, *Scorpaena guttata* Girard (211). Ranges from central California south into the Gulf of California.

SCORPIONFISH, *Scorpaena plumieri* Bloch (212). Inhabits the Atlantic coast from Massachusetts to the West Indies and Brazil.

SCORPIONFISH, *Scorpaena mystes* Jordan and Starks (213). Length 30 centimeters (12 inches). It ranges from Mexico to Peru.

SCORPIONFISH, RASCASSE, or SEA PIG, *Scorpaena porcus* (Linnaeus) (214). Inhabits the Atlantic coast of Europe from the English Channel to the Canary Islands, Morocco, and the Mediterranean and Black seas. Length 30 centimeters (12 inches).

Figure 16. Anterior view of the first dorsal sting of the stonefish *Synanceja*. The thick, warty integumentary sheath has been peeled back to show the large venom glands situated on either side of the spine shaft. Length of spine 36 millimeters (1.4 inches) (R. Kreuzinger)

DEVIL SCORPIONFISH or FALSE STONE-FISH, *Scorpaenopsis diabolus* (Cuvier) (215a, b), is sometimes confused with the true stonefishes (*Synanceja*) because of their close resemblance.

Many of the rockfish of the genus *Sebastes* found along the coastal areas of North America are now known to possess venom organs similar to those of *Pterois, Scorpaena,* and *Synanceja,* but are somewhat reduced in size. Nevertheless, they can inflict painful stings and should be handled with care. The following are two such attractive examples:

CHINA ROCKFISH, *Sebastes nebulosus* Ayres (216). Ranges along the Pacific coast from Alaska south to Point Conception, California. Length 30 centimeters (12 inches).

COPPER ROCKFISH, *Sebastes caurinus* Richardson (217). This species may be found along the Pacific coast from Puget Sound to California. Length 30 centimeters (12 inches).

STONEFISH

DEVIL SCORPIONFISH, *Inimicus barbatus* (DeVis) (218). This fish is also called the "bearded ghoul." Recent studies have shown that the venom apparatus closely resembles that of the stonefishes. It is found along the coast of Queensland, Australia. Length 20 centimeters (8 inches).

JAPANESE DEVIL SCORPIONFISH, *Inimicus japonicus* (Cuvier and Valenciennes) (219). The devil scorpionfishes present a variety of color combinations within a single species. The Japanese species is a classical example of camouflage coloration. This camouflage makes these fish extremely difficult to detect when they are in their natural habitat. *I. japonicus* can inflict a very painful wound with its venomous spines. Length 20 centimeters (8 inches).

FILAMENTOUS DEVIL SCORPIONFISH, *Inimicus filamentosus* (Cuvier and Valenciennes) (220a, b), of the Indo-Pacific region is a species closely related to *I. japonicus.*

STONEFISH, *Choridactylus multibarbis* Richardson (221). Found along the coastal areas of India, China, the Philippines Islands, and Polynesia. Length 10 centimeters (4 inches).

HIME-OKOZE, *Minous monodactylus* (Bloch and Schneider) (222). Inhabits the Indo-Pacific, and coasts of China, Japan. Length 15 centimeters (6 inches).

DEADLY or PRICKLY STONEFISH, *Synanceja horrida* (Linnaeus) (223, 224a, b). Inhabits coastal areas of India, the East Indies, China, the Philippine Islands, and Australia. This stonefish is an extremely dangerous species. Length 60 centimeters (24 inches).

WARTY DEADLY STONEFISH, *Synanceja verrucosa* Bloch and Schneider (225, 226, 227). This stonefish resembles *S. horrida,* but lacks the deep impression just back of the eyes. It is also smaller in size. Length 30 centimeters (12 inches). Inhabits the Indo-Pacific region, Indian Ocean, and Red Sea. Members of the genus *Synanceja* probably possess the most highly developed venom apparatus of any of the fishes.

Symptoms produced by the sting of the various species of scorpionfishes are essentially the same, varying in degree, rather than in quality. The pain is usually described as immediate, intense, sharp, shooting, or throbbing, and radiates from the affected part. The area around the wound becomes ischemic, and then cyanotic. The pain produced by most scorpionfishes generally continues for only a few hours, but wounds produced by *Synanceja* may be extremely painful and pain may continue for a number of days. Pain caused by *Synanceja* is sometimes so severe as to cause the victim to thrash about wildly, scream, and finally lose consciousness. The area in the immediate vicinity of the wound gradually becomes cyanotic, surrounded by a zone of redness, swelling, and heat (228). Subsequent sloughing of the tissues around the site may occur. In the case of *Synanceja* stings, the wound becomes numb, and the skin, some distance from the site of injury, becomes painful to touch. In some instances, complete paralysis of the limb may ensue. Swelling of the entire affected member may take place, frequently to such an extent that movement of the part is impaired. Other symptoms that may be present are cardiac failure, delirium, convulsions, various nervous disturbances, nausea, vomiting, lymphangitis, or swelling of the lymph nodes, joint aches, fever, respiratory distress, convulsions, and death. Complete recovery from a severe *Synanceja* sting may require many months and may have an adverse effect on the general health of the victim.

A special antivenin has been developed by the Commonwealth Serum Laboratories in Melbourne, Australia, for the treatment of stonefish stings.

## TOADFISHES

The toadfishes are all members of the family Batrachoididae. All are small bottom fishes that inhabit the warmer waters of the coasts of America, Europe, Africa, and India. With broad, depressed heads and large mouths, toadfishes are somewhat repulsive in appearance. Most of them are marine, but some are estuarine, or entirely freshwater, ascending rivers for great distances. They hide in crevices, burrows, under rocks, debris, among seaweed, or lie almost completely buried under a few centimeters of sand or mud. Toadfishes tend to migrate to deeper water during the winter months, where they remain in a torpid state. They are experts at camouflage. Their ability to change to lighter or darker shades of color at will and their mottled pattern make these fishes difficult to see.

### Venom Apparatus of Toadfishes

The venom apparatus of toadfishes consists of two dorsal fin spines, two gill cover spines, and their associated venom glands. The dorsal spines are slender and hollow, slightly curved, and terminate in sharp, needlelike points. At the base and tip of each spine is an opening through which the venom passes. The base of each dorsal spine is surrounded by a glandular mass from which the venom is produced. Each gland empties into the base of its respective spine (Figure 17a–d). The

operculum, or gill cover, is also highly specialized as a defensive organ for the introduction of venom. The horizontal limb of the operculum is a slender hollow bone, which curves slightly and terminates in a sharp tip. Openings are present at each end of the spine for the passage of venom. With the exception of the outer tip, the entire gill spine is encased within a glistening, whitish, pear-shaped mass. The broad, rounded portion of this mass is situated at the base of the spine, and it tapers rapidly as the tip of the spine is approached. This mass is the venom gland. The gland empties into the base of the hollow gill spine that serves as a duct.

### Toadfishes Dangerous to Humans

COMB TOADFISH, *Batrachoides cirrhosus* (Klunzinger) (229). Inhabits the Red Sea. Length 25 centimeters (10 inches).

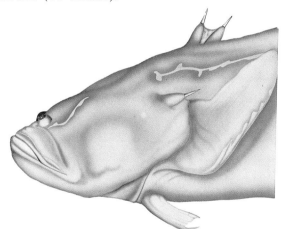

a. Head of toadfish showing location of dorsal and opercular stings;

b. Details of the left opercular sting. Note venom gland surrounding the opercular sting. The integumentary sheath has been removed to show the venom glands.

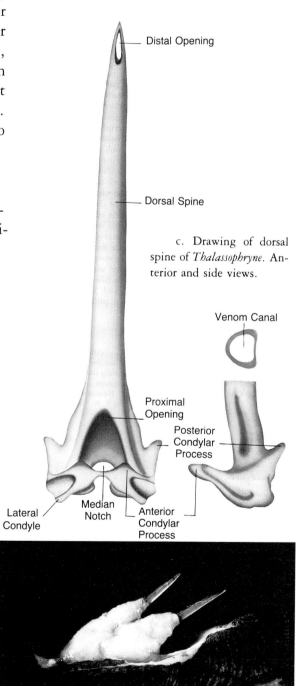

Figure 17a, b, c, d. The venom apparatus of the toadfish *Thalassophryne* consists of two opercular stings as depicted in these drawings:

c. Drawing of dorsal spine of *Thalassophryne*. Anterior and side views.

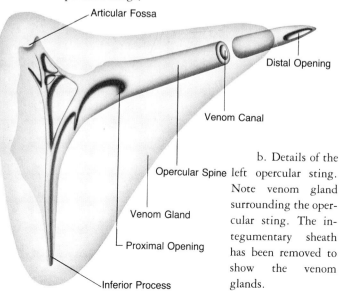

d. Photograph of dorsal stings of *Thalassophryne*. The integumentary sheath has been removed to expose the large venom glands at the base of the dorsal spines.

(R. Kreuzinger)

Figure 18. Tail of surgeonfish, *Acanthurus glaucopareius,* showing the caudal spine in an extended position and ready to inflict a cut. (D. Ollis)

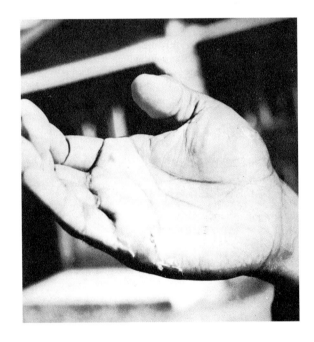

Figure 19. Surgeonfish wound inflicted by *Acanthurus olivaceus.* The victim was attempting to remove the surgeonfish from the shaft of a spear when he was struck by one of the caudal spines. Bleeding was immediate and profuse. Severe swelling began about one hour later and involved most of his hand. Swelling and drainage of the wound continued for about ten days; it finally healed in about three weeks. (G. Mote)

TOADFISH, *Batrachoides didactylus* (Bloch) (230). Inhabits the Mediterranean Sea and nearby Atlantic coasts. Length 19 centimeters (7.5 inches).

GRUNTING TOADFISH, or MUNDA, *Batrachoides grunniens* (Linnaeus) (231). Inhabits the coasts of Ceylon, India, Burma, and Malaysia. Length 20 centimeters (8 inches).

TOADFISH, *Batrachoides didactylus* (Bloch) (231). Inhabits the Mediterranean Sea and nearby Atlantic coasts. Length 19 centimeters (7.5 inches).

TOADFISH, OYSTERFISH, *Opsanus tau* (Linnaeus) (232). Found along the Atlantic coast of the United States, from Massachusetts to the West Indies. Length 30 centimeters (11.7 inches).

TOADFISH, or SAPO, *Thalassophryne maculosa* Günther (233). Found in the West Indies. Length 14 centimeters (5.5 inches).

TOADFISH, BAGRE SAPO, or SAPO, *Thalassophryne reticulata* Günther (234). Inhabits the Pacific coast of Central America. Length 25 centimeters (10 inches).

In addition to the foregoing, there are several other closely-related species inhabiting certain coastal areas of Central and South America.

The pain from toadfish wounds develops rapidly, is radiating and intense. Some victims have described the pain as being similar to that of a scorpion sting. The pain is soon followed by swelling, redness, and heat. No fatalities have been recorded in the literature. Little is known about the effects of toadfish venom.

## SURGEONFISHES

The family of surgeonfishes, or tangs, known as the Acanthuridae, derive their name from the presence of a compressed spine that is on either side of the tail. The spine resembles a surgeon's scalpel or lancet, which can be erected at right angles to the body of the fish, thus forming a formidable cutting weapon (Figure 18). When the spines are extended and the fish becomes aggravated, it swims rapidly about, lashes out with its tail, and can readily inflict a deep, painful wound

(Figure 19). These wounds are of the laceration type. On one occasion at Canton Island, Central Pacific, several fishermen corralled a school of large surgeonfish in a net. The fish became agitated and lashed out, cutting large gashes in the groin of one of the fishermen. A second fisherman then walked over and urinated into the wound. The victim claimed it helped relieve the pain and aided healing. The technique of urinating into wounds has since been recommended to the medical profession, but this therapeutic modality has never gained much acceptance.

The surgeonfishes are divided into two major groupings on the basis of their caudal armament: those that have folding spines on the caudal peduncle (*Acanthurus, Ctenochaetus, Zebrasoma, Paracanthurus*) and those that have one to six fixed spines or plates on each side of the peduncle (*Naso, Prionurus*). Some of these peduncular spines are reputed to be venomous, but documentation on this matter is lacking.

Surgeonfishes are circumtropical in distribution, but are best represented in the Indo-Pacific. Relatively few species are found in the tropical Atlantic and West Indies, and none inhabit the Mediterranean. A few representative species are presented here:

WHITE-FACE SURGEONFISH, *Acanthurus japonicus* Schmidt (235). Inhabits the tropical Indo-Pacific. Length 25 centimeters (10 inches).

ACHILLES SURGEONFISH, *Acanthurus achilles* Shaw (236). Inhabits the central Pacific. Length 19 centimeters (7.5 inches).

SURGEONFISH, *Acanthurus dussumieri* Cuvier (237). Inhabits the tropical Indo-Pacific. Length 30 centimeters (12 inches).

UNICORNFISH, *Naso lituratus* Bloch and Schneider (238). Inhabits the Indo-Pacific region. Length 38 centimeters (15 inches).

## FLYING GURNARDS

The flying gurnards, members of the family Dactylopteridae, are a small family of marine fishes with a distinctive arrangement of their head bones. They are characterized by large bony heads, greatly enlarged pectoral fins, and a single isolated dorsal spine attached to the nape of the neck. The head is blunt, and the top and sides are encased in a bony shield, which is deeply concave between the eyes. A long-keeled spine extends backward from the bony shield on the nape to below the midbase of the first dorsal fin. There is also a long spine at the angle of the preopercle, bearing a serrate keel. Whether these spines comprise a true venom apparatus has not been determined, but they may inflict a wound if the fish is improperly handled. Otherwise, this magnificent fish is generally thought to be quite harmless.

Gurnards may be observed "walking" on the bottom in search of food. When disturbed, they may extend their large pectoral fins laterally and are reputed to leap free of the surface and glide short distances on their expanded pectorals. However, it is doubtful that they are successful fliers because of their heavy armament and bottom-dwelling habits. At times, this fish emits a harsh noise, and when alarmed it can display a spectacular flash of color. The species represented here is:

FLYING GURNARD, *Dactylopterus volitans* (Linnaeus) **(239)**. Inhabits the Atlantic Ocean. Length 40 centimeters (16 inches).

Sea robins, members of the family Triglidae, resemble the flying gurnards, with which they are said to be distantly related. Sea robins also have bony heads armed with spines, and large pectoral fins. However, there are a number of features that separate these two families. It is doubtful that sea robins are venomous, despite their imposing head spines.

SEA ROBIN, *Trigla lyra* Linnaeus **(240)**. Inhabits the eastern Atlantic Ocean and the Mediterranean Sea. Length 60 centimeters (23.5 inches).

# DRAGONETS

Dragonets are small, scaleless fishes with flat heads, bearing a preopercle that is armed with a strong spine. Dragonets are members of the family Callionymidae. These fishes are brightly variegated in color and have high and often filamentous dorsal fins. Some species are found in deep water, whereas others are shore fishes inhabiting shallow bays and reefs. Dragonets are considered to be capable of inflicting serious wounds and should be handled with care. The spines of at least one species are said to be venomous:

DRAGONET, or LYRE FISH, *Callionymus lyra* Linnaeus **(241)**. Distributed along the Atlantic coast of Europe and the Mediterranean Sea. Length 10 centimeters (4 inches).

LYRE FISH, *Callionymus festivus* Pallas **(242)**. Closely related to *C. lyra*, it is found in the same region.

# RABBITFISHES

Rabbitfishes, which belong to the family Siganidae, are a group of spiny-rayed fishes closely resembling the surgeonfishes. They are termed rabbitfishes because of their rounded, blunt snouts and rabbit-like appearance of the jaws. They differ from all other fishes in that the first and last ray of the pelvic fins are spinous. Usually valued as food, rabbitfishes are of moderate size and abound around rocks and reefs from the Red Sea to Polynesia. They feed on algae and are sometimes poisonous to eat.

### Venom Apparatus of Rabbitfishes

The venom apparatus of *Siganus* consists of 13 dorsal, 4 pelvic, and 7 anal spines and their associated venom glands. A groove extends along both sides of the midline of the spine for almost its entire length. These grooves are generally deep and contain the venom glands, which are located in the outer one-third of the spine, near the tip (Figure 20a, b).

### Rabbitfishes Dangerous to Humans

RABBITFISH, *Siganus doliatus* (Cuvier) **(243)**. Inhabits the tropical Indo-Pacific. Length 25 centimeters (10 inches).

BROWN RABBITFISH, *Siganus fuscescens* (Houttuyn) **(244)**. Found throughout the Indo-Pacific region. Length 25 centimeters (9.7 inches).

Figure 20a, b. Venom apparatus of the rabbitfish *Siganus*.

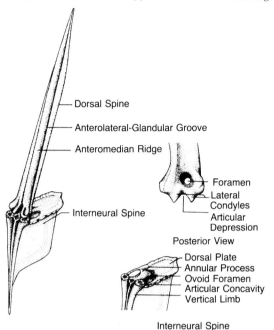

Dorsal Spine
Anterolateral-Glandular Groove
Anteromedian Ridge
Foramen
Lateral Condyles
Articular Depression
Interneural Spine
Posterior View
Dorsal Plate
Annular Process
Ovoid Foramen
Articular Concavity
Vertical Limb
Interneural Spine

a. Representative dorsal spine of *Siganus*. The venom glands are located in the glandular grooves.

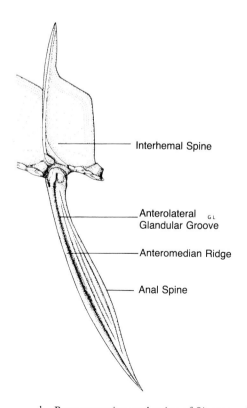

Interhemal Spine
Anterolateral GL Glandular Groove
Anteromedian Ridge
Anal Spine

b. Representative anal spine of *Siganus*, which also contains venom glands. (P. Mote)

STRIPED RABBITFISH, *Siganus lineatus* (Valenciennes) (245). Inhabits the Philippines, Santa Cruz Islands, New Guinea, Solomon Islands, Australia, Okinawa, and the Ryukyu Islands. Length 30 centimeters (11.7 inches).

PRETTY RABBITFISH, *Siganus puellus* (Schlegel) (246). Inhabits the East Indies, the Philippines, Palau, and the Gilbert, Marshall, and Solomon islands. Length 27 centimeters (10.5 inches).

CUNNING RABBITFISH, *Lo (Siganus) vulpinus* (Schlegel and Muller) (247). Inhabits the Indo-Pacific region. Length 20 centimeters (8 inches).

The symptoms produced as a result of envenomations by rabbitfishes are similar to those inflicted by scorpionfishes.

## SCATS

The scats, or spadefishes, are a small family of perch-like Indo-Pacific fishes. Members of the family Scatophagidae consist of about three species, all less than 35 centimeters (13.7 inches) in length. They are primarily marine, but commonly invade brackish and freshwater streams. Little appears to be known about their habits, but they inhabit inshore coastal areas, particularly around sewer outlets of coastal cities, where they are frequently observed ingesting excrement and refuse—hence the name of the genus *Scatophagus* (excrement eaters). Because of the ability of the young to adapt readily to freshwater, scats have become a popular aquarium fish. The young feed upon algae. Scats tend to be soft-bodied, but are nevertheless valued as food by some people. They are difficult to breed in captivity and are said to be oviparous.

### Venom Apparatus of Scats

The venom apparatus of scats is associated with the dorsal, anal, and ventral spines. All of the spines are equipped with venom glands, but these are largely confined to juveniles and gradually disappear with age. The venom glands appear as a slender, elongate, tapered

strand of gray or pinkish tissue lying within the anterolateral glandular grooves on either side of the spine.

### Scats Dangerous to Humans

SPOTTED SCAT, *Scatophagus argus* (Linnaeus) (248). Inhabits the Indo-Pacific region. Length 15 centimeters (6 inches).

MANY-BANDED SCAT, *Selenotoca multifasciata* (Richardson) (249). Inhabits warm-water coasts of Australia and New Guinea. Length 40 centimeters (16 inches).

Scatophagid stings cause painful wounds. The pain has been described as an intense shooting or throbbing sensation.

## STARGAZERS

Stargazers are bottom-dwelling fishes, members of the family Uranoscopidae, having a cuboid head, an almost vertical mouth with fringed lips, and eyes on the upper surface of the head. Uranoscopids spend a large part of their time buried in the mud or sand with only their eyes and a portion of the mouth protruding.

### Venom Apparatus of Stargazers

The venom apparatus of *Uranoscopus* is said to consist of two shoulder spines, one on each side, which protrude through a sheath of skin (Figure 21). Venom glands are attached to these spines. The spine is said to have a double groove through which the venom flows.

### Stargazers Dangerous to Humans

STARGAZER or MISHMIMAO KOZE, *Uranoscopus japonicus* Houttuyn (250). Inhabits southern Japan, southern Korea, China, the Philippine Islands, and Singapore. Length 25 centimeters (9.7 inches).

STARGAZER, *Uranoscopus scaber* (Linnaeus) (251). Inhabits the eastern Atlantic and Mediterranean Sea. Length 15 centimeters (6 inches).

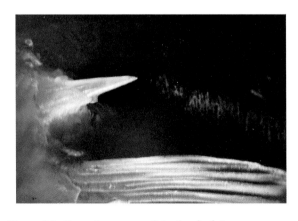

Figure 21. Posterior aspect of the head of the stargazer, *Uranoscopus scaber*, showing the left cleithral spine. The integumentary sheath has been removed to expose the spine.    (R. Kreuzinger)

STARGAZER, *Uranoscopus oligolepis* Bleeker (252). Inhabits the eastern Atlantic, Mediterranean, and Red Sea.

Very little is known concerning the clinical effects of stargazer stings, but *U. scaber* stings are said to be potentially lethal; however, this has not been determined.

## LEATHERBACKS (Leatherjackets)

The leatherback, or lae, is a member of the family Carangidae, which includes the jacks, scads, and pompanos. A particular characteristic of this family of fishes is the presence of two separate spines in front of the anal fins. Several other species of carangids are believed to possess venomous spines, but the venom apparatus has been described in only the single species *Scomberoides (Sanctipetri) lysan* (Forskål). The leatherback is found throughout the tropical Indo-Pacific region. Carangids are a group of fast-swimming oceanic fishes generally encountered in the vicinity of coral reefs and islands.

### Venom Apparatus of Leatherbacks

The venom apparatus consists of seven dorsal spines and two anal spines, their associated musculature, venom glands, and enveloping integumentary sheaths (Figure 22a, b).

### Leatherbacks Dangerous to Humans

LEATHERJACKET, or RUNNER, *Oligoplites saurus* (Bloch and Schneider) (253). Inhabits the Indo-Pacific region. Length 26 centimeters (10.2 inches).

LEATHERBACK, *Scomberoides (Sanctipetri) lysan* (Forskål) (254). Inhabits the Indo-Pacific region. Length 65 centimeters (25.5 inches).

Stings from leatherback spines result in intense pain that may last for several hours. The anal spines are believed to inflict the most serious stings. The wounds are of the puncture-wound variety and may be accompanied by redness and swelling.

## *VENOMOUS SNAKES*

### SEA SNAKES

Sea snakes are members of the family Hydrophiidae. Sea snakes are aquatic inhabitants of the tropical Pacific and Indian oceans, ranging from the Samoan Islands westward to the east coast of Africa, Japan to the Persian Gulf, along the coasts of Asia, and through

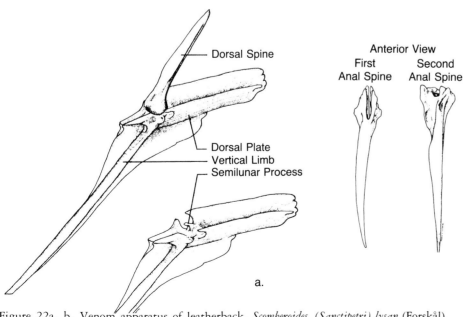

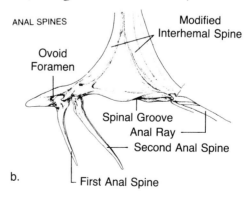

a. The dorsal spines are equipped with venom glands. This is a drawing of the fourth dorsal spine and its supporting interneural spine. This spine, which is the longest of the dorsal spines, is only 8 millimeters (.2 inches) in length.

b. Anal spines of *S. lysan* are also venomous and slightly longer than the dorsal spines. Length of spine in drawing is 12 millimeters (.36 inches). (S. K. Galloway)

Figure 22a, b. Venom apparatus of leatherback, *Scomberoides (Sanctipetri) lysan* (Forskål).

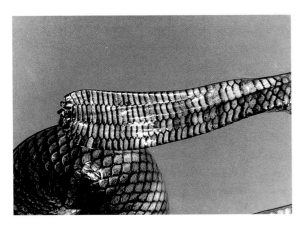

Figure 23. Note the flat, paddle-like tail, which is characteristic of sea snakes. The flattened tail is used to propel the sea snake through the water, providing considerable thrust. This specimen is *Laticauda semifasciata* (Reinwards), which attains a length of 1.3 meters (52 inches) and inhabits the tropical Indo-Pacific region.

(Courtesy R. E. Kuntz)

Indo-Australian seas to Australia. One species, *Pelamis platurus*, has an enormous geographical range, extending from the west coast of Latin America across the Pacific and Indian oceans to the east coast of Africa, and from the Sea of Japan to Tasmania. With the exception of a single freshwater species, *Hydrophis semperi*, which lives in freshwater Lake Taal, Luzon, Philippine Islands, all are marine. *Laticauda crockeri* is limited to the brackish water of Lake Tungano, Rennel Island, Solomon Islands.

Sea snakes generally prefer sheltered coastal waters and are particularly fond of river mouths. Around shore, sea snakes may inhabit rock crevices, tree roots, coral boulders, or pilings. In regions where sea snakes are plentiful, more than a hundred snakes may be taken by fishermen in a single net haul.

Most sea snake envenomations are the result of handling net loads of fish in which sea snakes become entangled. In the process of removing the snakes from the nets, fishermen are frequently bitten. Sea snakes are equipped with a well-developed venom apparatus; however, all bites do not necessarily result in envenomation. Consequently, the victim is observed for a period of several hours. If any clinical evidence of poisoning develops, the patient is immediately given sea snake antivenom. (*See* p. 250, "Emergency Treatment.")

A factor governing the distribution of most sea snakes seems to be the depth of water in which they feed. The depth must be shallow enough for them to be able to go to the bottom to feed and to rise to the surface for air. However, sea snakes have been observed 160 to 240 kilometers (100 to 150 miles) from land. A large group of Stoke's sea snakes (*Astrotia stokesi*) was once observed migrating between the Malay Peninsula and Sumatra. The mass of snakes was estimated to be about 3 meters (10 feet) wide and at least 96 kilometers (60 miles) long, consisting of several million individuals. Sea snakes are said to be the most abundant of all the reptiles.

With their compressed, paddle-shaped tails, sea snakes are well adapted for locomotion in the marine environment (Figure 23). Swimming is accomplished by lateral undulatory movements of the body. Sea snakes are able to float, lying motionless for long periods of time. They are also able to move backward or forward with amazing rapidity, but when placed on land they are very awkward and move about with difficulty.

The bodies of sea snakes are more or less compressed posteriorly, with a flat, paddle-shaped tail. They are covered with scales and have no limbs, ear openings, sternum, or urinary bladder. Their eyes are immobile, covered by transparent scales, and without lids. The tongue is slender, forked, and can protrude from the mouth.

Sea snakes are able to remain submerged for hours, but are unable to utilize oxygen from the water as fish do. They are equipped with an extended right lung, but the left lung is either vestigial or absent. Sea snakes capture food underwater, usually swallowing the fish head first. They feed on or near the bottom, around rocks, holes, or crevices, where they capture eels and other small fishes, which are promptly killed with a vigorous bite of their venomous jaws.

The disposition of sea snakes is a subject of controversy, but of practical importance to those coming in contact with them. After reviewing the experiences of numerous writers and divers, one can only conclude that the docility of a sea snake varies with the species, the season of the year, and the manner in which the snake is approached. Generally speaking, sea snakes tend to be docile, but under some circumstances may be quite aggressive. One should not become overconfident and should always be aware that a set of fully functional fangs and an extremely virulent venom (more toxic than king cobra venom) accompany an apparently gentle nature. In addition to envenomations while handling nets, bites may be contracted while sorting fish, wading, swimming, or accidentally stepping on them. Most species of sea snakes are .9 to 1.2 meters (3 to 4 feet) in length but may attain 2.7 meters (9 feet) or more.

## Venom Apparatus of Sea Snakes

Sea snakes inflict their wounds with the use of

fangs, which are comparatively small in size, but are of the cobra type (Figure 24). Compared with other venomous snakes, sea snake dentition is relatively feeble, but nevertheless specialized for venom conduction. The venom apparatus consists of the venom glands and fangs. The venom glands are situated behind and below the eye, one on either side, and in front of the tympanic bones. They are ovate and have an elongated venom duct that terminates at the base of the fangs (Figures 24, 25). Most sea snakes have two fangs on each side, but some have only one. The venom duct enters at the base of the fang through a relatively broad, triangular opening of the canal. Sea snake venom has neurotoxic, myotoxic, and hemotoxic properties. One drop (.03 milliliter) contains sufficient poison to kill three adult men. Some species can inject up to eight drops in a single bite.

### Sea Snakes Dangerous to Humans

There are about fifty species of sea snakes. The following species are reputed to be particularly dangerous to humans:

OLIVE-BROWN SEA SNAKE, *Aipysurus laevis* Lacépède (**255, 256**). This snake is large, heavy-bodied, and generally docile. It inhabits coastal tropical Australia and New Guinea. Length 1.8 meters (6 feet).

SEA SNAKE, *Enhydrina schistosa* (Daudin) (**257**). Inhabits the Persian Gulf to Southeastern Asia and the north coast of Australia. Length 1.2 meters (47.2 inches).

ORNATE SEA SNAKE, *Hydrophis ornatus* (Gray) (**258**). Inhabits the coast of northern Australia. Length 95 centimeters (37.5 inches).

SEA SNAKE, *Hydrophis cyanocinctus* (Daudin) (**259**). Inhabits the Bay of Bengal. Length 1 meter (39.3 inches).

HARDWICK'S SEA SNAKE, *Lapemis hardwicki* (Gray) (**260**). Ranges from southern Japan to the Merguri Archipelago and along the coast of northern Australia. Length 85 centimeters (33.5 inches).

SEA SNAKE, *Laticauda colubrina* (Schneider) (**261**

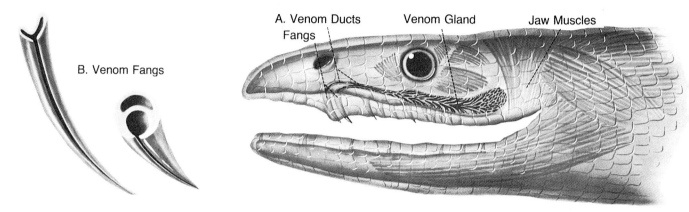

Figure 24. Venom apparatus of sea snake. The fangs are hollow with an open groove throughout most of their length.

(L. Barlow, after West)

**a, b, c**). This snake is generally docile, but extremely venomous. Widely distributed throughout the tropical Indo-Pacific region. Length 1.4 meters (55 inches).

YELLOW-BELLIED SEA SNAKE, *Pelamis platurus* (Linnaeus) (**262**). This species has the greatest range of any sea snake, extending from East Africa, throughout the Indo-Australian area, eastward to the Gulf of Panama. Length 85 centimeters (33.5 inches).

Symptoms caused by the bite of a sea snake characteristically develop rather slowly, taking from twenty minutes to several hours. It usually takes about one hour before definite symptoms begin. Aside from the initial prick, there is no pain or reaction at the site of the bite (**263**). The victim may even fail to connect the bite with the symptoms.

In some instances, the initial generalized symptom consists of a mild euphoria, whereas in others there is aching and anxiety. A sensation of thickening of the tongue and a generalized feeling of stiffness of the muscles usually develops. Common complaints during the early stages are aching, stiffness, or pain upon movement. There may be little indication of actual weakness at this time. The paralysis that soon follows is usually generalized, but of the ascending type, beginning with the legs; within an hour or two it involves the trunk, arms, and neck muscles. Lockjaw is one of the outstanding symptoms. Drooping of the eyelids is also an early and characteristic sign. The pulse becomes weak and

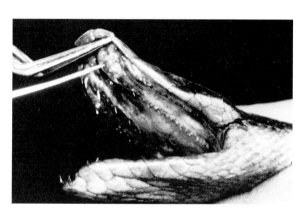

Figure 25. Side view of fangs of the yellow-bellied sea snake, *Pelamis platurus* (Linnaeus). Human fatalities from this sea snake have been reported.

(P. Saunders)

irregular, and the pupils dilate. Speaking and swallowing become increasingly difficult. Thirst, burning, or dryness of the throat may also be present. Nausea and vomiting are not uncommon. Muscle twitchings, twisting movements, and spasms have been noted. Ocular and facial paralysis may later develop. In severe intoxication, the symptoms become progressively more intense: the skin of the patient is cold, clammy, and cyanotic; convulsions begin and are frequent; respiratory distress becomes very pronounced; and finally the victim succumbs in an unconscious state. The overall fatality rate has been estimated to be about 28 percent.

## Freshwater Snakes

Although all snakes are capable of swimming, and at times may be found swimming across a pond or stream, there are only a few species that are commonly encountered in the freshwater aquatic environment. Two families of snakes are represented: Crotalidae, the pit vipers (two species), and Elapidae, which includes the water cobras (one species).

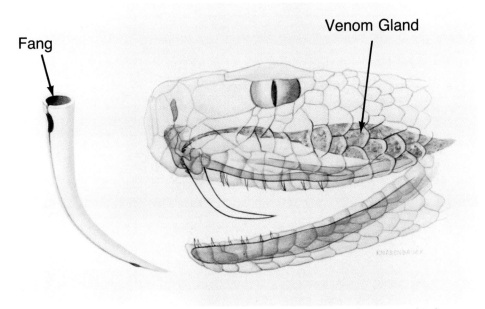

Figure 26. Venom apparatus of pit vipers (Crotalidae), which consists of long, movable fangs.
(R. H. Knabenbauer)

## Freshwater Aquatic Snakes Dangerous to Humans

CROTALIDAE

COTTONMOUTH WATER MOCCASIN, *Agkistrodon piscivorous* (Lacépède) **(264)**. This pit viper is related to the copperhead and commonly confused with nonvenomous semiaquatic snakes of the genus *Natrix*. The cottonmouth is often seen basking during the day on logs, stones, or branches near the water. It is also active at night in warm weather. This snake is aggressive at times and may not attempt to escape when confronted, throwing back its head with the white mouth wide open. (Most nonvenomous snakes usually swim or crawl away when alarmed.) Fatalities from this snake are rare, but the venom has strong proteolytic activity and can cause a nasty wound if treated improperly. Tissue destruction can be quite massive. The cottonmouth accounts for about 10 percent of all the snake bites in the United States. Symptoms consist of swelling, edema, and pain. Weakness, sweating, faintness, and nausea are common. A polyvalent crotalid antivenin is used in the treatment of cottonmouth bites. The species ranges from Virginia to Florida, south to central Texas, and is found only in wetlands. It attains a length of 1.83 meters (6 feet).

JARARACUSSU, *Bothrops jararacussu* Lacerda **(265)**. This is not a very common snake, but it is amphibious and may be encountered in the water. It is a dangerous species and produces large amounts (about 400 mg per bite) of a highly toxic venom. It is one of four species that cause most of the snake bite fatalities in Brazil. The symptoms are similar to other crotalid envenomations, but one of the earliest is blindness. Deaths are rare from this snake, but tissue damage may be extensive. It attains a length of 1.68 meters (5.5 feet).

A polyvalent antivenin made for *B. jararacussu* venom is produced in Argentina, Brazil, Colombia, France, Germany, and the United States.

The venom apparatus of Crotalids consists of long, movable fangs on each side of the head, which are sheathed in a whitish membrane to which is attached a venom gland and duct (Figure 26).

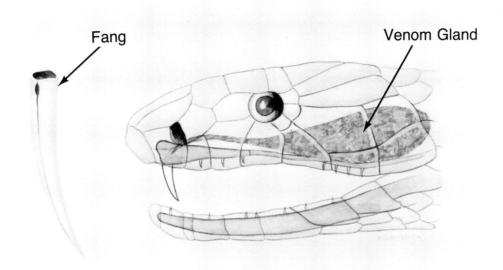

Fang

Venom Gland

Figure 27. Venom apparatus of cobras (Elapidae). The fangs are smaller than those of the vipers (Crotalidae), as in Figure 26. The fangs are located in the front of the jaw and are fixed.

(R. H. Knabenbauer)

ELAPIDAE

BANDED WATER COBRA, *Boulengerina annulata* (Buchholz and Peters) (266). This is a large fish-eating cobra that is always found in or near water. It is especially common along the shores of Lake Tanganyika. Water cobras raise the anterior part of the body and spread a narrow hood in a threatening manner similar to other cobras. These cobras are not aggressive and generally appear to offer little danger to persons who do not provoke them. Little is known about their bites, but it is said that their envenomations invoke more systemic than local effects, affecting the nervous system. Their fangs are smaller than those of the pit vipers, are located in the front of the jaws, and are fixed (Figure 27). No specific antivenin is available for this cobra. It inhabits central Africa and attains a length of 2.13 meters (7 feet).

## FRESHWATER VENOMOUS MAMMAL

### DUCK-BILLED PLATYPUS

The platypus was once considered by zoologists as a "fake," a creature that couldn't be. An early French naturalist claimed that the platypus was a bird, since it laid eggs. The fact that it had a bill and webbed feet like a duck further confirmed his diagnosis. On the other hand, this beast also has hair and suckles its young, which obviously makes it a mammal. But, since this zoological monstrosity has the spurs of a rooster and the venom of a snake, this gives one pause to think that all was not right in Paradise, or the evolutionary train got derailed for a certainty! The issue over the zoological identity of the platypus was debated in European scientific circles for over eighty years.

DUCK-BILLED PLATYPUS, *Ornithorhynchus anatinus* Shaw and Nodder (267), is a true mammal, a member of the order Monotremata, to which the spiny anteater also belongs. The platypus, however, is said to be more closely related to reptiles morphologically than most other mammals. Milk is produced by paired ducts on the abdomen of the females and is lapped up by the young. The usual presence of teats, as found in most mammals, is lacking in the platypus.

The duck-billed platypus was discovered in 1797 on the banks of a lake near the Hawkesbury River, New South Wales, Australia. The early settlers of Australia referred to it as a "water mole," a term that is now seldom used. It is also called the "duckbill" or "duckmole."

Figure 28. Duck-billed platypus, *Ornithorhynchus anatinus* Shaw and Nodder, is shown in its natural habitat feeding on one of its favorite foods, worms. The male platypus has venomous spurs on its hind legs. The spurs are capable of inflicting a painful sting.                    (J. E. Wapstra, Australian Museum)

The geographical range of the platypus is confined to the region of Australia east of 138° east longitude and to Tasmania.

The platypus seems to enjoy a wide range of water temperatures, from clear and icy rapids to alpine streams at a height of 1,800 meters (6,000 feet) on the Kosciusko Plateau, to the warm and turbid waters of the Queensland coastal plain, which includes lakes as well as small waterholes.

The male platypus may attain a length of about 61 centimeters (2 feet). The female is slightly smaller. The bill superficially resembles that of a duck, but instead of being hard and horny it is a soft leathery skin that corresponds to the nose and lips of other mammals. The bill is equipped with sensitive nerve endings that are a substitute for the sensory whiskers of most furred animals.

The platypus is well equipped for an aquatic existence with its beaver-like tail and the webbing of the forefeet. The webbed feet are useful in both swimming and burrowing. The hind feet are also webbed, but to a lesser extent. The bill-like muzzle is without teeth and is adapted for nuzzling in the mud in search for food, which consists of snails, shrimp, worms, and insects. The platypus can remain submerged for about a minute. Then the animal comes up to the surface for a similar period of time to chew up the catch. It generally feeds twice a day, early morning and late twilight.

Platypuses spend no more than a couple of hours each day in the water. They live in burrows, which they dig beneath the roots of large trees, with the entrances concealed by overhanging ledges. The females build special elaborate breeding burrows with a nesting chamber where her eggs are laid and hatched. Two eggs are laid, which are soft-shelled and dirty white in color. The incubation period is said to be about 14 days or less. The mother does not leave the nest between laying and hatching. During incubation the mother holds the eggs in the middle of her curled body. This close contact enables the young to feed by stimulating with their movements the flow of milk that exudes from the enlarged pores in the mother's breast. The milk is then sucked from the fur.

Attacks by platypuses on humans are rare. Only about 10 envenomations have been reported in the literature. The effects of platypus envenomations are generally mild. When the platypus was hunted for its fur, envenomations sometimes occurred, but since the symptoms were mild, people seldom paid much attention to the problem. Nowadays, people are seldom in contact with the animal since it is rigorously protected by law. When attacking, the platypus drives its hind legs together with considerable force and thereby embeds the spurs into the flesh of the victim. At times, the spurs become so deeply embedded that there is difficulty in separating the legs of the animal from the victim. All recorded attacks have been on the hands or wrists of the person.

The usual symptoms consist of extensive swelling and edema, which may extend up the arms to the shoulder. The swelling subsides within a few days. The pain is immediate and intense. Generalized symptoms of shock may be present. A few persons have reported numbness in the vicinity of the wound. There may be an absence of bleeding from the wound. Swelling of the lymph nodes may occur. Usually, no special treatment is required.

### Venom Apparatus of the Platypus

The venom apparatus of the platypus is confined to the male. It consists of a moveable horny spur on the inner side of each hind leg near the heel (Figure 29). Young females also have small spurs, but these disappear with maturity. The spur projects out for a distance of about 15 millimeters (.5 inch) and is tapered, conical, and slightly curved. The venomous spur is enclosed at the base in a fleshy sheath and normally lies against the leg, but can be erected into a rigid position more or less at right angles to the leg. The spur is attached to a bony plaque formed around its base, which articulates by a small synovial joint with the leg bone.

The venom gland, referred to as the crural, or poison, gland, is a whitish, roughly kidney-shaped body situated at the dorsal aspect of the thigh that is covered by cutaneous muscle. The size of the gland seems to vary with the season, but averages about 30 millimeters (1.2 inches) by 20 millimeters (.75 inch) in size. The venom gland is connected to the spur by a duct that extends under the flexor leg muscles and empties into a small reservoir through the center of the spur and finally empties at the tip.

Platypus venom is said to resemble a weak viperine venom, with an absence of specific neurotoxic properties, but it acts as an anticoagulant, having feeble hemolytic and cytolytic properties.

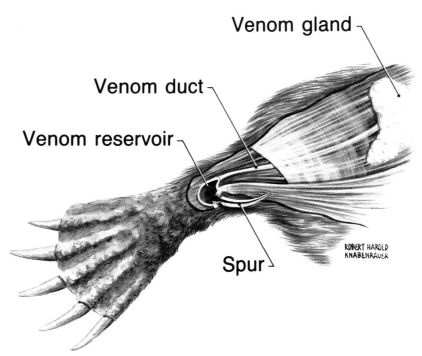

**Venom gland**

**Venom duct**

**Venom reservoir**

**Spur**

ROBERT HAROLD KNABENRAUER

Figure 29. Horny venomous spines are present on the inner side of each hind leg of the male platypus. Drawing shows the venom apparatus of the male platypus. (R. Kreuzinger)

**PLATE 166.** Spiny dogfish, *Squalus acanthias* Linnaeus. This small shark is equipped with a sharp spine on each of its dorsal fins. Contact with these spines can result in painful puncture wounds. Fortunately, the venom is mild, but the wound may become infected. *S. acanthias* inhabits northern regions of both the Pacific and Atlantic oceans. It attains a length of one meter (39 inches) or more.    (R. H. Knabenbauer)

167

168
169

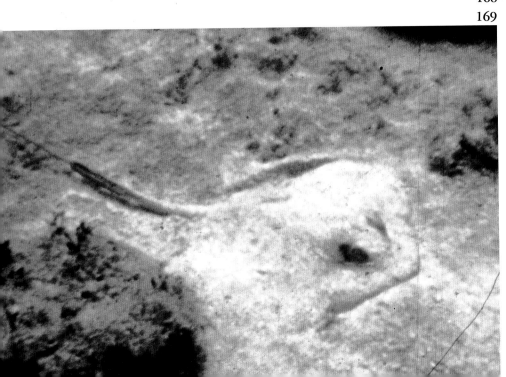

170

**PLATE 167.** Hornshark, *Heterodontus francisci*, (Girard). This is a distant relative of *S. acanthias*. Note the distinct white spine in front of each of the dorsal fins. The venom is believed to be quite mild. Taken in the Sea of Cortez, Baja California. Attains a length of 1.2 meters (4 feet). (Courtesy E. T. Rulison)

**PLATE 168.** Close-up view of *H. francisci*, focusing on one of the venomous dorsal spines. The spines are too blunt to be dangerous. (Courtesy E. T. Rulison)

**PLATE 169.** Stingrays seen hiding in the sand. These creatures can disappear rapidly into the sand by using their pectoral fins to scoop up large quantities of sand, which they throw over their backs. Taken from a motion picture film. (Courtesy P. Saunders)

**PLATE 170.** Australian giant stingray, *Dasyatis brevicaudata* (Hutton). This is the largest stingray in the world. Attains a length of 4.5 meters (15 feet) or more in length, a width of 2.2 meters (7 feet), and a weight of more than 325 kilograms (715 pounds). The sting may measure more than 37 centimeters (14.5 inches). This creature inhabits the Indo-Pacific region.
(M. Holmes)

**PLATE 171.** Valerie Taylor swimming alongside the Australian giant stingray, *Dasyatis brevicaudata*. The head of a small shovel-nose ray is seen in the foreground. Great Barrier Reef, Australia.
(R. and V. Taylor)

**PLATE 172.** Diamond stingray, *Dasyatis dipterurus* (Jordan and Gilbert). As stingrays go, this is a rather attractive species, named because of its diamond shape. Length 2 meters (6.5 feet). Its range extends from British Columbia south to Central America.
(M. Shirao)

**PLATE 173.** European stingray, *Dasyatis pastinaca* (Linnaeus). This is the famous European stingray of antiquity, known to Pliny and other writers of ancient Greece and Rome. The specimen pictured is rather small but is capable of delivering a very painful sting. Found in the northeastern Atlantic Ocean, Mediterranean Sea, and Indian Ocean. Length 2.5 meters (8 feet). Taken in an aquarium, Zoological Station of Naples. (P. Giacomelli)

**PLATE 174.** Southern stingray, *Dasyatis americana* Hildebrand and Schroeder. A diver approaching the stingray slowly and without commotion may be able to stroke the beast—and the ray seems to enjoy the process. San Salvador, Bahamas. (D. Woodward)

**PLATE 175.** A large specimen of the stingray *Dasyatis americana* Hildebrand and Schroeder is preparing to "take off" in a cloud of sand. Note the prominent sting on the tail. It ranges in the western Atlantic from New Jersey to southern Brazil. Length 2 meters (6.5 feet). Taken at Culebra Island, Puerto Rico.
(Courtesy R. Mandojana)

171

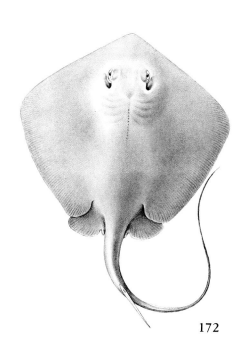

172

173
175

174

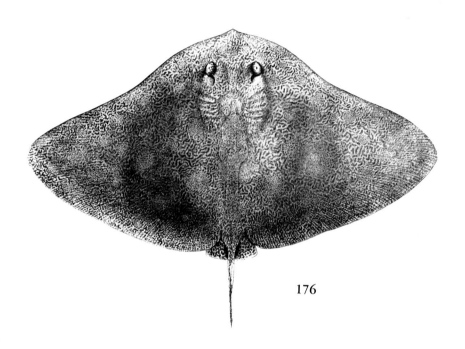

176

**PLATE 176.** Butterfly ray, *Gymnura marmorata* (Cooper). This is an interesting ray with very broad pectoral fins and a short tail. Although the sting is well developed, it is too small to be effective. Wing-span may reach 2.2 meters (7 feet). (S. Arita)

**PLATE 177.** Spotted eagle ray, *Aetobatis narinari* (Euphrasen). This is one of the most handsome of the stingrays. It ranges throughout tropical and warm temperate regions of the Atlantic, Pacific, and Indian oceans. The wingspan is about 2 meters (6.7 feet). (Courtesy R. Murphy, The Cousteau Society, Inc. )

**PLATE 178.** California bat ray, *Myliobatis californicus* (Gill). This ray ranges from Oregon south to Magdalena Bay, Baja, California. It is frequently seen resting in sandy areas in the midst of a kelp forest or swimming in a gliding motion near the bottom. Taken at San Diego, California. It attains a length of 1.2 meters (47 inches). (R. Church)

**PLATE 179.** *M. californicus* resting. Taken at Coronado Island, California. (C. Micklin)

177

178  179

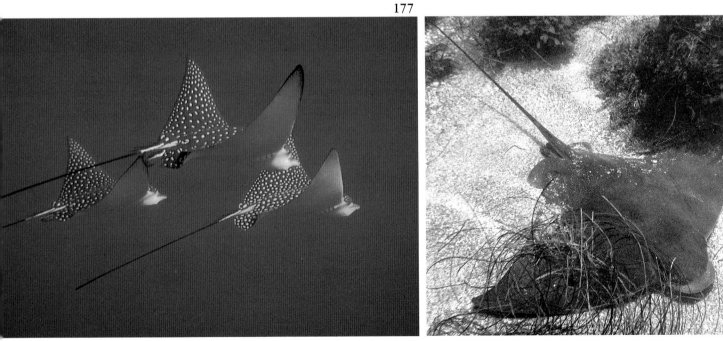
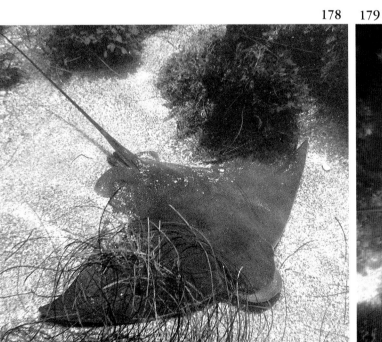
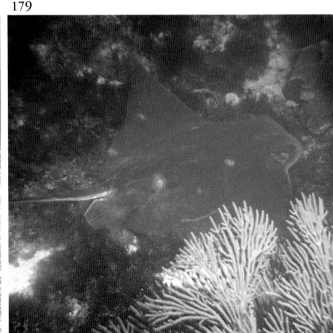

**PLATE 180.** Cow-nosed ray, *Rhinoptera bonasus* (Mitchill). These rays are frequently observed swimming in small schools like a squadron of graceful gliders, such as seen in this photograph. This is a swimming characteristic of the myliobatid rays. Ranging along the coastal western Atlantic, from New England to Brazil, it attains a width of about 2 meters (6.5 feet). (Courtesy J. B. Siebenaler, Gulfarium)

**PLATE 181.** Round stingray, *Urolophus halleri* Cooper. Taken in southern California. Length 50 centimeters (19.7 inches). (D. W. Gotshall)

**PLATE 182.** *U. halleri* shown in the process of striking a "plumber's friend"—taken from a film clip showing the accuracy of the ray in striking an object (or foot) placed on the back of the ray. This is a reflex action. The sting of this ray is attached to a powerful muscular tail that is used to drive the sting into the flesh of the victim. (Courtesy P. Saunders)

**PLATE 183.** Spotted round stingray, *Urolophus nebulosus* (Garman), is believed to be a color variant of *Urolophus halleri*. Taken in the Gulf of California. (D. W. Gotshall)

**PLATE 184.** Yellow stingray, *Urolophus jamaicensis* (Cuvier). This is a small ray, attaining a length of about 67 centimeters (2.2 feet). Found in the western tropical Atlantic, its range extends from Florida southward into the West Indies. Taken at San Salvador, Bahamas. (B. W. Halstead)

180

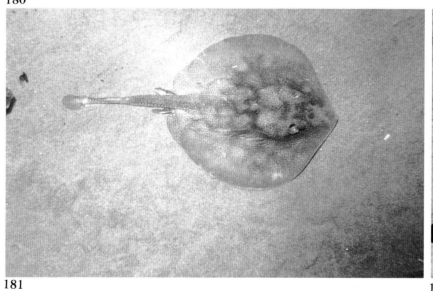

181

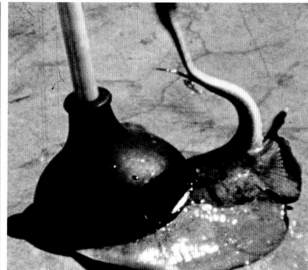

182

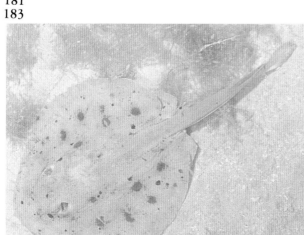

183

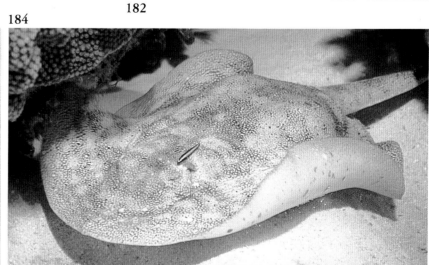

184

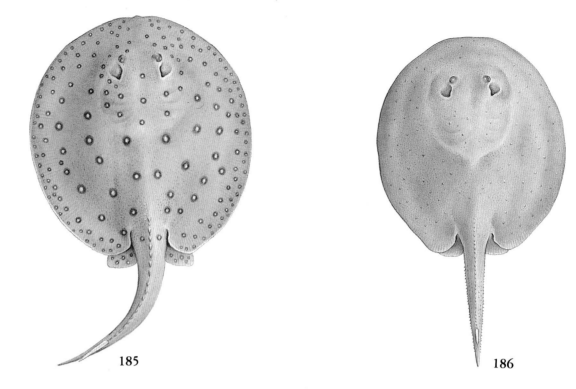

**PLATE 185.** South American freshwater stingray, *Potamotrygon motoro* (Müller and Henle). Freshwater stingrays can inflict extremely painful stings. This particular species has a reputation for having caused numerous envenomations. Found in the freshwater rivers of Paraguay and the Amazon River, south to Rio de Janeiro, Brazil. The width of the disc is 54 centimeters (21 inches). (M. Shirao, after M. Castex)

**PLATE 186.** Paucke's freshwater stingray, *Potamotrygon pauckei* Castex. This freshwater ray produces a very potent venom. It inhabits freshwater rivers of Argentina, Paraguay, and Uruguay. The width of the disc is 43 centimeters (17 inches).
(M. Shirao, after M. Castex)

**PLATE 187.** European ratfish, *Chimaera monstrosa* Linnaeus. This fish can inflict a painful puncture wound with its sharp dorsal spines. In fact, most wounds are contracted by fishermen in the process of removing the fish from their nets. It ranges in the north Atlantic Ocean from Norway and Iceland to Cuba, the Azores, Morocco, Mediterranean Sea, and South Africa. Taken at the aquarium, Zoological Station, Naples, Italy. Length 1 meter (39 inches).
(Courtesy P. Giacomelli)

**PLATE 188a, b.** Pacific ratfish, *Hydrolagus colliei* (Lay and Bennett). Found along the Pacific coast of North America. Length 1 meter (39 inches).
a. Male; b. Female. (M. Shirao)

187

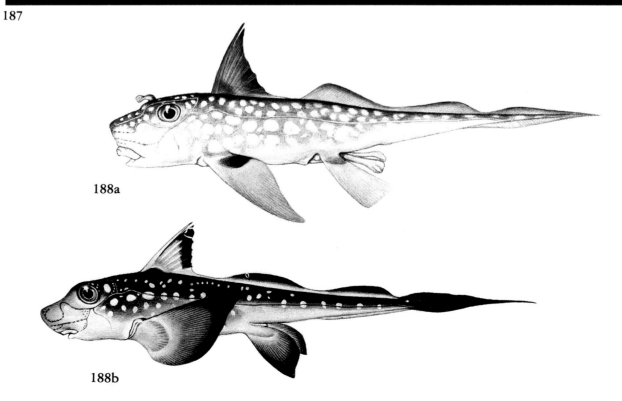

188a

188b

189

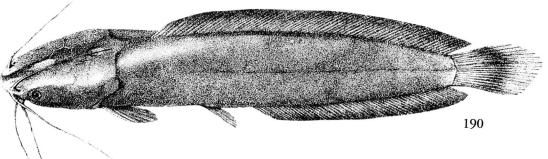

190

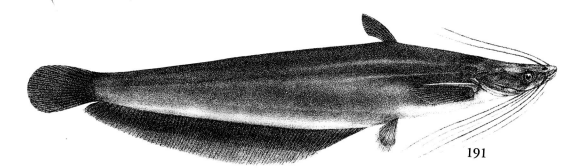

191

192

**PLATE 189.** Catfish, *Galeichthys felis* (Linnaeus). This marine catfish is more active than most of its freshwater relatives. It is generally observed moving about in large schools along sandy beach areas, in shallow bays, and in brackish river mouths. The pectoral and dorsal spines are very sharp and can inflict painful wounds. This fish ranges from Cape Cod to the Gulf of Mexico. Length 40 centimeters (15.7 inches).

(Courtesy Miami Seaquarium)

**PLATE 190.** Labrynthic catfish, *Clarias batrachus* (Linnaeus). This catfish is equipped with an auxilliary breathing apparatus contained in a pocket that extends from the gill cavity. It is in the form of a tree-like breathing organ that is attached to the second and fourth gill arches, which extend into the pocket. This permits these catfish to live out of water for longer periods of time than other catfishes. The species inhabits India, Indonesia, and the Philippine Islands. It has been introduced into the Hawaiian and Guam islands. Length 30 centimeters (11.7 inches).

(From Day)

**PLATE 191.** East Indian catfish, *Heteropneustes fossilis* (Bloch). Ranges along the coasts of India, Sri Lanka, and Vietnam. Length 25 centimeters (9.7 inches).

(From Day)

**PLATE 192.** Oriental catfish, *Plotosus lineatus* (Thunberg). Found in the vicinity of river mouths throughout the Indo-Pacific region. Length 30 centimeters (11.7 inches).

(R. and V. Taylor)

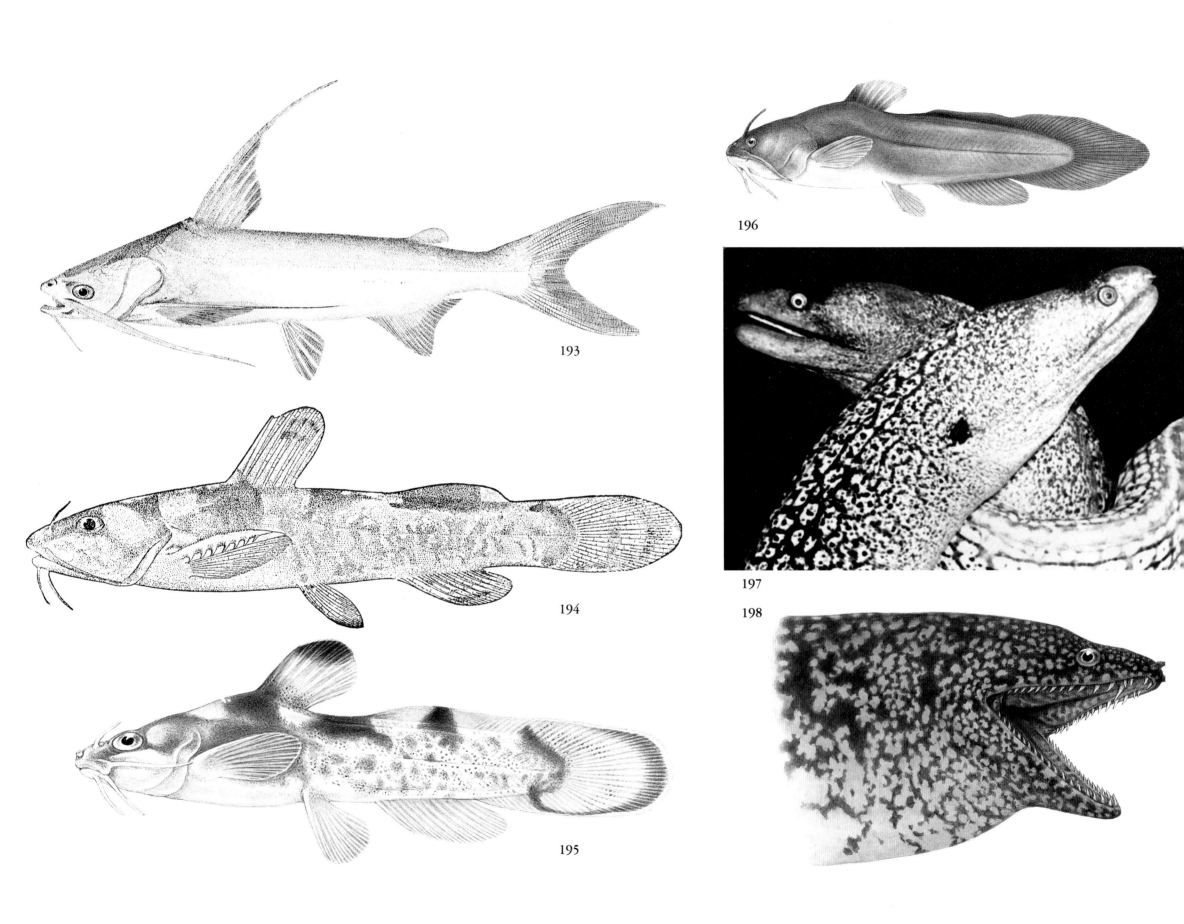

193

194

195

196

197

198

**PLATE 193.** Sea catfish, *Bagre marinus* (Mitchill). Ranges along the east coast of America from Cape Cod to Rio de Janeiro, Brazil. Length 35 centimeters (13.7 inches). (From Goode).

**PLATE 194.** Carolina madtom, *Noturus furiosus* Jordan and Meek. Inhabits the freshwater streams of eastern North Carolina. Length 12 centimeters (4.7 inches). (From Jordan)

**PLATE 195.** Brindled madtom, *Noturus miurus* (Jordan). Length 10 centimeters (4 inches). Ranges from Illinois to Lake Erie, Lake St. Claire drainage, Allegheny drainage, and Mississippi River drainage. (M. Shirao)

**PLATE 196.** Tadpole madtom, *Noturus mollis* (Mitchill). Inhabits the eastern and central North American river drainages. Length 10 centimeters (4 inches). (M. Shirao)

**PLATE 197.** European moray eel, *Muraena helena* Linnaeus. The teeth of moray eels have been considered to be venomous from ancient times, but modern research fails to confirm this. However, there is evidence that the palatine mucosa lining the mouths of these eels may secrete a toxic substance. The bite of a moray can be a very painful experience. *M. helena* is found along the coastal areas of the eastern Atlantic Ocean and Mediterranean Sea. Attains a length of 1.5 meters (5 feet). (From Cervigon)

**PLATE 198.** The mouth of the moray is fearsome to behold. Despite their toothy appearance and biting abilities, they respond to kindness and make great pets. When working on coral reefs, keep your fingers out of the holes in which they may burrow, and they will probably leave you alone. (M. Shirao)

**PLATE 199.** Greater weeverfish, *Trachinus draco* Linnaeus. This is one of the most aggressive and venomous of the fishes. Stings from the dorsal or opercular stings of this fish are extremely painful. It ranges along the coast of Norway and the British Isles southward to the Mediterranean Sea, and along the coast of North Africa. Taken at the aquarium of the Zoological Station, Naples, Italy. Attains a length of 45 centimeters (17.7 inches). (P. Giacomelli)

**PLATE 200.** *T. draco* takes an aggressive attack stance. Note that the gill covers are flared out and the dorsal stings are erected. This fish is ready for action, and any person coming near is likely to be stung. Taken at the aquarium, University of Kiel, Germany. (Courtesy L. Béress)

**PLATE 201.** Close-up of head of *T. draco*. Note that the fish is at rest with the dorsal fin depressed. The opercular spine is clearly evident on the gill cover. (P. Giacomelli)

199

200

201

202

203

PLATE 202. Lesser weeverfish, *Trachinus vipera* Cuvier. The term "lesser" is in name only. Although this fish is smaller (15 centimeters) in size than the greater weeverfish, it can inflict an extremely painful sting. It ranges from the North Sea southward along the coast of Europe and into the Mediterranean Sea.

(P. Giacomelli)

PLATE 203. Short-finned zebrafish, *Brachirus zebra* (Quoy and Gaimard). This fish ranges throughout the Indo-Pacific region from Polynesia to East Africa. Length 12 centimeters (4.7 inches). Taken at Sharm-Al-Sheikh, Red Sea. (Courtesy R. A. Ames)

PLATE 204. Lionfish, *Pterois antennata* (Bloch). This is a closely related venomous species frequently confused with *P. volitans*, but the markings differ. It ranges throughout the Indo-Pacific and Indian Ocean. Length 15 centimeters (6 inches) or more. Taken at Heron Island, Great Barrier Reef, Queensland, Australia. (A. Powers)

PLATE 205. Turkeyfish, lionfish, or zebrafish, *Pterois volitans* (Linnaeus). A very attractive and enticing fish but dangerous to touch since its fins are equipped with venom. It inhabits the Indo-Pacific region. Taken at Sharm-Al-Shaikh, Red Sea. Length 28 centimeters (11 inches). (Courtesy R. Mandojana)

PLATE 206. Lionfish, *Pterois radiata*, is truly one of the most magnificent show pieces of the zebrafish complex. Note the difference in marking compared with those of *P. volitans*. Length 15 centimeters (6 inches) or more. Taken at Sharm-Al-Sheikh, Red Sea.

(Courtesy R. Mandojana)

PLATE 207. *P. radiata*. Taken at Eniwetok, Marshall Islands. (Courtesy C. Arenson)

204

205

206

207

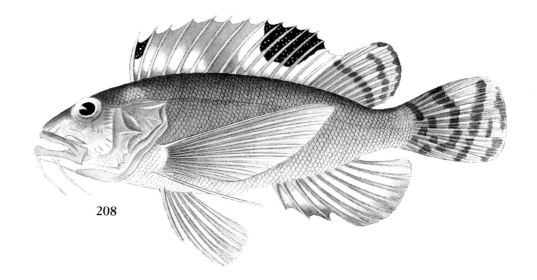

208

209

**PLATE 208.** Bullrout or sulky, *Apistus carinatus* (Bloch and Schneider). Dorsal and anal spines are venomous. Found in the Indo-Pacific and Indian Ocean. Length 16 centimeters (6.2 inches) or more.

(M. Shirao)

**PLATE 209.** Waspfish or fortesque, *Centropogon australis* (White). This fish has been appropriately named the "waspfish" because of the painful stings that it is capable of inflicting with its dorsal spines. It inhabits the coastal areas of New South Wales and Queensland, Australia. Length 15 centimeters (6 inches).

(Courtesy Justice F. Myers)

**PLATE 210.** Bullrout, *Notesthes robusta* (Günther). This fish inhabits New South Wales and Queensland coasts, Australia. Length 25 centimeters (9.7 inches).

(S. Arita, after Bleeker)

210

**PLATE 211.** California scorpionfish, *Scorpaena guttata* Girard. The color of this fish changes greatly depending upon the background upon which the fish is resting. The scorpionfish is adept at camouflage and may be difficult to detect, which in itself presents problems in attempting to avoid contact with venomous spines. It ranges from central California southward into the Gulf of California. Length 43 centimeters (17 inches).
(A. Giddings, Ocean Images, Inc.)

**PLATE 212.** Scorpionfish, *Scorpaena plumieri* Bloch. When the dorsal spines are erected, the fish is taking on an aggressive stance getting ready to strike its victim. This species ranges along the Atlantic coast from Massachusetts to the West Indies and Brazil. Length 30 centimeters (12 inches). Taken at Crashboat Beach Pier, Puerto Rico. (R. Mandojana)

211

212

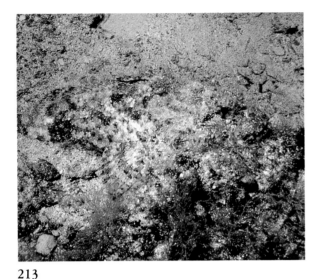

213

214

215a
215b

PLATE 213. The difficulty in detecting scorpionfish is exemplified in this photo of a closely related species, *Scorpaena mystes* Jordan and Starks. It is sometimes almost impossible to spot the beast until one is almost on top of it. Length 35 centimeters (13.7 inches)—if one can find where the nose starts and the tail ends. Taken in the Gulf of California.

(Courtesy E. T. Rulison)

PLATE 214. Scorpionfish, rascasse, or sea pig, *Scorpaena porcus* (Linnaeus). This scorpionfish has been a notorious stinger from the days of antiquity. It inhabits the Atlantic coast of Europe from the English Channel to the Canary Islands, Morocco, Mediterranean and Black seas. Length 30 centimeters (12 inches). Taken at the aquarium, Zoological Station, Naples, Italy.

(P. Giacomelli)

PLATE 215a, b. Devil scorpionfish or false stonefish, *Scorpaenopsis diabolus* (Cuvier). A number of the scorpionfishes, particularly of the genus *Scorpaenopsis*, closely resemble in appearance the deadly stonefish, *Synanceja*, and are confused with them. Both groups possess venom organs and are capable of inflicting painful stings. This scorpionfish is found throughout the tropical Indo-Pacific. Length 25 centimeters (10 inches).

    a. Taken at Oahu, Hawaii.     (R. F. Myers)
    b. Taken at Heron Island, Great Barrier Reef, Australia.     (K. Gillett)

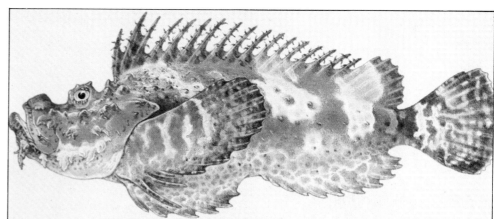

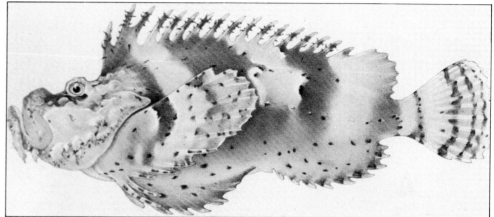

216

219

217

218

**PLATE 216.** China rockfish, *Sebastes nebulosus* Ayres. This species ranges along the Pacific coast from Alaska south to Point Conception, California. Length 30 centimeters (12 inches). (D. W. Gotshall)

**PLATE 217.** Copper rockfish, *Sebastes caurinus* Richardson. This species ranges along the Pacific coast from Puget Sound to California. Length 30 centimeters (12 inches). Taken at St. Nicholas Island, California. (D. W. Gotshall)

**PLATE 218.** Devil scorpionfish, *Inimicus barbatus* (DeVis). This ghoulish-appearing fish possesses a potent set of venomous spines. Found along the coast of Queensland, Australia. Length 20 centimeters (8 inches). (From McCulloch)

**PLATE 219.** Japanese devil scorpionfish, *Inimicus japonicus* (Cuvier and Valenciennes). Notice some of the color variations that may be present in this species. The color varies with the environmental background at the time. Found in the waters of Japan. Length 20 centimeters (8 inches). (M. Shirao)

221

220a

220b

222

223

**PLATE 220a, b.** Filamentous devil scorpionfish, *Inimicus filamentosus* (Cuvier and Valenciennes). This species ranges throughout the Indo-Pacific region. Length 16 centimeters (6.3 inches).

**a.** Side view, showing the erect venomous dorsal spines. Taken in the Gulf of Aqaba, Red Sea.

**b.** Same specimen with the fins extended and ready to attack. When a scorpionfish takes this stance, it is dangerous to approach.    (Courtesy D. Masry)

**PLATE 221.** Stonefish, *Choridactylus multibarbis* Richardson. This stonefish ranges along the coastal areas of India, China, the Philippine Islands, and Polynesia. Length 10 centimeters (4 inches).

(Courtesy J. E. Randall)

**PLATE 222.** Hime-Okoze, *Minous monodactylus* (Bloch and Schneider). This creature inhabits the Indo-Pacific, China, and Japan and can change into a variety of color phases. Length 15 centimeters (6 inches).

(S. Arita)

**PLATE 223.** Deadly or prickly stonefish, *Synanceja horrida* (Linnaeus). This is not only one of the most repulsive looking of marine organisms, but also one of the most venomous. Stonefish are dangerous to encounter because of their ability to hide in the sand and their close resemblance to the coral habitat in which they conceal themselves. There are at least four different species, but only two of the more common ones are shown. *S. horrida* can be recognized by the deep indentation on the head immediately behind the eyes. This species inhabits the Indo-Pacific, Polynesia westward into the Indian Ocean. Length 60 centimeters (24 inches). Photo taken at Heron Island, Great Barrier Reef, Australia.    (K. Gillett)

**PLATE 224.** Large dorsal venom glands of *S. horrida*.

**a.** Side view, showing two of the dorsal stings in which the integumentary sheaths have been removed. Note the large size of the venom glands in comparison to the size of the shaft of the spine.

**b.** Head view, showing the ensheathed venom glands, one on either side of the shaft of the dorsal spine. Taken at Heron Island, Great Barrier Reef, Queensland, Australia.    (K. Gillett)

**PLATE 225.** Warty deadly stonefish, *Synanceja verrucosa* Bloch and Schneider. Resembles *S. horrida*, but lacks the deep depression behind the eyes. It is also smaller is size. This creature inhabits the Indo-Pacific. Length 30 centimeters (12 inches). Photo taken at Torres Strait, Northern Australia.    (K. Gillett)

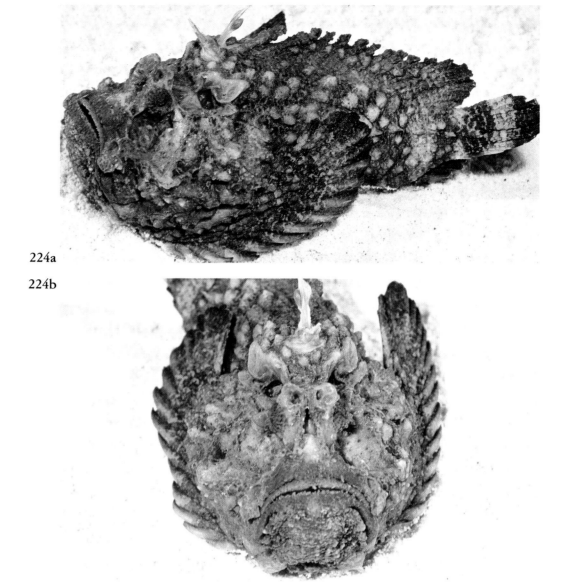

224a

224b

225

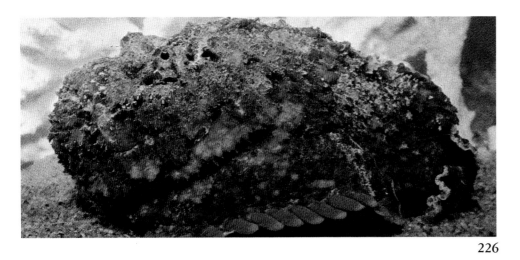

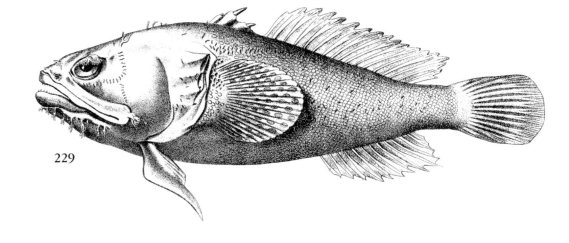

229

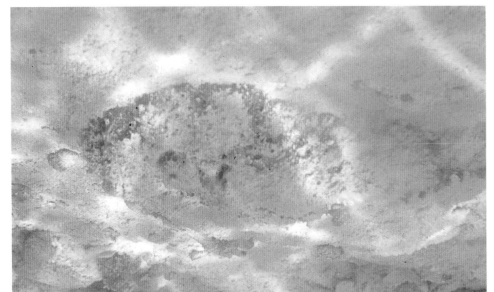

226

230

227

228

231

PLATE 226. Side view of *S. verrucosa*. Note the rounded head. Taken at Heron Island, Great Barrier Reef, Australia. (K. Gillett)

PLATE 227. *S. verrucosa* buried in the sand and a real hazard to anyone wading. This creature doesn't always move out of the way, and the sharp spines can readily penetrate sandals. Photo taken at Palau, Western Caroline Islands. (D. Ludwig)

PLATE 228. This victim was stung by a stonefish, *Synanceja*, on the little finger of the right hand. The finger became swollen and then, due to improper treatment, became gangrenous and necessitated amputation. The accident occurred at Guam, Marianas Islands. (Courtesy R. C. Schoening)

PLATE 229. Comb toadfish, *Batrachoides cirrhosus* (Klunzinger). Very little is known about the clinical aspects of toadfish stings. However, all of the toadfish species included in this *Atlas* are equipped with venomous spines and are reputed to inflict painful stings. This species inhabits the Red Sea. Length 25 centimeters (10 inches). (From Klunzinger)

PLATE 230. Toadfish *Batrachoides didactylus* (Bloch). The species inhabits the Mediterranean Sea and nearby Atlantic coasts. Length 19 centimeters (7.5 inches). (From Smitt)

PLATE 231. Grunting toadfish, or munda, *Batrachoides grunniens* (Linnaeus). The species inhabits the coasts of Sri Lanka, India, Burma, and Malaysia. Length 20 centimeters (8 inches). (From Blegvad)

PLATE 232. Toadfish, or oysterfish, *Opsanus tau* (Linnaeus). Although reputed to have venomous spines, anatomical studies have not confirmed this belief. The species ranges along the Atlantic coast of the United States, from Massachusetts to the West Indies. Length 30 centimeters (11.7 inches). (From Storer)

PLATE 233. Toadfish, bagre sapo, or sapo, *Thalassophryne maculosa* Günther. This creature inhabits the West Indies. Length 14 centimeters (5.5 inches). (From Collette)

PLATE 234. Toadfish, bagre sapo, or sapo, *Thalassophryne reticulata* Günther. The species inhabits the Pacific coast of Central America. Length 25 centimeters (10 inches). (M. Shirao)

232

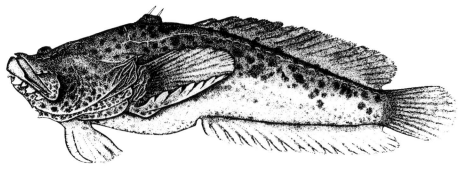

233

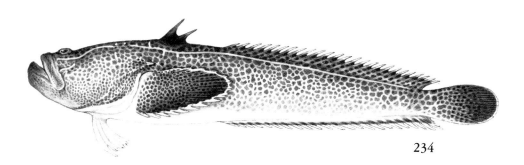

234

**238**

**235**

**239**

**236**
**237**

**240**

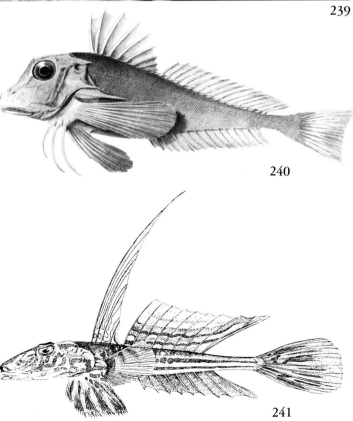

**241**

PLATE 235. White-face surgeonfish, *Acanthurus japonicus* Schmidt. This handsome species is found in the tropical Indo-Pacific regions. The moveable caudal lance is situated in the yellow patch at the base of the tail. Length 25 centimeters (10 inches).

(R. and V. Taylor)

PLATE 236. Achilles surgeonfish, *Acanthurus achilles* Shaw. Photo taken at Wake Island, Central Pacific. Length 19 centimeters (7.5 inches).    (D. Ollis)

PLATE 237. Surgeonfish, *Acanthurus dussumieri* Cuvier. The moveable caudal spine is readily apparent. It inhabits the tropical Indo-Pacific region. Length 30 centimeters (12 inches).    (J. Randall)

PLATE 238. Unicornfish, *Naso lituratus* Bloch and Schneider. This surgeonfish has fixed, nonmoveable forward-curved caudal spines at the base of the caudal fin, which can inflict a nasty cut. The species inhabits the Indo-Pacific region. Length 38 centimeters (15 inches). Taken at Oahu, Hawaii.    (R. Russo)

PLATE 239. Flying gurnard, *Dactylopterus volitans* (Linnaeus). The gurnards are very distinctive because of their large bony heads and their greatly enlarged pectoral fins. On their heads are spines that can inflict cuts, but there is no evidence that they are venomous. Gurnards are particularly impressive when they expand their pectorals and plod along the bottom looking for food such as seen in this photo. These fish inhabit the Atlantic Ocean. Length 40 centimeters (16 inches). Taken at San Salvador, Bahamas.    (D. Woodward)

PLATE 240. Sea robin, *Trigla lyra* Linnaeus. The sea robins resemble the flying gurnards but are members of a separate family. They have imposing head spines, but they are nonvenomous. This species inhabits the eastern Atlantic and Mediterranean Sea. Length 60 centimeters (23.5 inches).    (From Joubin)

PLATE 241. Dragonet, or lyre fish, *Callionymus lyra* Linnaeus. The lyre fish are said to have venomous spines, although this has not been authenticated, but they can inflict painful wounds. The species ranges along the Atlantic coast of Europe and the Mediterranean Sea. Length 10 centimeters (4 inches). This is a male specimen.    (From Poll)

PLATE 242. Lyre fish, *Callionymus festivus* Pallas. This is a species closely related to *C. lyra* and is found in the same general region. Taken at the aquarium of the Zoological Station, Naples, Italy.    (P. Giacomelli)

PLATE 243. Rabbitfish, *Siganus doliatus* (Cuvier). This species inhabits the tropical Indo-Pacific region. Length 25 centimeters (10 inches).    (R. and V. Taylor)

PLATE 244. Brown rabbitfish, *Siganus fuscescens* (Houttuyn). The dorsal and anal spines are venomous and can inflict painful wounds. The species inhabits the tropical Indo-Pacific. Length 25 centimeters (9.7 inches).    (S. Arita)

242

244

245

243

246

247

248

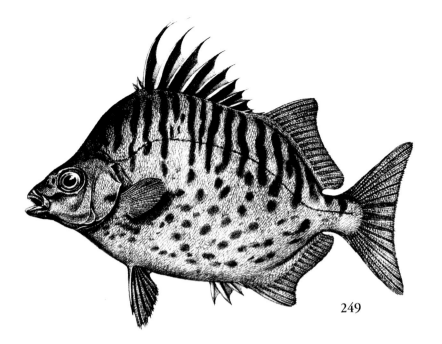

249

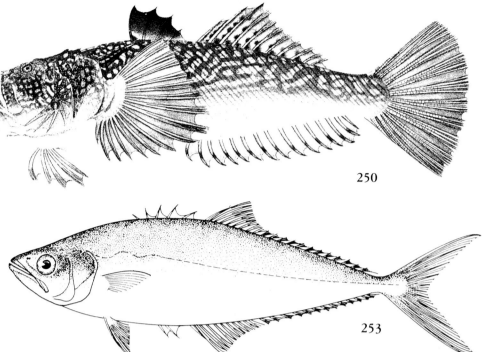

250

253

252

251

PLATE 249. Many-banded scat, *Selenotoca multifasciata* (Richardson). This fish is found along the warm-water coasts of Australia and New Zealand.

(From Richardson)

PLATE 250. Stargazer, or mishmimao koze, *Uranoscopus japonicus* Houttuyn. The shoulder or cleithral spines are quite venomous. The species inhabits the waters of Japan, China, Korea, and the Indo-Pacific. Length 25 centimeters (9.7 inches).

(From Temminck and Schlegel)

PLATE 251. Stargazer, *Uranoscopus scaber* (Linnaeus). Note the venomous cleithral spine on the shoulder area. This species inhabits the eastern Atlantic Ocean and Mediterranean Sea.     (R. H. Knabenbauer)

PLATE 252. Stargazer, *Uranoscopus oligolepis* Bleeker. Stargazers are usually found buried in the sand or mud, and are not commonly observed resting on the bottom, such as seen in this photograph. Length 18 centimeters (7 inches). Taken at the Nature Reserve, Eliat, Gulf of Aqaba, Israel.     (WLRI photo)

PLATE 253. Leatherjacket, or runner, *Oligoplites saurus* (Bloch and Schneider). Inhabits the tropical Indo-Pacific region. Length 26 centimeters (10.2 inches).     (From Jordan and Evermann)

PLATE 254. Leatherback, *Scomberoides* (*Sanctipetri*) *lysan* (Forskål). The dorsal and anal spines of the leatherback are venomous. The tough, leather-like skin of this fish is used by native fishermen as fishing lures, because of its small, tightly-adhering scales and bright silvery appearance. These fish are found throughout the tropical Indo-Pacific region. Length 65 centimeters (25.5 inches). Taken in the Red Sea.

(J. Randall)

PLATE 255. Olive-brown sea snake, *Aipysurus laevis* Lacépède. This is a large, heavy-bodied and active sea snake. It is generally not aggressive, but it is venomous and potentially dangerous. This species inhabits tropical Australia and New Guinea. Length 1.8 meters (6 feet). (R. and V. Taylor)

PLATE 256. Close up of head of *A. laevis*. Taken at Marion Reef, Coral Sea. (R. and V. Taylor)

PLATE 257. Sea snake, *Enhydrina schistosa* (Daudin). This snake is usually docile, but during the reproductive season it can be quite aggressive. It has produced human fatalities. Its range extends from the Persian Gulf to southeast China, and the north coast of Australia. Length 1.2 meters (47.2 inches) (R. H. Knabenbauer)

PLATE 258. Ornate sea snake, *Hydrophis ornatus* (Gray). This species has caused human fatalities. It inhabits northern Australia. Length 95 centimeters (37.5 inches). (Shirao)

PLATE 259. Sea snake, *Hydrophis cyanocinctus* (Daudin). This snake inhabits the Bay of Bengal and has caused human fatalities. Length 1 meter (39.3 inches). (R. Kuntz)

PLATE 260. Hardwick's sea snake, *Lapemis hardwicki* (Gray). This species ranges from Japan to the Merguri Archipelago and along the coast of northern Australia. Length 85 centimeters (33.5 inches). (M. Shirao)

PLATE 261a, b, c. Sea snake, *Laticauda colubrina* (Schneider). Although generally docile, this snake is venomous. It is widely distributed throughout the tropical Indo-Pacific region. Length 1.4 meters (55 inches).

a. Sea snakes are frequently seen swimming in and out of holes and crevices and amongst debris throughout the coral reefs that they inhabit. They appear to be in constant search of food.

b. Sea snake swimming near the surface of the water. Periodically they must surface for air since they breathe with the use of lungs.

c. *L. colubrina* basking out of water on a coral ledge. Taken in Palau, Western Caroline Islands. (D. Ludwig)

PLATE 262. Yellow-bellied sea snake, *Pelamis platurus* (Linnaeus). This is an attractive, but dangerous, species that has caused numerous human fatalities. The geographical range of this species is the most extensive of any of the sea snakes, extending from the western Indian Ocean eastward to the Gulf of Panama. Length 85 centimeters (33.5 inches). (M. Shirao)

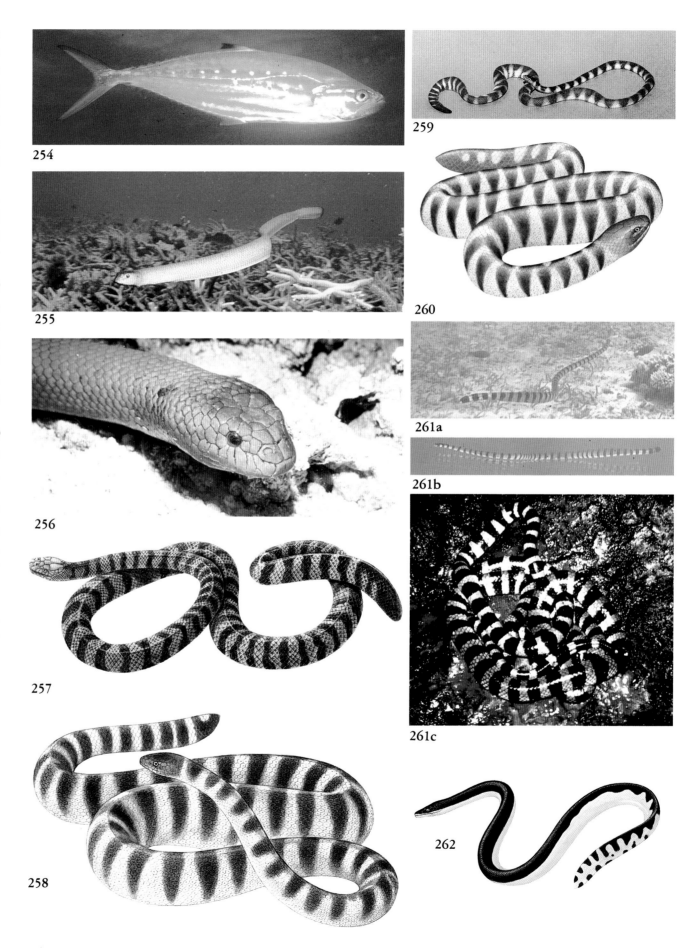

254

255

256

257

258

259

260

261a

261b

261c

262

263

264

265

266

267

PLATE 263. Sea snake bite on side of the foot of a fisherman who was bitten while stepping into a net full of fish that also contained several sea snakes. Note the small fang marks and the absence of swelling and tissue reaction. Taken at Penang, Malaysia.

(Courtesy H. A. Reid)

PLATE 264. Cottonmouth water moccasin, *Agkistrodon piscivorous* (Lacépède). Called the "cottonmouth" because of its white mouth, which it may open wide when confronted, this snake is frequently seen basking in the sun on logs or rocks. Generally found in wetlands, it can be quite aggressive and must be regarded as a dangerous venomous species that can cause massive tissue damage because of a potent proteolytic enzyme in its venom. It ranges from Virginia to Florida, south to central Texas. Attains a length of 1.83 meters (6 feet).     (Courtesy J. Tashjian and F. Russell)

PLATE 265. Jararacussu, *Bothrops jararacussu* Lacerda. This is a dangerous species and is responsible for numerous fatal snake bites in Brazil each year. It produces a large quantity of toxic venom. It ranges throughout the rivers and lakes in southern Brazil, eastern Bolivia, Paraguay, and northern Argentina. Length 1.68 meters (5.5 feet).

(Courtesy J. Tashjian and F. Russell)

PLATE 266. Banded water cobra, *Boulengerina annulata* (Buchholz and Peters). This cobra is not an aggressive species, but like other cobras it will spread its hood and raise its head in a threatening manner. Little seems to be known concerning the effects of its bite. It inhabits central Africa. Length 2.13 meters (7 feet).     (Courtesy J. Tashjian and F. Russell)

PLATE 267. Duck-billed platypus, *Ornithorhynchus anatinus* Shaw and Nodder, is shown in its natural habitat feeding on one of its favorite foods, worms. The male platypus has venomous spurs on its hind legs that are capable of inflicting painful stings.

(R. H. Knabenbauer)

# CHAPTER V

# Poisonous Aquatic Animals—Invertebrates

THE TERM "poisonous" can be confusing because "venomous" organisms are also poisonous since they are equipped with specialized poison glands. In this chapter, however, only those organisms that are poisonous to eat or those that release their poisons freely into the aquatic environment are included. In other words, this is a group of organisms that are poisonous but do not have a wound-producing device (i.e., tooth, fang, or spine) with which to inject or introduce the poison into the victim. Thus, all venoms are poisons, but not all poisons are venoms.

## Classification of Poisonous Aquatic Invertebrates

This outline will be helpful in appreciating the enormous scope and variety of poisonous aquatic organisms. This section includes the poisonous animals without a backbone. Poisonous aquatic invertebrates can be conveniently divided into the following groups, or phyla:

PROTISTA (PROTOZOA): The planktonic plant-animals. This group includes the planktonic one-celled organisms that are encountered by humans as a result of ingesting mollusks or fishes that have been feeding on toxic dinoflagellates. Two very important types of intoxications are produced in humans as a result of ingesting these organisms—namely, paralytic shellfish poisoning (from eating mollusks), and ciguatera fish poisoning (from eating fishes)—all of which have been feeding on toxic dinoflagellates.

†PORIFERA: The sponges. This group will not be included in this section since sponges are not generally eaten by humans. However, as shown in Chapter III, "Aquatic Animals That Sting—Invertebrates," some sponges can produce a severe contact dermatitis.

CNIDARIA (COELENTERATA): The hydroids, jellyfishes, sea anemones, and corals. Although hydroids, jellyfishes, corals, and sea anemones are best known because of their stinging abilities, a few species are poisonous to eat. Members of the genus *Palythoa*, which are soft corals or zoanthids, are among the most toxic aquatic organisms known. The poison is produced within the body of the organism rather than in the stinging nematocysts of the tentacles.

ECHINODERMATA: Starfishes, sea urchins, sea cucumbers. Poisonous echinoderms are limited to certain species of sea urchins having toxic eggs and sea cucumbers, which are sometimes eaten by humans.

†MOLLUSCA: Univalves, bivalves, octopuses, and squids. Paralytic shellfish poisoning is the best known of the mollusk intoxications. (*See* under "Protista.") However, poisonings have also resulted from ingesting abalone *(Haliotis)*; turban *(Turbo)* shells; whelks *(Neptunea)*; venerupin *(Tapes)*; giant tridacna clams *(Tridacna)*; and, on rare occasions, even octopuses.

†ANNELIDA: Segmented worms. One of the Japanese polychaete worms, *Lumbriconereis*, is known to be poisonous when eaten by insects. The effect of the poison on humans is unknown.

ARTHROPODA: Joint-legged animals, Asiatic horseshoe crabs, tropical reef crabs, and freshwater true bugs (Hemiptera). Some species of Asiatic horseshoe

---

†These are not discussed in this chapter, but may be referred to in the appropriate sections in Chapter III.

crabs and tropical reef crabs may be poisonous to eat. There are only a few toxic aquatic insect species, and these are found largely in five families of true bugs of the order Hemiptera that inhabit freshwater.

PLATYHELMINTHES: Flatworms. Some species of flatworms, such as the turbellarians, are believed to be poisonous to eat, but the poisons are apparently produced by specialized poison glands or crinotoxic organs.

## PROTISTA (PROTOZOA)
### Plant-Animals

The protozoa, or protista, are single-celled microscopic organisms, most of which are free-living; they inhabit an aquatic environment, but a few live in the body fluids of other animals. It is estimated that there are about 30,000 species. One group of protozoans, members of the order Dinoflagellata, includes a number of toxin-producing species. Since the dinoflagellates contain green coloring matter (chlorophyl), characteristic of plants, and flagella for locomotion, characteristic of animals, they are claimed by both zoologists and botanists and are known as "plant-animals."

When temperature and nutrient conditions are ideal, dinoflagellates may proliferate in large numbers and cause an actual discoloration of the water. Over a period of time, it has been observed that the toxic planktonic blooms, or "red tide," are most likely to take place during the warm season of the year, which varies somewhat with the geographical locality (in north temperate regions, March to November). During high peaks of red tide the dinoflagellates are present in such vast numbers as to cause a mass mortality of fishes. Dinoflagellate blooms have been known to kill upwards of a hundred tons of fish per day. Conditions such as this may pose serious economic and public health problems (272d).

Toxic dinoflagellates affect human health by being ingested by a variety of mollusks that are plankton feeders. The mollusks then become poisonous, since the poisons derived from the dinoflagellates are stored in the digestive glands of clams, mussels, and other shellfish. Humans then become intoxicated from eating shellfish. The Alaskan butter clam, *Saxidomus giganteus* (Deshayes) (274), may have dangerous toxicity levels in certain coastal areas of Alaska at almost any time of the year. One species of microorganism, *Gymnodinium (Ptychodiscus) breve*, may affect humans when ingesting shellfish, and may act as a respiratory irritant when present in windblown ocean spray.

### Dinoflagellates Poisonous to Humans

Several species of toxic dinoflagellates have been incriminated in human intopxication but only the species listed below are discussed:

POISONOUS DINOFLAGELLATE, *Gymnodinium (Ptychodiscus) breve* Davis (268, 272a). Found in the Gulf of Mexico and along the coast of Florida.

POISONOUS DINOFLAGELLATE, *Gonyaulax (Protogonyaulax) catenella* Whedon and Kofoid (269, 271, 272b). Found along the Pacific coast of North America, Japan, and the northern coast of South America.

POISONOUS DINOFLAGELLATE, *Gonyaulax (Protogonyaulax) tamarensis* Lebour (270, 272c). Found along the eastern coast of North America and Japan.

### Paralytic Shellfish Poisoning

This is one of the more important types of marine poisonings throughout the world and deserves particular attention by the public since it is a potentially serious health problem.

### Geographical Distribution

Paralytic shellfish poisoning has a spotty worldwide geographical distribution. Outbreaks have occurred in North America (East Coast, Alaska, California, Washington), Europe, Japan, Chile, Venezuela, South Africa, New Zealand, New Guinea, and Brunei.

There are no accurate global statistics as to the overall incidence, but for 1974 it was estimated that there were about 1,600 cases with more than 300 deaths. Paralytic shellfish poisoning is one of the more common lethal forms of marine intoxications.

## Economic and Environmental Aspects

Economic loses resulting from an outbreak of paralytic shellfish poisoning may be catastrophic. The closure of harvesting areas leads to severe economic loss to fishermen, processors, and related industries. Since there is no known way of rendering toxic shellfish safe for human consumption, public health authorities may be forced to close a contaminated shellfish bed for weeks or months, during which time the toxin is depleted naturally. In some areas, certain shellfish beds may remain toxic for a year or more, during which time no shellfish can be harvested. Under these conditions, the economic loss to the community can be devastating. The toxin is quite heat stable, and cooking, including canning procedures, only partially destroys it, but not sufficiently to permit any degree of safety.

The occurrence of an outbreak of paralytic shellfish poisoning in one region often leads to a decline in consumer demand for fish and shellfish in other areas. This is usually the result of an emotional reaction by the public stemming from widespread reporting by the news media. For example, one outbreak that was reported in North America resulted in losses to the fish and shellfish industry of more than $1 million within a few weeks time.

The severity of the effects of paralytic shellfish poisoning on man and the difficulty of predicting its occurrence have led many countries to institute costly surveillance and enforcement activities in the field and in the laboratory with the hope of providing adequate safety measures. In some areas surveillance techniques must be utilized on a year-round basis.

The occurrence of paralytic shellfish poisoning may also have severe repercussions on tourism where fishing is an important tourist activity. International trade relations have also been hampered because of the threat of toxic shellfish being exported to other countries.

In addition to these economic aspects, there are undesirable environmental consequences, including the transfer of dinoflagellate toxins through the food chain, resulting in the death of fish and seabirds.

Recent studies have shown that paralytic shellfish poison may also occur in reef crabs and other marine organisms in Okinawa. Japanese scientists have also found paralytic shellfish poison in the red alga *Jania*. This highly toxic poison complex has an amazingly wide distribution throughout the marine environment.

There are at least seven types of shellfish poisoning:

(1) *Gastrointestinal type*, involving symptoms of nausea, vomiting, diarrhea, and abdominal pain. This type usually develops about ten to twelve hours after eating the shellfish and is believed to be caused by bacterial contamination.

(2) *Allergic type*, characterized by redness of the skin, swelling, development of a hive-like rash, itching, headache, nasal congestion, abdominal pain, dryness of the throat, swelling of the tongue, palpitations, and difficulty in breathing, due to hypersensitivity to shellfish.

(3) *Paralytic type*, caused by paralytic shellfish poison. The disease has been designated as paralytic shellfish poisoning—(PSP). The early symptoms are a tingling or burning sensation of the lips, gums, tongue, and face, which gradually spreads elsewhere to the body. The tingling areas later become numb, and movements of the muscles of the body may become very difficult. Other symptoms frequently present are weakness, dizziness, joint aches, increased salivation, intense thirst, difficulty in swallowing. Nausea, vomiting, diarrhea, and abdominal pain are relatively rare. The muscular paralysis may become increasingly severe until death ensues.

(4) *Neurotoxic shellfish poisoning* (NSP), or *Brevitoxic shellfish poisoning* (BSP), due to ingestion of shellfish containing brevitoxins from *Gymnodium breve*. Symp-

toms include tingling, numbness, muscular aches, gastrointestinal (G.I.) upset, and dizziness. Inhalation of toxic products contained in windblown ocean spray from red tide areas of *Gymnodium breve* may cause irritation of the mucous membranes of the nose and throat, resulting in coughing, sneezing, and respiratory distress.

(5) *Diarrhetic shellfish poisoning* (DSP), caused by ingestion of shellfish that have been feeding on the dinoflagellate *Dinophysis fortii* and related species. Symptoms include gastrointestinal upset.

(6) *Amnesic shellfish poisoning* (ASP), caused by eating shellfish that have fed on the toxic diatom *Nitzchia pungens*. Symptoms include gastrointestinal upset, disorientation, memory loss, and death. The poison is domoic acid.

(7) *Venerupin shellfish poisoning* (VSP), which is discussed below. Other symptoms of shellfish poisoning have been reported, but are poorly understood at this time. There is no specific treatment available for paralytic shellfish poisoning and no known antidotes. Evacuation of the gastrointestinal tract should be instituted as soon as possible if shellfish have been ingested. Vomiting can be stimulated by swallowing large quantities of saltwater, egg white, or by merely placing one's finger down the throat. Alkaline fluids, such as a solution of ordinary baking soda, are said to be of value since the poison is rapidly destroyed by these fluids. Artificial respiration may be required. See a physician at once if you are fortunate enough to be near one.

The extremely toxic nature of this poison cannot be overemphasized. Most areas where paralytic shellfish poisoning is likely to occur are examined by local public health authorities. When toxic shellfish are discovered, the area is placed under quarantine. One should adhere strictly to local quarantine regulations. Since poisonous shellfish cannot be detected by their appearance, smell, or by discoloration of a silver object or garlic placed in cooking water (as many believe), it is only by careful scientific procedures that paralytic shellfish poison can be determined with any degree of certainty.

The digestive organs, or dark meat, gills, and in some shellfish species the siphon, contain the greatest concentration of the poison (273a, b). The musculature or white meat is generally harmless; however, it should be thoroughly washed before cooking. The broth or bouillon in which the shellfish is boiled is especially dangerous since the poison is water-soluble. The broth should be discarded if there is the slightest doubt. The tidal location from which these shellfish were gathered cannot be used as a criterion for whether the shellfish are safe to eat. Poisonous shellfish may be found in either low or high tidal zones. If in doubt—throw them out!

Shellfish most commonly involved in paralytic shellfish poisoning are:

SOLID SURF CLAM, *Spisula solidissima* (Dillwyn) (274a). Occurs from Labrador to North Carolina.

SOFT-SHELLED CLAM, *Mya arenaria* Linnaeus (274b). Inhabits Britain, Scandinavia, Greenland, Atlantic coast of North America south to Carolina, Alaska south to Japan, and Vancouver, British Columbia, California, and Oregon coasts.

COMMON MUSSEL, *Mytilus californianus* Conrad (274c). Inhabits Unalaska, Aleutian Islands, eastward and southward to Socorro Island.

BAY MUSSEL, *Mytilus edulis* Linnaeus (274d). Ranges from the Arctic Ocean to South Carolina, Alaska to Cape San Lucas, Baja California; practically worldwide in temperate waters.

NORTHERN HORSE MUSSEL, *Modiolus modiolus* (Linnaeus) (274e). Ranges from the Gulf of St. Lawrence River to Florida.

ROCK COCKLE or COMMON LITTLE NECK, *Protothaca staminea* (Conrad) (274f). Ranges from the Aleutian Islands to Cape San Lucas, Baja California.

ALASKAN BUTTER CLAM, SMOOTH WASHINGTON, or BUTTER CLAM, *Saxidomus giganteus* (Deshayes) (274g). Ranges from Sitka, Alaska to San Francisco Bay, California.

COMMON WASHINGTON or BUTTER CLAM, *Saxidomus nuttalli* Conrad (274h). Ranges from Humboldt Bay, California to San Quentin Bay, Baja California.

### Venerupin Shellfish Poisoning

Dinoflagellates also cause a type of shellfish poisoning that is found only in certain restricted areas in the Kanagawa and Schizuoka prefectures in Japan during the period of January through April. Two species of shellfish have been involved:

JAPANESE OYSTER, *Crassostrea gigas* (Thunberg) (275), and

ASARI, *Tapes semidecussata* Reeve (276).

The poison in these two species is concentrated in the digestive gland, or "liver," of the mollusk. The poison is believed to be produced by the dinoflagellate *Prorocentrum mariae-lebouriae* (Parke and Ballantine).

The symptoms of venerupin shellfish poisoning usually develop in 24 to 48 hours after ingestion of the toxic mollusks, but the incubation period is believed to extend up to 7 days. The initial symptoms are anorexia, gastric pain, nausea, vomiting, constipation, headache, and malaise. Within 2 to 3 days, nervousness, hematemesis, and bleeding of the mucous membranes of the nose, mouth, and gums develop. Halitosis is a dominant part of the clinical picture. Jaundice, petechial hemorrhages, and ecchymoses of the skin are generally present, particularly about the chest, neck, and upper portion of the arms and legs. Increased white blood count, anemia, retardation of blood-clotting time, and evidence of disturbances in liver function have been noted. The liver is generally enlarged, but painless. In fatal cases the victim usually becomes extremely excitable, delirious, and comatose. There is no evidence of paralysis or other neurotoxic effects usually observed in paralytic shellfish poisoning. In the outbreaks that have been reported, an average case fatality rate of about 33 percent resulted in severe cases; death occurs within one week. In mild cases, recovery is slow, with the victim showing extreme weakness.

# CNIDARIA (COELENTERATA)
## Sea Anemones, Soft Corals (Zoanthids)
### Sea Anemones

Intoxications resulting from the ingestion of poisonous sea anemones are extremely rare. However, poisonings have occurred in Samoa and other parts of the tropical Indo-Pacific region. Sea anemones are commonly eaten by the natives of Samoa, but only certain species, and only after the anemones are cooked. Poisonings occur most frequently in children who eat raw anemones when adults carelessly leave their catch within their reach. Generally considered to be poisonous when raw, but safe when cooked, are:

POISONOUS SEA ANEMONE, *Rhodactis howesi* Kent (277c, 278a, b), known locally as *matalelei*, and

POISONOUS SEA ANEMONE, *Physobrachia douglasi* Kent (277b), known locally as *lumane*.

Considered to be poisonous either raw or cooked is:

POISONOUS SEA ANEMONE, *Radianthus paumotensis* (Dana) (277a), known locally as *matamala sama-sama*.

Initial symptoms are those of acute gastritis, cyanosis, and prostration. Shortly after ingestion the victim may become stuporous, with an absence of superficial reflexes, but with a normal pulse rate and blood pressure. Eventually, the patient may go into prolonged shock and die with pulmonary edema. There is no known treatment, and the nature of the poison is not known.

### Soft Corals

Some of the soft corals, or zoanthids, of the genus *Palythoa* have been found to contain one of the most deadly poisons known to science. This poison is produced within the body of the organism rather than in the stinging nematocysts of the tentacles. The poison, designated as *palytoxin*, has been demonstrated to have a potent action on the nervous and muscular systems of experimental animals. There is some clinical evidence that palytoxin can depress the immune system. The poison can be inactivated by heat and acids and is probably destroyed by gastric juices. When swimming in closed tidal pools containing large numbers of *Palythoa*, a person may develop a sensation of numbness and tingling of the lips and mouth. If ingested it may cause respiratory distress and death.

Species of the soft coral *Palythoa* are found both in the Caribbean and the tropical Pacific. In the Hawaiian Islands, *Palythoa* is referred to as the "deadly seaweed of Hana" (*limu-make o hana*). *Palythoa* (277d, 279a, b) are generally found growing in tidal pools or other shallow water protected areas and may be encrusted on shells, seaweed, corals, or rocks.

Persons working for prolonged periods in confined tidal pools inhabited by this coelenterate should do so with caution.

# ECHINODERMATA
## Sea Urchins, Sea Cucumbers

There are relatively few echinoderms (starfishes, sea urchins, sea cucumbers) known to produce human oral intoxications. Only two groups have been incriminated to any significant extent, namely:

### Sea Urchins
POISONOUS EUROPEAN SEA URCHIN, *Paracentrotus lividus* Lamarck (280), inhabiting the Atlantic coasts of Europe and the Mediterranean, and

WHITE SEA URCHIN or POISONOUS WEST INDIAN SEA URCHIN, *Tripneustes ventricosus* (Lamarck) (281a, b), inhabiting the West Indies.

It is believed that the poison is contracted from toxic algae upon which the sea urchins have been feeding. Reports have also appeared from time to time of poisoning due to the ingestion of sea urchin eggs.

Poisonings usually occur during the reproductive season of the year. Symptoms consist of acute gastritis, nausea, vomiting, diarrhea, abdominal pain, and severe migraine-like headaches. Little else is known about sea urchin poisoning in humans, or the nature of the poison.

### Sea Cucumbers
These are a group of sluggish creatures that move over the bottom of the sea by means of rhythmic contractions of a sausage-like body. They have a series of tentacles circling the mouth at the anterior end of the body. Sea cucumbers, members of the class Holothuridae, serve as important food items in some parts of the world, where they are sold under the name of *trepang* or *bêche-de-mer*. They are boiled and then dried in the sun or smoked. *Trepang* are used to flavor soups and stews, or are eaten whole.

Contact with the liquid ejected from the visceral cavity of some sea cucumber species may result in dermatitis or blindness. The poison of sea cucumbers is termed *holothurin* and is generally concentrated in the organs of Cuvier. Intoxications may also occur as a result of ingestion of sea cucumbers, but poisonings of this type are rare. Nothing is known concerning the symptoms produced, but fatalities have been reported. Treatment of sea cucumber poisoning is symptomatic. There is no known antidote. A representative group of poisonous sea cucumbers appears in Plate 282a-j.

# ARTHROPODA
## Horseshoe Crabs, Reef Crabs,
## Lobsters, Aquatic Bugs

The phylum Arthropoda is the largest single group in the animal kingdom, having more than 800,000 species. Unfortunately, very little is known concerning the toxicity of most aquatic arthropods, the joint-legged animals that include the horseshoe crabs, reef crabs, lobsters, and a few aquatic insects. Some of the Asiatic horseshoe crabs, tropical lobsters, and reef crabs are occasionally quite poisonous to eat. There are a few toxic aquatic insect species that are members of the order Hemiptera, or true bugs.

### Asiatic Horseshoe Crabs
ASIATIC HORSESHOE CRAB, *Carcinoscorpius rotundicauda* (Latreille) (283a, b, c). Poisoning from ingestion of this creature is due to eating of the unlaid green eggs or viscera during the reproductive season of the year. Most of the intoxications have occurred in southeast Asia. Despite their period of toxicity, the large masses of green unlaid eggs are highly esteemed by Asiatic peoples.

Horseshoe crab poisoning, or mimi poisoning, usually occurs within 30 minutes after ingestion of the toxic eggs. Symptoms consist of dizziness; headaches; nausea; vomiting; abdominal cramps; diarrhea; cardiac palpitation; numbness of the lips; tingling of the lower extremities; weakness; loss of speech; sensation of heat in the mouth, throat, and stomach; muscular paralysis; hypersalivation; drowsiness; and loss of consciousness. The mortality rate is very high. Death may occur within sixteen hours or less. The treatment is symptomatic; there is no known antidote. Asiatic horseshoe crabs are eaten in many parts of southeast Asia, but should be avoided during the reproductive season.

TROPICAL REEF CRABS

Although violent intoxications have been periodically reported from eating tropical reef crabs, it is only within the last few years that a serious scientific effort has been made to study the occurrence and nature of crab poisons.

There are numerous crab species that occur in tropical waters, but only a few species have been found to be toxic:

COCONUT CRAB, *Birgus latero* (Linnaeus) (284). This toxic species is terrestrial and found in damp jungle areas on tropical islands of the Indo-Pacific. Intoxications from the coconut crab have been reported in the Ryukyu Islands. It is believed this crab becomes toxic as a result of feeding on poisonous plants. The symptoms of coconut crab poisoning include nausea, vomiting, headache, chills, fever, joint aches, exhaustion, and muscular weakness. Deaths have been reported.

Several species of tropical Indo-Pacific reef crabs have produced violent intoxications:

POISONOUS REEF CRAB, *Atergatus floridus* (Linnaeus) (285).

RED SPOTTED CRAB, *Carpilius maculatus* (Linnaeus) (286).

POISONOUS REEF CRAB, *Demania toxica* Garth (287).

POISONOUS REEF CRAB, *Eriphia sebana* (Shaw and Nodder) (288).

POISONOUS REEF CRAB, *Platypodia granulosa* (Rüppell) (289).

POISONOUS REEF CRAB, *Zozymus aeneus* (Linnaeus) (290).

The symptoms produced by tropical reef crabs differ from those of the coconut crab. The symptoms include nausea, vomiting, collapse, numbness, tingling, and muscular paralysis. Death may occur in severe intoxications.

The poison is believed to be chemically identical to paralytic shellfish poison, which is commonly found in shellfish. Treatment is symptomatic, and there is no known antidote.

Avoid eating tropical reef crabs unless you are certain they are safe to eat. If in doubt, check with the local natives or public health authorities.

LOBSTERS

Several reports have appeared from time to time on the toxicity of lobsters found in southern Polynesia.

SPINY LOBSTER, *Panulirus interruptus* (Randall) (291). This specimen is a close relative of the Polynesia species.

The symptoms seem to resemble ciguatera fish poison, but little is known concerning the nature of the poison. This lobster is usually safe to eat.

POISONOUS AQUATIC BUGS

The order Hemiptera, or true bugs, are a large group of insects with representative species in abundance throughout the world. The group contains more than 55,000 known species. The Hemiptera are equipped with beaks containing an ensheathed stylet-like maxillae and mandibles. They use the beak to pierce plant or animal tissues; salivary fluids are forced into the tissue through one tube, and partially digested materials are withdrawn through the other. Bugs make themselves felt in a wide variety of ways by serving as important plant pests and by transmitting diseases to plants, animals, and man. They are an interesting group of organisms. There are five freshwater aquatic families in this group that are known to produce poisons by means of specialized glands. The structure of these glands varies somewhat from one species to the next. The glands are situated within the body of the bug, either ventrally or dorsally, and the poison is released through minute ducts via openings through the cuticle. Some of these bugs appear to possess a venom apparatus, whereas others seem to merely release their poisons into the water. The chemical structures of some of these compounds have been determined; the effect of these poisons on humans has not been determined.

Some representatives of the poisonous aquatic bugs are:

CREEPING WATERBUG, *Ilyocoris cimicoides* (Linnaeus) (292a). This is a predacious bug that lives in both still and running water. The members of this family, of which *Ilyocoris* is representative, are medium size, 5 to 16 millimeters (⅝ inch) in length, and have a cosmopolitan distribution. They produce two toxic substances known as hydroxybenzaldehyde and hydroxybenzoate. Their effects on humans are unknown.

GIANT WATERBUG, *Lethocerus fakir* (Gistel) (292b, 293). These are predacious aquatic bugs, mostly found in still water, although some live in running streams. They inhabit all major zoogeographic locations. They attain a length of up to 70 millimeters (2.7 inches). The poison contains two toxic substances known as trans-hex-2-enylacetate and trans-hex-2-enyl-butyrate. Their effects on humans are unknown.

BACKSWIMMER, *Notonecta undulata* Say (292c, 294). These bugs are predacious and swim with the ventral surface up. They are found in all zoogeographic regions of the world. Their length is up to 17 millimeters (⅝ inch). The poison contains two toxic substances, hydroxybenzaldehyde and methyl-p-hydroxybenzoate. Their effects on humans are unknown.

TOADBUG, *Gelactocoris oculatus* (Fabricius) (292d, 295). These bugs are predacious and found in moist shores of streams, marshes, and ponds. They are cosmopolitan in distribution. They attain a length of up to 10 millimeters (⅜ inch). The poison contains a toxic substance, trans-4-o-o-hex-2-enal. Its effect on humans is unknown.

## PLATYHELMINTHES
### Flatworms

There is another category of poisonous organisms about which little is known but is deserving of mention; namely, the *crinotoxic* organisms. There appears to be a large number of marine organisms that are provided with specialized poison glands, but there is no mechanical device available through which the poison can be purveyed into the victim. The poison is generally released into the environment by means of integumentary pores in a manner somewhat comparable to the action of sweat glands. For the most part, little is known about the chemical or pharmacological properties of these poisons.

Crinotoxins are found in invertebrates such as:

NEMERTEAN WORM, *Drepanophorus crassus* (Quatrefages) (296).

TURBELLARIAN FLATWORM, *Thysanozoon brocchi* Grube (297). This European turbellarian has a highly specialized glandular structure found in crinotoxic turbellarians as shown in Figure 1. (*See* Chapter VI for vertebrates containing crinotoxic poisons: Icthyocrinotoxic Fishes.)

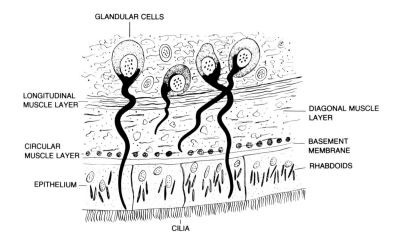

Figure 1. Histological structure of the integument of the polyclad turbellarian, *Thysanozoon brocchi*, showing the glandular cells and rhabdoids that are believed to produce the poison present in some species of marine turbellarians. Semidiagrammatic.    (R. Kreuzinger, after Lang)

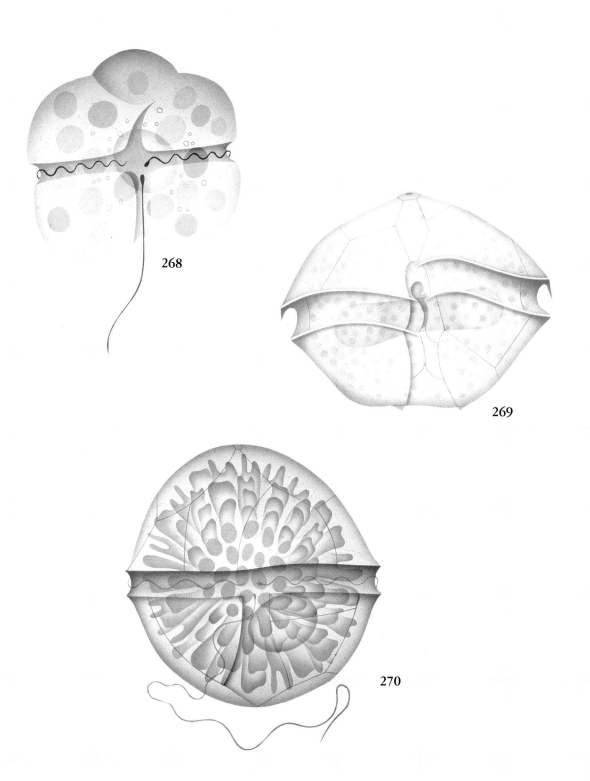

**PLATE 268.** Poisonous dinoflagellate, *Gymnodinium (Ptychodiscus) breve* Davis. This microscopic dinoflagellate may cause a mass mortality of fishes. It has been known to kill over 100 tons of fish in a single day when a toxic red tide bloom occurs. It may cause poisonings in humans, both as a severe respiratory irritant when present in a windblown ocean spray and as a form of neurotoxic shellfish poisoning involving ingestion of mollusks. Enlarged x 1,350.

(R. Kreuzinger)

**PLATE 269.** Poisonous dinoflagellate, *Gonyaulax (Protogonyaulax) catenella* Whedon and Kofoid. This microscopic dinoflagellate is ingested by a variety of shellfish and has been incriminated as a causative agent of paralytic shellfish poisoning. Paralytic shellfish poison is a complex substance and is extremely toxic to humans. One must be careful about eating shellfish wherever this organism is found. Fortunately, the problem of shellfish poisoning is under careful surveillance by most public health agencies involved. It inhabits the Pacific coast of North America, Japan, the northern coast of South America. Enlarged x 1,350.

(R. Kreuzinger)

**PLATE 270.** Poisonous dinoflagellate, *Gonyaulax (Protogonyaulax) tamarensis* Lebour. This microscopic dinoflagellate has also been incriminated in paralytic shellfish poisoning. It inhabits the eastern coast of North America and Europe. Enlarged x 1,350.

(R. Kreuzinger)

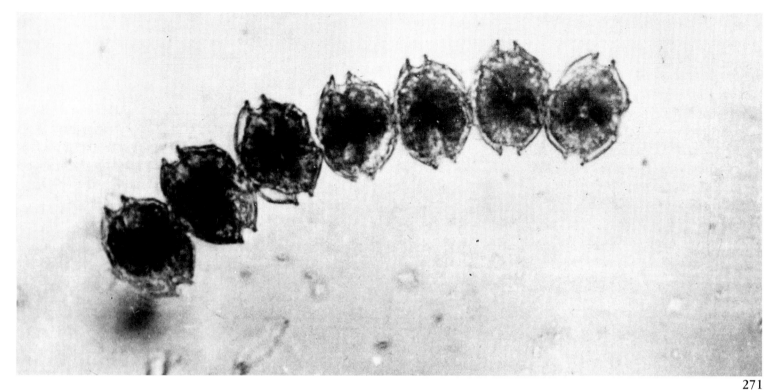

271

PLATE 271. Photomicrograph of living specimens of *Gonyaulax catenella* Whedon and Kofoid in a typical chain formation. Taken from a culture. Enlarged x 500. (H. Sommer, courtesy of K. F. Myer, George Williams Hooper Foundation)

PLATE 272a–d. Electron micrographs of poisonous dinoflagellates.

a. *Gymnodinium (Ptychodiscus) breve* Davis. May cause severe allergies when present in windblown sprays and neurotoxic shellfish poisoning. (Courtesy K. Steidinger, Florida Department of Natural Resources)

b. *Gonyaulax (Protogonyaulax) catenella* Whedon and Kofoid. From Owase Bay, Mie Prefecture, Japan. Enlarged x 1,800.

c. *Gonyaulax (Protogonyaulax) tamarensis* Lebour. From Lynher River, England. Enlarged x 2,200. (Courtesy A. R. Loeblich III and L. A. Loeblich)

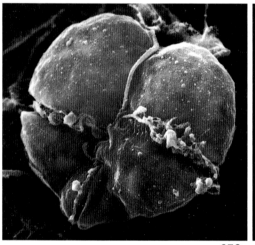
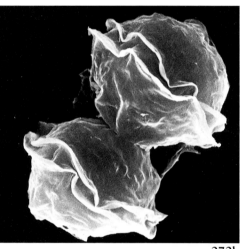
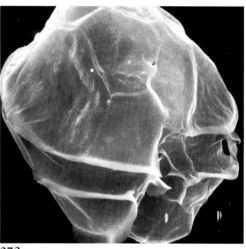

272a    272b 272c    272d

d. A spectacular example of a red tide caused by *Noctiluca scintilans* (McCartney) in Lake Macquarie, New South Wales, Australia. Toxic dinoflagellate red tides can cause mass mortality of fishes and may be lethal to humans. (Courtesy B. Magrath)

PLATE 273a, b. Anatomy of shellfish involved in paralytic shellfish poisoning.

a. Internal anatomy of the mussel *Mytilus*, showing parts of the body of the shellfish likely to contain paralytic shellfish poison.

b. Internal anatomy of the clam *Saxidomus*, showing parts of the body of the shellfish likely to contain paralytic shellfish poison. In certain parts of Alaska, the butter clam, *Saxidomus*, may be poisonous the year round, whereas in most other parts of the world paralytic shellfish poisoning tends to be seasonal. (R. Kreuzinger)

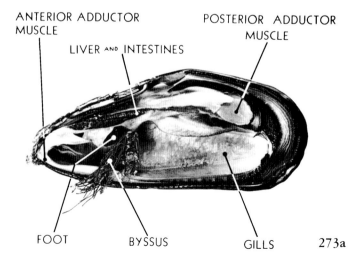

ANTERIOR ADDUCTOR MUSCLE
LIVER AND INTESTINES
POSTERIOR ADDUCTOR MUSCLE
FOOT
BYSSUS
GILLS
273a

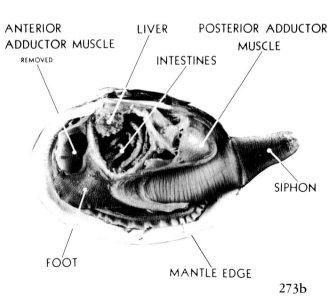

ANTERIOR ADDUCTOR MUSCLE REMOVED
LIVER
INTESTINES
POSTERIOR ADDUCTOR MUSCLE
SIPHON
FOOT
MANTLE EDGE
273b

PLATE 274a–h. Representative series of shellfish involved in paralytic shellfish poisoning:

**a.** Solid surf clam, *Spisula solidissima* (Dillwyn). Occurs from Labrador to North Carolina. x 0.4.

**b.** Soft-shelled clam, *Mya arenaria* Linnaeus. Inhabits Britain, Scandinavia, Greenland, the Atlantic coast of North America south to the Carolinas, Alaska south to Japan and to Vancouver, British Columbia, and the California and Oregon coasts. x 0.2.

**c.** Common mussel, *Mytilus californianus* Conrad. Inhabits Unalaska, Aleutian Islands, eastward and southward to Socorro Island. x 0.3.

**d.** Bay mussel, *Mytilus edulis* Linnaeus. Ranges from the Arctic Ocean to South Carolina, Alaska to Cape San Lucas, Baja California; practically worldwide in temperate waters. x 0.9.

**e.** Northern horse mussel, *Modiolus modiolus* (Linnaeus). Ranges from the Gulf of St. Lawrence River to Florida. x 0.4.

**f.** Rock cockle or common little neck, *Protothaca staminea* (Conrad). Ranges from the Aleutian Islands to Cape San Lucas, Baja California. x 0.8.

**g.** Alaskan butter clam, smooth Washington, or butter clam, *Saxidomus giganteus* (Deshayes). Ranges from Sitka, Alaska to San Francisco Bay, California. x 0.3. (R. Kreuzinger, courtesy S. S. Berry)

**h.** Common Washington or butter clam, *Saxidomus nuttalli* Conrad. Ranges from Humboldt Bay, California, to San Quentin Bay, Baja California.

274a–h

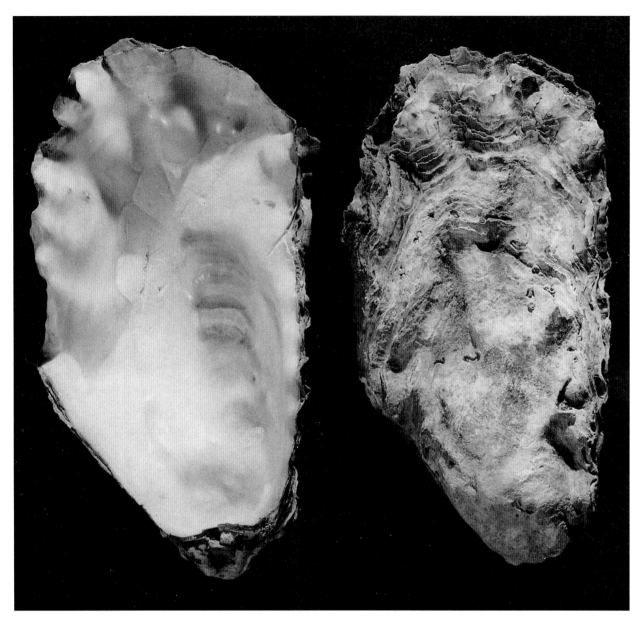

**PLATE 275.** Japanese oyster, *Crassostrea gigas* (Thunberg). This oyster has been known to be poisonous in certain localities in Japan due to the ingestion of a poisonous dinoflagellate, *Prorocentrum mariae-lebouriae,* which it feeds upon. Length up to 25 centimeters (9.7 inches). Causes venerupin poisoning.

(R. Kreuzinger, courtesy S. S. Berry)

**PLATE 276.** Asari, *Tapes semidecussata* Reeve. The asari may become poisonous from feeding on the poisonous dinoflagellate *Prorocentrum mariae-lebouriae.* Ingestion of the asari may cause venerupin poisoning in some areas of Japan. Length 5 centimeters (2 inches). Symptoms of venerupin poisoning may consist of severe gastrointenstinal upset, anemia, halitosis, jaundice, and other evidence of liver damage. It may be fatal. (R. Kreuzinger, courtesy S. S. Berry)

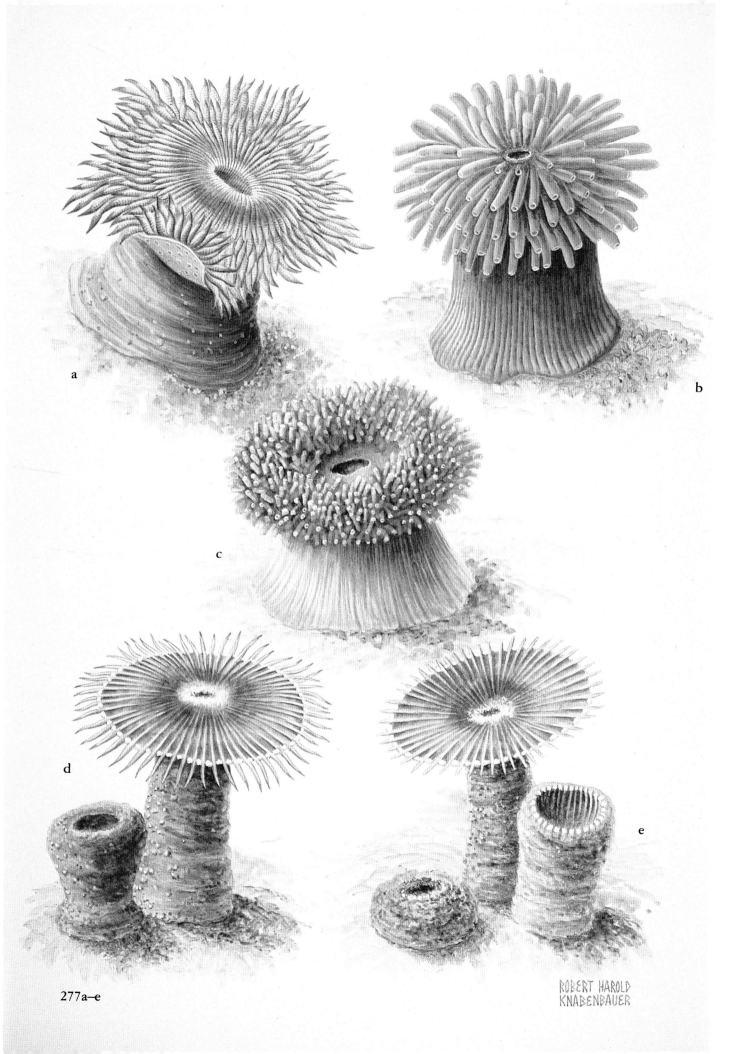

PLATE 277a–e. Poisonous sea anemones and soft corals:

a. Poisonous sea anemone, *Radianthus paumotensis* (Dana). This sea anemone is safe to eat when cooked, but may be poisonous when eaten raw. It has caused fatalities in children in Samoa. Found in the tropical Indo-Pacific. Diameter 8 centimeters (3.2 inches).

b. Poisonous sea anemone, *Physobrachia douglasi* Kent. It is said to be safe to eat when cooked but poisonous raw. Found in the tropical Indo-Pacific. Diameter 5 centimeters (2 inches).

c. Poisonous sea anemone, *Rhodactis howesi* Kent. This species is safe to eat when cooked, but there are some closely related species that are poisonous to eat either raw or cooked. Diameter 7 centimeters (2.5 inches).

d. Poisonous soft coral, *Palythoa toxica* Walsh and Bowers. The members of the genus *Palythoa* contain the deadly palytoxin, one of the most poisonous substances known. The poison is not released by the stinging nematocysts, but appears to be produced in the tissues of the anemone.

e. Poisonous soft coral, *Palythoa tuberculosa* Esper. A species closely related to *P. toxica*, *P. tuberculosa* is widely distributed throughout tropical seas. The diameter of the disk is 9 centimeters (3 inches).

(R. H. Knabenbauer)

277a–e

ROBERT HAROLD
KNABENBAUER

PLATE 278a, b. Close-up showing beds of *Rhodactis howesi* Kent. The size of the anemone can be determined by comparing it with the man's hand.

(Courtesy E. J. Martin)

PLATE 279a, b. Poisonous soft coral, *Palythoa* (species undetermined). *Palythoa* contains the deadly palytoxin. The effects on humans are not known, but there is a possible detrimental effect on the immune system. Palytoxin has been found to have neurotoxic and cardiotoxic effects in laboratory animals.

    a. Taken in an aquarium.

       (Courtesy Sea World, San Diego, California)

    b. Taken in an aquarium in New Caledonia.

(Courtesy R. Catala,
Aquarium de Noumea, New Caledonia)

278a

278b

279a

279b

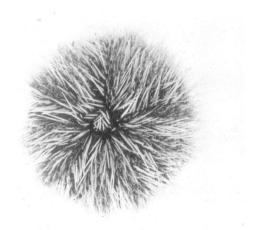

281a
281b

280

PLATE 280. Poisonous European sea urchin, *Paracentrotus lividus* Lamarck. The pedicellariae of this sea urchin are venomous, and the gonads contain a poison that produces paralysis, convulsions, and death in laboratory animals. The effects of the poison on humans are unknown. The diameter of the test is 7 centimeters (2.7 inches). Color varies from a deep violet to green. Living specimen taken at the Zoological Society of Naples, Italy.          (Courtesy P. Giacomelli)

PLATE 281a, b. White sea urchin, or poisonous West Indian sea urchin, *Tripneustes ventricosus* (Lamarck). The eggs of this sea urchin may be poisonous to eat, causing severe gastrointestinal disturbances, pain, nausea, vomiting, and diarrhea. However, at times, the eggs are eaten without ill effect and sold as "white sea eggs." The eggs are said to be safe to eat during September through April. Living specimen taken at the Bermuda Biological Station.          (G. Lower)

**PLATE 282a–j.** Representative group of poisonous sea cucumbers. All of the sea cucumbers illustrated here have been found to contain holothurin, a toxic saponin. Visceral liquid ejected by some sea cucumbers may produce a skin rash or blindness if it contacts the eyes. Although some of the sea cucumbers are commonly eaten in certain areas, eating them should be done with a degree of caution.

a. *Afrocucumis africana* (Semper). Japan. Length 8 centimeters (3.1 inches).

(H. Baerg, after Kuroda and Uchida; Utinomi)

b. *Stichopus japonicus* Selenka. Japan. Length 40 centimeters (15.7 inches). (H. Baerg, after Utinomi)

c. *Holothuria vagabunda* Selenka. Tropical western Pacific. (H. Baerg, after Kuroda and Uchida)

d. *Paracaudina chilensis* (Von Marenzeller). Japan. Length 20 centimeters (8 inches).

(H. Baerg, after Utinomi)

e. *Thelenota ananas* (Jaeger). Japan. Length 75 centimeters (29.5 inches). (H. Baerg, after Utinomi)

f. *Holothuria monocaria* Lesson. Japan. Length 40 centimeters (15.7 inches).

(H. Baerg, after Fisheries Society of Japan)

g. *Stichopus japonicus* Selenka. Japan. Length 30 centimeters (12 inches).

H. Baerg, after Fisheries Society of Japan)

h. *Pentacta australia* (Ludwig). Japan, Length 8 centimeters (3 inches). (H. Baerg, after Utinomi)

i. *Holothuria impatiens* (Forskål). Australia. Length 40 centimeters (15.7 inches).

(H. Baerg, after Clark)

j. *Cucumaria japonica* Semper. Japan. Length 20 centimeters (8 inches).

(H. Baerg, after Fisheries Society of Japan)

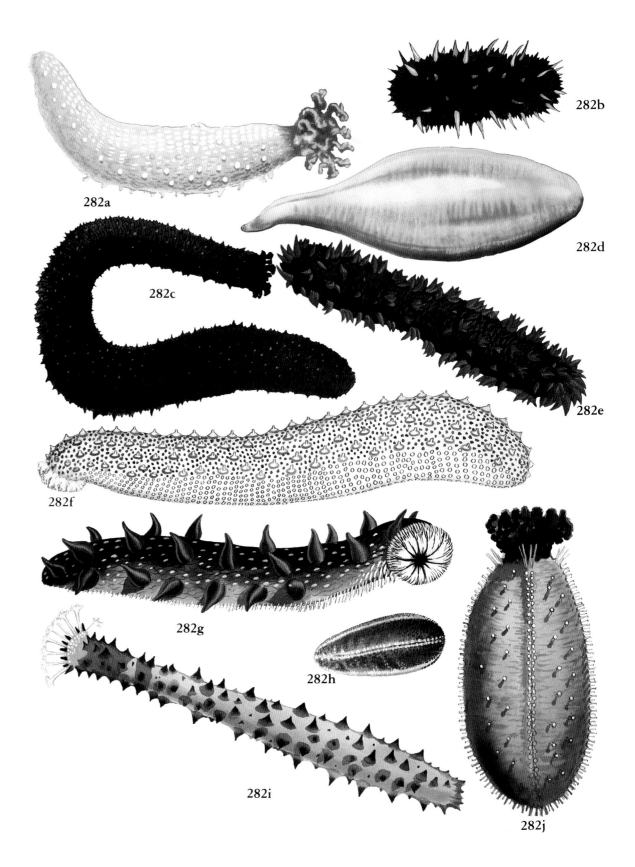

282a 282b 282c 282d 282e 282f 282g 282h 282i 282j

PLATE 283a, b, c. Asiatic horseshoe crab, *Carcinoscorpius rotundicauda* (Latreille). The flesh, viscera, and eggs of this horseshoe crab may be extremely toxic to eat during the reproductive season of the year. Tropical Indo-Pacific, southeast Asia. a) Side, b) dorsal, and c) ventral views of the adult male. Total length 33 centimeters (13 inches). From the collection of the Osborn Zoological Laboratory, Yale University.

(Courtesy H. Waterman)

PLATE 284. Coconut crab, *Birgus latero* (Linnaeus). This crab may be poisonous in certain localities. Poisoning resembles ciguatera fish poisoning. Tropical Indo-Pacific. Length of carapace 11 centimeters (4.2 inches) or more.          (M. Shirao)

PLATE 285. Poisonous reef crab, *Atergatis floridus* (Linnaeus). This crab may be extremely poisonous to eat. The poison within the crab is believed to be chemically identical to tetrodotoxin, which is found in puffer fish. Tropical Indo-Pacific. Width of carapace 5 centimeters (2 inches) or more.          (M. Shiaro)

PLATE 286. Red spotted crab, *Carpilius maculatus* (Linnaeus). This crab has caused the death of several persons who have eaten it. Tropical Indo-Pacific. Width of carapace 14 centimeters (5.5 inches).

(From Guinot)

PLATE 287. Poisonous reef crab, *Demania toxica* Garth. This crab has been responsible for the deaths of several persons who have eaten it. Tropical Indo-Pacific. Width of carapace 43 millimeters (1.7 inches).

(From Garth)

PLATE 288. Poisonous reef crab, *Eriphia sebana* (Shaw and Nodder). It may cause death when eaten. Indo-Pacific. Width of carapace 3.5 centimeters (1.3 inches).          (M. Shirao)

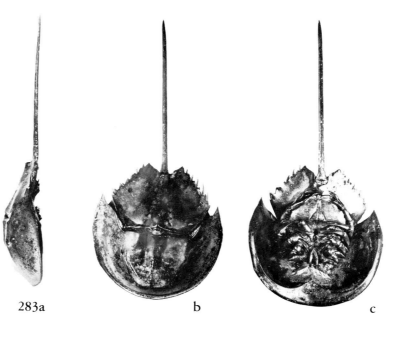

283a                    b                    c

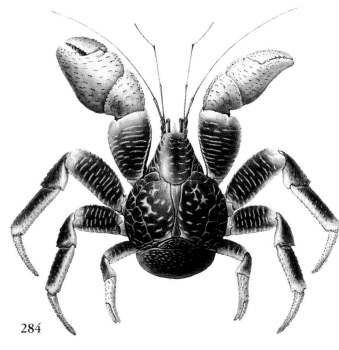

284

285

286

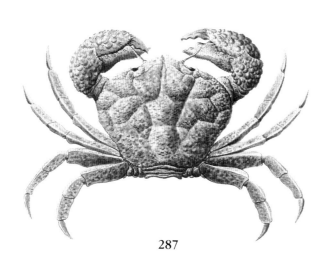

287

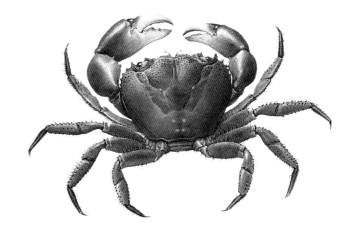

288

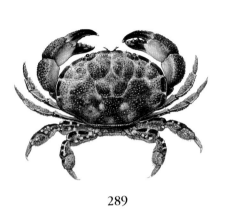

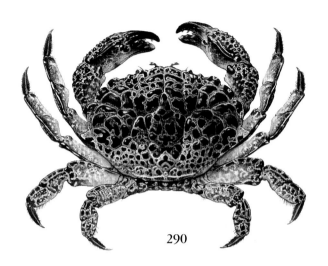

289

290

291

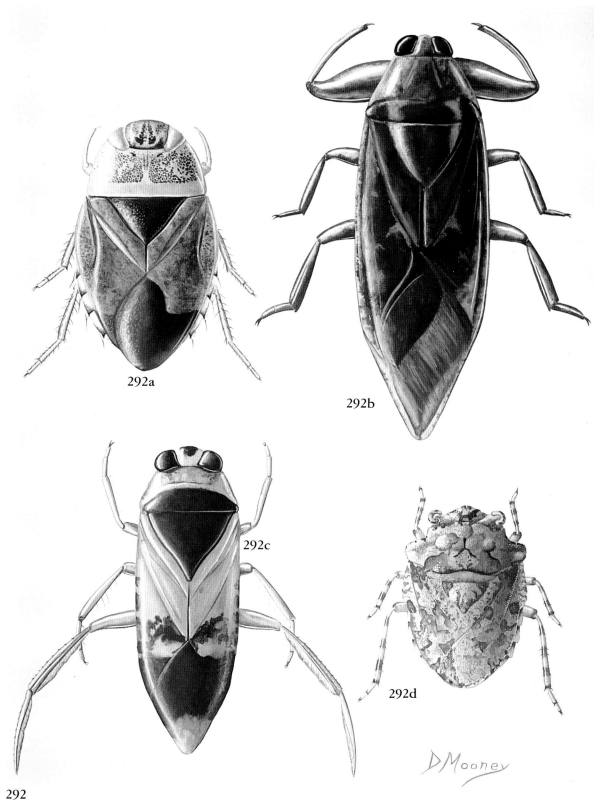

292a

292b

292c

292d

292

D.Mooney

293

294

295

296

PLATE 296. Nemertean worm, *Drepanophorus crassus* (Quatrefages). Two toxic substances from the tissues of this worm, "amphiporine" and "nemertine," have had effects on laboratory animals. Length 14 centimeters (5.5 inches). (H. Baerg, after Lang)

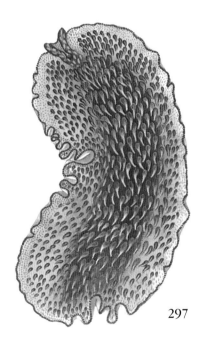

297

PLATE 297. Turbellarian worm, *Thysanozoon brocchi* Grube. The European turbellarians secrete a toxic substance believed to be produced by their rhabdoids and certain poison glands, although little is known about the nature of the poison or its effects on humans. Length 60 millimeters (1.5 inches). (H. Baerg, after Lang)

# CHAPTER VI

# Poisonous Aquatic Animals—Vertebrates

THIS CHAPTER INCLUDES all toxic aquatic animals having a backbone that are poisonous to eat, namely, poisonous fishes, amphibians, reptiles, and marine mammals; they are categorized as follows:

## POISONOUS FISHES

This section includes fishes that when ingested cause biotoxications.

## ICHTHYOSARCOTOXIC FISHES

Those fishes that contain a poison within the flesh (i.e., in the broadest sense), musculature, viscera, skin, or slime, which when ingested by humans will produce a biotoxication.

### Lampreys, Hagfishes
### (Cyclostome Poisoning)

CLASS AGNATHA—Lampreys and hagfishes that cause *cyclostome poisoning*.

### Toxic Sharks, Rays, Chimaeras
### (Elasmobranch Poisoning)

CLASS CHONDRICHTHYES—Sharks, rays, and chimaeras that cause poisoning as a result of one's eating their flesh or viscera. The poisoning is sometimes referred to as *elasmobranch poisoning* when involving sharks or rays or as *chimaera poisoning* when involving ratfishes (chimaeras).

CLASS OSTEICHTHYES—The true bony fishes, including a wide range of species having poisonous flesh, gonads, or other viscera:

### Ciguatoxic Fishes

About 400 species of poisonous marine tropical reef fishes have been incriminated as ciguatoxic. Only a few representative species are shown in this *Atlas*. The intoxication, ciguatera, is caused by a complex nerve poison known as *ciguatoxin*.

### Clupeotoxic Fishes

This group includes some of the herrings, anchovies, and related species. Apparently, the fish become poisonous after eating certain planktonic organisms. The poison appears to resemble paralytic shellfish poison, but its chemical nature is unknown.

### Gempylotoxic Fishes

This group includes the gempylid fishes, otherwise known as the escolars, or pelagic mackerels. They contain an oil resembling castor oil, which has a very pronounced purgative effect.

### Scombrotoxic Fishes

This group involves intoxications resulting from inadequately preserved scombroid fishes, i.e., tunas, skipjack, mackerels, albacore, and related species. The poison, *histamine*, develops in the flesh of the fish due to bacterial activity on the musculature.

### Hallucinogenic Fishes

A group of tropical reef fishes whose flesh produces hallucinations; however, no fatalities have been reported. The nature of the poison is unknown.

### Tetrodotoxic Fishes

This group includes the puffer fishes and is commonly known as puffer poisoning. This is one of the most violent forms of fish poisoning and carries a high degree of lethality. The poison is known as *tetrodotoxin*.

### Ichthyootoxic Fishes

Many freshwater and a few saltwater species develop a poison within their gonads, particularly during the reproductive period of the year, just before spawning. This is sometimes referred to as fish roe poisoning. There is a definite relationship between gonadal activity and toxin production. The nature of the poison is known only in a few instances.

### Ichthyohemotoxic Fishes

This group includes fishes having poisonous blood. Intoxications are quite rare because the poison is destroyed by gastric juices and heat. The nature of the poison is unknown.

## ICHTHYOCRINOTOXIC FISHES

This second major category of toxic fishes includes those species that release a poison through their skin by means of specialized secretory organs. This includes the soapfish and trunkfishes, as well as some puffers and toadfish. No venom apparatus is involved.

## *OTHER POISONOUS VERTEBRATES*

## AMPHIBIANS

Some amphibians produce extremely violent poisons:

Toxic Salamanders or Newts
Toxic Frogs and Toads

## REPTILES

Some species of marine turtles may become poisonous as a result of feeding on toxic marine plants; the exact source and nature of the poison is unknown.

## MARINE MAMMALS

The livers of some marine mammals—whales, dolphins, and porpoises; polar bears; walruses, seals, and sea lions—may be toxic to eat.

\* \* \* \* \* \*

## *POISONOUS FISHES*

This section includes those fishes that, when ingested, cause an intoxication. The poisons of these fishes are contracted as a result of the feeding habits of the fish, or because of certain adverse conditions in the preservation of the fish (scombroid fish poisoning). It does not include those conditions in which there has been accidental bacterial food poisoning. These marine biotoxins are naturally occurring poisons derived directly from marine organisms.

## ICHTHYOSARCOTOXIC FISHES

Included within this group are those fishes that contain a poison within the flesh (includes muscle, viscera, skin, and even slime). Tropical reef fishes contain some of the most violent poisons known to science. One of the most striking features of this form of poisoning is the wide phylogenetic range of organisms involved and the spectacular array of fish species. A complex of poisons are found in ichthyosarcotoxic fishes.

### Lampreys, Hagfishes
### (Cyclostome Poisoning)

CLASS AGNATHA

The slime and flesh of certain lampreys and hagfishes are reported to produce gastrointestinal disturbances, nausea, vomiting, and diarrhea. The nature of the poison is unknown.

The cyclostomes include the hagfishes and lampreys. These fish-like vertebrates are unique since they have only a cartilaginous or fibrous skeleton, no definite jaws or bony teeth, and a cranium of a primitive type. They are considered the most primitive of true vertebrates. They have 6–14 pairs of gill pouches opening directly into the pharynx or into a separate respiratory tube. Only a single nostril is present. The skin is scaleless. Examples of this group include:

RIVER LAMPREY, *Lampetra fluviatilis* (Linnaeus) (298), of the Baltic and North Sea basins. Length 36 centimeters (14 inches).

ATLANTIC HAGFISH, *Myxine glutinosa* Linnaeus (299), of the North Atlantic. Length 79 centimeters (31 inches).

## Toxic Sharks, Rays, Chimaeras (Elasmobranch Poisoning)

### CLASS CHONDRICHTHYES

This form of ichthyosarcotoxism is most commonly caused by eating shark livers and the flesh of some tropical sharks, but the Greenland shark, *Somniosus microcephalus*, which inhabits arctic waters, has caused intoxications in humans and sled dogs. The chemical nature of these shark poisons is unknown.

The most severe forms of poisoning usually result from eating the liver. The musculature in most instances is only mildly toxic, with diarrhea and other symptoms resembling a mild gastrointestinal upset. Symptoms from liver poisoning usually develop within 30 minutes and consist of nausea, vomiting, diarrhea, abdominal pain, headache, joint aches, tingling about the mouth, and a burning sensation of the tongue, throat, and esophagus. As time goes on, the symptoms involving the nervous system may become progressively severe, resulting in muscular incoordination and difficulty in breathing due to muscular paralysis, coma, and finally death. Ciguatoxin may also be involved in some shark poisonings.

Avoid eating the liver of any shark unless it is known with certainty to be edible. The livers of large tropical sharks are said to be especially dangerous. The flesh of tropical and arctic sharks should be indulged in only with caution. These is no specific treatment available.

The following sharks are only a few representative species reported as poisonous to man:

GREAT WHITE SHARK, *Carcharodon carcharias* (Linnaeus) (Chapter II, 2, 3, 4). Cosmopolitan distribu-tion: tropical, subtropical, and warm-temperate belts of all oceans.

BLACKTIP REEF SHARK, *Carcharhinus melanopterus* (Quoy and Gaimard) (Chapter II, 14). The flesh and liver of this species may be toxic. Found in the tropical Indo-Pacific region. Length 2 meters (6.5 feet).

SEVEN-GILLED SHARK, *Heptranchus perlo* (Bonnaterre) (300). Atlantic, Mediterranean, South Africa, and Japan. Length 2 meters (6.3 feet).

SIX-GILLED SHARK, *Hexanchus grisseus* (Bonnaterre) (301). Atlantic, Pacific coast of North America, Chile, Japan, Australia, southern Indian Ocean, and South Africa. Length 5 meters (15.5 feet).

GREENLAND SHARK, *Somniosus microcephalus* (Bloch and Schneider) (302). Arctic Atlantic, North Sea east to the White Sea and west to the Gulf of St. Lawrence, Greenland. Length 2 meters (6.3 feet).

HAMMERHEAD SHARK, *Sphyrna zygaena* (Linnaeus) (Chapter II, 20). Tropical to warm temperate belt of the Atlantic and Pacific Oceans. Length 4 meters (14 feet).

The musculature and viscera of some of the ratfishes, or chimaeras, have been found to be toxic, but the nature of the poison and its effects in humans are not known. An example of this group of fishes is:

EUROPEAN RATFISH, *Chimaera monstrosa* Linnaeus (Chapter IV, 187), which inhabits the North Atlantic and Mediterranean Sea. Length 1 meter (39 inches).

### CLASS OSTEICHTHYES

#### Ciguatoxic Fishes

These fishes harbor one of the most serious and widespread forms of ichthyosarcotoxism. Biotoxication is caused largely by tropical shorefishes, with more than 400 species incriminated. Because many of the toxic species are generally regarded as valuable food, ciguatoxic fish constitute a serious threat to the development of tropical shore fisheries. In many instances, useful food fishes suddenly, and without warning, become poisonous within a matter of hours and may remain toxic for a period of years or decades. Fishes become poisonous because they have been feeding upon some noxious material such as toxic algae, invertebrates, other fishes, or dinoflagellates.

The diagram (Figure 1) depicts the biogenesis, or transvector mechanism, by which ciguatoxin is obtained through the food chain. There is now evidence that a dinoflagellate (*Gambierdiscus toxicus* Adachi and Fukuyo) frequently found on the surface of a benthic brown seaweed (*Turbinaria ornata* J. Agardh), and other algae species, may produce ciguatoxin (Figure 2). This dinoflagellate, and possibly other species as well, may

serve as the primary source of ciguatoxin. These dinoflagellates may be ingested by filter-feeding invertebrates, plankton-feeding fishes, herbivorous fishes feeding on marine plants, and indirectly by carnivorous fishes feeding on herbivorous fishes. It is evident that the source of ciguatoxin is due to a complex food web involvement in which a variety of environmental factors play a role. The food web interactions account for the widespread phylogenetic distribution of ciguatoxin among marine animals. Ciguatera is most prevalent in subtropical and tropical latitudes, but the greatest concentration of ciguatoxic fishes seems to be around islands in the Caribbean, tropical Pacific, and Indian oceans. Ciguatoxin is one of the most potent marine poisons, and may involve other poisons, such as maitotoxin and scaritoxin.

Symptoms of ciguatera poisoning consist of paresthesias (or numbness) of the lips, tongue, and limbs and gastrointestinal distrurbances. Victims frequently complain of myalgia (joint aches) and profound muscular weakness. The so-called paradoxical sensory disturbance in which the victim interprets cold as "tingling, burning, dry-ice, or electric-shock sensation," or hot objects as cold, is characteristic of this form of poisoning. Severe neurological disturbances consisting of ataxia (generalized motor incoordination), diminished reflexes, muscular twitching, tremors, dysphagia, clonic and tonic convulsions, coma, and muscular paralysis may be present. The case fatality rate is said to be about twelve percent. Complete recovery may require many months, and even years in some cases.

Clupeoid fishes (such as anchovies and herrings) have been known to cause violent poisonings at sporadic intervals in the Caribbean Sea, tropical Atlantic, and Pacific and Indian oceans. It is believed that clupeoid fishes contract the poison from eating dinoflagellates. (*See* section on Clupeotoxic Fishes, pp. 156–57 for further details.) The relationship of clupeotoxism to ciguatera fish poisoning, if any, has not been determined since nothing is known concerning the nature of clupeotoxin.

One cannot detect a poisonous fish by its appearance. Moreover, there is no known simple chemical test

Figure 1. Diagram showing the transvector mechanism by which ciguatoxin is spread through the food chain and finally affects man. The poison is produced by the dinoflagellate *Gambierdiscus toxicus*, which adheres to the brown alga *Turbinaria ornata*, which in turn is ingested by a fish. (*See also* Figure 2.)

(R. H. Knabenbauer)

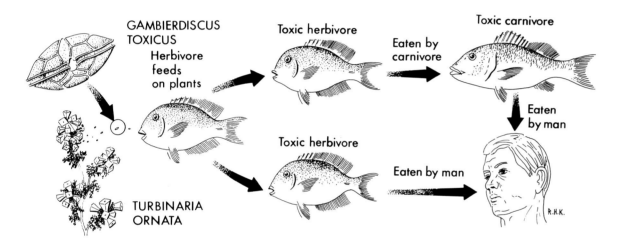

Figure 2. *Gambierdiscus toxicus* Adachi and Fukuyo, with the brown alga *Turbinaria ornata* J. Agardh.

(R. H. Knabenbauer)

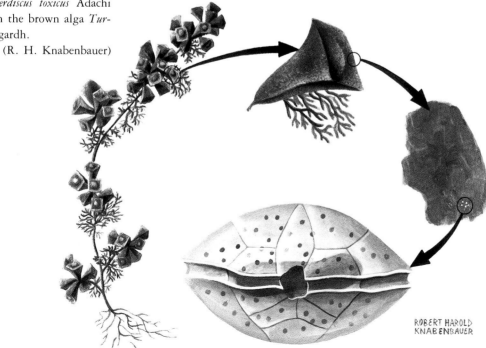

to detect the poison. However, an enzyme immunoassay has now been developed that appears to be a reliable method of detecting ciguatoxin. Another reliable method involves the preparation of tissue extracts, which are injected into mice, or feeding samples of the viscera and flesh to cats or dogs, and observing the animal for the development of toxic symptoms. The viscera—liver and intestines—of tropical marine fishes should *never* be eaten. Also, the roe of most marine fishes is potentially dangerous, and in some cases may produce rapid death. Fishes unusually large for their size should not be eaten. This is particularly true for barracuda (*Sphyraena*), jacks (*Caranx*), and grouper (*Epinephelus*) during their reproductive seasons. Do not eat moray eels. Even some of the "safe" species may at times be violently poisonous.

If one is living under survival conditions, and questionable fishes must be eaten, it is advisable to cut the fish into thin fillets and to soak the fillets in several changes of water—fresh or salt—for at least 30 minutes. Do not use the rinse water for cooking purposes. This may serve to leach out the poison, which is somewhat water-soluble. If a questionable species is cooked by boiling, the water should always be discarded. It must be emphasized that ordinary cooking procedures do not destroy or significantly weaken the poison. The advice of native people on eating tropical marine fishes is sometimes conflicting and erroneous, particularly if they have not lived within a particular region over a period of time. Nevertheless, one should always check with the local peoples as to the edibility of fish products in any tropical island area. Keep in mind that an edible fish in one region may be deadly poisonous in another.

The following is a representative list of tropical insular fishes that have been incriminated in human outbreaks of ciguatera fish poisoning. They are arranged alphabetically according to the scientific name of the fish family. A brief commentary on the biology of each group is also presented.

## Surgeonfishes or Tangs

Family ACANTHURIDAE: Surgeonfishes or tangs are a group of shore fishes inhabiting warm seas.

The principal genus, *Acanthurus*, is characterized by the presence of a sharp, lance-like, moveable spine, located on each side of the caudal peduncle, at the tail. Surgeonfishes are particularly common in surge channels and shoal areas in the vicinity of coral patch reefs. They are predominantly herbivores, feeding mostly on fine filamentous algae of numerous species. Most surgeonfishes are small to moderate in size. The eggs and larvae of at least some species are pelagic.

SURGEONFISH, *Acanthurus glaucopareius* Cuvier (303). Tropical Indo-Pacific. Length 30 centimeters (12 inches).

STRIPED SURGEONFISH, *Acanthurus lineatus* (Linnaeus) (304). Tropical Indo-Pacific. Length 30 cen- (12 inches).

CONVICT SURGEONFISH, TANG, *Acanthurus triostegus* (Linnaeus) (305). Tropical Indo-Pacific. Length 26 centimeters (10 inches).

SURGEONFISH, TANG, *Acanturus xanthopterus* (Cuvier and Valenciennes) (306). Tropical Indo-Pacific. Length 35 centimeters (14 inches).

COMMON BRISTLE-TOOTHED TANG, *Ctenochaetus striatus* (Quoy and Gaimard) (307). Tropical Indo-Pacific. Length 20 centimeters (8 inches).

UNICORNFISH, *Naso lituratus* Bloch and Schneider (Chapter IV, 238). Tropical Indo-Pacific. Length 38 centimeters (15 inches).

## Filefishes

Family ALUTERIDAE: Filefishes are a group of small-sized, shallow-water shore fishes of temperate and tropical seas characterized by compressed lean bodies covered by shagreen-like prickles. The musculature is generally too meager to make these fishes useful as food. However, some natives do skin and eat them. The flesh is considered to be dry, bitter, and offensive to the taste. Filefishes are omnivorous, but frequently make a meal of a single item if available in sufficient quantity. Corals appear to be their main dietary item.

UNICORN FILEFISH, *Alutera monoceros* (Linnaeus) (308). All warm seas. Length 30 centimeters (12 inches).

SCRAWLED FILEFISH, *Alutera scripta* (Osbeck) (309). All warm seas. Length 50 centimeters (20 inches).

## Triggerfishes

Family BALISTIDAE: Triggerfishes are a group of small to moderate-sized shore fishes, characterized by their deep compressed body covered with a thick layer of enlarged bony scales. The first two dorsal spines are modified into a trigger-like device. Triggerfishes are widely distributed throughout all warm seas. They seem to prefer shallow reef areas, although some are found in fairly deep water. They are omnivorous in their eating habits, ingesting corals, sponges, urchins, algae, and various other small organisms. Despite their slow swimming movement, they travel long distances by floating with the currents. Some species bite eagerly on almost any bait, whereas others are difficult to take.

UNDULATED TRIGGERFISH, *Balistapus undulatus* (Mungo Park) (310). Tropical Indo-Pacific. Length 35 centimeters (14 inches).

BOAR TRIGGERFISH, *Balistes capriscus* (Gmelin) (311). Tropical Atlantic and Mediterranean Sea. Length 50 centimeters (20 inches).

OLD WOMAN TRIGGERFISH, *Balistes vetula* Linnaeus (312). Tropical Atlantic, Mediterranean Sea, and Indian Ocean. Length 38 centimeters (15 inches).

CLOWN TRIGGERFISH, *Balistoides conspicillum* Bloch and Schneider (313). Tropical Indo-Pacific and Red Sea. Length 35 centimeters (14 inches).

TRIGGERFISH, *Melichthys buniva* (Lacépède) (314). Tropical Indo-Pacific. Length 35 centimeters (14 inches).

BLACK TRIGGERFISH, *Odonus niger* (Rüppell) (315). Tropical Indo-Pacific, Red Sea. Length 30 centimeters (12 inches).

YELLOW-MARGINED TRIGGERFISH, *Pseudobalistes flavimarginatus* (Rüppell) (316). Tropical Indo-Pacific and Red Sea. Length 30 centimeters (12 inches).

PAINTED TRIGGERFISH, *Rhinecanthus aculeatus* (Linnaeus) (317). Tropical Indo-Pacific. Length 30 centimeters (12 inches).

RECTANGULAR TRIGGERFISH, *Rhinecanthus rectangulus* (Bloch) (318). Tropical Indo-Pacific. Length 20 centimeters (8 inches).

## Jacks, Scads, Pompanos

Family CARANGIDAE: Jacks, scads, and pompanos are a large group of swift-swimming, oceanic fishes, which are cosmopolitan in distribution. They are particularly common in the vicinity of coral reefs. Some of the Pacific species are especially noted for their long migrations in quest of food. They are mostly carnivorous in their eating habits. Many are desirable game fishes, and most of them are valued as food.

CREVALLE or JACK, *Caranx bartholomaei* Cuvier and Valenciennes (319). West Indies, northward to North Carolina. Length 38 centimeters (15 inches).

CREVALLE or JACK, *Caranx hippos* (Linnaeus) (320). Tropical Atlantic. Length 75 centimeters (29.5 inches).

JACK, *Caranx ignobilis* (Forskål) (321). Tropical Indo-Pacific. Length 75 centimeters (29.5 inches).

HORSE-EYE JACK, *Caranx latus* Agassiz (322). Tropical western Atlantic. Length 90 centimeters (35.5 inches).

BLACK JACK, *Caranx lugubris* Poey (323). Circumtropical in distribution. Length 60 centimeters (23.5 inches).

BLUE CREVALLE or JACK, *Caranx melampygus* Cuvier (324). Tropical Indo-Pacific. Length 65 centimeters (25.5 inches).

SIX-BANDED JACK, *Caranx sexfasciatus* (Quoy and Gaimard) (325). Tropical Indo-Pacific. Length 50 centimeters (19.5 inches).

RAINBOW RUNNER, *Elagatis bipinnulatus* (Quoy and Gaimard) (326). Circumtropical in distribution. Length 65 centimeters (25.5 inches).

LEATHERJACKET, *Scomberoides lysan* (Forskål) (formerly *S. sanctipetri*) (Chapter IV, 254). Tropical Indo-Pacific, Red Sea, East Africa. Length 65 centimeters (25.5 inches).

BIGEYE SCAD, *Selar crumenopthalmus* (Bloch) (327). Atlantic coast of tropical America. Length 60 centimeters (23.5 inches).

GREATER AMBERJACK, YELLOWTAIL, *Seriola dumerili* (Risso) (328). Tropical Indo-Pacific, Mediterrean Sea to West Indies. Length 90 centimeters (35.5 inches).

ALMACO JACK, *Seriola falcata* Valenciennes (329). West Indies, north to the Carolinas. Length 30 centimeters (12 inches).

## Butterfly Fishes

Family CHAETODONTIDAE: Butterflyfishes are among the most colorful reef inhabitants. They are most common in the warm waters of the West Indies and Pacific Ocean. Butterflyfishes are usually found around tidal pools, coral reefs, and lagoons, and at depths greater than 4 or 5 fathoms. The species are varied in their coloration, with yellow and black predominating, and are small in size. Their body is compressed and deep. Despite their morphology they are able to move about with great rapidity when frightened. Their diet is varied—largely animal, consisting of worms, small gastropods, sponges, and the polyps of a variety of coelenterates, which they easily remove with their brush-like teeth. Although most butterflyfishes are edible, few are considered of food value because of their small size.

THREADFIN BUTTERFLYFISH, *Chaetodon auriga* Forskål (330). Tropical Indo-Pacific, Red Sea. Length 16 centimeters (6.5 inches).

RETICULATED BUTTERFLYFISH, *Chaetodon reticulatus* Cuvier (331). Indo-Pacific, India, China, and Japan. Length 15 centimeters (6 inches).

LONGFIN BANNERFISH, *Heniochus acuminatus* (Linnaeus) (332). Tropical Indo-Pacific, India, Japan, Red Sea.

EMPEROR ANGELFISH, *Pomacanthus imperator* (Bloch) (333). Indo-Pacific, Red Sea, Zanzibar. Length 35 centimeters (14 inches).

## Dolphins (Dorads), Halfbeaks

Family CORYPHAENIDAE: Dolphins are large, fast-swimming, beautifully colored, predatory, oceanic fishes, found in all warm seas. They are usually observed swimming near the surface of the water and may enter bays and inlets. The flesh is fine-flavored, and they are an excellent game fish. They are carnivorous in their feeding habits.

DOLPHIN, *Coryphaena hippurus* Linnaeus (334). Pelagic, in all tropical and temperate seas. Length 1.2 meters (4 feet).

Family HEMIRAMPHIDAE: The halfbeaks have been appropriately named, having a spear-like, much prolonged lower jaw, and a greatly reduced upper one. Halfbeaks are widely distributed throughout warm and temperate seas. Their main food consists of planktonic organisms, vegetable matter, and crustaceans, which they skim off the surface of the water. Most of the species are small and seldom exceed 30 centimeters in length. A few are oceanic, but the majority of them are shore fishes.

HALFBEAK, *Hemiramphus archipelagicus* (Forskål) (formerly *H. marginatus*) (335). Tropical Indo-Pacific, Red Sea. Length 30 centimeters (12 inches).

BRAZILIAN HALFBEAK, *Hemiramphus brasiliensis* (Linnaeus) (336). Tropical Atlantic. Length 38 centimeters (15 inches).

## Squirrelfishes

Family HOLOCENTRIDAE: The squirrelfishes or soldierfishes are species characteristic of rocky or coral flats in tropical seas. Their ctenoid scales are very hard and remarkably spiny. They are further characterized by the presence of a spine at the angle of the preopercle. The coloration of these fishes is usually brilliant crimson, with or without stripes. Squirrelfishes are predacious, active, and largely nocturnal in their habits, feeding on crustaceans, worms, and algae. During the day they may be observed hovering almost motionless in coral or rock crevices. At night they come out to feed on the reef flat or in the surf.

SPINY SQUIRRELFISH, *Holocentrus spinifer* (Forskål) (337). Indo-Pacific, from the Red Sea and

Madagascar to the Philippines, Hawaii, and Tuamotus. Length 38 centimeters (15 inches).

SOLDIERFISH, *Myripristis murdjan* (Forskål) (338). Tropical Indo-Pacific. Length 30 centimeters (12 inches).

## Wrasses

Family LABRIDAE: Wrasses are characterized by their large, separate, conical teeth in the front of the jaws. They have an extensive geographical range, but most are concentrated in warmer water. Most species are shore forms, inhabiting rocky areas, coral reefs, and growths of marine algae. Some species are herbivorous, but most of them are carnivores. They are among the most beautiful and gaily colored of the reef creatures. Their quality as food fishes varies considerably from one species to the next.

BANDED WRASSE, *Cheilinus fasciatus* (Bloch) (339). Tropical Indo-Pacific, Australia. Length 30 centimeters (12 inches).

GIANT GREEN WRASSE, *Cheilinus undulatus* Rüppell (340). Indo-Pacific, Red Sea. Length 1.5 meters (5 feet).

GAIMARD'S WRASSE, *Coris gaimardi* (Quoy and Gaimard) (341). Tropical Indo-Pacific. Length 30 centimeters (12 inches).

RAINBOW WRASSE, *Coris julis* (Linnaeus) (342). Eastern Atlantic and Mediterranean. Length 25 centimeters (10 inches).

WRASSE, *Epibulus insidiator* (Pallas) (343). Tropical Indo-Pacific. Length 30 centimeters (12 inches).

THREE-SPOTTED WRASSE, *Halichoeres trimaculatus* (Quoy and Gaimard) (344). Tropical Indo-Pacific. Length 22 centimeters (8.5 inches) or more.

HOGFISH, *Lachnolaimus maximus* (Walbaum) (345). Florida and West Indies. Length 48 centimeters (19 inches).

## Snappers

Family LUTJANIDAE: Snappers are carnivorous, voracious, gamy shore fishes, abundant in all warm seas. They take the hook readily. Their food consists largely of smaller fishes. Common in rocky coral reef areas, snappers are usually good food fishes and of commercial value in some places. Certain members of the genus *Lutjanus* are among the most serious offenders as ciguatoxic fishes.

BLUEGREEN SNAPPER, *Aprion virescens* Cuvier and Valenciennes (346). Tropical Indo-Pacific. Length 72 centimeters (28 inches).

GOLDEN-STRIPED SNAPPER, *Gnathodentex aureolineatus* (Lacépède) (347). Tropical Indo-Pacific. Length 25 centimeters (10 inches).

GRAY SNAPPER, *Gymnocranius griseus* (Temminck and Schlegel) (348). Tropical Indo-Pacific. Length 25 centimeters (10 inches).

SCAVENGER SNAPPER, *Lethrinus harak* (Forskål) (349). Indo-Pacific, Red Sea. Length 30 centimeters (12 inches).

GREY SNAPPER, *Lethrinus miniatus* (Forster) (350). Tropical Indo-Pacific, Japan, East Africa. Length 45 centimeters (18 inches).

SMOKEY SNAPPER, *Lethrinus nebulosus* (Forskål) (351). Tropical Indo-Pacific, East Africa. Length 30 centimeters (12 inches).

VARIEGATED SNAPPER, *Lethrinus variegatus* Cuvier and Valenciennes (352). Tropical Indo-Pacific. Length 35 centimeters (14 inches).

SILVER-SPOTTED SNAPPER, *Lutjanus argentimaculatus* (Forskål) (353). Indo-Pacific. Length 50 centimeters (19.5 inches).

RED SNAPPER, *Lutjanus aya* (Bloch) (354). Western tropical Atlantic. Length 76 centimeters (30 inches).

RED SNAPPER, *Lutjanus bohar* (Forskål) (355). Indo-Pacific, Red Sea. Length 90 centimeters (35.5 inches).

DARK-TAILED SNAPPER, *Lutjanus janthinuropterus* (Bleeker) (356). Indo-Pacific. Length 60 centimeters (2 feet).

DOG SNAPPER, *Lutjanus jocu* (Bloch and Schneider) (357). Florida and West Indies, south to Brazil. Length 75 centimeters (29.5 inches).

BLACK-SPOTTED SNAPPER, *Lutjanus monostigmus* (Cuvier and Valenciennes) (358). Tropical Indo-Pacific, Red Sea. Length 30 centimeters (12 inches).

CHINAMAN, *Lutjanus nematophorus* (Bleeker) (359). Australia. Length 68 centimeters (27 inches).

SNAPPER, *Lutjanus semicinctus* Quoy and Gaimard (360). Tropical Indo-Pacific, east coast of Africa, Australia. Length 50 centimeters (20 inches).

RED SNAPPER, *Lutjanus vagiensis* (Quoy and Gaimard) (361). Tropical Indo-Pacific, east coast of Africa and Australia. Length 50 centimeters (20 inches).

LARGE-EYE SNAPPER, *Monotaxis grandoculis* (Forskål) (362). Tropical Indo-Pacific. Length 32 centimeters (12.5 inches.)

\* \* \*

Family MONACANTHIDAE: The family Aluteridae is sometimes included in the Monacanthidae. The habits of the fishes of these two families are essentially the same. *See* Aluteridae, p. 149.

\* \* \*

## Mullets

Family MUGILIDAE: Mullets are small to moderate-sized fishes with broad heads and a mouth fringed with very feeble teeth. They are tropical and temperate zone inhabitants of shallow bays, estuaries, and lagoons, although a few are confined to freshwater. Mullets are largely herbivores. They are frequently observed in schools swimming near the surface of the water. In some areas they are a valuable food fish and are often raised in large numbers in ponds. They have a phenomenal ability to jump over the cork line of a seine and give the fisherman a real test of his ability.

MULLET, *Chelon vaigiensis* (Quoy and Gaimard) (363). Tropical Indo-Pacific. Length 32 centimeters (12.5 inches).

COMMON MULLET, *Mugil cephalus* Linnaeus (364). Cosmopolitan in distribution. Length 30 centimeters (12 inches).

## Surmullets or Goatfishes

Family MULLIDAE: Surmullets or goatfishes are small to moderate-sized shore fishes of warm seas. A variety of forms may be seen swimming about coral reefs, many gaily colored. They are usually observed as a few scattered individuals or in small schools. With the use of their feelers they feel their way along a sandy bottom in quest of food. They are carnivorous, feeding largely on a variety of small animals. Surmullets serve as food for a variety of predatory fishes. Their flesh is usually excellent.

GOLDEN FLAMMED GOATFISH, *Mulloidichthys auriflamma* (Forskål) (365). Tropical Indo-Pacific, Red Sea. Length 35 centimeters (14 inches).

SAMOAN GOATFISH, *Mulloidichthys samoensis* (Günther) (366). Tropical Indo-Pacific. Length 30 centimeters (12 inches).

GOATFISH, *Parupeneus chryserydros* (Lacépède) (367). Tropical Indo-Pacific, East Africa. Length 30 centimeters (12 inches).

GOATFISH, *Upeneus arge* Jordan and Evermann (368). Tropical Indo-Pacific. Length 32 centimeters (12.5 inches).

## Moray Eels

Family MURAENIDAE: Moray eels are a group of savage, moderate-sized marine fishes, which, surprisingly, can be readily tamed. Their bathymetric range extends from intertidal reef flats to depths of more than a hundred meters. They are found throughout temperate and tropical seas. Moray eels inhabit a large variety of ecological biotopes—surge channels, coralline ridges, inter-islet channels, reef flats, and lagoon patch reefs. They are nocturnal in their habits, hiding in crevices, holes, and under rocks or coral during the day, and coming out at night. With the aid of a light one can observe morays wriggling over a reef flat at night in large numbers. They may often be seen thrusting their heads out of coral holes, their mouths slowly opening and closing, waiting for some unwary victim to pass by their lair. They are able to strike with great rapidity and ferocity. Their long, fang-like, depressible teeth are exceedingly sharp and can inflict serious lacerations. Their powerful muscular development, tough leathery skin, and dangerous jaws make them formidable animals. Some of the larger morays attain a length of 3 meters or more and may constitute a real hazard to divers, particularly when poking one's hands into holes and crevices. Morays are carnivorous and predacious. They can be readily lured out by placing dead fish in front of their lair. Natives use spears, hook and line, snares, and traps in capturing them. The flesh of some species is used by some peoples as food. The flesh is said to be agreeable, but oily and not readily digestible. Some species are violently poisonous to eat.

SPOTTED MORAY EEL, *Echidna nebulosa* (Ahl) (369). Tropical Indo-Pacific, coasts of Australia, East Africa, China. Length 75 centimeters (29.5 inches).

YELLOW-MARGINED MORAY EEL, *Gymnothorax flavimarginatus* (Rüppell) (370). Tropical Indo-Pacific, coast of East Africa. Length 1.5 meters (5 feet).

GREEN MORAY EEL, *Gymnothorax funebris* Ranzani (371). Caribbean Sea south to Brazil. Length 1.8 meters (6 feet).

MORAY EEL, *Gymnothorax javanicus* (Bleeker) (372). Tropical Indo-Pacific, coast of East Africa. Length 1.5 meters (5 feet).

MORAY EEL, *Gymnothorax meleagris* (Shaw and Nodder) (373). Tropical Indo-Pacific, coast of Japan. Length 1 meter (3.2 feet).

PAINTED MORAY EEL, *Gymnothorax pictus* (Ahl) (374). Tropical Indo-Pacific. Length 75 centimeters (29.5 inches).

UNDULATED MORAY EEL, *Gymnothorax undulatus* (Lacépède) (375). Tropical Indo-Pacific, Red Sea, coast of East Africa. Length 1.5 meters (5 feet).

EUROPEAN MORAY EEL, *Muraena helena* Linnaeus (Chapter IV, 197). Eastern Atlantic Ocean and Mediterranean Sea. Length 1.5 meters (5 feet).

## Trunkfishes

Family OSTRACIONTIDAE: Trunkfishes are one of the most peculiarly constructed groups of plecto-gnaths. The body is enveloped within a bony box comprised of six-sided scutes, leaving openings only for jaws, fins, and tail. They live in tropical seas and are frequently seen swimming slowly along among the corals in shallow water. Many of them are brilliantly colored. The exoskeleton, which serves them well for protection, is also used by native peoples as a container for cooking them over a fire. Little is known of their habits.

HONEYCOMB COWFISH, *Acanthostracion quadricornis* (Linnaeus) (376). Western Atlantic, tropical coasts of the Americas and Caribbean Sea. Length 25 centimeters (10 inches).

TRUNKFISH, *Kentrocapros aculeatus* (Houttuyn) (377). Tropical Indo-Pacific, coasts of Japan, India. Length 15 centimeters (6 inches).

SMOOTH TRUNKFISH, *Lactophrys triqueter* (Linnaeus) (378). Western Atlantic, tropical coasts of the Americas, and Caribbean Sea. Length 30 centimeters (12 inches).

HORNED TRUNKFISH, *Lactoria cornuta* (Linnaeus) (379). Tropical Indo-Pacific, Japan, South Africa. Length 40 centimeters (16 inches)

TRUNKFISH, *Lactoria diaphana* (Bloch and Schneider) (380). Tropical Indo-Pacific, Japan, South Africa. Length 30 centimeters (12 inches).

SPECKLED TRUNKFISH, *Ostracion meleagris* Shaw (381). Tropical Indo-Pacific, coasts of Japan, South Africa. Length 20 centimeters (8 inches).

## Damselfishes

Family POMACENTRIDAE: Damselfishes are chiefly confined to coral reefs, although a few species are found in more temperate zones. They are most abundant around coral crevices and in holes and rocky areas, which they utilize for protection. Although gregarious, they do not form large schools. Damselfishes are omnivorous, and, although apparently preferring an herbivorous diet, they readily ingest any organism that is picked up in the process of their grazing. Most of these fishes are too small to be considered of food value.

SERGEANT MAJOR, *Abudefduf saxatilis* (Linnaeus) (382). Tropical Indo-Pacific, coasts of Australia, east Africa, China. Length 18 centimeters (17 inches).

## Parrotfishes

Family SCARIDAE: Parrotfishes are similar in appearance to the wrasses, but differ in that they have their teeth fused into plates. They are shallow-water shore fishes and very common in coral reefs, lagoons, and rocky areas of tropical waters. Their food consists of algae and small animals that are ingested along with corals, which make up the major part of their diet. Deep gouges and scratches may be observed on coral rocks where small schools of parrotfishes have browsed. They thus contribute significantly to the formation of fine sand by means of returning the pulverized rock and skeletal material to the bottom as fecal components.

BLUE PARROTFISH, *Scarus coeruleus* (Bloch) (383). Florida, West Indies, Panama. Length 90 centimeters (35.5 inches).

PARROTFISH, *Scarus ghobban* Forskål (384). Tropical Indo-Pacific, coasts of Japan, Red Sea, Australia. Length 1.1 meters (3.6 feet).

PARROTFISH, *Scarus gibbus* Rüppell (385). Tropical Indo-Pacific. Length 60 centimeters (24 inches).

BLUE PARROTFISH, *Scarus jonesi* (Streets) (386). Tropical Indo-Pacific. Length 38 centimeters (15 inches).

PARROTFISH, *Scarus microrhinus* Bleeker (387). Tropical Indo-Pacific. Length 33 centimeters (13 inches).

## Mackerels

Family SCOMBRIDAE: The great family of true mackerels, which includes the tunas, are distinguished by their streamlined bodies, smooth scales, magnificent metallic coloration, and by the presence of a number of detached finlets behind the dorsal and anal fins. Mackerels are for the most part swift-swimming pelagic fishes and are one of our most valuable fisheries resources. Most species run in large schools. Some of these schools have been reported to be "a half mile wide and 20 miles long." Although there are a large number of species in the Scombridae, only a few members of the genera *Acanthocybium, Euthynnus, Sarda,* and *Scomberomorus* have been incriminated in ciguatera poisoning. They, like most of their relatives, are oceanic fishes but during the reproductive season come in close to shore, and some species may at times be found in bays and lagoons. Apparently it is during this inshore migration period that they encounter ciguatoxin by means of their diet. They feed on a variety of foods: sardines, anchovies, plankton, etc.

WAHOO, *Acanthocybium solandri* (Cuvier) (388). Circumtropical in distribution. Length 2 meters (6.5 feet).

WAVYBACK SKIPJACK, *Euthynnus affinis* (Cantor) (389). Tropical Indo-Pacific. Length 1 meter (3.2 feet).

ATLANTIC BONITO, *Sarda sarda* (Bloch) (390). Atlantic Ocean. Length 91 centimeters (3 feet).

KING MACKEREL, *Scomberomorus cavalla* (Cuvier) (391). Tropical Atlantic. Length 1.5 meters (5 feet).

## Seabass or Groupers

Family SERRANIDAE: Seabass or groupers are robust, carnivorous, predacious shore fishes of tropical and temperate waters. A variety of biotopes are inhabited by this large family: coral reefs, rocks, sandy areas, and kelp. A few are found in fairly deep water, but most live in shallow water. Some attain great size. They are usually considered good food fishes.

ROCKCOD, *Anyperodon leucogrammicus* (Cuvier and Valenciennes) (392). Tropical Indo-Pacific. Length 40 centimeters (16 inches).

SPOTTED GROUPER, *Cephalopholis argus* Bloch and Schneider (393). Indo-Pacific. Length 50 centimeters (19.5 inches).

ROCKHIND, *Epinephelus adscensionis* (Osbeck) (394). Coasts of Florida and West Indies southward to Brazil. Length 38 centimeters (15 inches).

BROWN SPOTTED GROUPER, *Epinephelus fus-*

*coguttatus* (Forskål) (395). Tropical Indo-Pacific. Length 60 centimeters (23.5 inches).

SPOTTED GROUPER, *Epinephelus guttatus* (Linnaeus) (396). South Carolina to Brazil. Length 45 centimeters (17.5 inches).

GROUPER, *Epinephelus merra* Bloch (397). Tropical Indo-Pacific. Length 30 centimeters (12 inches).

SPOTTED SEABASS, *Epinephelus tauvina* (Forskål) (398). Tropical Indo-Pacific. Length 2.1 meters (6.8 feet).

TIGER GROUPER, *Mycteroperca tigris* (Valenciennes) (399). Western tropical Atlantic. Length 48 centimeters (19 inches).

POISONOUS GROUPER, *Mycteroperca venenosa* (Linnaeus) (400). Western tropical Atlantic. Length 90 centimeters (35.5 inches).

CREOLEFISH, *Paranthias furcifer* (Valenciennes) (401). Coasts of Cuba to Brazil. Length 35 centimeters (14 inches).

GROUPER, *Plectropomus oligacanthus* Bleeker (402). Tropical Indo-Pacific. Length 55 centimeters (21.5 inches).

GROUPER, *Plectropomus truncatus* Fowler and Bean (403). Tropical Indo-Pacific. Length 52 centimeters (20.5 inches).

GROUPER, *Variola louti* (Forskål) (404). Tropical Indo-Pacific. Length 60 centimeters (23.5 inches).

## Rabbitfishes

Family SIGANIDAE: Rabbitfishes are moderate-sized fishes, having compressed, ovate bodies with slippery skins and minute scales. They are found in tropical waters, traveling in dense schools, around coral reefs, where they browse on marine algae. However, they are not obligatory herbivores and at times may shift to a fleshy diet.

SILVER RABBITFISH, *Siganus argenteus* (Quoy and Gaimard) (405). Tropical Indo-Pacific. Length 35 centimeters (14 inches).

RABBITFISH, *Siganus fuscescens* (Houttuyn) (406). Tropical Indo-Pacific. Length 25 centimeters (10 inches).

PRETTY RABBITFISH, *Siganus puellus* (Schlegel) (407). Tropical Indo-Pacific. Length 27 centimeters (10.5 inches).

## Porgies

Family SPARIDAE: Porgies are a group of shore fishes having a perch-like appearance. They are closely related to the Pomadasyidae. They are found on tropical and temperate coasts, usually confined to shallow waters in a variety of habitats. Small fishes, crustaceans, and other invertebrates comprise their diet. They are among the more important food fishes.

PORGY, *Sparus sarba* Forskål (408). Tropical Indo-Pacific, Red Sea. Length 35 centimeters (14 inches).

## Barracuda

Family SPHYRAENIDAE: Barracuda are elongate, slender, swift-swimming, carnivorous, savage, and exceedingly voracious shore fishes of tropical and temperate waters. Their jaws contain long, knife-like canine teeth. Some attain large size. They are common in lagoons, passageways, and coral reefs. Their flesh is of excellent quality, but the larger specimens of some species may be very toxic, especially during the reproductive season.

GREAT BARRACUDA, *Sphyraena barracuda* (Walbaum) (Chapter II, 29). All tropical seas, with the exception of the eastern Pacific Ocean. Length 1.6 meters (5.5 feet).

## Moorish Idols

Family ZANCLIDAE: Moorish idols are handsome reef fishes having the same general appearance and habits as the butterflyfishes, Chaetodontidae.

MOORISH IDOL, *Zanclus cornutus* (Linnaeus) (409). Indo-Pacific, Mexico to East Africa. Length 15 centimeters (6 inches).

### Clupeotoxic Fishes

These fishes produce a form of ichthyosarcotoxism

caused by eating fishes of the order Clupeiformes, which includes the families Clupeidae (herrings), Engraulidae (anchovies), Elopidae (tarpons), Albulidae (bonefishes), Pterothrissidae (deep-sea bonefishes), and Alepicephalidae (deep-sea slickheads). The families most commonly incriminated in human clupeotoxications are Clupeidae and Engraulidae. Clupeotoxism is a sporadic, unpredictable public health problem of the tropical Atlantic Ocean, the Caribbean Sea, and the tropical Pacific Ocean. Most poisonings have occurred in tropical island areas and were caused by fishes that had been captured close to shore. The viscera are regarded as the most toxic part of the fish. Tropical clupeiform fishes are most likely to be toxic during the warm summer months. There is no possible way to detect a toxic clupeiform fish by its appearance, and the degree of freshness has no bearing on its toxicity. The clinical characteristics of clupeotoxism are distinct and usually violent. The first indication of poisoning is a sharp metallic taste, which may be present immediately after ingestion of the fish. This is rapidly followed by a severe gastrointestinal upset, which may be accompanied by a drop in blood pressure, cyanosis, and other evidences of a vascular collapse. Concurrently, or within a short period, a variety of neurological disturbances develop—nervousness, dilated pupils, violent headaches, numbness, tingling, hypersalivation, muscular cramps, respiratory distress, paralysis, convulsions, coma, and death. Death may occur in less than 15 minutes. There are no accurate statistics on the case fatality rate, but it is reported to be very high. Treatment is symptomatic. There is no information available on the nature of the poison, and the source of the poison is unknown.

The representatives of this group are:

## Herring

Family CLUPEIDAE: Herring are among the most cosmopolitan groups of fishes. Some species live in freshwater, whereas others enter rivers to spawn, but the majority are oceanic species. Herring are frequently found swimming in immense schools. They have been incriminated in both the ciguatera and clupeoid types of ichthyosarcotoxism. Two species, *Clupanodon thrissa* and *Clupea tropica,* have been reported as violently toxic species. Although these two species are considered to be valuable food fishes in most areas, they may be extremely poisonous at times elsewhere.

The dentition of herring is small and feeble, and their food consists largely of planktonic organisms, shrimp, crustaceans, worms, etc. They are greatly valued as food fishes. The economic significance of herring has been noted by Jordan (1905), viz.: "As salted, dried, or smoked fish the herring is found throughout the civilized world, and its spawning and feeding groups have determined the location of cities."

SPRAT, THREAD HERRING, *Clupanodon thrissa* (Linnaeus) (410). Tropical Indo-Pacific, China, Japan, Korea. Length 25 centimeters (10 inches).

RED-EAR SARDINE, *Harengula humeralis* (Cuvier) (411). Florida, Bermuda, West Indies to Brazil. Length 40 centimeters (16 inches).

SARDINE, *Harengula ovalis* (Bennett) (412). Indo-Pacific, Red Sea. Length 15 centimeters (6 inches).

HILSA, SABLEFISH, *Macrura ilisha* (Buchanan-Hamilton) (413). Persian Gulf, Indian Ocean. Length 25 centimeters (10 inches).

ATLANTIC THREAD HERRING, *Opisthonema oglinum* (LeSueur) (414). West Indies, occasionally to Cape Cod. Length 25 centimeters (10 inches).

MARQUESAN SARDINE, *Sardinella marquesensis* Berry and Whitehead (415). Tropical Indo-Pacific. Length 20 centimeters (8 inches).

SARDINE, *Sardinella perforata* (Cantor) (416). Tropical Indo-Pacific, Persian Gulf. Length 18 centimeters (7 inches).

## Anchovies

Family ENGRAULIDAE: Anchovies are small herring-like fishes, abundant in temperate and warm seas. Although generally found in the open seas, they enter bays and ascend rivers. They are characterized by their snout projecting beyond their very wide mouth.

The flesh of some species is of excellent flavor, and they are commercially canned in large numbers. Anchovies are valuable bait fishes and serve as an important food source for larger fishes.

ANCHOVY, *Engraulis encrasicholus* (Linnaeus) (417). Eastern Atlantic and Mediterranean. Length 20 centimeters (8 inches).

JAPANESE ANCHOVY, *Engraulis japonicus* Schlegel (418). China, Japan, Korea, Taiwan. Length 13 centimeters (5 inches).

ANCHOVY, *Thrissina baelama* (Forskål) (419). Tropical Indo-Pacific, Red Sea, enters river mouths. Length 12 centimeters (4.5 inches).

## Gempylotoxic Fishes

Gempylotoxism is caused by ingestion of the flesh of the fishes of the family Gempylidae—the escolares or pelagic mackerels—which contain an oil with a pronounced purgative effect. The purgative oil is present also in the bones, and sucking on the rich, oily bones may result in diarrhea. Gempylid poisoning is usually not a serious matter, and many native groups esteem these fishes for their purgative effects. Ordinary cooking procedures do not destroy the purgative effect of the oil.

Members of this group include:

### Snake Mackerels

Family GEMPYLIDAE: Snake mackerels may attain large sizes—60 kilograms (132 pounds) or more and a length of 2 meters (6.5 feet). They are fishes of the high seas and are most frequently found at depths up to 400 fathoms or more. They are nocturnal and carnivorous in their feeding habits. They will bite on a variety of baits, but jacks and flying fishes are especially good. The flesh of some species is quite oily and coarse. Ingestion of this oil produces a painless diarrhea.

CASTOR OILFISH, *Ruvettus pretiosus* Cocco (420). Tropical Atlantic and Indo-Pacific regions. Length 1.3 meters (4.25 feet).

## Scombrotoxic Fishes

Scombroid fishes include the tuna, mackerel, skipjack, and related species. These fishes are usually edible and a valuable commercial species. Scombroid poisoning is caused by improper preservation. Certain bacteria convert muscle histidine into histamine, which is potentiated by diamines. This is the only form of ichthyosarcotoxism in which bacteria play an active role in the production of the poison within the body of the fish. However, the poison is not a bacterial endotoxin.

Symptoms usually develop within a few minutes after ingestion of the fish. Frequently, toxic fish can be detected immediately upon tasting because of the "sharp or peppery" taste. The symptoms of scombroid poisoning resemble those of a histamine intoxication, including intense headaches, dizziness, throbbing of the large blood vessels of the neck, epigastric pain, flushing of the face, generalized erythema, urticarial eruptions, severe itching, bronchospasm, burning of the throat, cardiac palpitation, nausea, vomiting, diarrhea, abdominal pain, thirst, inability to swallow, suffocation, and severe respiratory distress. There is danger of shock, and deaths have been reported. This is reputed to be the most common form of fish poisoning on a worldwide basis. Treatment is with the use of antihistamines. Most of the victims recover.

A list of the species will not be given since any of the tuna, skipjack, bonito, mackerel, etc., may be involved. These fishes are worldwide in their distribution.

## Hallucinogenic Fishes

Certain types of reef fishes in the tropical Pacific and Indian oceans contain poisons capable of producing hallucinations (ichthyoallyeinotoxism). The families incriminated in ichthyoallyeinotoxism include the following: Acanthuridae (surgeonfish); Kyphosidae (rudderfish); Mugilidae (mullets); Mullidae (surmullets or goatfish); Pomacentridae (damselfish); Serranidae (seabass or groupers); and Siganidae (rabbitfish). Ichthyoallyeinotoxism may result from eating the flesh or the head of the fish, where the poison is reputedly concentrated. This biotoxication is sporadic and unpredictable in its occurrence. The poison affects primarily the central nervous system. The symptoms may develop within a few minutes to two hours and persist for 24 hours or longer. Symptoms are dizziness, loss of equilibrium, lack of motor coordination, hallucinations, and mental depression. A common complaint of the victim is that "someone is sitting on my chest," or there is a sensation of a tight constriction around the chest. The conviction that one is going to die, or some other frightening fantasy, is a characteristic part of the clinical picture. Other complaints consist of itching, burning of the throat, muscular weakness, and abdominal distress. No fatalities have been reported, and in comparison with other forms of ichthyosarcotoxism, hallucinogenic fish poisoning is relatively mild. There is no information available concerning the pharmacological and chemical properties of the poison. Ordinary cooking procedures do not destroy the poison.

Species in this group of fishes are:

### Sea Chub, Goatfish

SEA CHUB, *Kyphosus cinerascens* (Forskål) (421) Tropical Indo-Pacific. Length 50 centimeters (19.5 inches).

SAMOAN GOATFISH, SURMULLET, *Mulloidichthys samoensis* (Günther) (422). Tropical Indo-Pacific. Length 30 centimeters (12 inches).

WHITE GOATFISH, *Upeneus arge* Jordan and Evermann (423). Tropical Indo-Pacific. Length 32 centimeters (12.5 inches).

### Tetrodotoxic Fishes

Tetrodotoxic fishes are most common in subtropical and tropical areas. Tetraodontoid fishes produce one of the most violent forms of fish poisoning, which is characterized by rapidly-developing, violent symptoms.

This biotoxication is characterized by paresthesia, or numbness, of the lips and tongue, which gradually spreads to include the extremities and later develops into severe numbness. The numbness may later involve the entire body. Gastrointestinal disturbances may or may not be present. Respiratory distress is a prominent part of the clinical picture, and the victim later becomes intensely cyanotic. Petechial hemorrhages, blistering, and severe desquamation may develop. Ataxia, aphonia, dysphagia, muscular twitchings, tremors, incoordination, paralysis, and convulsions are frequently present. The victim may become comatose, but in most instances remains conscious until shortly before death. Treatment is symptomatic. The case fatality rate is about 60 percent. If death occurs, it usually takes place within the first 24 hours.

Pharmacological studies have shown that the primary action of tetrodotoxin is on the nervous system, producing both central and peripheral effects. Relatively low doses of the poison will readily inhibit neuromuscular function. Major effects include respiratory failure and hypotension. It is believed that puffer fish poisoning has a direct action on respiratory centers; there is some evidence that tetrodotoxin depresses the vasomotor center. The neuromuscular paralysis may be due to inhibition of nerve conductivity.

Members of this group are:

### Puffers
#### (Canthigasteridae)

Family CANTHIGASTERIDAE: The sharp-nosed puffers are small, brilliantly-colored marine fishes that abound in coral reefs and shoal areas. They are sometimes placed in the family Tetraodontidae. *Canthigaster amboinensis* is said to attain a length of 25 centimeters (10 inches) or more, but most of the species attain a maximum length of less than 13 centimeters (5 inches). These attractive little fishes generally travel singly or in pairs, hovering almost motionless for a time and then suddenly darting in and out among the corals with a speed that is unusual for most puffers. When frightened or injured, canthigasterids have the typical pufferlike habit of inflating themselves with water and grating their teeth together in a noisy manner.

CROWNED PUFFER, *Canthigaster coronata* (Vaillant and Sauvage) (424). Tropical Indo-Pacific, Red Sea. Length 10 centimeters (4 inches).

WHITE-SPOTTED PUFFER, *Canthigaster jactator* (Jenkins) (425). Tropical Indo-Pacific. Length 9 centimeters (3.5 inches).

SHARP-NOSED PUFFER, *Canthigaster rivulatus* (Temminck and Schlegel) (426). Tropical Indo-Pacific, Japan. Length 10 centimeters (4 inches).

BLUE-SPOTTED PUFFER, *Canthigaster solandri* (Richardson) (427). Tropical Indo-Pacific. Length 10 centimeters (4 inches).

VALENTINE'S PUFFER, *Canthigaster valentini* (Bleeker) (428). Tropical Indo-Pacific. Length 20 centimeters (8 inches).

## Porcupinefishes

Family DIODONTIDAE: The porcupinefishes are spiny marine fishes that are widely distributed in all warm seas. *Diodon hystrix* is said to attain a total length of 91 centimeters (3 feet) or more, but most diodontids range from 20 to 50 centimeters (8 to 20 inches) in length. Porcupinefishes inhabit coral reefs and shoal areas, generally traveling singly or in pairs. They also have the ability to inflate themselves until they are almost spherical in outline. During the inflation process the spines, which are usually depressed, are extended, giving the fish a formidable appearance. Porcupinefishes have been known to kill large carnivorous fishes by inflating themselves and becoming stuck in the throat of the would-be captor. Diodontids are also capable of giving a severe bite. Darwin (1945) stated that diodons have been found alive in the stomachs of sharks and in some instances have mortally wounded their captors by gnawing through the stomach walls and sides and thus escaping.

PORCUPINEFISH, *Chilomycterus affinis* Günther (429). Atlantic coast of tropical America, west and southern Africa. Length 17 centimeters (6.5 inches).

SPOTTED BURRFISH, *Chilomycterus atinga* (Linnaeus) (430). Florida Keys, West Indies, Bermuda. Length 20 centimeters (8 inches).

PORCUPINEFISH, *Chilomycterus orbicularis* (Bloch) (431). Tropical Indo-Pacific, westward to Cape of Good Hope. Length 26 centimeters (10 inches).

PORCUPINEFISH, *Diodon holacanthus* Linnaeus (432). All warm seas. Length 30 centimeters (12 inches).

PORCUPINEFISH, *Diodon hystrix* Linnaeus (433). All tropical seas. Length 90 centimeters (35.5 inches).

## Sunfish

Family MOLIDAE: The Molidae, the largest of the tetraodontoid fishes, are members of the genus *Mola*. They attain a length of more than 3 meters (10 feet) and weigh in excess of 16,500 kilograms (3.5 tons). However, *Ranzania*, another genus of this family, rarely exceeds a length of 61 centimeters (24 inches). Sunfishes inhabit open seas and are generally seen singly or in pairs, but seem to become gregarious at certain seasons when they band together in small schools of as many as a dozen individuals. The name "headfishes" is sometimes given to these grotesque creatures because they have the appearance of being composed of an enormous head to which small fins are attached. When swimming they are said to progress with a waving motion from side to side with the dorsal fin projecting from the water. The small specimens of *Mola mola* can move with surprising rapidity and at times have been observed jumping several feet clear of the surface of the water. During calm weather, these fishes may be observed basking in the sun at the surface of the sea, lying more or less on their sides. Large basking specimens are generally slow moving, unable to move faster than a boat can row, and are easily overtaken and harpooned. They are said to emit a grunting or groaning noise when captured. Most of the basking specimens are believed to be sick and dying as a result of heavy parasitic infestations. Molas have been found to contain in their stomachs fishes that are known to live at depths of at least 100 fathoms; hence it is believed that at times molas descend to considerable depths.

Some scientists believe that the inshore migrations of molas coincide with the invasion of medusae, salps, and ctenophores upon which they largely feed. However, specimens of molas taken inshore have usually been found to be feeding on littoral forms of crustacea, ophiuroids, mollusks, hydroids, ctenophores, corallines, and algae. *Mola mola* have been captured on hook and line with live anchovy bait in California waters. Relatively little is known about the breeding habits of molas.

OCEAN SUNFISH, *Mola mola* (Linnaeus) (434). Temperate and tropical seas. length 3 meters (9.8 feet) or more.

## Puffers
### (Tetraodontidae)

Family TETRAODONTIDAE: Some authors divide the puffer family Tetraodontidae into four separate families: Chonerhinidae, Colomesidae, Lagocephalidae, and Tetraodontidae. However, more recent studies suggest that these puffers should be combined into the single family Tetraodontidae. Tetraodontids thrive in a variety of ecosystems—marine, estuarine, as well as freshwater habitats. Most lagocephalids range in size from about 25 to 50 centimeters (10 to 20 inches), but *Lagocephalus lagocephalus* is said to attain an even greater size. *Arothron stellatus* has been reported to reach a total length of 90 centimeters (36 inches), but most tetraodontids range from about 20 to 40 centimeters (8 to 16 inches). Most puffers are considered to be shallow water fishes. However, it should be pointed out that some members inhabit relatively deep waters. *L. oceanicus* has been taken at 40 meters or more, *L. lagocephalus inermis* at 90 meters, *L. sceleratus* at 60 meters, and *Sphaeroides oblongus* at 100 meters. *Liosaccus cutaneus* is usually conceded to be a deep water species, and *Boesmanichthys firmamentum* has been taken at a depth of 100 fathoms. Species of *Lagocephalus* have been taken

hundreds of miles from shore at depths of 4,000 meters and are a common constituent in the stomachs of pelagic fishes such as tunas, wahoos, and other scombroids. It is not known whether these deep water puffers are nontoxic or whether the poison is transvectored by scombroids. The Indo-Pacific tetraodontids living around coral reef areas tend to travel singly or in small groups. *Sphaeroides* species tend to be more gregarious and are sometimes observed in large groups, but apparently they do not school in the manner that some fishes do. Stomach analyses conducted in our laboratories on *A. hispidus* indicate that this species is omnivorous, since fragments of corals, sponges, algae, mollusks, and fish have been found in their stomachs. At Tagus Cove, Isabela Island, during the Krieger Galapagos expedition, it was observed that hundreds of *Sphaeroides annulatus* were attracted to the surface of the water with a night light. Specimens could then be readily captured by spear or dip net. When puffers are at rest they appear to hover almost motionless with only their pectorals fanning the water. The pectoral, dorsal, and anal fins are the chief locomotory organs, the tail being used principally as a rudder. Despite their reputation of being slow-moving fishes, puffers are capable of moving with surprising rapidity when frightened. They are likewise capable of inflicting severe bites. They are quite vicious and readily snap at almost any bait offered them.

The inflating mechanism of puffers has been a subject of interest among anatomists for many years. Inflation is employed only as a defense mechanism. If a puffer is frightened or annoyed it will gulp down its fluid medium, thus causing inflation. There is no evidence that puffers come to the surface in order to inflate themselves with air, as is commonly believed. The inflating mechanism consists of the powerful muscles of the first branchiostegal ray; these muscles depress a pad covering the ceratohyals, thus expanding the mouth cavity and drawing in water or air if the fish is out of water. The elevation of the ceratohyals forces the fluid into the sac-like ventral diverticulum of the stomach, from which it is partially separated by a sphincter-like ring. Fluid is retained in the diverticulum by a strong esophageal sphincter and the pylorus, and not by the flap-like breathing valves present in the mouth. The opercular valves prevent leakage during compression, but the sac can remain distended when the valves are held open or removed. The water or air in the sac is released by relaxation of the esophageal sphincter, permitting escape through the oral or opercular openings. Puffers make considerable noise during inflation by grinding their heavy jaw teeth together. Some species of puffers are covered with short prickly bristles, which they appear to have the ability to withdraw or extend at will. Puffers have a distinctive offensive odor, which is particularly noticeable when they are being dressed or dissected.

The genus *Colomesus* is comprised of a single species, which inhabits the rivers of northern South America and the West Indies. Specimens have been taken from the mouth of the Amazon to the fringe of the Andes Mountains—a distance of more than 3,000 miles from the nearest saltwater. The colomesids likewise have the ability to inflate themselves with water or air. Judging from the literature, relatively little is known regarding its habits.

The *Xenopterus* is a small genus of freshwater fishes that, with the possible exception of a single African species, is restricted to the rivers of southern Asia and Indonesia. These fishes are said to attain a total length of about 28 centimeters (11 inches). Xenopterids are pugnacious and are capable of inflicting serious wounds with their sharp beak-like jaws. Burmese natives claim that if a person should fall into the water where the fishes abound, these puffers will attack in droves and kill the victim by their bites. Apparently little else has been reported on the habits of this interesting group.

PUFFER, BLOWFISH, *Amblyrhynchotes honckeni* (Bloch) (435). Indonesia, China, South Africa. Length 30 centimeters (12 inches).

PUFFER, BLOWFISH, *Arothron hispidus* (Linnaeus) (436). Panama, Indo-Pacific, Japan, Australia, South Africa, Red Sea. Length 53 centimeters (21 inches).

PUFFER, BLOWFISH, *Arothron manillensis* (Proce) (437). Tropical Indo-Pacific. Length 25 centimeters (10 inches).

PUFFER, BLOWFISH, *Arothron meleagris* (Lacépède) (438). West coast of Central America and throughout the Indo-Pacific. Length 32 centimeters (12.5 inches).

PUFFER, BLOWFISH, *Arothron nigropunctatus* (Bloch and Schneider) (439). Tropical Indo-Pacific, Japan, Australia, east coast of Africa, Red Sea. Length 25 centimeters (10 inches).

PUFFER, BLOWFISH, *Arothron stellatus* (Bloch and Schneider) (440). Tropical Indo-Pacific, Japan, Australia, Red Sea and east coast of Africa. Length 30 centimeters (12 inches).

FRESHWATER PUFFER, *Chelonodon fluviatilis* (Hamilton-Buchanan) (441). Freshwaters and coasts of India, Burma, Malaya, and Indonesia. Length 15 centimeters (6 inches).

PUFFER, *Fugu niphobles* (Jordan and Snyder) (442). Japan, China, the Philippines. Length 16 centimeters (6.25 inches).

PUFFER, *Fugu pardalis* (Temminck and Schlegel) (443). China and Japan. Length 36 centimeters (14 inches).

PUFFER, BLOWFISH, *Fugu poecilonotus* (Temminck and Schlegel) (444). Indo-Pacific, China, Korea, Japan. Length 25 centimeters (10 inches).

PUFFER, *Fugu rubripes rubripes* (Temminck and Schlegel) (445). Japan, China, Korea. Length 45 centimeters (17.5 inches).

PUFFER, *Fugu stictonotus* (Temminck and Schlegel) (446). Southern Korea, east China Sea and adjoining waters, Japan. Length 40 centimeters (16 inches).

PUFFER, *Fugu vermicularis vermicularis* (Temminck and Schlegel) (447). East China Sea, Japan. Length 33 centimeters (23.5 inches).

PUFFER, *Lagocephalus lunaris* (Bloch and Schneider) (448). Indo-Pacific, India, Red Sea, south and east coast of Africa, Australia, China, Japan. Length 30 centimeters (12 inches).

PUFFER, BLOWFISH, *Lagocephalus sceleratus* (Forster) (449). Indo-Pacific, southern Japan, Australia, east coast of Africa. Length 75 centimeters (29.5 inches).

PUFFER, *Sphaeroides annulatus* (Jenyns) (450). California to Peru, Galapagos Islands. Length 28 centimeters (11 inches).

PUFFER, *Sphaeroides maculatus* (Bloch and Schneider) (451). Atlantic coast of United States to Guiana. Length 25 centimeters (10 inches).

PUFFER, *Sphaeroides testudineus* (Linnaeus) (452). Atlantic coast of United States, West Indies, Brazil. Length 21 centimeters (8.25 inches)

PUFFER, *Tetraodon lineatus* Linnaeus (453). Rivers of northern and western Africa. Length 45 centimeters (17.5 inches).

PUFFER, BLOWFISH, *Torquigener hamiltoni* (Gray and Richardson) (454). Indo-Pacific, Australia. Length 3.5 inches).

### *Human Consumption of Poisonous Puffers*

The story of human consumption of poisonous puffers is a Japanese gourmet's paradox. Few organisms are known to be more deadly than puffers, and few organisms are considered to be a greater food delicacy than puffers. Puffers are considered to be a trash fish by the uninitiated and a gourmet's delight by connoisseurs. In ancient Japan, it was the fish of emperors, and commoners were forbidden to eat them. Yet, puffers have contributed more to the mortality statistics of food poisonings than any other food commodity in Japan.

Today, in Japan, the sale of poisonous puffers by fishermen and restaurant owners is rigidly controlled by health authorities. Fishermen, wholesalers, restaurant owners, and puffer cooks must follow rigid health regulations. Special restaurants are licensed as *fugu* (puffer) restaurants, and the fish are prepared by specially trained fugu cooks who are licensed as such (Figure 3). The Tokyo Metropolitan Office has even published a special cookbook for Japanese fugu cooks.

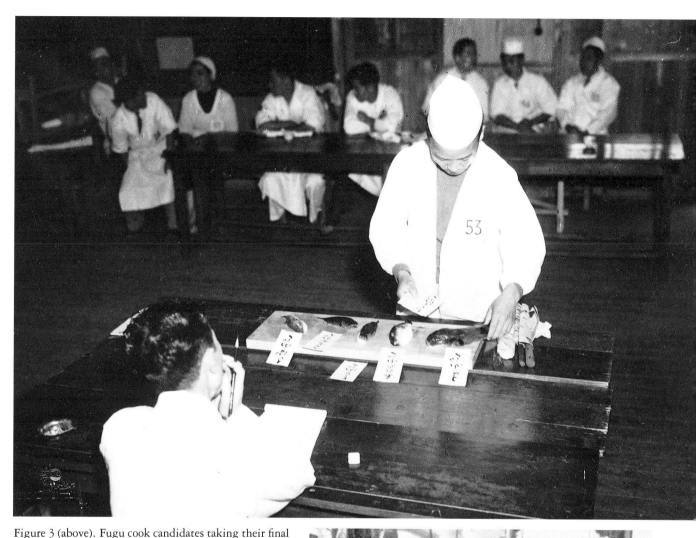

Figure 3 (above). Fugu cook candidates taking their final practical examination on the proper preparation of poisonous puffers for human consumption. Examinations are administered by licensed veterinarians that have had special training on the public health aspects of puffer cookery. Photo shows one of the students being examined on the identification of poisonous Japanese puffers. This culinary game is sometimes referred to as a form of Russian roulette. (Courtesy Tokyo Metropolitan Office)

Figure 4 (right). The danger of intoxications from ciguatoxic fishes is increasing in some parts of the world as fisheries operations are extended into tropical waters. The photograph shows a group of public health inspectors examining a shipment of snappers that has just arrived at the wharf of the Tokyo Central Wholesale Fish Market. Suspect fishes will be removed from the lot and samples tested by routine cat and mouse bioassays. This situation is unique because it is the only public health surveillance system presently in operation in any country.
(Courtesy M. Kainuma, Public Health Division, Tokyo Metropolitan Government)

Japan offers the finest screening and public health surveillance system of any country in the world for the purpose of detecting poisonous fishes. An outstanding example of this is the Tokyo Central Wholesale Fish Market (Figure 4), which maintains a continual surveillance program to insure the freshness and the elimination of any fisheries product suspected as poisonous. This procedure is particularly important in Japan since their fisheries catches are taken from every part of the world. Suspect fishes are sampled and then tested for toxicity by means of laboratory procedures.

**Ichthyootoxic Fishes**

Ichthyootoxism is one of the lesser known forms of fish poisoning. Ichthyootoxic fishes constitute a group of organisms that produce a poison that is generally restricted to the gonads of the fish. There is a definite relationship between gonadal activity and toxic production. The musculature and other parts of the fish are usually edible. Fishes in this group are mainly freshwater, but others are anadromous, that is, can live in both fresh and seawater or in brackish water. A cursory review of some of the freshwater forms has been included in this section in order to complete the overall picture of ichthyootoxications. Many of the fishes involved in ichthyootoxism are phylogenetically unrelated.

Symptoms develop soon after ingestion of the roe and consist of abdominal pain, nausea, vomiting, diarrhea, dizziness, headache, fever, bitter taste, dryness of the mouth, intense thirst, sensation of constriction of the chest, cold sweats, rapid irregular weak pulse, low blood pressure, cyanosis, pupillary dilatation, syncope, chills, dysphagia, and tinnitus. In severe cases there may be muscular cramps, paralysis, convulsions, coma, and death. *Barbus* roe usually does not cause death, but fatalities have resulted from eating the roe of the Japanese prickleback, *Stichaeus.* The victims generally recover within 3 to 5 days if they are given reasonable supportive therapy, but complete recovery may take longer. The nature of the poison is unknown.

These fishes include:

## Sturgeons

Family ACIPENSERIDAE: Sturgeons are a group of freshwater or anadromous fishes having elongate fusiform bodies covered with five rows of bony scutes. The head is covered with bony shields, and the snout is elongate, conical, or spatulate. The jaws are toothless. They are found in Europe, northern Asia, and North America. There are four genera and about 25 species. Sturgeons interbreed easily. Anadromous sturgeons have seasonal forms. The spring form ascends the rivers in spring, and spawns in spring or summer of the same year. The winter form ascends the rivers usually in autumn and spawns in the following year. They are clumsy, sluggish bottom feeders. Sturgeons feed on a variety of foods, including fishes, mollusks, crustaceans, and worms. They may attain large size, up to about 5.8 meters (18 feet), with a weight of 1,300 kilograms (2,860 pounds). Their flesh is coarse and beefy, but they are nevertheless of great economic importance in some regions. The fecundity rate of sturgeons is exceedingly high. A single fish may produce more than 7.5 million eggs in a single season. Spawning occurs usually in the central part of the river in a rocky area. The roe of sturgeons is used commercially in the preparation of caviar. Sturgeons are said to be long lived, attaining an age of more than 100 years.

RUSSIAN STURGEON, *Acipenser guldenstadti* Brandt (455). Persian and Siberian rivers, Caspian Sea, Danube. Length 1.4 meters (4.5 feet).

STURGEON, *Acipenser sturio* Linnaeus (456). Both coasts of the Atlantic, Mediterranean Sea, rivers of Europe and Russia. Length 3 meters (10 feet).

## Gars

Family LEPISOSTEIDAE: The gars are characterized by having an elongate body and a long snout covered with ganoid scales. The dorsal and anal fins are located in the posterior portion of the body near the caudal fin. They are found in North and Central America and on the island of Cuba. Gars are largely freshwater fishes inhabiting streams, lakes, and bayous, but may occur in brackish water. They are sluggish swimmers and voracious in their eating habits, feeding on crayfish and small fishes, and quite destructive to other fishes in general. The flesh of gars is usually considered to be of poor quality. Most species move whenever possible to coastal areas to spawn. Gars may attain large size, 6 meters (20 feet) or more in length. The eggs of two species, *Lepisosteus spatula* and *L. tristoechus*, have been reported to be toxic to humans. It is suspected that the eggs of other species may also be poisonous to eat.

ALLIGATOR GAR, *Lepisosteus tristoechus* (Bloch and Schneider) (457). Streams, brackish waters and coastal waters of the south Atlantic and Gulf states. Length 6 meters (20 feet).

## Whitefish

Family SALMONIDAE: The salmons and trouts are freshwater and anadromous fishes of the Northern Hemisphere. They are a group of outstanding fishes because of their beauty, activity, gaminess, and edibility. There are less than 100 species. They are characterized by an elongate, or moderately elongate, body covered with cycloid scales, by a naked head, and by the presence of an adipose fin. The salmonids are a commercially important group. They are active and voracious feeders, living largely on smaller fishes and a variety of invertebrates. The roe of some European salmonids has been reported as toxic to humans.

WHITEFISH, *Stenodus leucichthys* (Guldenstädt) (458). Volga River, rivers of Siberia. Length 71 centimeters (28 inches).

## Cyprinids

Family CYPRINIDAE: This is the largest of all fish families, containing more than 2,000 species. Minnows are found scattered throughout the north temperate zone except the Arctic Circle and extend only to a limited extent south of the Tropic of Cancer in the Western Hemisphere. They are particularly abundant in the rivers of southern Asia and tropical Africa. The family is characterized by highly specialized pharyngeal teeth. With few exceptions, cyprinids are small and relatively feeble fishes. They constitute most of the food of the predatory river fishes. The diet of cyprinids varies greatly according to the species; some are strictly herbivorous, whereas others are carnivorous. Most cyprinids are freshwater fish; only a few species are able to tolerate any degree of salinity. Some species are found in cold waters of melting snows (*Schizothorax*, etc.), whereas others are found in stagnant ponds. Some of the cyprinids found in the clear, swift streams of eastern Europe and central Asia contain toxic roe during the reproductive season.

BREAM, *Abramis brama* (Linnaeus) (459). Europe north of the Pyrenees and Alps to the Volga River and Caspian Sea. Length 35 centimeters (13.5 inches).

BARBEL, *Barbus barbus* (Linnaeus) (460). Northern and central Europe. Length 85 centimeters (33.5 inches).

TENCH, *Tinca tinca* (Linnaeus) (461). Europe. Length 60 cm (23.5 inches).

## Catfishes

Family ARIIDAE: Most marine catfishes are members of the family Ariidae. It is a large family with numerous species. Ariid catfishes inhabit tropical and subtropical regions throughout the world. They are sleek silvery fishes covered with smooth skin, but the head is protected by a coat of mail pierced by a central fontanelle. They have four to six barbels around the mouth. The dorsal and pectoral spines of some species are very sharp and can inflict a painful venomous wound. They are more active than many of their freshwater counterparts and spend little time resting on the bottom, but may frequently be seen in schooling formation. Ariid catfishes are generally tough eating, since they have coarse flesh, but they are used as foodfishes in some regions. Sea catfishes are sometimes seen swarming in shallow water, in sandy bays, or in the vicinity of river-mouths. The roe of some species is reported to be toxic.

SEA CATFISH, *Bagre marinus* (Mitchill) (Chapter IV, 193). Seas of tropical America. Length 30 centimeters (12 inches).

Family SILURIDAE: The members of this catfish family are characterized by a scaleless body, a long anal fin, and the absence of an adipose fin. They are largely freshwater fishes that are widespread throughout Europe and Asia. Some species of this family are occasionally found in brackish water, particularly in the southern seas of the former U.S.S.R. They feed mainly on other fishes.

These catfishes vary greatly in size. *Siluris glanis*, for example, is one of the largest river fishes in Europe, attaining a weight of 200 kilograms (440 pounds) or more. Some of the silurids are commercially valuable in certain parts of Europe; the roe of some species, however, is reported as poisonous to eat.

CATFISH, MUDFISH, *Parasilurus asotus* (Linnaeus) (462). Japan, Korea, Manchuria, and China. Length 40 centimeters (16 inches).

## Codfishes

Family GADIDAE: The codfishes are among the most valuable of all food fishes. They are found in all seas of the Northern Hemisphere. One species is a freshwater fish. Codfishes among other things are characterized by one, two, or three dorsal fins without any spines. An unpaired barbel is usually present under the chin. The members of this family are largely deepwater fishes but are also found close in to shore. They tend to be voracious eaters and will feed on almost anything that is available. They are prolific breeders; a single fish may produce more than 9 million eggs in a single season. They are similar to salmon in that, unlike most fishes, they spawn in cooling waters. The liver produces an oil of considerable economic value. Some species may attain a weight of about 75 kilograms (165 pounds). The freshwater *Lota* of Europe and Asia is reported to have toxic roe.

BURBOT, EELPOUT, *Lota lota* (Linnaeus) (463). Freshwaters of northern and central Europe. Length 1 meter (3 feet).

## Killifishes

Family CYPRINODONTIDAE: The killifishes are a family of small fishes, most of which are freshwater fish, and range from New England south to Argentina and to Asia and Africa. Among other things they are characterized by a small protractile mouth. There are about 200 species. The largest species rarely reaches a length of 30 centimeters (12 inches). Most of them are found in swamps, ditches, reservoirs, lakes, or small ponds. Some species are herbivorous, but many of them are insectivorous. Because of their insectivorous habits, some species are used quite extensively in mosquito abatement. *Fundulus* inhabits both freshwater and salt-water. The marine species are usually found in shallow bays or protected areas close to shore. Cyprinodonts are generally too small to be considered of much food value.

KILLIFISH, *Aphanius calaritanus* (Cuvier and Valenciennes) (464). Southern Europe and north Africa. The roe may be toxic. Length 5 centimeters (2 inches).

### Ichthyohemotoxic Fishes

Although the subject of ichthyohemotoxins, or fish serum poisoning, is actually concerned with a variety of phylogenetically unrelated fishes, most of the research has been concerned with toxins derived from three types of eels—morays, congers, and anguillids—which are members of the single order Anguilliformes (Apodes). The members of this group are characterized by an eel-like body, abdominal pelvic fins (when present), and an air bladder connected with the intestines by a duct. There are no spines in the fins. The scales, if present, are cycloid. The vertebrae are numerous. Gill openings are narrow or slit-like. The dorsal and anal fins are very long, and usually confluent posteriorly.

In reviewing the research on ichthyohemotoxins, it is noteworthy that most reports deal with the immunological, toxicological, and chemical aspects, and that the usual array of clinical reports are absent.

Fish serum intoxications may be of two types:

(1) Systemic, a form that results from drinking fresh, uncooked fish blood. The symptoms consist of diarrhea, bloody stools, nausea, vomiting, frothing at the mouth, skin eruptions, cyanosis, apathy, irregular pulse, weakness, paresthesia, paralysis, respiratory distress, and possibly death.

(2) Local, a form that produces severe inflammatory response when raw eel serum is placed in the eye or on the tongue. Oral symptoms consist of burning, redness of the mucosa, and hypersalivation. Ocular symptoms are manifested in severe burning and redness of the conjunctivae, which develop within five to twenty minutes after contamination. Lacrimation and swelling of the eyelids are usually present. A sensation as though a foreign body was present in the eye may persist for several days. Repeated inoculations of eel serum in the eye gradually result in an immunity, with progressing decrease in the severity of symptoms with each subsequent inoculation.

Very little is known regarding the symptomatology of ichthyohemotoxism in humans. Treatment is symptomatic, and there is no specific antidote.

This group of fishes includes:

## Freshwater Eels

Family ANGUILLIDAE: Freshwater eels are widely distributed throughout the world, with the exception of the Arctic, Antarctic, west coast of Africa, Pacific coast of America, and Atlantic coast of South America, from which areas they are absent. Anguillids are primarily freshwater and brackishwater fishes, but they migrate to the depths of the sea for the purpose of breeding. When the common freshwater eel of Europe attains a length of about 30 centimeters (12 inches), it changes from its usually yellow color to a silvery appearance. "Silver eels" make their way down to the mouths of rivers. Migration from estuaries and into the open sea takes place during late summer and autumn. Then starts the extended journey in the deep waters of the central Atlantic, to an area known as the Sargasso Sea.

Reproductive activities take place within this area. The young leaf-shaped eels, which are termed leptocephalids, slowly make their way to Europe. It is estimated that this migration takes about three years. During this period the leptocephalids gradually change into the true eel-like appearance. Upon reaching the shores of Europe, they ascend the rivers as typical little eels, known as "elvers." They remain in freshwater for a period of five to twenty years and finally return to the sea to spawn and die. The American eel has a similar life history, but the leptocephalids are believed to require only about one year for their migration. Eels are reputed to be among the more voracious of carnivorous fishes. Their bill of fare consists of a large variety of bony fishes, shrimp, and crayfish. They are powerful, rapid swimmers and somewhat nocturnal in their habits. During the day they may hide in crevices, under rocks, under logs, or burrow in the mud. Freshwater eels are generally considered to be excellent food fishes. The females, which are larger than the males, may attain a length of about a meter.

COMMON EUROPEAN EEL, *Anguilla anguilla* (Linnaeus) (465). Europe, fresh and saltwater. Length 1 meter (3 feet).

AMERICAN EEL, *Anguilla rostrata* (LeSueur) (466). Atlantic coast of the United States, from Maine to Mexico. Length 1 meter (3 feet).

## Conger Eels, Moray Eels

Family CONGRIDAE: Conger eels are similar in appearance to anguillids but are without scales, have a somewhat different mouth, and have the dorsal fin beginning nearer the head. They are widely distributed in marine, brackish, or freshwater, in warm and temperate zones. The principal species, *Conger conger,* with which this chapter is concerned, is largely marine. Congers prefer deep water rocky bottoms or sandy areas surrounded by rocks, although its bathymetric range extends from tidal zones to 50 fathoms or more. They may enter lobster pots to secure their contents and prey upon flatfishes, pilchard, hake, herring, crabs, and a large variety of other types of marine animals. Congers may attain a length of more than 2 meters (6.5 feet) and a weight of more than 45 kilograms (100 pounds).

CONGER EEL, *Conger conger* (Linnaeus) (467). Atlantic Ocean, Mediterranean. Length 2 meters (6.5 feet).

Family MURAENIDAE: See Chapter IV, p.84 for biology of Moray eels.

EUROPEAN MORAY EEL, *Muraena helena* Linnaeus (Chapter IV, 197). Eastern Atlantic Ocean and Mediterranean Sea. Length 1.5 meters (5 feet).

## ICHTHYOCRINOTOXIC FISHES

The fishes included in this section comprise a recently established category of ichthyotoxic fishes. Ichthyocrinotoxic fishes produce their poisons by glandular secretion but lack a venom apparatus, i.e., the glandular structures are not associated with spines, teeth, or some other mechanical traumatogenic device. The toxic glandular contents are merely secreted into the water. There is no mechanism whereby the poison can be injected into the victim. Our present knowledge of this group of fishes is meager, but their role in the marine ecosystem may ultimately prove to be of great significance. With the exception of a few preliminary studies, ichthyocrinotoxic fishes have been largely overlooked by marine biotoxicologists. The number and phylogenetic distribution of ichthyocrinotoxic fishes is unknown, but they are probably widely distributed among piscine organisms.

The poison glands of ichthyocrinotoxic fishes undoubtedly assist in the defensive mechanism of the fish as warning or repellent substances. However, these glands may exert some of their most profound effects in the marine exosystem by secreting toxic metabolites into the ocean environment. (*See* Figures 5; 6a, b; 7; and 8a, b, c).

In the case of cyclostome poisoning, it is not certain whether intoxication is due to poisons that are present primarily in the slime, flesh, or both. The symptoms consist of nausea, vomiting, dysenteric diarrhea, tenesmus, abdominal pain, and weakness. Symptoms usually begin to appear within a few hours after ingestion of the fish. Recovery generally takes place within a period of several days.

The ingestion of trunkfishes (Ostraciontidae) may result in unsteadiness of gait similar to drunkenness, and the effects may be serious. It is not known whether this is the result of ostracitoxin or ciguatoxin.

The toxicity of the skin of puffers is well known to the public health officials familiar with tetrodotoxications in Japan. In a series of 129 cases of puffer poisoning, 10 were due to eating the skin of the fish. The symptoms of puffer poisoning have been discussed at length on p. 159.

When the mucus of grammistid fishes comes into contact with the tongue, it has an immediate unpleasant bitter taste and produces a slight stinging sensation. Moreover, when the fish are confined to a small volume of water and agitated, an unpleasant odor associated with this taste may be detected in the water.

The ichthyocrinotoxic fishes include:

## Lampreys, Hagfishes

Family PETROMYZONTIDAE: The members of the family Petromyzontidae are inhabitants of marine and fresh waters of the Northern Hemisphere. Some species are marine and anadromous, whereas others are confined to fresh waters. The habits of *Petromyzon marinus* are representative of the marine and anadromous species. Since lampreys are seldom seen in the open sea, little is known about this phase of their life. When encountered in the sea, they are usually close to the land or in estuaries or other comparatively shallow water areas. Lampreys have been taken at 547 fathoms off Nantucket, Massachusetts. Life history studies indicate that lampreys tolerate a wide range of temperatures and salinities.

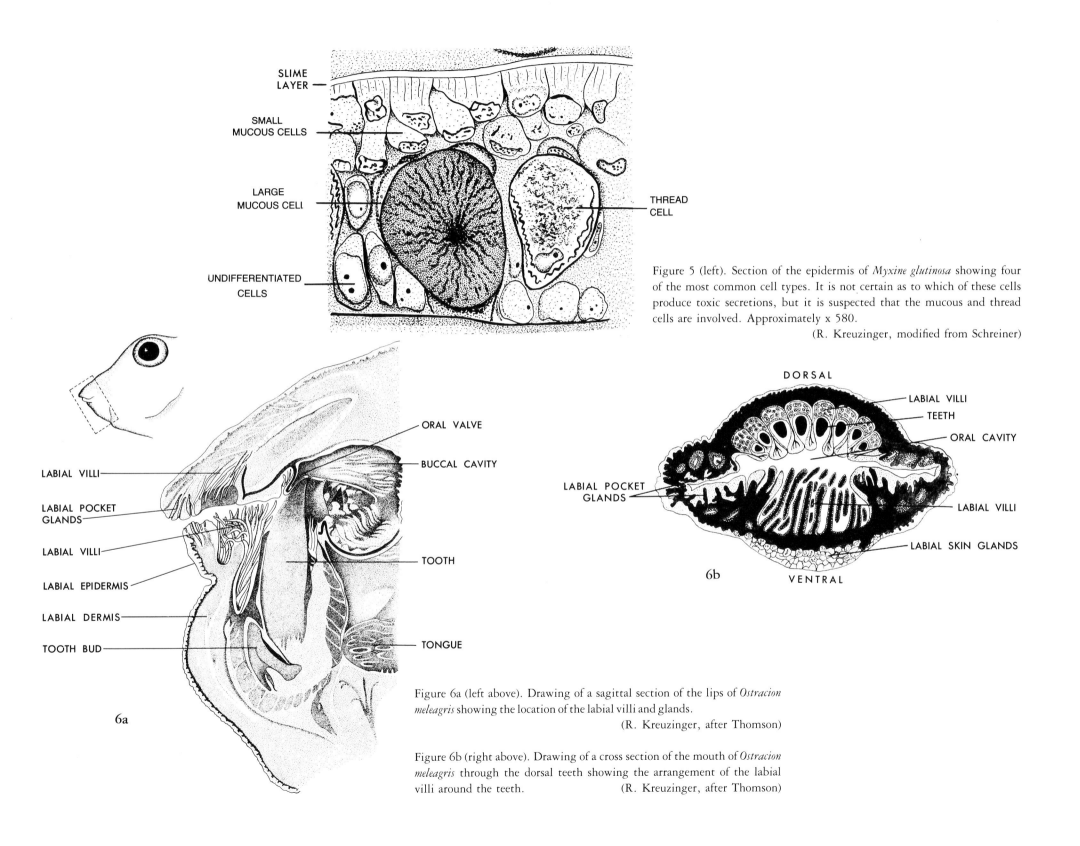

SLIME LAYER

SMALL MUCOUS CELLS

LARGE MUCOUS CELL

UNDIFFERENTIATED CELLS

THREAD CELL

Figure 5 (left). Section of the epidermis of *Myxine glutinosa* showing four of the most common cell types. It is not certain as to which of these cells produce toxic secretions, but it is suspected that the mucous and thread cells are involved. Approximately x 580.

(R. Kreuzinger, modified from Schreiner)

LABIAL VILLI

LABIAL POCKET GLANDS

LABIAL VILLI

LABIAL EPIDERMIS

LABIAL DERMIS

TOOTH BUD

ORAL VALVE

BUCCAL CAVITY

TOOTH

TONGUE

6a

DORSAL

LABIAL VILLI

TEETH

ORAL CAVITY

LABIAL POCKET GLANDS

LABIAL VILLI

LABIAL SKIN GLANDS

6b

VENTRAL

Figure 6a (left above). Drawing of a sagittal section of the lips of *Ostracion meleagris* showing the location of the labial villi and glands.

(R. Kreuzinger, after Thomson)

Figure 6b (right above). Drawing of a cross section of the mouth of *Ostracion meleagris* through the dorsal teeth showing the arrangement of the labial villi around the teeth. (R. Kreuzinger, after Thomson)

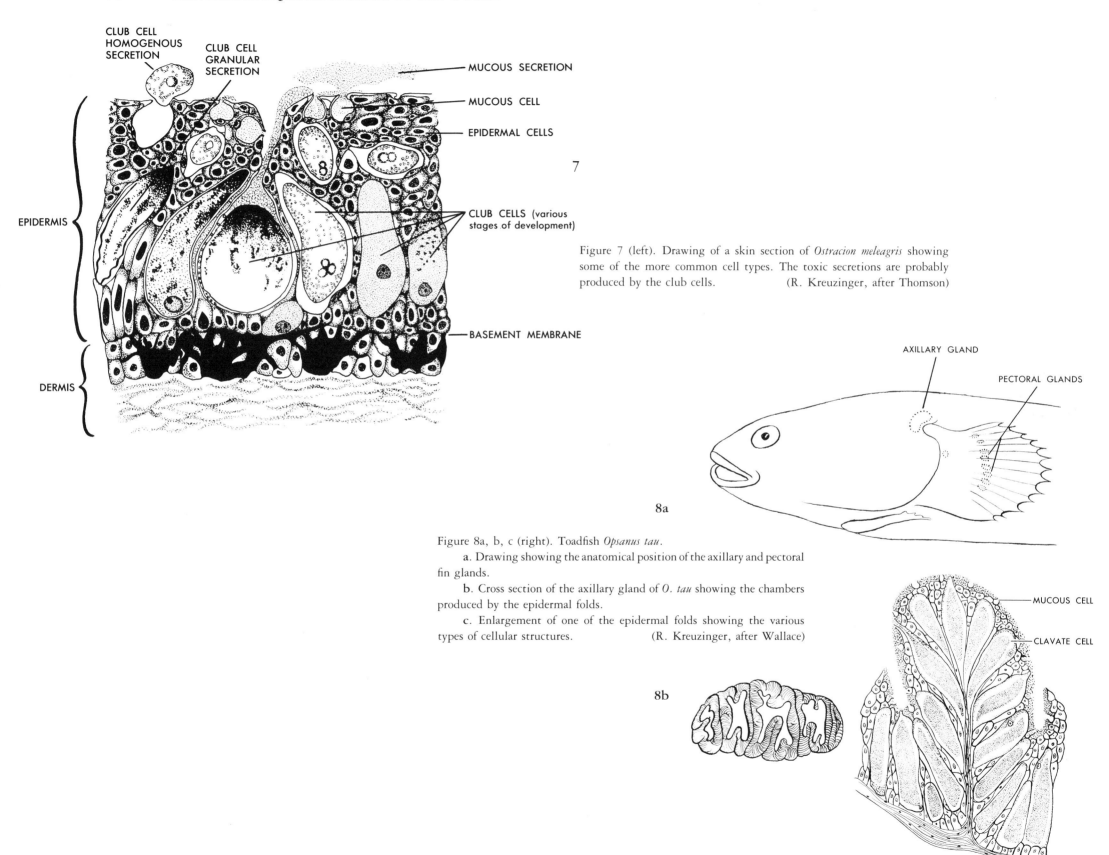

CLUB CELL HOMOGENOUS SECRETION

CLUB CELL GRANULAR SECRETION

MUCOUS SECRETION

MUCOUS CELL

EPIDERMAL CELLS

7

CLUB CELLS (various stages of development)

EPIDERMIS

BASEMENT MEMBRANE

DERMIS

Figure 7 (left). Drawing of a skin section of *Ostracion meleagris* showing some of the more common cell types. The toxic secretions are probably produced by the club cells.          (R. Kreuzinger, after Thomson)

AXILLARY GLAND

PECTORAL GLANDS

8a

Figure 8a, b, c (right). Toadfish *Opsanus tau*.
      a. Drawing showing the anatomical position of the axillary and pectoral fin glands.
      b. Cross section of the axillary gland of *O. tau* showing the chambers produced by the epidermal folds.
      c. Enlargement of one of the epidermal folds showing the various types of cellular structures.          (R. Kreuzinger, after Wallace)

MUCOUS CELL

CLAVATE CELL

8b

8c

Adult lampreys are parasitic, feeding on the blood of other fishes. They attach themselves to the body of a host fish by sucking with the oral disk; by means of their horny teeth they rasp through the skin and scales and then suck the blood until the host is dry. Studies have shown that the buccal secretion of lampreys contains an anticoagulant that facilitates the flow of blood. Mackerel, shad, cod, pollock, salmon, basking sharks, herring, swordfish, hake, sturgeon, and eels are favorite preys of lampreys. Larval lampreys feed largely on microscopic organisms.

*P. marinus,* an anadromous species, seeks a river having a gravelly bottom with rapid running water for spawning beds and a muddy or soft sandy bottom in quiet water for the larvae. In the New England states, migration up the rivers usually takes place during the spring and early summer months. The parents die soon after spawning. The larval lampreys remain in the parent stream living in mud burrows for a period of three to five years. When they reach a length of 10 to 13 centimeters (4 to 5 inches), they migrate to the sea, usually during the autumn.

RIVER LAMPREY, *Lampetra fluviatilis* (Linnaeus) (298). Baltic and North Sea basins, westward to Ireland and France; enters the rivers from the sea. Length 36 centimeters (14 inches) or more.

ATLANTIC HAGFISH, *Myxine glutinosa* Linnaeus (299). Length 79 centimeters (31 inches).

## Seabass or Groupers

Family SERRANIDAE: Seabass or groupers are robust, carnivorous, predacious shore fishes of tropical and temperate waters. A variety of biotopes are inhabited by this large family, including coral reefs, rocks, sandy areas, and kelp. A few are found in fairly deep waters, but most live in shallow water. Some attain a weight of 300 kilograms (660 pounds) or more. They are usually considered good food fishes, although some seabass are poisonous to eat.

GOLDEN STRIPED BASS, *Grammistes sexlineatus*

(Thunberg) (468). Indo-Pacific. Length 15 centimeters (6 inches).

SOAPFISH, *Rypticus saponaceus* (Bloch and Schneider (469). Tropical and subtropical Atlantic. Length 45 centimeters (17.5 inches).

## Trunkfishes

Family OSTRACIONTIDAE: Trunkfishes are especially peculiar in construction. The body is enveloped within a bony box, comprised of six-sided scutes, leaving openings only for the jaws, fins, and tail. They live in tropical seas and are frequently seen swimming slowly among the corals in shallow water. Many of them are brilliantly colored. The "exoskeleton," which serves them well for protection, is used by primitive peoples as a container in which the trunkfish is cooked over a fire. Little is known of the habits of trunkfishes.

SPECKLED TRUNKFISH, *Ostracion meleagris* Shaw (381). Tropical Indo-Pacific, Japan, South Africa. Length 20 centimeters (18 inches).

TRUNKFISH, *Lactoria diaphana* (Bloch and Schneider) (380). Tropical Indo-Pacific, Japan, South Africa. Length 30 centimeters (12 inches).

TRUNKFISH, *Ostracion cubicus* Linnaeus (470). Tropical Indo-Pacific. Length 20 centimeters (8 inches).

## Puffers
### (Tetraodontidae)

Family TETRAODONTIDAE: See p. 161 for the biology of puffer fishes.

PUFFER, BLOWFISH, *Arothron hispidus* (Linnaeus) (436). Panama, Indo-Pacific, Japan, Australia, South Africa, Red Sea. Length 53 centimeters (21 inches).

PUFFER, BLOWFISH, *Arothron nigropunctatus* (Bloch and Schneider) (439). Indo-Pacific, Japan, Australia, East Africa, Red Sea. Length 25 centimeters (10 inches).

PUFFER, *Spaeroides maculatus* (Bloch and Schneider) (451). Atlantic coast of United States to Guiana. Length 25 centimeters (10 inches).

## Toadfishes

Family BATRACHOIDIDAE: See p. 89 for the biology of Toadfishes.

OYSTER TOADFISH, *Opsanus tau* (Linnaeus) (Chapter IV, 232). Atlantic coast of United States, Massachusetts to West Indies. Length 30 centimeters (12 inches).

## OTHER POISONOUS VETEBRATES

### AMPHIBIANS

Amphibians are poikilothermic ("cold-blooded"), usually small vertebrates. There are about 2,400 living species of amphibians, which involve the chordate class Amphibia—the frogs, salamanders, sirens, and caecilians. They have moist skins, are scaleless, and have four limbs that are rudimentary in some species. The hands have four fingers and the feet five toes. The skull is flat and wide, and the arrangement of the skull bones tends to be reptilian and attached to the vertebral column by two bony protuberances. They are equipped with true teeth in the jaw bones and roof of the mouth, but the teeth are without roots and are replaced continuously. Chromatophores with brown, yellow, and red pigmentation enable the body to change color.

Amphibians lay their eggs in the water or in moist surroundings. The egg is covered by several gelatinous envelopes rather than a shell and usually hatches into a larva. Poisons may be present in the eggs or larvae. The larva differs structurally from the adult and will metamorphose rather abruptly into the adult body form. The larvae have gills, which may be enclosed within a gill chamber. In the adults, respiration takes place by means of lungs, through gills, through the skin or mucous membrane lining the mouth and pharynx, or by a combination of these mechanisms.

The skin of amphibians is of particular interest to toxicologists because of its role in poison production. The epidermis or upper horny layer of the skin produces horny claws, thorn pads, horned teeth, jaws, and other horny structures. The dermis or lower skin layer is rich in glands producing slime or poison. The skin organs that secrete these poisons are granular glands whose minute openings are scattered over the surface of the skin among the openings of the mucous glands. Granular glands seem to be a primitive type of gland common to amphibians that synthesize, store, and release these toxic substances. Some of the poisons produced are among the most toxic substances known. The chemical nature of these poisons is complex and includes, among others, alkaloids, which are substances usually found in plants. Other poisons include such agents as salamandarin, bufotoxin, tetrodotoxin, and batrachotoxin. Some of these poisons are now used in biomedical research on nerve, muscle, and heart function studies.

The effect of some of these amphibian poisons on humans due to ingestion is not known, since people do not generally eat amphibian skins. The blow-gun dart poisons derived from frogs are known to be extremely toxic, and if injected into a human would undoubtedly produce death.

The living amphibians are generally grouped into four orders as follows:

Order ANURA, or frogs and toads. They have well-developed legs, the hind ones being longer than the front ones. Anurans lack tails in the adult stage. They are the lowest form of vertebrates to have a middle ear cavity. Moveable eyelids protect the eyes, and glands are present to keep them moist. Most anurans require moist surroundings and cannot stand prolonged exposure to low humidities, but a few, such as the giant toad, *Bufo marinus,* are able to adapt to rather arid conditions. Fertilization is almost always external. Usually the eggs are laid in the water and hatch into aquatic larvae, but in some species the eggs are laid on land and the young hatch resembling miniature adults. There are about 1,900 species. Some of the frogs and toads produce extremely toxic substances, which are used by natives as arrow poisons.

Order CAUDATA, or salamanders and newts, which retain the tail throughout life instead of losing it during metamorphosis as do frogs. There are about 300 species. The skin and eggs of salamanders and newts are toxic.

Order GYMNOPHIONA, or caecilians, which are slimy, worm-like creatures with no limbs or limb girdles and practically no tail. There are about 160 species.

Order TRACHYSTOMATA, or sirens. There are only three aquatic species, and they remain in the larval form for life.

## Salamanders or Newts

The skin of salamanders or newts produces a variety of toxic substances in specialized skin glands. These poisons include alkaloids, steroids, amino acids, and other toxic products, some of which involve extremely complex molecules. One of the most remarkable finds is the presence of tetrodotoxin, the same poison that is found in pufferfish of the family Tetraodontidae. This poison, when first detected in freshwater newts, was referred to as "tarichatoxin."

Some of the salamanders or newts are strikingly ornate in their coloration. Most species require a habitat of cool streams and lakes in which the water is clean and well oxygenated, with submerged vegetation, and adjacent humid forest and grasslands.

The following salamander or newt species are representative of those known to contain tetrodotoxin in their skin:

JAPANESE SWORDTAIL NEWT, *Cynops (Triturus) ensicauda* (Hallowell) (471). Japan. Length 16 centimeters (6.2 inches).

JAPANESE RED-BELLIED NEWT, *Cynops (Triturus) pyrrhogaster* (Boie) (472). Japan. Length 14 centimeters (5.5 inches).

BLACK-SPOTTED NEWT, *Notophthalmus meri-*dionalis (Cope) (473). South Texas and Mexico. Length 11 centimeters (4 inches).

ROUGH-SKINED NEWT, *Taricha granulosa* (Skilton) (474). California to Alaska, Idaho. Length 21 centimeters (8 inches).

RED-BELLIED NEWT, *Taricha rivularis* (Twitty) (475). California. Length 21 centimeters (8 inches).

CALIFORNIA NEWT, *Taricha torosa* (Rathke) (476; 477a, b). Southwestern United States. Length 19 centimeters (7 inches).

ALPINE NEWT, *Titurus alpestris* (Laurenti) (478). Central Europe, Germany, French Alps, Italy, Switzerland, Greece. Length 11 centimeters (4 inches).

CRESTED NEWT, *Triturus cristatus* (Laurenti) (479). Northern and Middle Europe, Russia. Length 18 centimeters (7 inches).

MARBLED NEWT, *Triturus marmoratus* (Laetreille) (480). France, Spain. Length 15 centimeters (6 inches).

SMOOTH NEWT, *Triturus vulgaris* (Linnaeus) (481). Europe, Urals, Turkey. Length 11 centimeters (4.2 inches).

## Frogs and Toads

The skin of certain frogs and toads is known to contain a variety of very toxic substances known as batrachotoxins, pumiliotoxins, and histrionicotoxins. These are alkaloids and are among the most poisonous nonprotein poisons known. Some of these poisons are of sufficient potency as to be useful in tipping darts used in the blowguns of South American Indians for hunting purposes. One of the most toxic of these poisons is contained in the skin of the tree frog *Phyllobates terribilis,* so named because of its extreme toxicity. (See the excellent work on the poison-dart frogs by Myers and Daly [1976] for further information on these poisons.) Tetrodotoxin has also been found in the skin of some of the atelopid frogs, such as *Atelopus varius* and others found in Costa Rica. *Atelopus zeteki* contains an unusually potent cardiovascular poison known as atelopidtoxin.

Some of the toads, such as *Bufo marinus,* contain toxic steroidal peptides known as bufotoxins that are present in their skin and parotid glands. The eggs of some toads are also extremely poisonous and may cause death in humans if eaten.

The following is a partial list of frogs and toads known to possess skin poisons of various types:

POISON-DART FROGS[1]

*Atelopus varius* Stannius (482). Colombia, Central America. Body length 4.4 centimeters (1.7 inches).

*Atelopus zeteki* Dunn (483). Central America. Body length 4 centimeters (1.5 inches).

*Dendrobates auratus* (Girard) (484). Colombia. Body length 4.2 centimeters (1.6 inches).

*Dendrobates bombates* Myers and Daly (485). Colombia. Body length 3 centimeters (1.2 inches).

*Dendrobates histrionicus* Berthold (486). Colombia, Ecuador. Body length 3 centimeters (1.2 inches).

*Dendrobates lehmanni* Myers and Daly (487). Colombia. Body length 3 centimeters (1.2 inches).

*Dendrobates leucomelas* Fitzinger (488). Colombia. Body length 3.7 centimeters (1.4 inches).

*Dendrobates silverstonei* Myers and Daly (489). Colombia. Body length 3 centimeters (1.2 inches).

*Phyllobates terribilis* Myers and Daly (490). Colombia. Length 4.5 centimeters (1.7 inches).

*Dendrobates trivittatus* (Spix) (491). Colombia. Body length 4.9 centimeters (2 inches).

*Phyllobates aurotaenia* (Boulenger) (492). Colombia. Body length 3 centimeters (1.2 inches).

*Phyllobates lugubris* (Schmidt) (493). Colombia. Length 2.5 centimeters (1 inch).

GIANT TOAD, *Bufo marinus* (Linnaeus) (494). Central and South America, Texas. Body length 20 centimeters (8 inches).

---

[1] There are no common English names available.

# REPTILES
## Turtles

Reptiles of the order Chelonia (Testudinata) are characterized by a broad body encased in a bony shell comprised of a rounded dorsal carapace and a flat ventral plastron, joined at the sides and covered by polygonal laminae (scutes, scales) or leathery skin. The jaws are edentulous and equipped with horny sheaths. The quadrate bone is united to the skull. The ribs are fused to the shell, and the sternum is absent. All turtles (tortoises, terrapins) are oviparous in their reproduction. Although there are about 265 species in the order Chelonia, only five marine species of turtles have been reported as poisonous to man.

The symptoms of chelonitoxication vary with the amount of flesh ingested and the individual. Symptoms generally develop within a few hours to several days after eating the turtle. In one large outbreak involving 100 persons, most of the victims developed symptoms about twelve hours after eating the turtle. Initial signs and symptoms usually consist of nausea, vomiting, diarrhea, tachycardia, pallor, severe epigastric pain, sweating, coldness of the extremities, and vertigo. Victims frequently report an acute stomatitis consisting of a dry, burning sensation of the lips, tongue, lining of the mouth, and throat; some may complain of a sensation of tightness of the chest. The victim frequently becomes lethargic and unresponsive. Swallowing becomes very difficult, and hypersalivation is pronounced. The oral symptoms may be slow to develop, but become increasingly severe after several days. The tongue develops a white coating, the breath becomes foul, and later the tongue may become covered with multiple pinhead-size, reddened pustular papules. The pustules may persist for several months, whereas in some instances they break down into ulcers.

Desquamation of the skin over most of the body has been reported. Some victims develop a severe hepatomegaly, with right upper quadrant tenderness.

The conjunctivae become icteric. Headaches and a feeling of "heaviness of the head" are frequently reported. Deep reflexes may be diminished. Somnolence is one of the more pronounced symptoms present in severe intoxications and is usually indicative of an unfavorable prognosis. At first the victim is difficult to awaken and then gradually becomes comatose, which is followed rapidly by death. The symptoms present are typical of a hepatorenal death. The overall case fatality rate on reported outbreaks is about 28 percent.

Family CHELONIIDAE: The green sea turtle *Chelonia* usually inhabits water less than 25 meters (80 feet) in depth and prefers areas sheltered by reefs where it feeds on algae. It is also common in bays and lagoons. Occasionally *Chelonia* will make its way into freshwater lakes. Green turtles are sometimes seen basking on reefs and beaches of islands uninhabited by man. They are omnivorous but primarily vegetarian, feeding upon *Cymodocea, Thalassia, Zostera, Halophila,* and other algae. When kept in captivity, they seem to show a preference for a diet of meat and fish. Green turtles nest between latitudes 30° north and 30° south of the equator. They will migrate considerable distances, leaving their usual haunts to get to their breeding grounds. The nest site is usually selected on a beach having loose sand within reach of the waves. When the exact spot is selected, the loose sand is brushed away with the front flippers, but the actual digging is done with the hind ones. About 60 to 190 eggs may be laid at a time. Upon completion of laying, the turtle covers her nest completely with sand. She obliterates her tracks by throwing sand over her back with the front flippers as she moves away. The entire nesting process requires about two hours. The breeding season seems to be from July to November in Ceylon, but from October to mid-February in Australia. This species is considered one of the more food-valuable turtles.

The hawksbill turtle, *Eretmochelys*, is generally found close to land in tropical and subtropical oceans. Seldom does it enter lagoons. Although usually consid-

ered carnivorous, it is omnivorous and at times may subsist entirely upon algae. The breeding range is between 25° north and 25° south of the equator. Eggs are laid on sandy beaches in a manner similar to that used by *Chelonia*. As many as 115 eggs or more are laid at a time. The egg-laying season extends from November to February in some areas, but seems to take place during April to June in others. *Eretmochelys* is of commercial importance because of its overlapping scutes, which unfortunately are utilized in the manufacturing of jewelry and ornaments.

GREEN TURTLE, *Chelonia mydas* (Linnaeus) (495; 496; 499a) . All tropical and subtropical oceans. May attain a weight of over 25 kilograms (55 pounds) and a carapace length of about 120 centimeters (47 inches).

HAWKSBILL TURTLE, *Eretmochelys imbricata* (Linnaeus) (497, 499b). All tropical and subtropical oceans. May attain a weight of about 125 kilograms (275 pounds) and a carapace length of about 85 centimeters (33.5 inches).

Family DERMOCHELIDAE: The leatherback turtle, *Dermochelys*, usually inhabits relatively deep water near the edge of the Continental Shelf and is said to be the swiftest and the largest of living chelonians. Newly hatched leatherbacks head directly for the open ocean and do not return to shallow water until they are ready for egg-laying. An adult may attain a weight of more than 780 kilograms (1,716 pounds). Their food consists of algae, crustaceans, and fishes. *Dermochelys* is believed to lay eggs three or four times a year, which in Ceylon takes place during May to June. The eggs are laid on sandy beaches at night. Often several females will deposit their eggs in close proximity to each other.

LEATHERBACK TURTLE, LEATHERY TURTLE, *Dermochelys coriacea* (Linnaeus) (498; 499c). Largely circumtropical in distribution, but occasionally taken in temperate seas off the coasts of North and South America, Mediterranean area, British Isles, and Japan. May attain a weight of over 250 kilograms (550 pounds) and a carapace length of about 120 centimeters (47 inches).

## MARINE MAMMALS

The species presented in this section comprise a small, diverse group of poisonous marine mammals: whales, dolphins, and porpoises; polar bears; and walruses, seals, and sea lions. Most of the species involved inhabit cold temperate or arctic waters.

### Whales, Dolphins, and Porpoises

Mammals of the order Cetacea are characterized by their spindle-shaped body form. The head is long, often pointed, and joined directly to the body. Some species have a fleshy dorsal fin. The flippers or fore-limbs are broad and paddle-like; the digits are embedded and have no claws. There are no hind limbs. The tail is long and ends in two broad, transverse, fleshy flukes notched in the midline. The teeth, when present, are all alike and lack enamel. The nostrils are on top of the head. The ear openings are minute. The body surface is smooth, without hairs except for a few on the muzzle. There are no skin glands except mammary and conjunctival glands. A thick layer of fat (blubber) under the skin affords insulation.

The living cetaceans comprise thirty-eight genera and about ninety species, distributed among eight families. They occur in all seas of the world and in certain rivers and lakes.

Intoxications have been reported from eating the liver of the sei whale, *Balaenoptera borealis*. The signs and symptoms of sei whale liver poisoning develop within 24 hours after ingestion and consist of severe occipital headaches, neck pain, flushing and swelling of the face, nausea, vomiting, abdominal pain, diarrhea, fever, chills, photophobia, epiphora, and an erratic blood pressure. After a day or two the patient's lips become dry, and desquamation develops around the mouth, gradually spreading to the cheeks, forehead,

and neck. The desquamation usually does not involve the entire body. The chemical and pharmacological properties of sei whale poison are unknown, but it is believed to be a histamine-like substancee, since methanol extracts of the poison give a marked histamine-like reaction on isolated rabbit intestine. If the poison is a histamine-like substance, the use of epinephrine should be considered since it is a specific physiological antagonist to histamine. Antihistamines should prove of value. The remainder of the treatment is symptomatic.

Asiatic porpoise poisoning is caused by eating the viscera or flesh of the Asiatic porpoise *Neophocaena phocaenoides*. The signs and symptoms consist of abdominal pain, abdominal distention, swelling and numbness of the tongue, loss of vision, cyanosis, a sensation of numbness of various areas of the skin, hypersalivation, with the saliva having a greenish tinge, and finally muscular paralysis. Death may be rapid; the case fatality rate is said to be very high. There is no specific antidote. The treatment is symptomatic. The natives claim that aqueous extracts of the plants *Mirabilis jalapa* Linnaeus, *Mimosa corniculata* Loureiro, Chinese olive (*Canarium* sp.), and camphor are effective antidotes.

Ingestion of the flesh of the white whale may cause human fatalities. Clinical characteristics are unknown. Treatment is symptomatic.

The flesh of the sperm whale is said to be poisonous, but there is no information available concerning the clinical characteristics of this biotoxication. Treatment is symptomatic.

Family BALAENOPTERIDAE: The fin-back whales are the largest of living animals. The largest member of this group, the blue or sulphur-bottom whale, *Sibbaldus musculus* (Linnaeus), attains a length of 30 meters (98 feet) and a weight of 112,500 kilograms (123.7 tons). The family is composed of three genera and six species and occurs in all oceans. This is one of two families of baleen whales in which the embryonic teeth are replaced by baleen plates in the adult animal. Fin-back whales are frequently called "rorquals," which refers to "a whale having folds or pleats." The rorquals are equipped with longitudinal furrows, usually 10 to 100 in number and 2.5 to 5 centimeters (1 to 2 inches) deep, which are present in the throat or chest. These furrows increase the capacity of the mouth when opened. The members of this family are the fastest swimmers of the baleen whales, some of them attaining speeds up to 48 kilometers (30 miles) per hour. They usually travel singly or in pairs, but several hundred individuals may congregate where food is abundant. Their food consists largely of krill, copepods, amphipods, and other zooplankton. Some species even include fishes and penguins in their diet. The zooplankton are captured by gulping and swallowing or skimming. When skimming, the whale swims through the zooplankton with its mouth open and its head above the surface of the water. When a mouthful of organisms has been filtered from the water by the baleen plates, the whale dives, closes its mouth, and swallows the plankton. Rorquals breed and give birth in the warmer waters within their range. The larger species give birth to a single calf every other year, but the smaller forms breed more frequently.

Several of the members of this family are hunted commercially for their oil and meat. These whales are considered to be among the most healthy of all living mammals since evidence of pathology is seldom observed. The liver may be poisonous to eat.

SEI WHALE, *Balaenoptera borealis* Lesson (500, top). Atlantic Ocean, coast of Labrador southward to Campeche; Pacific Ocean, Bering Sea southward to Baja California. Length 18 meters (59 feet).

Family DELPHINIDAE: This family of dolphins and porpoises comprises eighteen genera and about sixty-two species. They inhabit all the oceans and the estuaries of many large rivers; some species may ascend the rivers for great distances. Some species seem to prefer warm coastal waters and are never found in polar regions. The term "dolphin" generally refers to small cetaceans having a beak-like snout and a slender streamlined body, whereas the term "porpoise" refers to small cetaceans having a blunt snout and rather stout stocky body form. Dolphins are among the most agile and swiftest swimming of all the cetaceans. They are capable of speeds up to 25 knots. They are frequently seen following ships and frolicking about the bow. They usually associate in schools as large as five hundred to seven hundred individuals. Migration is known to occur in some species. They utter a wide variety of underwater calls and noises. Cooperative behavior has often been observed in which one or more individuals will come to the aid of a fellow in distress or a cow giving birth, pushing it to the surface so that it can breathe. It is the opinion of those that have studied their behavior that they are highly intelligent animals; they can readily be trained to perform tricks and even useful functions. The killer whale, *Orcinus*, feeds on almost any type of animal food, but other members of this family feed mainly on cephalopods and fishes. The gestation period in most species is from 9 to 12 months; the calf is born underwater and usually swims unaided to the surface to breathe. Some species are commercially hunted.

*Neophocaena phocaenoides* ascends estuaries and rivers long distances from the mouth. This species is usually seen singly or in pairs. They are sluggish in their movements and roll when rising to breathe. Birth of the young occurs about October. Their food consists of fishes, crustaceans, and cuttlefish.

SOUTHEAST ASIATIC PORPOISE, BLACK FINLESS PORPOISE, *Neophocaena phocaenoides* (Cuvier) (501, top). Frequents the coasts, estuaries, rivers and lakes of China, Japan, Borneo, Java, Sumatra, Pakistan, India, and South Africa. It has been reported 1,600 kilometers (990 miles) from the mouth of the Yangtze River and reaches Tungting Lake. Length 1.5 meters (5 feet).

Family MONODONTIDAE: The family of white whales consists of only two genera, each having a single species, *Delphinapterus leucas,* the white whale, and *Monodon monoceros,* the narwhal. Both species are found in arctic seas but may ascend rivers. Ingestion of the flesh of the white whale has caused fatalities. There is no information available concerning the edibility of the narwhal. The white whale attains a length of more than 4 meters (13 feet) and a weight of about 900 kilograms (1,985 pounds). The body shape of the white whale resembles that of the members of the Delphinidae. The snout is blunt and there is no beak. There are no external grooves on the throat. White whales usually live in schools, sometimes consisting of more than 100 individuals. They migrate in response to the shifting pack ice and rigorous winters. The white whale can swim for hours at a speed of 9 kilometers (6 miles) per hour and can remain underwater for periods of 15 minutes. They emit various sounds, which are probably produced by the emission of a stream of bubbles rather than by the voicebox. They feed mainly on benthic organisms, cephalopods, crustaceans, and fishes. The gestation period is about 14 months, and the calf is about 1.5 meters (5 feet) in length at birth. White whales are of economic importance and are hunted mainly for their skins, which are sometimes sold as "porpoise leather."

WHITE WHALE, BELUGA, *Delphinapterus leucas* (Pallas) **(501, bottom)**. Arctic and subarctic seas. Length 5.5 meters (18 feet).

Family PHYSETERIDAE: The family of sperm whales consists of two genera and two species, which inhabit all oceans. The sperm whale, *Physeter catodon,* attains a large size up to 20 meters (65 feet) and more than 55 metric tons. The other member of the family, the pygmy sperm whale, *Kogio breviceps,* is small and attains a length of about 4 meters (13 feet) and a weight of about 320 kilograms (705 pounds). The characteristic features of *Physeter* are its tremendous barrel-shaped head and the underslung lower jaw. The sperm whale is said to be the only cetacean with a gullet large enough to swallow a man. It sometimes lifts its head out of the water to look and listen. When necessary, it can swim at speeds up to 12 knots. They usually travel in groups of up to twenty individuals, but large schools may number in the hundreds. The gestation period in *Physeter* is about sixteen months. They feed on squid, cuttlefish, fishes, and elasmobranchs. *Physeter* is hunted

primarily for the oil and spermaceti, used for making candles and ointments. Ambergris is a substance that is unique to the sperm whale and is believed to be formed from solid wastes coalescing around a matrix of indigestible matter. The meat of the sperm whale is usually discarded by pelagic whalers, but some of the Pacific coast stations freeze the meat as food for fur-bearing animals or treat it to yield oil and meat meal. The flesh and oil may be poisonous to eat in some localities.

SPERM WHALE, *Physeter catodon* Linnaeus **(500, bottom)**. Polar, temperate, and tropical seas. Length 18 meters (59 feet).

## Polar Bears

Carnivores are a group of small to large animals, having four or five toes, claws, mobile limbs, a complete and separate radius and ulna, tibia and fibula, small incisors, and canines as slender fangs. The only marine carnivore toxic to man is the polar bear, *Thalarctos maritimus* (Phipps) (Chapter II, 56). Most mammalogists are of the opinion that there is but a single species.

The symptoms of polar bear poisoning usually begin about two to five hours after ingestion. The predominant symptoms are intense throbbing or dull frontal headaches, nausea, vomiting, diarrhea, abdominal pain, dizziness, drowsiness, irritability, weakness, muscle cramps, visual disturbances, and collapse. The headaches may become intensified during the first eight hours and cause insomnia, since they are aggravated by lying down. Gradually the headache lessens in severity and may disappear by the following day. Numerous cases have been cited in which desquamation occurred in various parts of the body, particularly the face, arms, legs, and feet. Tonic and clonic convulsions may be present. If fatalities do occur from these ingestions, they are very rare. The amount of liver ingested appears to have a direct bearing upon the severity of the symptoms produced. Eskimos believe that ingestion of polar bear liver may result in depigmentation of the skin, but this has not been substantiated.

Toxicological and biochemical assays have revealed that the liver contains toxic concentrations of vitamin A and that the toxicity in humans is probably due to a hypervitaminosis A. Treatment is symptomatic; emetics and laxatives are sometimes useful if promptly administered.

## Walruses, Seals, and Sea Lions

Pinnipeds are a group of small to large mammals having a spindleshaped body and limbs modified into flippers for aquatic locomotion. The toes are included in webs, and the tail is very short. The males are usually larger than the females. The livers of walruses and certain species of seals may at times be poisonous to eat. The symptoms of walrus and seal liver poisoning are believed to be similar to those of polar bear liver poisoning (see p. 178).

Family ODOBENIDAE: Walruses inhabit the open waters of the Arctic Ocean near the edge of the polar ice. They migrate south in the winter with the advance of the ice and move north in the spring as the ice retreats. Walruses are frequently observed riding the ice floes during their migration. Walruses have a thick swollen body, rounded head and muzzle, a short neck, and a tough wrinkled skin. There is no tail. They have a conspicuous mustache consisting of large bristles that are richly supplied with blood vessels and nerves. They are especially characterized by their large, protruding ivory tusks. The bulls attain a length of about 3.7 meters (12 feet) and a weight of more than a metric ton. The cows are about one-third the size of the bulls. They are generally found in mixed herds consisting of bulls, cows, and calves and numbering 100 or more individuals. Walruses can swim about 24 kilometers (15 miles) per hour. They may be observed using their tusks to haul themselves out of the water. Walruses make a bellowing noise and at times may sound like a herd of trumpeting elephants. They seem to have poor senses of smell and hearing but fairly good eyesight. Walruses feed on the bottom and are thought to use their bristles and possibly their tusks to forage for food, which consists mainly of mollusks and other marine life.

Rogue walruses, individuals who remain separate from the rest of the herd, may feed on seals, narwhal, white whales, or other dead cetaceans. It is the rogue walruses that are most likely to have toxic livers. The rogue is a solitary bull and feeds almost exclusively on vertebrates. It has a characteristic appearance: relatively lean and slender with shoulders and forelimbs that appear unusually large and powerfully developed. The chin, neck, and breast are impregnated with oil from frequent contact with seal blubber; the oxidized oil imparts an amber color to these parts. The tusks are unusually long, slender, and sharp-pointed; their surfaces are covered with scratches. Rogues are said to constitute less than 0.1 percent of the walrus population. Eskimos claim that rogues develop from calves that are separated from their mothers in the first year or two of life and are not sufficiently familiar with bottom feeding techniques to sustain themselves that way. Consequently, only a few of the stronger bulls are able to survive by scavenging and preying on whatever vertebrates they are able to capture. Actually no one knows exactly how rogues originate in the normal herd.

Walruses are polygamous. The gestation period is about 12 months, and most of the births take place from April to June. Eskimos use every part of the walrus, either for food, shelter, or boats, and the tusks are used extensively in ivory carvings.

WALRUS, *Odobenus rosmarus* (Linnaeus) (Chapter II, 55). Arctic Ocean—northeast coast of Siberia, the northwest coast of Alaska and north to northwest Greenland and Ellesmere Island. Length 3.5 meters (11.5 feet). It attains a weight of about 1,300 kilograms (1.4 tons).

Family PHOCIDAE: The family of true seals consists of thirteen genera and eighteen species that are widely distributed throughout the coastal and oceanic waters of polar, temperate, and tropical regions of the world.

Bearded seals (*Erignathus*) are solitary creatures, living alone on ice floes not far from land, except during the mating season. They derive their name from the beard-like tuft of stout white bristles growing down on each side of their muzzles. Their food consists largely of crustaceans and mollusks. Fishes are sometimes eaten but are apparently less desirable. Bearded seals seek their food on the bottom of the sea and may dive to great depths. The single pup is born about late March. The adult male attains a length of about 3 meters (10 feet) and a weight exceeding 360 kilograms (794 pounds). The flesh is said to be tough, coarse, and most appreciated by the Eskimos when it is decomposed and frozen. The liver is toxic to eat, apparently because of the excessive vitamin A content.

The Australian sea lion (*Neophoca*) is the largest of its kind, inhabiting rocky coastal areas along the southern shore of Australia. For the most part, these seals are nonmigratory, usually remaining in the immediate environs of their birthplace throughout their life. They are generally docile, except during the mating season, when they become somewhat ill-tempered. Their food consists mainly of penguins, which are available in abundance, and fishes. They also have an interesting habit of ingesting stones, apparently used as an aid in digesting their food. The breeding season is from October to early December, during which time the community spends most of its time inshore. The harems are relatively small, consisting of one to four females to each male. The females give birth to a single pup. The male attains a maximum length of about 3.7 meters (12 feet). The flesh of some specimens has been reported to be highly toxic.

AUSTRALIAN FUR SEAL, *Arctocephalus doriferus* Wood Jones (502). South Australia and Tasmania. Length 1.83 meters (6 feet). The liver may be poisonous to eat.

BEARDED SEAL, *Erignathus barbatus* (Erxleben) (503). Inhabits the edge of the ice along the coasts and islands of North America and northern Eurasia. Length 2.7 meters (9 feet).

AUSTRALIAN SEA LION, HAIR SEAL, *Neophoca cinerea* (Peron) (504). Rocky islands off the south and southwest coasts of Australia. Length 2.4 meters (8 feet).

RINGED SEAL, *Pusa hispida* (Schreber) (505). Circumboreal near the edge of the ice, to the North Pole. Length 1.4 meters (4.5 feet).

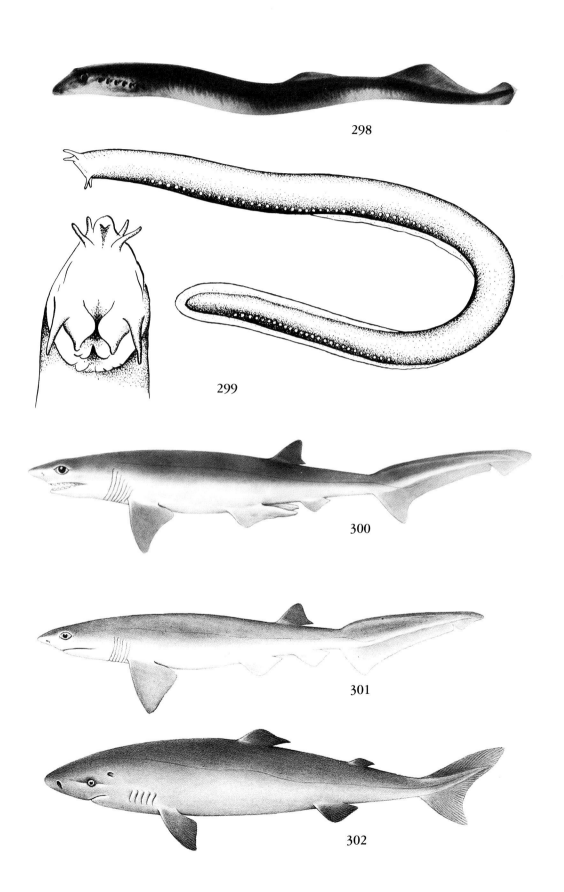

298

299

300

301

302

**PLATE 298.** River lamprey, *Lampetra fluviatilis* (Linnaeus). This lamprey has been incriminated in human intoxications. The slime is reputed to be toxic. Found in the Baltic and North Sea basins, westward as far as Ireland and France. Enters the rivers from the sea. Length 36 centimeters (14 inches).　　(From Berg)

**PLATE 299.** Atlantic hagfish, *Myxine glutinosa* Linnaeus. Side view and buccal cavity. The slime of this jawless vertebrate is reputed to be toxic. However, it is not generally considered to be a food fish. Length 79 centimeters (31 inches). North Atlantic Ocean.

(R. Kreuzinger, after Bigelow and Schroeder)

**PLATE 300.** Seven-gilled shark, *Heptranchus perlo* (Bonnaterre). The flesh is sometimes poisonous to eat. Found in the Atlantic, Mediterranean, South Africa, and Japan. Length 2 meters (6.5 feet).　(M. Shirao)

**PLATE 301.** Six-gilled shark, *Hexanchus grisseus* (Bonnaterre). The flesh and liver may be poisonous to eat. Found in the Atlantic Ocean; off the Pacific coast of North America, Chile, Japan, Australia; in the Indian Ocean; and off the coast of South Africa. Length 5 meters (15.5 feet).　　　　　(M. Shirao)

**PLATE 302.** Greenland shark, *Somniosus microcephalus* (Bloch and Schneider). The flesh of this shark may be poisonous to eat. Found in the Arctic, North Sea, east to the White Sea and west to the Gulf of St. Lawrence. There is a closely related but distinct species in the Pacific. Length 2 meters (6.5 feet).　　(M. Shirao)

**PLATE 303.** Surgeonfish, *Acanthurus glaucopareius* Cuvier. Tropical Indo-Pacific. Length 30 centimeters (12 inches). Taken at Haputo, Guam. (R. F. Myers)

**PLATE 304.** Striped surgeonfish, *Acanthurus lineatus* (Linnaeus). Tropical Indo-Pacific. Length 30 centimeters (12 inches). Taken in Guam. (R. F. Myers)

**PLATE 305.** Convict surgeonfish, tang, *Acanthurus triostegus* (Linnaeus). Tropical Indo-Pacific. Length 26 centimeters (10 inches). Taken in the Red Sea. (D. Ollis)

**PLATE 306.** Surgeonfish, tang, *Acanthurus xanthopterus* (Cuvier and Valenciennes). Tropical Indo-Pacific. Length 35 centimeters (14 inches). Taken in Hawaii. (J. Randall)

**PLATE 307.** Common bristle-toothed tang, *Ctenochaetus striatus* (Quoy and Gaimard). Tropical Indo-Pacific. Length 20 centimeters (8 inches). (K. Tomita)

**PLATE 308.** Unicorn filefish, *Alutera monoceros* (Linnaeus). All warm seas. Length 30 centimeters (12 inches). (From Hiyama)

**PLATE 309.** Scrawled filefish, *Alutera scripta* (Osbeck). All warm seas. Length 50 centimeters (20 inches). (T. Kumada)

**PLATE 310.** Undulated triggerfish, *Balistapus undulatus* (Mungo Park). Tropical Indo-Pacific. Length 35 centimeters (14 inches). Taken in Guam. (R. F. Myers)

303
304

305

308

306

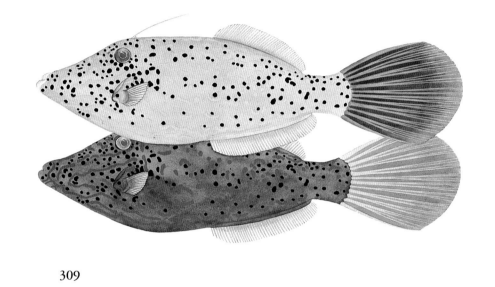

309

307

310

311

314

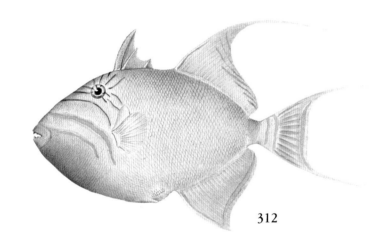

312

315

313

316

317

318

319

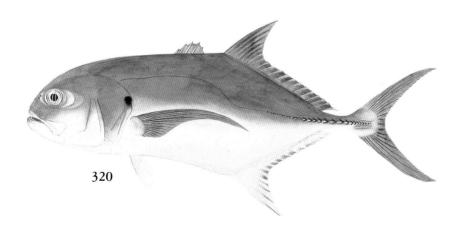

320

PLATE 311. Boar triggerfish, *Balistes capriscus* (Gmelin). Tropical Atlantic and Mediterranean Sea. Length 50 centimeters (20 inches). Taken in an aquarium, Zoological Station, Naples, Italy. (P. Giacomelli)

PLATE 312. Old woman triggerfish, *Balistes vetula* Linnaeus. Tropical Atlantic, Mediterranean Sea, and Indian Ocean. Length 38 centimeters (15 inches).
(From Evermann and Marsh)

PLATE 313. Clown triggerfish, *Balistoides conspicillum* Bloch and Schneider. Tropical Indo-Pacific and Red Sea. Length 35 centimeters (14 inches). (T. Kumada)

PLATE 314. Triggerfish, *Melichthys buniva* (Lacépède). Tropical Indo-Pacific. Length 35 centimeters (14 inches). (From Jordan and Evermann)

PLATE 315. Black triggerfish, *Odonus niger* (Rüppell). Tropical Indo-Pacific, Red Sea. Length 30 centimeters (12 inches). (K. Tomita)

PLATE 316. Yellow-margined triggerfish, *Pseudobalistes flavimarginatus* (Rüppell). Tropical Indo-Pacific, Red Sea. Length 30 centimeters (12 inches).
(S. Arita)

PLATE 317. Painted triggerfish, *Rhinecanthus aculeatus* (Linnaeus). Tropical Indo-Pacific. Length 30 centimeters (12 inches). Taken at Tepungan Channel, Guam. (R. F. Myers)

PLATE 318. Rectangular triggerfish, *Rhinecanthus rectangulus* (Bloch). Tropical Indo-Pacific. Length 20 centimeters (8 inches). (From Jordan and Evermann)

PLATE 319. Crevalle or jack, *Caranx bartholomaei* Cuvier and Valenciennes. West Indies, northward to North Carolina. Length 38 centimeters (15 inches).
(J. Randall)

PLATE 320. Crevalle or jack, *Caranx hippos* (Linnaeus). Tropical Atlantic. Length 75 centimeters (29.5 inches). (T. Kumada)

PLATE 321. Jack, *Caranx ignobilis* (Forskål). Tropical Indo-Pacific. Length 55 centimeters (21.5 inches). Taken at mouth of Pago River, Guam.     (R. F. Myers)

PLATE 322. Horse-eye jack, *Caranx latus* Agassiz. Tropical Western Atlantic. Length 90 centimeters (35.5 inches).     (J. Randall)

PLATE 323. Black jack, *Caranx lugubris* Poey. Circumtropical. Length 60 centimeters (23.5 inches). Taken in Palau.     (R.F. Myers)

PLATE 324. Blue crevalle or jack, *Caranx melampygus* Cuvier. Tropical Indo-Pacific. Length 65 centimeters (25.5 inches). Taken at Eniwetok Atoll.

(R. F. Myers)

PLATE 325. Six-banded jack, *Caranx sexfasciatus* (Quoy and Gaimard). Circumtropical. Length 50 centimeters (19.5 inches).     (T. Kumada)

PLATE 326. Rainbow runner, *Elegatis bipinnulatus* (Quoy and Gaimard). Circumtropical. Length 65 centimeters (25.5 inches).     (R. F. Myers)

PLATE 327. Bigeye scad, *Selar crumenophthalmus* (Bloch). Atlantic coast of tropical America. Length 60 centimeters (23.5 inches).     (T. Kumada)

PLATE 328. Greater amberjack, yellowtail, *Seriola dumerili* (Risso). Tropical Indo-Pacific, Mediterranean, West Indies. Length 90 centimeters (35.5 inches).

(From Palombi and Santarelli)

PLATE 329. Almaco jack, *Seriola falcata* Valenciennes. West Indies, north to the Carolinas. Length 30 centimeters (12 inches).     (J. Randall)

PLATE 330. Threadfin butterflyfish, *Chaetodon auriga* Forskål. Tropical Indo-Pacific. Length 16 centimeters (6.5 inches).     (R. F. Myers)

PLATE 331. Reticulated butterflyfish, *Chaetodon reticulatus* Cuvier. Tropical Indo-Pacific, India, China, Japan. Length 15 centimeters (6 inches).

(R. F. Myers)

PLATE 332. Longfin bannerfish, *Heniochus acuminatus* (Linnaeus). Tropical Indo-Pacific, India, Japan, Red Sea. Length 20 centimeters (8 inches).     (R. F. Myers)

321

322

323

324

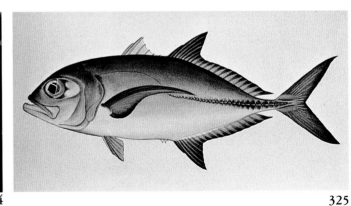

325

326

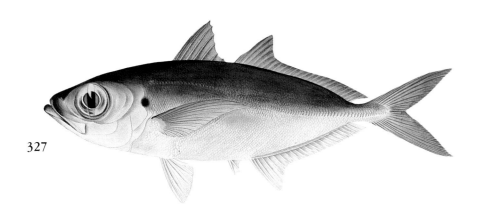

327

328

329

330

331
332

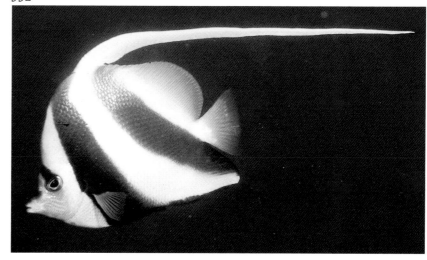

PLATE 333. Emperor angelfish, *Pomacanthus imperator* (Bloch). Tropical Indo-Pacific, Red Sea, Zanzibar. Length 35 centimeters (14 inches). (R. F. Myers)

PLATE 334. Dolphin, *Coryphaena hippurus* Linnaeus. Pelagic, in all temperate and tropical seas. Length 1.2 meters (4 feet). (R. F. Myers)

PLATE 335. Halfbeak, *Hemiramphus archipelagicus* (Forskål). Tropical Indo-Pacific, Red Sea. Length 30 centimeters (12 inches). (R. F. Myers)

PLATE 336. Brazilian halfbeak, *Hemiramphus brasiliensis* (Linnaeus). Tropical Atlantic. Length 38 centimeters (15 inches). (From Jordan and Evermann)

333

334

335

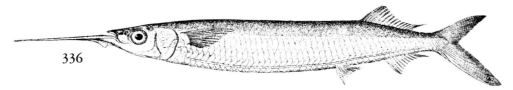

336

PLATE 337. Spiny squirrelfish, *Holocentrus spinifer* (Forskål). Tropical Indo-Pacific, Red Sea. Length 38 centimeters (15 inches).                (R. F. Myers)

PLATE 338. Soldierfish, *Myripristis murdjan* (Forskål). Tropical Indo-Pacific. Length 30 centimeters (12 inches).                (From Jordan and Evermann)

PLATE 339. Banded wrasse, *Cheilinus fasciatus* (Bloch). Tropical Indo-Pacific, Australia. Length 30 centimeters (12 inches).                (R. F. Myers)

PLATE 340. Giant green wrasse, *Cheilinus undulatus* Rüppell. Tropical Indo-Pacific, Red Sea. Length 1.5 meters (5 feet).                (R. F. Myers)

PLATE 341. Gaimard's wrasse, *Coris gaimardi* (Quoy and Gaimard). Tropical Indo-Pacific. Length 30 centimeters (12 inches).                (R. Russo)

PLATE 342. Rainbow wrasse, *Coris julis* (Linnaeus). Eastern Atlantic and Mediterranean. Length 25 centimeters (10 inches).                (K. Fogassy)

PLATE 343. Wrasse, *Epibulus insidiator* (Pallas). Tropical Indo-Pacific. Length 30 centimeters (12 inches).                (R. F. Myers)

PLATE 344. Three-spotted wrasse, *Halichoeres trimaculatus* (Quoy and Gaimard). Tropical Indo-Pacific. Length 22 centimeters (8.5 inches) or more.                (R. F. Myers)

337

338

339

340

341

342

343

344

345

346

348

347

349

350

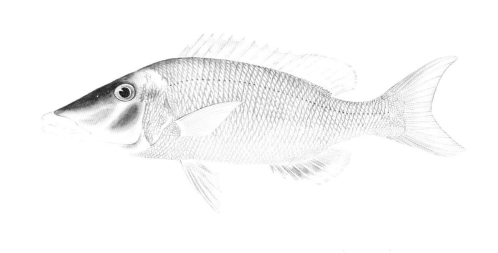

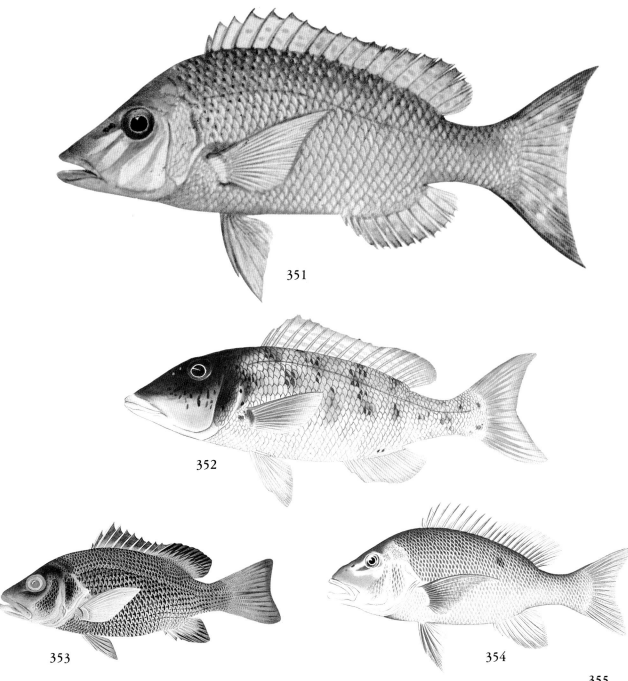

351

352

353

354

355

PLATE 345. Hogfish, *Lachnolaimus maximus* (Walbaum). Florida and West Indies. Length 48 centimeters (19 inches). (J. Randall)

PLATE 346. Bluegreen snapper, *Aprion virescens* Cuvier and Valenciennes. Tropical Indo-Pacific. Length 72 centimeters (28 inches). (T. Kumada)

PLATE 347. Golden-stripped snapper, *Gnathodentex aureolineatus* (Lacépède). Tropical Indo-Pacific. Length 25 centimeters (10 inches). Taken at Guam. (R. F. Myers)

PLATE 348. Gray snapper, *Gymnocranius griseus* (Temminck and Schlegel). Tropical Indo-Pacific. Length 35 centimeters (14 inches). (From Hiyama)

PLATE 349. Scavenger snapper, *Lethrinus harak* (Forskål). Tropical Indo-Pacific, Red Sea. Length 30 centimeters (12 inches). Taken at Agana Reef, Guam. (R. F. Myers)

PLATE 350. Grey snapper, *Lethrinus miniatus* (Forster). Tropical Indo-Pacific, off the coast of Japan, and East Africa. Length 45 centimeters (18 inches). (K. Tomita)

PLATE 351. Smokey snapper, *Lethrinus nebulosus* (Forskål). Tropical Indo-Pacific. Length 30 centimeters (12 inches). (From Marshall)

PLATE 352. Variegated snapper, *Lethrinus variegatus* Cuvier and Valenciennes. Tropical Indo-Pacific. Length 35 centimeters (14 inches). (T. Kumada)

PLATE 353. Silver-spotted snapper, *Lutjanus argentimaculatus* (Forskål). Tropical Indo-Pacific. Length 50 centimeters (19.5 inches). (T. Kumada)

PLATE 354. Red snapper, *Lutjanus aya* (Bloch). Western tropical Atlantic. Length 76 centimeters (30 inches). (S. Arita)

PLATE 355. Red snapper, *Lutjanus bohar* (Forskål). Tropical Indo-Pacific. Length 90 centimeters (35.5 inches). Taken in a fish trap, Orote Cliffs, Guam. (R. F. Myers)

356

357

358

359

360

361

362

363

364

365

366

PLATE 356. Dark-tailed snapper, *Lutjanus janthinuropterus* (Bleeker). Tropical Indo-Pacific. Length 60 centimeters (2 feet). (T. Kumada)

PLATE 357. Dog snapper, *Lutjanus jocu* (Bloch and Schneider). Florida and West Indies, south to Brazil. Length 75 centimeters (29.5 inches). (S. Arita)

PLATE 358. Black-spotted snapper, *Lutjanus monostigmus* (Cuvier and Valenciennes). Tropical Indo-Pacific, Red Sea. Length 30 centimeters (12 inches). Taken at Palau, Western Caroline Islands.
(R. F. Myers)

PLATE 359. Chinaman, *Lutjanus nematophorus* (Bleeker). Australia. Length 68 centimeters (27 inches). (G. Coates)

PLATE 360. Snapper, *Lutjanus semicinctus* Quoy and Gaimard. Tropical Indo-Pacific. Length 30 centimeters (12 inches). (T. Kumada)

PLATE 361. Red Snapper, *Lutjanus vagiensis* (Quoy and Gaimard). Tropical Indo-Pacific, east coast of Africa, Australia. Length 50 centimeters (20 inches).
(K. Tomita)

PLATE 362. Large-eye Snapper, *Monotaxis grandoculis* (Forskål). Tropical Indo-Pacific. Length 32 centimeters (12.5 inches). Taken at Palau. (R. F. Myers)

PLATE 363. Mullet, *Chelon vaigiensis* (Quoy and Gaimard). Tropical Indo-Pacific. Length 32 centimeters (12.5 inches). (From Marshall)

PLATE 364. Common Mullet, *Mugil cephalus* Linneaus. Cosmopolitan in distribution. Length 30 centimeters (12 inches). (From Hiyama)

PLATE 365. Golden flammed goatfish, *Mulloidichthys auriflamma* (Forskål). Tropical Indo-Pacific, Red Sea. Length 35 centimeters (14 inches).
(From Jordan and Evermann)

PLATE 366. Samoan goatfish, *Mulloidichthys samoensis* (Günther). Tropical Indo-Pacific. Length 30 centimeters (12 inches). (From Jordan and Evermann)

PLATE 367. Goatfish, *Parupeneus chryserydros* (Lacépède). Tropical Indo-Pacific, East Africa. Length 30 centimeters (12 inches). (From Jordan and Evermann)

PLATE 368. Goatfish, *Upeneus arge* Jordan and Evermann. Tropical Indo-Pacific. Length 32 centimeters (12.5 inches). (From Jordan and Evermann)

PLATE 369. Spotted moray eel, *Echidna nebulosa* (Ahl). Tropical Indo-Pacific, coast of Australia, East Africa, China. Length 75 centimeters (29.5 inches). Taken at Oahu, Hawaii. (R. F. Myers)

PLATE 370. Yellow-margined moray eel, *Gymnothrax flavimarginatus* (Rüppell). Tropical Indo-Pacific, coast of East Africa. Taken at Palau.
(R. F. Myers)

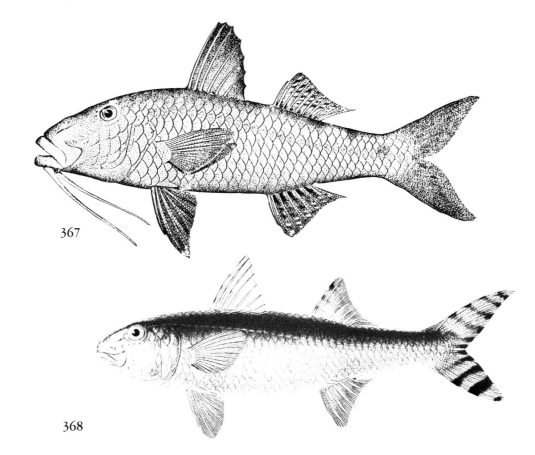

367

368

369
370

371

372

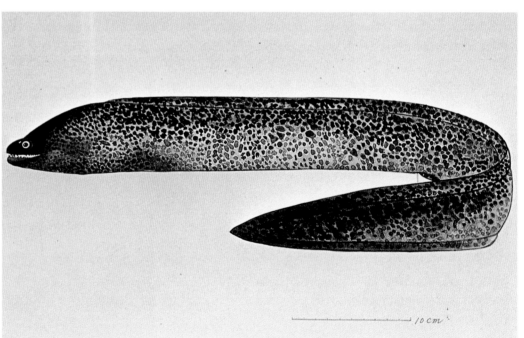

373

374

375

PLATE 371. Green moray eel, *Gymnothorax funebris* Ranzani. West Indies, south to Brazil. Length 1.8 meters (6 feet). (WLRI photo)

PLATE 372. Moray eel, *Gymnothorax javanicus* (Bleeker). Tropical Indo-Pacific, coast of East Africa. Length 1.5 meters (5 feet). Taken at Palau. This species is noted for its high levels of ciguatera poison and should never be eaten. (R. F. Myers).

PLATE 373. Moray eel, *Gymnothorax meleagris* (Shaw and Nodder). Tropical Indo-Pacific, coast of Japan. Length 1 meter (3.2 feet). (R. F. Myers)

PLATE 374. Moray eel, *Gymnothorax pictus* (Ahl). This moray has several different color phases. Tropical Indo-Pacific. Length 75 centimeters (29.5 inches). (T. Kamada)

PLATE 375. Moray eel, *Gymnothorax undulatus* (Lacépède). Tropical Indo-Pacific, coast of East Africa, Red Sea. Length 1.5 meters (5 feet). (R. F. Myers)

PLATE 376. Honeycomb cowfish, *Acanthostracion quadricornis* (Linnaeus). Western Atlantic, tropical coasts of the Americas and Caribbean. Length 25 centimeters (10 inches). (WLRI photo)

PLATE 377. Trunkfish, *Kentrocapros aculeatus* (Houttuyn). Tropical Indo-Pacific, coast of Japan, and India. Length 25 centimeters (10 inches) (From Tomiyama and Abe)

PLATE 378. Smooth trunkfish, *Lactophrys triqueter* (Linnaeus). Western Atlantic, tropical coasts of the Americas and Caribbean. Length 30 centimeters (12 inches). (WLRI photo)

376

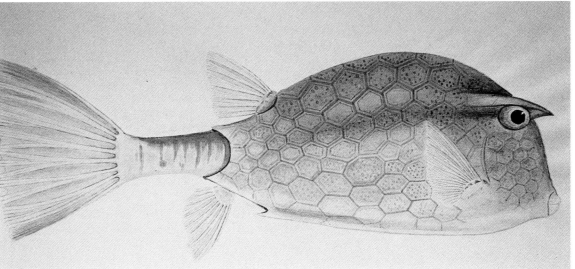

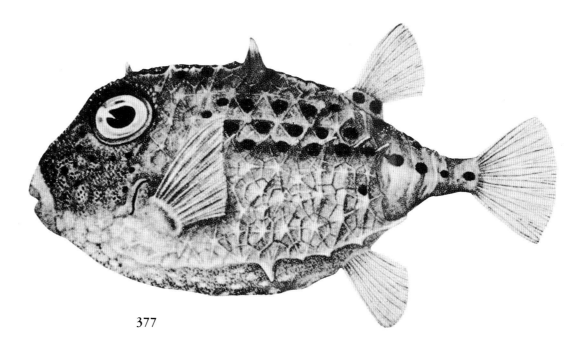
377

378

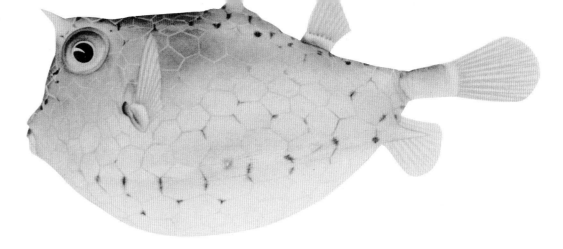

379 380

381 382

383 384

PLATE 379. Horned trunkfish, *Lactoria cornuta* (Bloch and Schneider). Tropical Indo-Pacific, coasts of Japan, and South Africa. Length 30 centimeters (12 inches). (From Hiyama).

PLATE 380. Trunkfish, *Lactoria diaphana* (Bloch and Schneider). Tropical Indo-Pacific, coasts of Japan and South Africa. Length 30 centimeters (12 inches).

(From Hiyama)

PLATE 381. Speckled trunkfish, *Ostracion meleagris* Shaw. Tropical Indo-Pacific, coasts of Japan and South America. Length 20 centimeters (8 inches). Taken at Oahu, Hawaii. (R. F. Myers)

PLATE 382. Sergeant major, *Abudefduf saxatilis* (Linnaeus). Tropical Indo-Pacific, coast of Australia, East Africa, and China. Length 18 centimeters (17 inches).

(R. F. Myers)

PLATE 383. Blue parrotfish, *Scarus coeruleus* (Bloch). From the coast of Florida to the West Indies and Panama. Length 90 centimeters (35.5 inches). Taken at Virgin Gorda, British Virgin Islands.

(B. W. Halstead)

PLATE 384. Parrotfish, *Scarus ghobban* Forskål. Tropical Indo-Pacific, coasts of Japan and Australia; Red Sea. Length 1.1 meters (3.5 feet). Taken at Palau, Western Caroline Islands. (R. F. Myers)

PLATE 385. Parrotfish, *Scarus gibbus* Rüppell. Tropical Indo-Pacific. Length 60 centimeters (24 inches). Taken at Eniwetok, Marshall Islands. (R. F. Myers)

PLATE 386. Blue parrotfish, *Scarus jonesi* (Streets). Tropical Indo-Pacific. Length 38 centimeters (15 inches). (From Bleeker)

PLATE 387. Parrotfish, *Scarus microrhinus* Bleeker. Tropical Indo-Pacific. Length 33 centimeters (13 inches). (T. Kumada)

PLATE 388. Wahoo, *Acanthocybium solandri* (Cuvier). Circumtropical in distribution. Length 2 meters (6.5 feet). (From Walford)

386

385

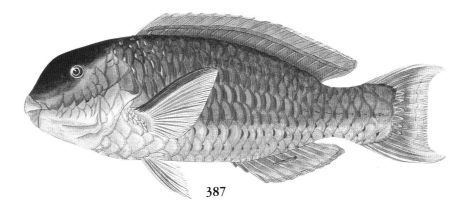

387

388

389

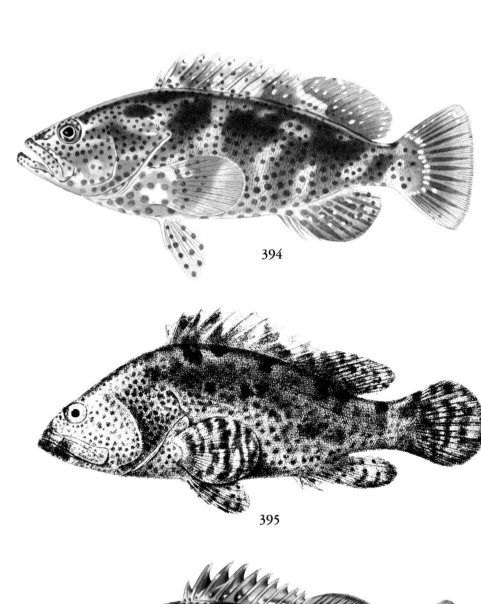

394

390

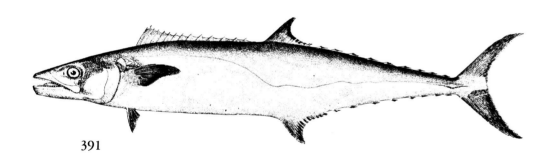

391

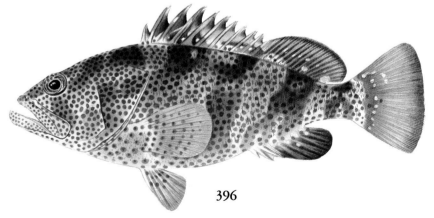

395

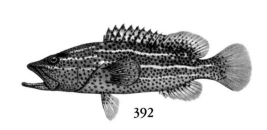

392

393

396

397 398

399

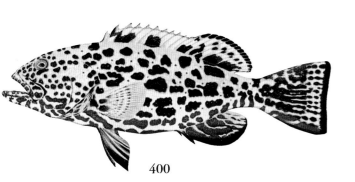

400

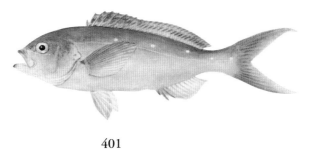

401

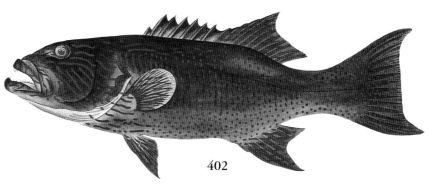

402

PLATE 389. Wavyback skipjack, *Euthynnus affinis* (Cantor). Tropical Indo-Pacific. Length 1 meter (3 feet).                                    (WLRI photo)

PLATE 390. Atlantic bonito, *Sarda sarda* (Bloch). Atlantic Ocean. Length 91 centimeters (3 feet).
(Courtesy National Geographic Society)

PLATE 391. King mackerel, *Scomberomorus cavalla* (Cuvier). Tropical Atlantic. Length 1.5 meters (5 feet).
(From Goode)

PLATE 392. Rockcod, *Anyperodon leucogrammicus* (Cuvier and Valenciennes). Tropical Indo-Pacific. Length 40 centimeters (16 inches).    (From Marshall)

PLATE 393. Spotted grouper, *Cephalopholis argus* Bloch and Schneider. Length 50 centimeters (19.5 inches).                                    (R. F. Myers)

PLATE 394. Rockhind, *Epinephelus adscensionis* (Osbeck). Coasts of Florida and West Indies, southward to Brazil. Length 38 centimeters (15 inches).
(S. Arita after Evermann and Marsh)

PLATE 395. Brown spotted grouper, *Epinephelus fuscoguttatus* (Forskål). Tropical Indo-Pacific. Length 60 centimeters (23.5 inches).          (From Day)

PLATE 396. Spotted grouper, *Epinephelus guttatus* (Linnaeus). South Carolina to Brazil. Length 45 centimeters (17.5 inches).                        (S. Arita)

PLATE 397. Grouper, *Epinephelus merra* Bloch. Tropical Indo-Pacific. Length 30 centimeters (12 inches). Taken at Tanguisson, Guam.      (R. F. Myers)

PLATE 398. Spotted seabass, *Epinephelus tauvina* (Forskål). Tropical Indo-Pacific. Length 2.1 meters (6.8 feet).                                    (R. F. Myers)

PLATE 399. Tiger gouper, *Mycteroperca tigris* (Valenciennes). Western tropical Atlantic. Length 48 centimeters (19 inches). Taken in San Salvador, Bahamas.
(B. W. Halstead)

PLATE 400. Poisonous grouper, *Mycteroperca venenosa* (Linnaeus). Western tropical Atlantic. Length 90 centimeters (35.5 inches).          (N. Erickson)

PLATE 401. Creolefish, *Paranthias furcifer* (Valenciennes). Coasts of Cuba to Brazil. Length 35 centimeters (14 inches).
(T. Asaeda, Courtesy California Academy of Sciences)

PLATE 402. Grouper, *Plectropomus oligacanthus* Bleeker. Tropical Indo-Pacific. Length 55 centimeters (21.5 inches).                              (T. Kumada)

PLATE 403. Grouper, *Plectropomus truncatus* Fowler and Bean. Tropical Indo-Pacific. Length 52 centimeters (20.5 inches). (T. Kumada)

PLATE 404. Grouper, *Variola louti* (Forskål). Tropical Indo-Pacific. Length 60 centimeters (23.5 inches). Taken at Guam. (R. F. Myers)

PLATE 405. Silver rabbitfish, *Siganus argenteus* (Quoy and Gaimard). Tropical Indo-Pacific. Length 35 centimeters (14 inches). Taken at Guam. (R. F. Myers)

PLATE 406. Rabbitfish, *Siganus fuscescens* (Houttuyn). Tropical Indo-Pacific. Length 25 centimeters (10 inches). (S. Arita)

PLATE 407. Pretty rabbitfish, *Siganus puellus* (Schlegel). Tropical Indo-Pacific. Length 27 centimeters (10.5 inches). Taken at Palau, Western Caroline Islands. (R. F. Myers)

PLATE 408. Porgy, *Sparus sarba* Forskål. Tropical Indo-Pacific. Length 35 centimeters (14 inches). (From Hiyama)

403

404

405

406

407

408

409

PLATE 409. Moorish idol, *Zanclus cornutus* (Linnaeus). Tropical Indo-Pacific, Mexico to coast of East Africa. Length 15 centimeters (6 inches).

(R. F. Myers)

PLATE 410. Sprat, thread herring, *Clupanodon thrissa* (Linnaeus). Tropical Indo-Pacific, China, Japan, Korea. Length 25 centimeters (10 inches).　(S. Arita)

PLATE 411. Red-ear sardine, *Harengula humeralis* (Cuvier). Florida, Bermuda, West Indies to Brazil. Length 41 centimeters (16 inches).　(From Rivas)

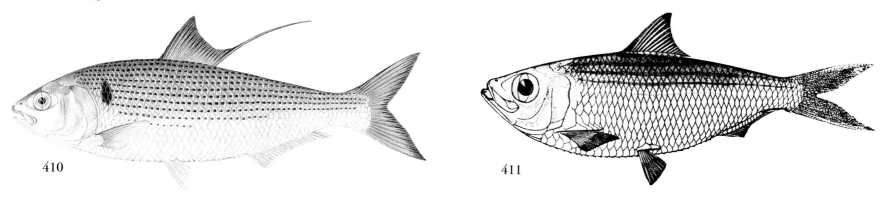

410　　　　　　　　　　　　　　411

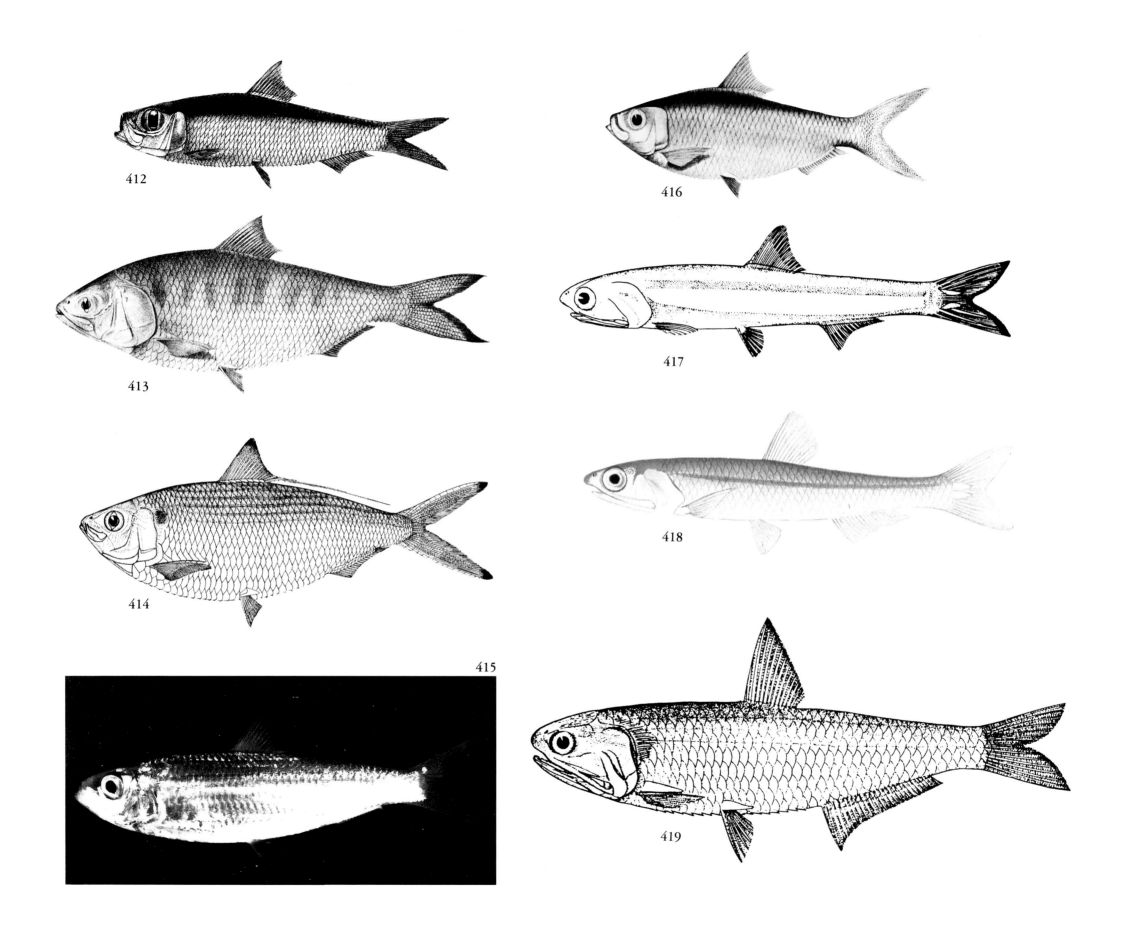

412

416

413

417

414

418

415

419

420

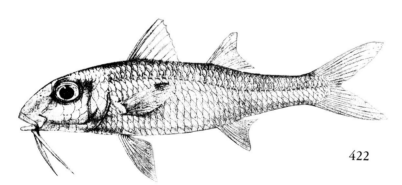

421

422

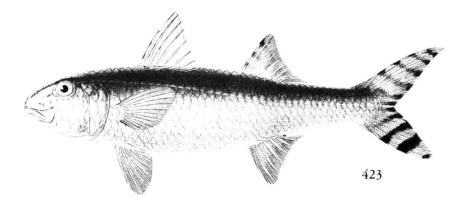

423

PLATE 412. Sardine, *Harengula ovalis* (Bennett). Tropical Indo-Pacific, Red Sea. Length 15 centimeters (6 inches). (From Day)

PLATE 413. Hilsa, sablefish, *Macrura ilisha* (Buchanan-Hamilton). Persian Gulf, Indian Ocean. Length 25 centimeters (10 inches). (From Day)

PLATE 414. Atlantic thread herring, *Opisthonema oglinum* (LeSueur). West Indies, Western Atlantic. Length 25 centimeters (10 inches).

(From Hildebrand)

PLATE 415. Marquesan sardine, *Sardinella marquesensis* Berry and Whitehead. Length 20 centimeters (8 inches). Taken at Hivaoa, Marquesas Islands.

(Courtesy J. E. Randall)

PLATE 416. Sardine, *Sardinella perforata* (Cantor). Tropical Indo-Pacific, Persian Gulf. Length 18 centimeters (7 inches). (From Bleeker)

PLATE 417. Anchovy, *Engraulis encrasicholus* (Linnaeus). Eastern Atlantic, Mediterranean. Length 20 centimeters (8 inches). (From FAO)

PLATE 418. Japanese anchovy, *Engraulis japonicus* Schlegel. China, Japan, Taiwan. Length 13 centimeters (5 inches). (S. Arita)

PLATE 419. Anchovy, *Thrissina baelama* (Forskål). Tropical Indo-Pacific, Red Sea, enters river mouths. Length 12 centimeters (4.5 inches). (From Daly)

PLATE 420. Castor oilfish, *Ruvettus pretiosus* Cocco. Length 1.3 meters (4.5 feet). (From Hiyama)

PLATE 421. Sea chub, *Kyphosus cinerascens* (Forskål). Tropical Indo-Pacific. Length 50 centimeters (19.5 inches). Taken at Guam. (R. F. Myers)

PLATE 422. Samoan goatfish, surmullet, *Mulloidichthys samoensis* (Günther). Tropical Indo-Pacific. Length 30 centimeters (12 inches).

(From Jordan and Evermann)

PLATE 423. White goatfish, *Upeneus arge* Jordan and Evermann. Chin barbels are not seen in this drawing. Tropical Indo-Pacific. Length 32 centimeters (12.5 inches). (From Jordan and Evermann)

PLATE 424. Crowned puffer, *Canthigaster coronata* (Vaillant and Sauvage). Tropical Indo-Pacific, Red Sea. Length 10 centimeters (4 inches). Taken at Guam.

(R. F. Myers)

PLATE 425. White-spotted puffer, *Canthigaster jactator* (Jenkins). Tropical Indo-Pacific. Length 9 centimeters (3.5 inches). (R. F. Myers)

PLATE 426. Sharp-nosed puffer, *Canthigaster rivulatus* (Temminck and Schlegel). Tropical Indo-Pacific, Japan. Length 10 centimeters (4 inches).

(R. F. Myers)

PLATE 427. Blue-spotted puffer, *Canthigaster solandri* (Richardson). Tropical Indo-Pacific. Length 10 centimeters (4 inches). Taken at Guam. (R. F. Myers)

PLATE 428. Valentine's puffer, *Canthigaster valentini* (Bleeker). Tropical Indo-Pacific. Length 20 centimeters (8 inches). Taken at Guam. (R. F. Myers)

PLATE 429. Porcupinefish, *Chilomycterus affinis* Günther. Atlantic coast of tropical America, west and South Africa. Length 17 centimeters (6.5 inches).

(M. Shirao)

PLATE 430. Spotted burrfish, *Chilomycterus atinga* (Linnaeus). Florida Keys, West Indies, Bermuda. Length 20 centimeters (8 inches). (M. Shirao)

424

425

426

427

428

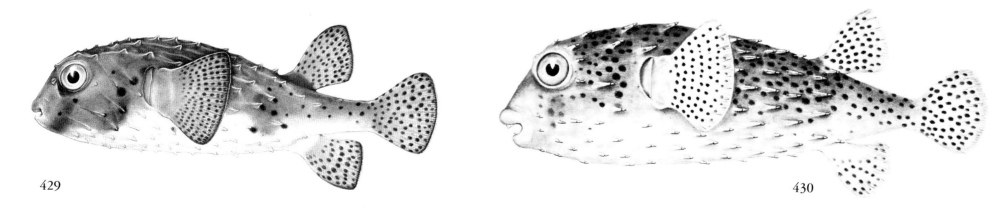

429

430

431

432

433

434

435

436

437

**438**

PLATE 431. Porcupinefish, *Chilomycterus orbicularis* (Bloch). Tropical Indo-Pacific, westward to Cape Good Hope. Length 26 centimeters (10 inches).     (S. Arita)

PLATE 432. Porcupinefish, *Diodon holancanthus* Linnaeus. All warm seas. Length 30 centimeters (12 inches). Taken at Oahu, Hawaii.     (R. F. Myers)

PLATE 433. Porcupinefish, *Diodon hystrix* Linnaeus. All tropical seas. Length 90 centimeters (35.5 inches). Taken at Oahu, Hawaii.     (R. F. Myers)

PLATE 434. Ocean sunfish, *Mola mola* (Linnaeus). Temperate and tropical seas. Length 3 meters (10 feet) or more.     (Courtesy D. Gotshall)

PLATE 435. Puffer, blowfish, *Amblyrhynchotes honckeni* (Bloch). Indonesia, China, South Africa. Length 30 centimeters (12 inches).     (M. Shirao)

PLATE 436. Puffer, blowfish, *Arothron hispidus* (Linnaeus). Panama, Indo-Pacific, Japan, Australia, South Africa, Red Sea. Length 53 centimeters (21 inches). Taken at Waikiki Aquarium, Hawaii.     (R. F. Myers)

PLATE 437. Puffer, blowfish, *Arothron manillensis* (Proce). Tropical Indo-Pacific. Length 25 centimeters (10 inches). Taken at Guam.     (R. F. Myers)

PLATE 438. Puffer, blowfish, *Arothron meleagris* (Lacépède). West coast of Central America and throughout the Indo-Pacific. Length 32 centimeters (12.5 inches). Taken at Oahu, Hawaii.     (R. F. Myers)

PLATE 439. Puffer, Blowfish, *Arothron nigropunctatus* (Bloch and Schneider). Tropical Indo-Pacific, Japan, Australia, east coast of Africa, Red Sea. Length 25 centimeters (10 inches).     (S. Arita)

PLATE 440. Puffer, blowfish, *Arothron stellatus* (Bloch and Schneider). Tropical Indo-Pacific, Japan, Australia, Red Sea and east coast of Africa. Length 30 centimeters (12 inches). Taken at Eniwetok Atoll.

(R. F. Myers)

**439**

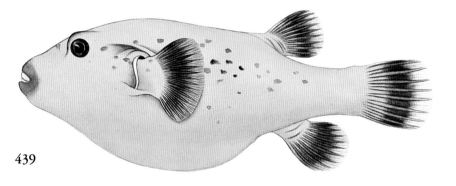

**440**

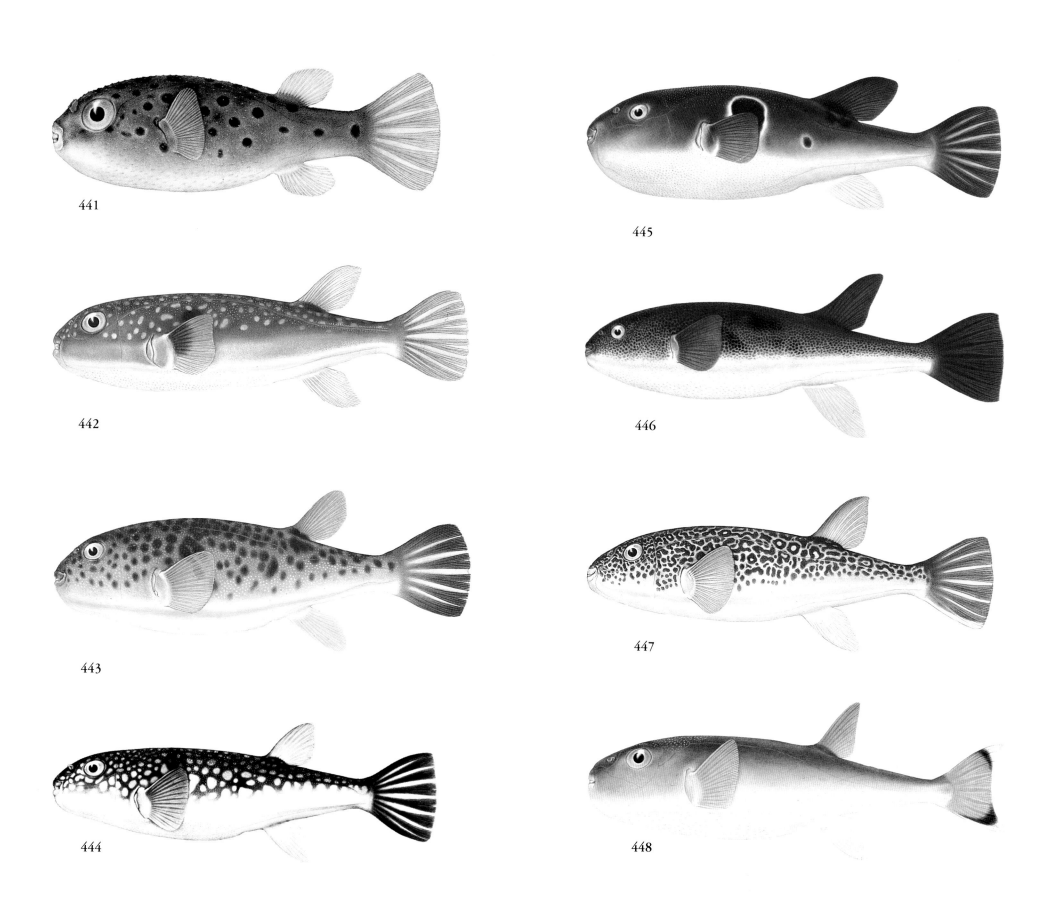

441

442

443

444

445

446

447

448

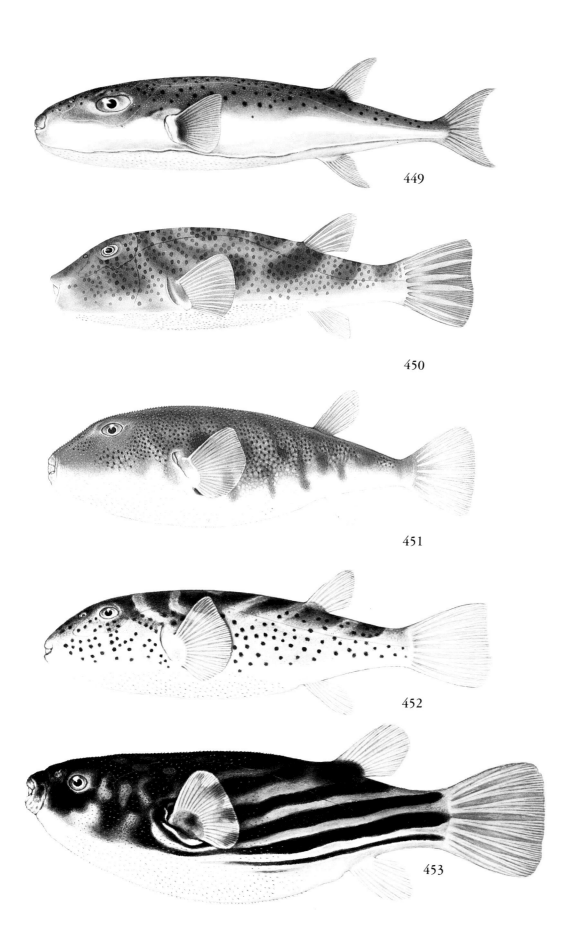

449

450

451

452

453

PLATE 441. Freshwater puffer, *Chelonodon fluviatilis* (Hamilton-Buchanan). Freshwaters and coasts of India, Burma, Malaya, and Indonesia. Length 15 centimeters (6 inches). (M. Shirao)

PLATE 442. Puffer, *Fugu niphobles* (Jordan and Snyder). Japan, China, the Philippines. Length 16 centimeters (6.25 inches). (M. Shirao)

PLATE 443. Puffer, *Fugu pardalis* (Temminck and Schlegel). China and Japan. Length 36 centimeters (14 inches). (M. Shirao)

PLATE 444. Puffer, blowfish, *Fugu poecilonotus* (Temminck and Schlegel). Indo-Pacific, China, Korea, Japan. Length 25 centimeters (10 inches). (M. Shirao)

PLATE 445. Puffer, *Fugu rubripes rubripes* (Temminck and Schlegel). Japan, China, Korea. Length 45 centimeters (17.5 inches). (M. Shirao)

PLATE 446. Puffer, *Fugu stictonotus* (Temminck and Schlegel). Southern Korea, east China Sea and adjoining waters, Japan. Length 40 centimeters (16 inches).
(M. Shirao)

PLATE 447. Puffer, *Fugu vermicularis vermicularis* (Temminck and Schlegel). East China Sea, Japan. Length 33 centimeters (23.5 inches). (M. Shirao)

PLATE 448. Puffer, *Lagocephalus lunaris* (Bloch and Schneider). Indo-Pacific, India, Red Sea, South and East coast of Africa, Australia, China, Japan. Length 30 centimeters (12 inches). (M. Shirao)

PLATE 449. Puffer, blowfish, *Lagocephalus sceleratus* (Forster). Indo-Pacific, southern Japan, Australia, east coast of Africa. Length 75 centimeters (30 inches).
(M. Shirao)

PLATE 450. Puffer, *Sphaeroides annulatus* (Jenyns). California to Peru, Galapagos Islands. Length 28 centimeters (11 inches). (T. Kumada)

PLATE 451. Puffer, *Sphaeroides maculatus* (Bloch and Schneider). Atlantic coast of United States to Guiana. Length 25 centimeters (10 inches). (M. Shirao)

PLATE 452. Puffer, *Sphaeroides testudineus* (Linnaeus). Atlantic coast of the United States, West Indies, Brazil. Length 21 centimeters (8.25 inches).
(M. Shirao)

PLATE 453. Puffer, *Tetraodon lineatus* Linnaeus. Rivers of northern and western Africa. Length 45 centimeters (17.5 inches). (M. Shirao)

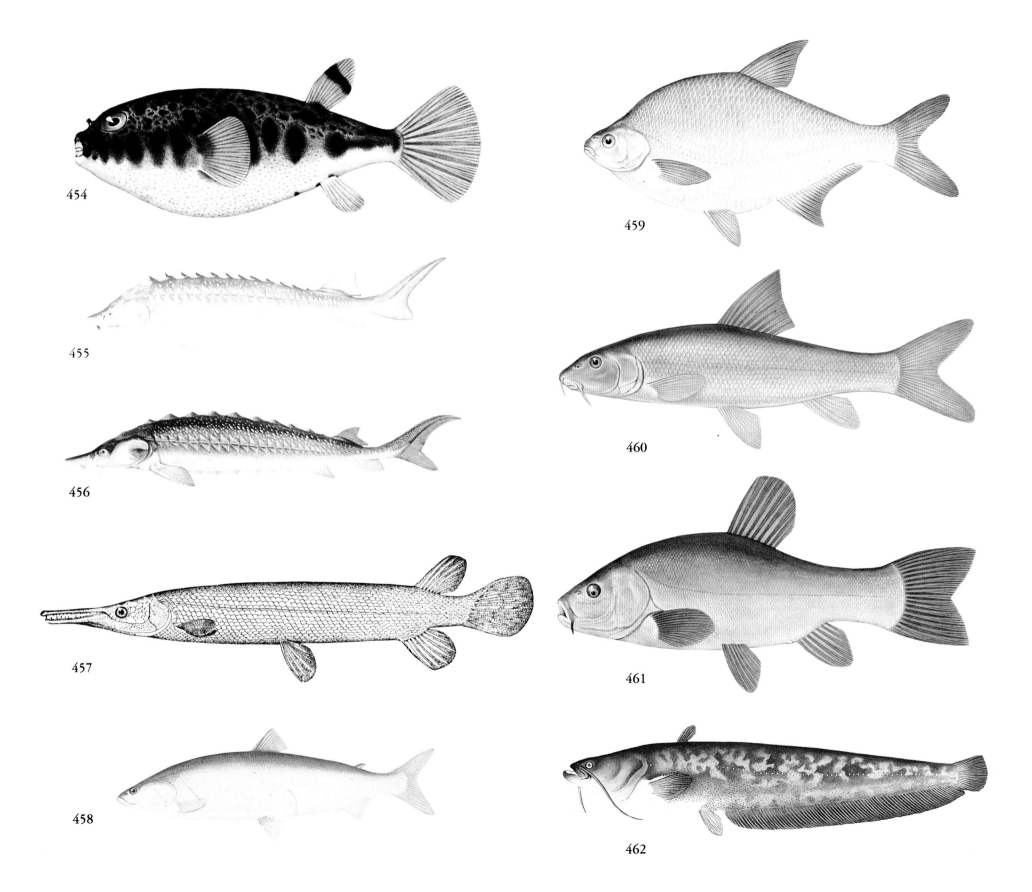

454

455

456

457

458

459

460

461

462

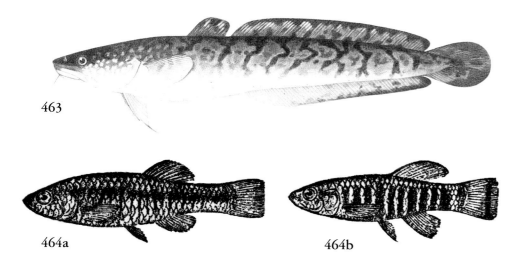

463

464a          464b

465

466

PLATE 454. Puffer, blowfish, *Torquigener hamiltoni* (Gray and Richardson). Indo-Pacific, Australia. Length 9 centimeters (3.5 inches).          (M. Shirao)

PLATE 455. Russian sturgeon, *Acipenser guldenstadti* Brandt. Persian and Siberian rivers, Caspian Sea, Danube. Length 1.4 meters (4.5 feet).
(From *Fish Resources of the U.S.S.R.*)

PLATE 456. Sturgeon, *Acipenser sturio* Linnaeus. Both coasts of the Atlantic, Mediterranean Sea, rivers of Europe and Russia. Length 3 meters (10 feet).
(From *Fish Resources of the U.S.S.R.*)

PLATE 457. Alligator gar, *Lepisosteus tristoechus* (Bloch and Schneider). South Atlantic and Gulf states of the United States. Length 6 meters (19.5 feet).
(From Jordan and Evermann)

PLATE 458. Whitefish, *Stenodus leucichthys* (Guldenstädt). Volga River, rivers of Siberia. Length 71 centimeters (28 inches).
(From *Fish Resources of the U.S.S.R.*)

PLATE 459. Bream, *Abramis brama* (Linnaeus). Europe, north of the Pyrenees and Alps to the Volga River and Caspian Sea. Length 35 centimeters (13.5 inches).          (M. Shirao)

PLATE 460. Barbel, *Barbus barbus* (Linnaeus). Northern and Central Europe. Length 85 centimeters (33.5 inches).          (M. Shirao)

PLATE 461. Tench, *Tinca tinca* (Linnaeus). Europe. Length 60 centimeters (23.5 inches).     (M. Shirao)

PLATE 462. Catfish, mudfish, *Parasilurus asotus* (Linnaeus). Japan, Korea, Manchuria, and China. Length 40 centimeters (16 inches).          (S. Arita)

PLATE 463. Burbot, eelpout, *Lota lota* (Linnaeus). Freshwaters of northern and central Europe. Length 1 meter (3 feet).   (From *Fish Resources of the U.S.S.R.*)

PLATE 464. Killifish, *Aphanius calaritanus* (Cuvier and Valenciennes). Southern Europe and north Africa. Length 5 centimeters (2 inches).
    a. Female.
    b. Male.          (From Boulenger)

PLATE 465. Common European eel, *Anguilla anguilla* (Linnaeus). Europe, fresh and saltwater. Length 1 meter (3 feet).     (From *Fish Resources of the U.S.S.R.*)

PLATE 466. American eel, *Anguilla rostrata* (LeSueur). Atlantic coast of the United States, from Maine to Mexico. Length 1 meter (3 feet).
(From Jordan and Evermann)

467

468

469

470

471

472

473

474

475

476

477a

477b

478

480

479

481

**PLATE 467.** Conger eel, *Conger conger* (Linnaeus). Atlantic Ocean, Mediterranean. Length 2 meters (6.5 feet). (From Goode)

**PLATE 468.** Golden striped bass, *Grammistes sexlineatus* (Thunberg). Tropical Indo-Pacific. Length 15 centimeters (6 inches). Taken at Guam. (R. F. Myers)

**PLATE 469.** Soapfish, *Rypticus saponaceus* (Bloch and Schneider). Length 45 centimeters (17.5 inches). Tropical and subtropical Atlantic. (From Bean)

**PLATE 470.** Trunkfish, *Ostracion cubicus* Linnaeus. Tropical Indo-Pacific. Length 20 centimeters (8 inches). Taken at Guam. (R. F. Myers)

**PLATE 471.** Japanese swordtail newt, *Cynops (Triturus) ensicauda* (Hallowell). Japan. Length 16 centimeters (6.2 inches). Male. (R. H. Knabenbauer)

**PLATE 472.** Japanese red-bellied newt, *Cynops (Triturus) pyrrhogaster* (Boie). Japan. Length 14 centimeters (5.5 inches). Male. (R. H. Knabenbauer)

**PLATE 473.** Black-spotted newt, *Notophthalmus meridionalis* (Cope). South Texas and Mexico. Length 11 centimeters (4 inches). (R. H. Knabenbauer)

**PLATE 474.** Rough-skinned newt, *Taricha granulosa* (Skilton). California to Alaska, Idaho. Length 21 centimeters (8 inches). (R. H. Knabenbauer)

**PLATE 475.** Red-bellied newt, *Taricha rivularis* (Twitty). California. Length 21 centimeters (8 inches). (R. H. Knabenbauer)

**PLATE 476.** California newt, *Taricha torosa* (Rathke). Southwestern United States. Length 19 centimeters (7 inches). (R. H. Knabenbauer)

**PLATE 477a.** California newt, *Taricha torosa* (Rathke). Male (right) with rough skin; female (left), with smooth skin. This is the species that was first discovered to contain tarichatoxin—now known to be identical to pufferfish poison, tetrodotoxin—in their skin.

b. Egg clusters of *T. torosa.* Diameter of each cluster about 2 centimeters (.75 inches). The eggs are also very poisonous. (Courtesy H. S. Mosher)

**PLATE 478.** Alpine newt, *Triturus alpestris* (Laurenti). Central Europe, Germany, French Alps, Italy, Switzerland, Greece. Length 11 centimeters (4 inches). Male. (R. H. Knabenbauer)

**PLATE 479.** Crested newt, *Triturus cristatus* (Laurenti). Northern and Middle Europe, Russia. Length 18 centimeters (7 inches). Male. (R. H. Knabenbauer)

**PLATE 480.** Marbled newt, *Triturus marmoratus* (Laetreille). France, Spain. Length 15 centimeters (6 inches). Male. (R. H. Knabenbauer)

**PLATE 481.** Smooth newt, *Triturus vulgaris* (Linnaeus). Europe, Urals, Turkey. Length 11 centimeters (4.2 inches). Male. (R. H. Knabenbauer)

**PLATE 482.** Poison-dart frog,* *Atelopus varius* Stannius. Colombia, Central America. Length 4.4 centimeters (1.7 inches body length). (Courtesy C. W. Myers, AMNH†)

**PLATE 483.** *Atelopus zeteki* Dunn. Central America. Length 4 centimeters (1.5 inches). (Courtesy C. W. Myers, AMNH)

**PLATE 484.** *Dendrobates auratus* (Girard). Colombia. Length 4.2 centimeters (1.6 inches). (Courtesy C. W. Myers, AMNH)

**PLATE 485.** *Dendrobates bombates* Myers and Daly. Colombia. Length 3 centimeters (1.2 inches). (Courtesy C. W. Myers, AMNH)

**PLATE 486.** *Dendrobates histrionicus* Berthold. Colombia, Ecuador. Length 3 centimeters (1.2 inches). (Courtesy C. W. Myers, AMNH)

**PLATE 487.** *Dendrobates lehmanni* Myers and Daly. Colombia. Length 3 centimeters (1.2 inches). (Courtesy C. W. Myers, AMNH)

**PLATE 488.** *Dendrobates leucomelas* Fitzinger. Colombia. Length 3.7 centimeters (1.4 inches). (Courtesy C. W. Myers, AMNH)

**PLATE 489.** *Dendrobates silverstonei* Myers and Daly. Colombia. Length 3 centimeters (1.2 inches). (Courtesy C. W. Myers, AMNH)

**PLATE 490.** *Phyllobates terribilis* Myers and Daly. Colombia. Length 4.5 centimeters (1.7 inches). (Courtesy C. W. Myers, AMNH)

**PLATE 491.** *Dendrobates trivittatus* (Spix). Colombia. Length 4.9 centimeters (2 inches). (Courtesy C. W. Myers, AMNH)

**PLATE 492.** *Phyllobates aurotaenia* (Boulenger). Rio San Juan, Nicaragua. Length 3 centimeters (1.2 inches). (Courtesy C. W. Myers, AMNH)

**PLATE 493.** *Phyllobates lugubris* (Schmidt). Colombia. Length 2.5 centimeters (1 inch). (Courtesy C. W. Myers, AMNH)

*There are no common English names available for **Plates** 482–93.
†AMNH = American Museum of Natural History.

482  483

484  485

486  487

488  489

490  491

492  493

494

495

496

497
498

499a

499b

499c

500a

500 (top)

500 (bottom)

501 (bottom)

PLATE 494. Giant toad, *Bufo marinus* (Linnaeus). Central, South America, Texas. Length 20 centimeters (8 inches).                    (R. H. Knabenbauer)

PLATE 495. Green turtle, *Chelonia mydas* (Linnaeus). All tropical and subtropical oceans. The flesh of this turtle may be poisonous to eat in some localities. May attain a weight of over 25 kilograms (55 pounds) and a carapace length of about 1.2 meters (4 feet). Taken at Heron Island, Australia.          (D. Perrine)

PLATE 496. Close-up of head of a large female *C. mydas* laying eggs in the sand. Taken at Heron Island. The flesh may be poisonous to eat.          (K. Gillett)

PLATE 497. Hawksbill turtle, *Eretmochelys imbricata* (Linnaeus). May attain a weight of about 125 kilograms (275 pounds) and a carapace length of about 85 centimeters (33.5 inches). Female. Taken on the beach at Heron Island, Australia.          (J. Booth)

PLATE 498. Leatherback turtle, *Dermochelys coriacea* (Linnaeus). The flesh may be poisonous to eat. Largely circumtropical in distribution, but occasionally taken in temperate seas. Attains large size, over 250 kilograms (551 pounds) and a carapace length of about 1.2 meters (4 feet). Taken near Kuala Dungan, Malaysia.          (Courtesy H. Hobard)

PLATE 499a, b, c. Drawing showing a comparison of the three sea turtles: (a) *Chelonia mydas*; (b) *Eretmochelys imbricata*; and (c) *Dermatochelys coriacea*. All three species may be poisonous to eat at certain places and seasons. The toxicity is unpredictable.          (H. Baerg)

PLATE 500 (top). Sei whale, *Balaenoptera borealis* Lesson. The liver may be poisonous to eat, probably due to excessively high levels of vitamin A. Atlantic Ocean, Labrador southward to Campeche; Pacific Ocean, Bering Sea southward to Baja California. Length 18 meters (59 feet).          (R. H. Knabenbauer)

PLATE 500 (bottom). Sperm whale, *Physeter catodon* Linnaeus. The flesh and oil may be poisonous to eat in some localities. Polar, temperate, and tropical seas. Length 18 meters (59 feet).          (R. H. Knabenbauer)

PLATE 501 (top). Southeast Asiatic porpoise, or black finless porpoise, *Neophocaena phocaenoides* (Cuvier). The liver may be poisonous to eat. China, Japan, Indonesia, Pakistan, India, South Africa. Length 1.5 meters (5 feet).          (R. H. Knabenbauer)

PLATE 501 (bottom). White whale, beluga, *Delphinapterus leucas* (Pallas). The flesh may be poisonous to eat. The nature of the poison is unknown. Arctic and subarctic seas. Length 5.5 meters (18 feet).

(R. H. Knabenbauer)

502

503

504
505

PLATE 502. Australian fur seal, *Arctocephalus doriferus* Wood Jones. South Australia and Tasmania. Length 1.83 meters (6 feet). Liver may be poisonous to eat. Male specimen. Taken at Seal Rocks, Phillip Island, Victoria, Australia. (Courtesy B. J. Marlow)

PLATE 503. Bearded seal, *Erignathus barbatus* (Erxleben). The liver may be toxic to eat, apparently because of the excessive vitamin A content. Inhabits the edge of the ice along the coasts and islands of North America and Northern Eurasia, and polar areas. Length 2.7 meters (9 feet). (R. H. Knabenbauer)

PLATE 504. Australian sea lion, *Neophoca cinerea* (Peron). The liver may be poisonous to eat. Rocky Islands off the south and southwest coasts of Australia. Length 2.4 meters (8 feet). (B. J. Marlow)

PLATE 505. Ringed seal, *Pusa hispida* (Schreber). The liver of older specimens may at times be toxic to eat. Circumboreal near the edge of the ice, to the North Pole. Length 1.4 meters (4.7 feet).

(R. H. Knabenbauer)

# CHAPTER VII

# Electric Aquatic Animals

ELECTRIC FISHES are small in number, but constitute a fascinating assemblage of dangerous aquatic animals. Although most plants and animals produce electrical discharges of some type, there are only about 250 species of fishes known to possess actual specialized electric organs. However, many other species of fishes are known to emit electrical discharges through their lateral line system.

Electricity is an important constituent in the metabolic activity of living things. The amount of current is so small in many instances that these currents can be detected only by extremely sensitive instruments. In land animals, the air acts as a good insulator, and these small discharges are very difficult to detect at any distance from the body. With animals living in an aquatic medium, the water acts as a good conductor, and some aquatic animals possess a specialized organ system that discharges electricity through the water at surprisingly high voltages.

The best known and most studied of the electric aquatic organisms are the following—

## ELECTROPHORIDAE

There is only a single species in this family:
ELECTRIC EEL, *Electrophorus electricus* (Linnaeus) (506). This eel inhabits the streams and swamps of South American jungles, and is the most powerful of the electric fishes. An air breather, it must periodically surface for a gulp of air, or it will drown. This eel is able to produce an enormous amount of electricity—up to about 650 volts, with an average 40 watts—sufficient to light up an electric bulb. When this current is discharged into the water, the electrical field that it sets up is sufficient to stun a man or even a horse.

When at rest, *Electrophorus* gives off no electricity, but when swimming it will emit a discharge of about 50 volts at a rate of about 50 per second. Since this eel develops cataracts at an early age, possibly due to the electrical discharges, the electrolocation system is of considerable importance in its survival. Although the discharge lasts only two one-thousandths of a second, the eel can send out 400 or more per second. An eel can give out a steady series of discharges for 20 minutes, rest for 5 minutes, and then continue the shocking process again. It is truly one of the world's most efficient batteries.

Another well known group of electric fishes are the marine torpedo rays, which include species that are the second most potent dischargers of electricity. Large torpedo rays can give off more than 200 volts. One such species is:

## NARCINIDAE: TORPEDO RAYS

LESSER ELECTRIC RAY, *Narcine brasiliensis* (Olfers) (Figure 1), is found in the inshore waters of the

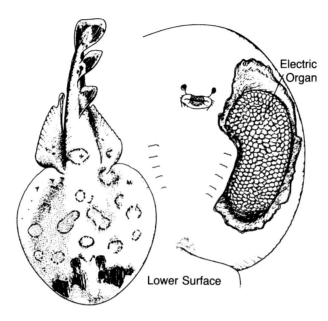

Figure 1. Lesser electric ray, *Narcine brasiliensis* (Olfers) with the skin removed to show the arrangement of the electric organs. Contact with the skin can result in a severe electric shock long to be remembered. It can discharge up to 200 volts. The polarity of the electric organ is positive on the dorsal side and negative on the underside. This fish inhabits the western Atlantic from Brazil to Florida and Texas, south to Argentina. Length 45 centimeters (11 inches).

(After Bigelow and Schroeder)

Electric Organ

Lower Surface

western Atlantic, from Brazil to Florida and Texas, south to Argentina.

Other representative species are:

BULL'S EYE TORPEDO or ELECTRIC RAY, *Diplobatis omata* (Jordan and Gilbert) (507), which ranges in the inshore waters of the southern California coast.

TORPEDO or CRAMPFISH, *Torpedo torpedo* (Linnaeus) (508), which inhabits the Mediterranean Sea.

MARBLED CRAMPFISH or TORPEDO RAY, *Torpedo marmorata* Risso (509), which also inhabits the Mediterranean Sea.

CALIFORNIA TORPEDO RAY, *Torpedo californica* (Ayres) (510), which ranges along the California coast.

The electric rays are sluggish, feeble swimmers that spend most of their time lying on the bottom partially buried in the mud or sand at shallow depths.

The Greeks knew the torpedo rays and referred to them as the "narke," a term from which the words narcotic and narcosis are derived. Many Roman physicians used these torpedo rays to shock their patients. Thus, electrotherapy is a very ancient modality.

There are numerous other electric fishes that are not as well known as the electric eels and torpedos. One of these is:

ELECTRIC CATFISH, *Malopterurus electricus* Lacépède (511). This electric catfish inhabits a wide range of streams and rivers of Africa, extending from the Nile to the Zambesi rivers, but is absent from most of the rivers of East Africa. Electric catfishes are also sluggish creatures, spending much of their time on the bottom in the mud. Larger specimens of *Malopterurus* are said to produce a discharge of up to 450 volts. They have been observed in an aquarium shocking other fishes, causing them to vomit up their meals, which are quickly ingested by *Malopterurus*. Certainly this is one of the world's most unique methods of procuring food. Normally they feed chiefly on decomposing vegetable and animal matter.

Electric catfish were well known to ancient Eygptians and were depicted on the murals and tombs of Ti at Sakkara and in the great fishing scene at Giza. The electric catfish, which was referred to as the "torpedo," was also known to ancient Abyssinians and was noted as follows in the book *Abassia*, viz.: "In thefe Rivers and Lakes is alfo found the Torpedo, which if any man hold in his hand, if it ftirse not, it doth produce no effect, but if it mouv it felfe never fo little, it fo tormenth the body of him which holds it, that his Arteries, Joints, Sinewes, & all his numbers feele exceeding paine. . . ." (*See* Wu, 1984.)

Because of its unique electrical properties, *Malopterurus* was used for its medicinal properties by physicians of ancient Middle Eastern countries. The shocking process by electric fishes was used in ancient times for the treatment of rheumatism. The Arab physician Ibn-Sidah claimed that a live electric catfish placed on the brow of an epileptic victim was beneficial. It is significant that in World War II, the electric organs of the electric eel, *Electrophorus*, were used as a potential anti-war gas agent. Maybe the ancient "witch doctors" were ahead of their time.

Another interesting group of electric fishes includes the stargazers of the family Uranoscopidae:

SOUTHERN STARGAZER, *Astroscopus y-graecum* (Cuvier and Valenciennes) (512), which inhabits the south Atlantic coast from Cape Hatteras to the Caribbean Sea, has been studied to only a limited extent. The electrogenic organs of stargazers are located in a specialized pouch just behind the eyes. The uranoscopids are also equipped with venomous shoulder spines. Their electrogenic organs are said to be modified eye muscles. When at rest, *Astroscopus* discharges only about 90 millivolts, but is capable of releasing up to 50 volts when necessary.

Some of the electric fishes are quite bizarre in their appearance. The elephantfishes of the family Mormyridae have an oddly-shaped mouth that is extremely variable in appearance. In some species, there is a very elongate proboscis-like snout with a terminal mouth. An example of the *Mormyrus* species is:

ELEPHANTNOSE or SNOUTFISH, *Mormyrus tapirus* Pappenheim (513), which is known to produce low voltage discharges at a rather steady rate. Mormyrids have poor eyesight and live in the murky water in the Nile River and tropical Africa. They set up an electrical field around them so that when anything breaks this field, they are readily able to detect an object. The mormyrids are closely related to another species of electric fish:

UBANGI MORMYRID, *Gnathonemus petersi* (Günther) (514), which also discharges low voltage electricity.

Another species producing an electrical discharge is:

JERFAR, *Gymnarchus niloticus* Cuvier (515), which is the only species in the family Gymnarchidae. Laboratory studies have shown that this fish can distinguish between objects having identical geometric and optical properties but having different conductivities. The mormyrids and *Gymnarchus* appear to have small specialized electrical organs located in the posterior part of their bodies.

CARAPO, *Gymnotus carapo* Linnaeus (516), a member of the family Gymnotidae, or naked-back knifefish, is an air breather like *Electrophorus*. It inhabits the freshwaters of Central and South America. The carapo discharges electricity as a continuous series of low-intensity impulses at the rate of 65 per second.

The knifefish family Rhamphichthyidae of the freshwater streams of South America also possess electrogenic organs:

KNIFEFISH, *Gymnorhamphichthys hypostomus* Ellis (517) produces a discharge of about 50 volts.

BLACK AFRICAN KNIFEFISH, *Xenomystus nigri* (Günther) (518), another fish in this family, emits low voltage discharges.

Numerous other fishes also possess specialized electric organs. The following is a partial list of fish genera known to have electric organs: The elephantfishes, *Genyomyrus, Gnathoneumus, Hyperopisus, Marcusenius, Mormyrops, Mormyrus, Petrocephalus*; the knifefish *Hypopomus*; glass knifefish, *Eigenmania*; naked knifefish, *Adontosternarchus, Sternarchus*; and the electric rays, *Raja*.

## Electric Organs of Fishes

The electric organs of fishes are said to be derived from muscle or nerve tissue. Although a few fish such as the electric eel, *Electrophorus*, can produce potent discharges of up to 650 volts, most electric fishes emit discharges in the range of millivolts up to several volts. Strong discharges are emitted infrequently and are used to deter as a defense mechanism or to stun their prey. Weak discharges are emitted continuously and are used as a system of electrolocation and social communication.

The answer to the question as to how do fishes generate electricity has intrigued scientists for many years and has stimulated an enormous amount of research. The electric organs of fishes are believed to function on the following principles:

Specialized electrocytes (electric cells) that are arranged in series are synchronously excited by spinal nerve signals to generate small voltage gradients in the direction of their linear arrangement. Since each stack

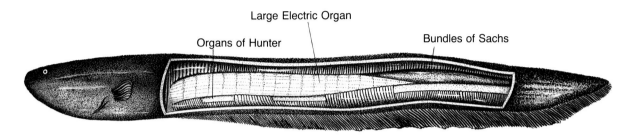

Large Electric Organ

Organs of Hunter

Bundles of Sachs

Figure 2. Illustration of the general anatomical arrangement of the electric eel, *Electrophorus electricus*. There are three separate electric organs. The *large electric organ* is the main battery. This is the electric organ from which the large discharges are released. This organ is paired, one on either side or the tail of the fish. It starts just behind the body of the fish and continues to a point about two-thirds down the tail. At this point, the large electric organ diminishes in size and is replaced by two smaller paired electric organs known as the *bundles of Sachs*. The arrangement of cells is similar in both organs, but the cells of the bundles of Sachs are larger. There is a third set of electric organs known as the *organs of Hunter*. They are very slender, extending throughout the entire length of the anal fin along the base of the fin. The discharge of the organs of Hunter appears to be influenced by the large electric organ. The electric cells that fill the organs are arranged in series-parallel in the fish, but prevail in series. Their voltage is about 0.1 volt. They vary in size depending upon the size of the fish. The polarity in the eel is positive at the head and negative at the tail. There is no reversal of polarity.

(R. Kreuzinger, after Coates)

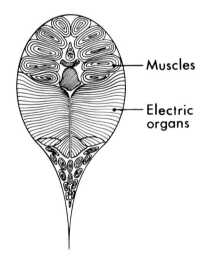

Muscles

Electric organs

Figure 3. Cross section of the tail of the electric eel, showing the anatomical relationship of electric organs to muscle mass. (R. Kreuzinger, after Coates)

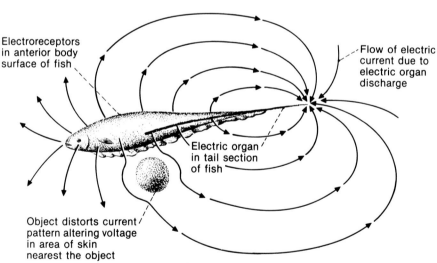

Electroreceptors in anterior body surface of fish

Flow of electric current due to electric organ discharge

Electric organ in tail section of fish

Object distorts current pattern altering voltage in area of skin nearest the object

Figure 4. Diagram showing the principles of electrolocation. The longitudinal black bar in the tail of the fish indicates the location of the electric organ. The electroreceptors are situated in a series of pores on the anterior body surface of the fish. (R. H. Knabenbauer)

of electrocytes is tightly surrounded by insulating tissues, the voltage contributions of the electrocytes add linearly, as with a series of small batteries. Figures 2 and 3 show the general anatomical structure of the electric eel.

The electric ray is arranged differently (Figure 1). Here, the electric organs constitute about one-sixth of the total body weight and are situated one on either side of the anterior part of the disc between the anterior extension of the pectoral fin and the head, and extend from about the level of the eye backward past the gill region.

The process of electrolocation (Figure 4) resembles echo or sonar location in the sense that the animal assesses its environment by actively emitting signals and monitoring their feedback. One of the benefits of the systems used by electro- and echolocating animals is that they can operate effectively in total darkness. The fish generates a current field that emanates from its anterior body and then converges on the tip of its tail. Electroreceptors distributed over the anterior body surface monitor local current flowing over the skin produced by the electric organ discharge. The electroreceptors are derived from the lateral line organs and are supplied by lateral line nerves. It is interesting to note that the lateral line system is comprised of sensory cells that resemble hair cells of the inner ear of humans. An object that differs in impedance (opposition in an electrical circuit) from the surrounding water distorts the electric field and thereby alters the pattern of electrical current intensities over the body of the fish that is closest to the object. Thus, by monitoring local changes in electroreceptor activity, the fish is able to perceive the presence and nature of objects. Electric fishes are truly one of the marvels of the aquatic world and offer a wealth of material for future research into the phenomena of electrolocation.

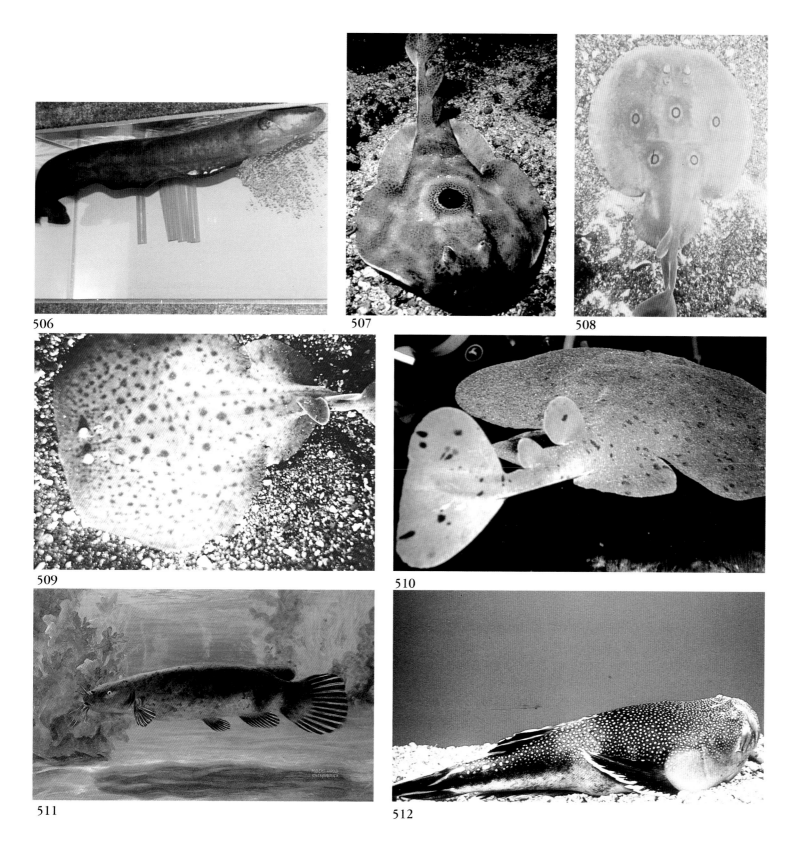

506

507

508

509

510

511

512

**PLATE 506.** Electric eel, *Electrophorus electricus* (Linnaeus). The head and body comprise only the anterior, or one-fifth of the fish. The electric organs are all located in the tail. This eel can deliver an electrical discharge up to 650 volts, which is sufficient to stun a man or a horse. Inhabits the streams and swamps of tropical South America. Attains a length of 1.2 meters (4 feet) or more. Taken in an aquarium.

(Courtesy G. D. Ruggieri, New York Aquarium, New York Zoological Society)

**PLATE 507.** Bull's eye torpedo or electric ray, *Diplobatis omata* (Jordan and Gilbert). Contact with this attractive ray can result in an unpleasant shocking experience. Taken in the Gulf of California. Length 61 centimeters (24 inches). (Courtesy E. T. Rulison)

**PLATE 508.** Torpedo or crampfish, *Torpedo torpedo* (Linnaeus). Inhabits the Mediterranean Sea. Length 60 centimeters (23.5 inches). (P. Giacomelli)

**PLATE 509.** Marbled crampfish or torpedo ray, *Torpedo marmorata* Risso. All of the torpedo rays are able to shock. This species inhabits the Mediterranean Sea. Taken in the Bay of Naples, Italy. Length 70 centimeters (27.5 inches). (P. Giacomelli)

**PLATE 510.** California torpedo ray, *Torpedo californica* (Ayres). This electric ray can deliver a very painful shock, as the author can attest from personal experience. Ranges along the coast of California. Attains a length of 91 centimeters (3 feet).

(Courtesy A. Giddings, Ocean Images, Inc.)

**PLATE 511.** Electric catfish, *Malopterurus electricus* Lacépède. This species spends much of its time on the muddy bottom. It can discharge up to 450 volts and shock other fish, causing them to vomit up their food, which it then eats! It inhabits the streams and rivers of Africa, from the Nile to the Zambesi rivers, but is absent from East Africa. Length 61 centimeters (2 feet). (R. H. Knabenbauer)

**PLATE 512.** Southern stargazer, *Astroscopus y-graecum* (Cuvier and Valenciennes). This fish can discharge up to 50 volts. The electric organs are located in a specialized pouch behind the eyes. Inhabits the south Atlantic coast, from Cape Hatteras to the Caribbean Sea. Length 38 centimeters (15 inches). Taken at the Miami Seaquarium. (Courtesy Miami Seaquarium)

513

514

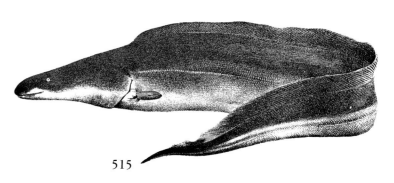

515

516

517

518

PLATE 513. Elephantnose or snoutfish, *Mormyrus tapirus* Pappenheim. The snoutfish emits low levels of electrical discharges. It inhabits the freshwaters of central Africa. Length 28 centimeters (11 inches).

(R. H. Knabenbauer)

PLATE 514. Ubangi mormyrid, *Gnathonemus petersi* (Günther). This fish has a unique look, with the lower jaw cylindrical, having a tapering dermal appendage, giving the fish a "Ubangi" appearance. The mormyrids usually discharge only low-voltage electricity. These fish have poor eyesight and live in murky water. Most of their food detection and avoidance of enemies is by means of electrolocation. It inhabits the waters of central Africa. Length 23 centimeters (9 inches) or more. Taken at the New York Aquarium.

(Courtesy G. D. Ruggieri, New York Aquarium, New York Zoological Society)

PLATE 515. Jerfar, *Gymnarchus niloticus* Cuvier. The only member of its family, this bizarre-looking fish releases a low discharge of electricity; it has the ability to distinguish between objects having identical geometric and optical properties but with different conductivities. It inhabits the freshwaters of tropical Africa and the Nile. Length 1 meter (39 inches).

(From Boulenger)

PLATE 516. Carapo, *Gymnotus carapo* Linnaeus. The carapo discharges electricity as a continuous series of low-intensity impulses at the rate of 65 per second. It inhabits the freshwaters of Central and South America. Length 38 centimeters (15 inches).

(From Coates, New York Zoological Society)

PLATE 517. Knifefish, *Gymnorhamphichthys hypostomus* Ellis. This fish produces an electrical discharge of about 50 volts. It inhabits the freshwater streams of South America. Length 61 centimeters (2 feet).

(From Coates, New York Zoological Society)

PLATE 518. Black African knifefish, *Xenomystus nigri* (Günther). This species emits low-voltage discharges. Usually the fish is dark brown in color, as seen in this specimen at the left side of the aquarium tank. It inhabits freshwaters of central Africa. Length 20 centimeters (8 inches). (Courtesy G. D. Ruggieri, New York Aquarium, New York Zoological Society)

# CHAPTER VIII

# Human Parasitic Catfish (Candirú)

MEDICAL-ICHTHYOLOGICAL facts are frequently stranger than fiction. Fragmentary stories concerning a fish that penetrates the human urethra by swimming up the urinary stream while a person is voiding have issued from the Amazon jungles for centuries. However, it was not until the researches of ichthyologist Dr. E. W. Gudger, formerly of the American Museum of Natural History, that these wild tales achieved scientific credence.

Urinophilous fishes are commonly designated by the natives of the tropical lowland regions of South America as the *candirú* or *carnero*. However, the species identity of the candirú continues to elude scientists because no specimen removed from the urogenital or rectal orifices of humans have ever found their way to a reputable ichthyological museum for scientific identification. Despite this paucity of data, most ichthyologists who have worked in the Amazon region are in agreement that the true candirú is a member of the catfish family Pygidiidae. Among the genera *Acanthopoma, Vandellia, Steophilus, Branchioica, Urinophilus, Cetopsis, Hemicetopsis,* and *Tridens* are one or more species of minute, elongate catfishes that are believed to exhibit a positive tropism toward human urine—that is, will follow a trail of urine—and have a tendency to enter the urethra, vagina, rectum, or some natural opening of the body of humans and other animals.

The pygidiid catfishes are distributed throughout South America and abound in moderate to extremely high elevations in the Andes Mountains, but most of the reports concerning their parasitic inclinations have stemmed from the tropical lowland portions of South America. To the best of our knowledge, these strange fishes are found in no other part of the world.

Most pygidiid culprits capable of urinary misconduct are either juvenile or small specimens. They are generally elongate or eel-like in form, cylindrical to terete in cross section, and have a rounded, depressed head and an inferiorly placed mouth. The body of these fishes is scaleless and slimy, having a transparent or flesh to brown color. The dangerous pygidiids range from 3 millimeters to 5 centimeters (⅛ inch to 2 inches) in total length.

The general structure of some of these species of pygidiids shows them to be uniquely adapted for an intrusive or parasitic existence. An example of a species having a most typical urinophiloid morphology is:

PARASITIC CATFISH or CANDIRÚ, *Urinophilus erythrurus* Eigenmann (519).

Some of the anatomical features of this species are shown in (520). It possesses nine fang-like erectile teeth, pointing backward and forward immediately in front of the mouth. The buccal cavity has a number of papillae, and the lips are laterally thickened and devoid of teeth. Behind the lower lip is a membranous mask-like structure that can be drawn forward to enclose all of the anterior part of the buccal cavity. There is a group of about 15 opercular spines situated on either gill cover. The spines are sharp and toothlike, pointing upward and backward. On the lower side of the head, below and behind each eye, is a patch of spines that also point backward and inward. The gill openings in these fishes are greatly reduced. The mouth is small and inferior in position, leading into a short, straight intestinal tract best suited for a carnivorous or hemophagous diet. Examination of the intestinal tract of specimens of *U. erythrurus* and related species have revealed guts engorged with blood. Truly, the pygidiid makes a formidably-armed urethral instrument.

The history of urinophilous fishes is an interesting one. Hair-raising reports on the activities of these fishes are said to have been brought back to the Old World by some of the early Spanish and Portuguese Amazonian explorers. The German naturalist explorer Phillip Von Martius is generally credited as the first to have prepared a scientific account on these urine-loving creatures in *Itinere per Brasiliam annis, 1817–20.* The author states, "By a singular instinct it is incited to enter the excretory openings of the human body when it can get at these parts in those who are bathing in the river. With great violence it forces its way in, and desiring to eat the flesh, it unfortunately brings danger to human life." Similar accounts have been published by numerous other naturalists.

To what extent pygidiids are truly urinophilous is not readily known. However, it is generally accepted among the natives that one is in greatest danger if urinating in the water. The preponderance of evidence thus far would indicate that these catfishes may on occasion invade the human urethra, and that women, because of the nature of their anatomy, run a greater risk than men.

The statement that "an ounce of prevention is worth a pound of cure" certainly applies to the ever-urine-loving catfish of the Amazon. Natives have developed several devices (521) that reputedly afford the necessary safety. Probably one of the most widespread preventive techniques is a protective ligature around the penis. Another method is to cover the genitalia with a small minutely perforated coconut shell suspended in a bag of palm fibers. Some of the tribes along the Xingu River, in Brazil, wear a device called the "inoba." This is a sheath woven of dried palm leaves. The prepuce is drawn through the lower opening, which serves as a constricting device. The women of the Bakairai tribe, who live at the headwaters of the Xingu River, wear a device called the "uluri." This device is made of bark, folded and worn as a pudendal belt. The men of the Kenapo and Tapirape tribes wear a penis sheath of woven palm leaf strips called the "imudje." Although the penis sheaths are used by primitive tribes the world over, it is believed by some scholars that the candirú and the piraña had a stimulating influence in their development in the Amazon region.

Injuries produced by the candirú are caused by the retrose teeth of the jaws and mouth and by the opercular spines. The teeth and spines are so oriented that forward movement of the fish in the urethral canal takes place with facility, but any attempt to remove the fish results in lacerations of the surrounding tissues. Hemorrhaging and secondary infections are the most common complications. The usual treatment is by mechanical removal of the fish, and at times requires surgical intervention and even amputation of the penis.

Although there are many unknowns regarding the biology and medical aspects of the candirú problem, there appears to be sufficient scientific evidence to justify their reputation as a "human vertebrate parasite" in a rather general sense of the term.

The French ichthyologist Clement Jobert (1898) published a lengthy account on urinophilous fishes. Although somewhat skeptical that such fishes actually existed, he was much impressed with the fear exhibited by the Tapyos Indians while collecting fishes in the vicinity of Pará. He observed that the males religiously tied a tight ligature around their penis in order to prevent attacks from these fishes. Jobert became even more impressed with the reality of the situation when he bathed in a nearby stream infested by candirús and was bitten by them. He later had his fish wounds examined by one of the local physicians, who informed him that the marks were those of the dreaded candirú. The doctor further remarked that he had previously removed a small catfish from the urethra of a woman who had made the serious blunder of urinating while bathing in the river.

There is one case on record in which one of the physicians at Remate de Males, Brazil, removed a "kandiroo" from the urethra of a man, who subsequently died from hemorrhage following the operation.

Carl H. Eigenmann, who was one of the greatest authorities on South American fishes, has written extensively on these fishes in his 1918 monograph, "The Pygidiidae, a Family of South American Catfishes." Eigenmann states that specimens of pygidiids are sometimes taken from the gill covers of large catfishes, where apparently they have established a commensal or parasitic existence. The fact that their intestinal tracts are engorged with blood would indicate that they are more parasitic than commensalistic. Eigenmann was sufficiently impressed with their urinotropic tendencies that he appropriately named a genus of pygidiids *Urinophilus*—a lover of urine.

Other cases have been cited in which candirús had penetrated into the anal and urinary openings of men and women bathers. One of the most interesting cases is one in which a group of Indian women removed their garments and squatted down Indian fashion to do their washing. They were not long at work when one of their number gave a shriek of pain, jumped up and ran out on the bank. Her companions ran to her, and upon examination found that a candirú had entered the external genital orifice and had penetrated some distance into the vagina. She was led to a nearby hut, where her companions extracted the fish mechanically. The retrose hooks on the opercular apparatus tore into the flesh causing great pain and considerable loss of blood. The crude method of extraction seemed to cause no lasting ill effects, for the woman was soon about her work.

Eigenmann reported several cases of candirús that had attacked the anus, nose, ears, vagina, and penis. In Eigenmann and Allen's work on the *Fishes of Western South America,* the authors include a chronological list of all the known reported attacks of the candirú on human beings.

While teaching at the School of Tropical and Preventive Medicine in the 1950s at Loma Linda, California, I discussed periodically with our students in medical zoology the subject of the candirú. Several students who had worked as missionaries in the Amazon Basin stated that they were personally acquainted with instances in which catfishes had become lodged in the urethra of the victim and had to be surgically removed in order to save the life of the patient.

Most catfishes tend to be bottom dwellers and are constantly seeking a hiding place under a log or rock, in the mud, or in a crevice or burrow of some type. The habits of the candirú follow this general pattern, but only more so. With their elongate, slimy, eel-like bodies and retrose teeth, they are peculiarly adapted for an intrusive existence. Although it is a well-established fact that pygidiids have the remarkable ability to climb the perpendicular sides of a slippery waterfall by means of their opercular spines and suctorial mouths, the reports of their swimming up the urinary stream while the person is urinating in the Amazon River is stretching the aquatic ability of even the famed candiru.

Catfishes are carnivorous in their eating habits and are readily attracted by flesh and blood, and the candirú offers the dreaded pirañhas some very close competition. Most ichthyologists are agreed that pygidiids are definitely blood suckers. If a dead animal falls into the stream, it is promptly consumed by pirañhas and candirús. The ectoparasitic habits of this fish appear to be well established by several zoologists who have observed them clinging to fishes, humans, and other animals that invade their aquatic environment. The lesion that they produce has best been described as a "cuppingglasslike wound." They fasten themselves on the victim, painlessly cut the skin, and then gorge themselves with blood. It has also been observed that in their ectoparasitic operations on large fishes they will sometimes burrow their way into the abdominal cavity of the victim.

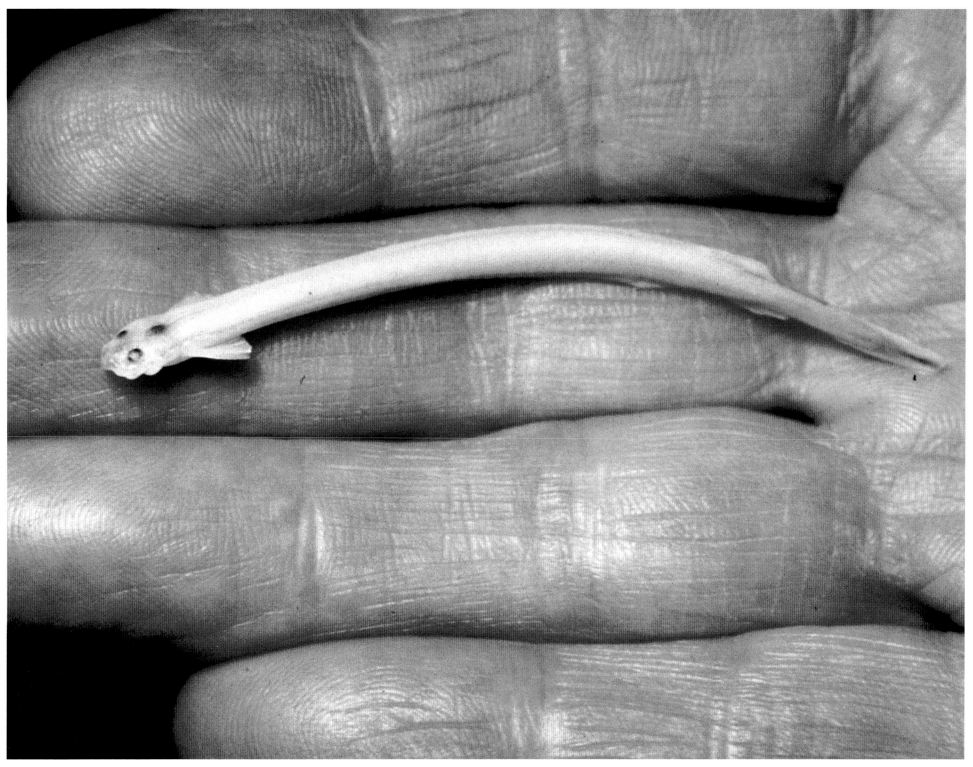

PLATE 519. Parasitic catfish or candirú, *Urinophilus erythrurus* Eigenmann. This urine-loving, blood-sucking catfish may be small in size, but is capable of creating a tremendous amount of genito-urinary havoc. The shape of this little beast permits it to penetrate the urethra, vagina, or any other body opening that is accessible to it. Once the fish reaches its goal, it then proceeds to gouge the victim with its sharp, fang-like teeth and opercular spines. Vampire-like, it then engorges itself with blood. This delightful creature inhabits the tropical lowland streams of tropical South America, and attains a length of up to 20 centimeters (8 inches), but the smaller specimens are the more dangerous ones. Taken at the Steinhart Aquarium, California Academy of Sciences.   (J. Tashijan)

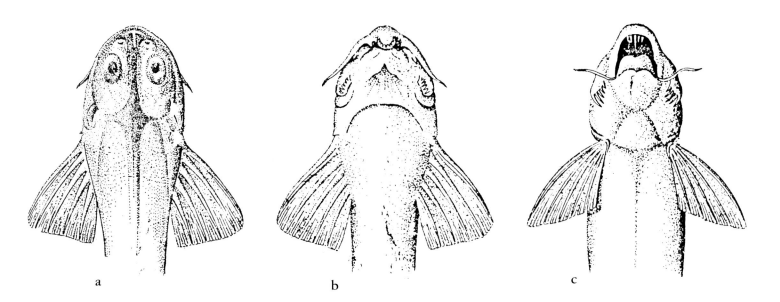

PLATE 520a, b, c, d. Drawing of the Amazonian parasitic candirú catfish.

   a. Dorsal view of the head of *Urinophilus*.

   b. Ventral view of the head, showing opercular spines.

   c. Ventral view of the head of *Vandellia cirrhosa* Cuvier and Valenciennes, a related species of candirú. Note the teeth of the upper jaw and gill covers.

   d. Side view of *U. erythrurus*.

   (R. Kreuzinger, after Gudger)

PLATE 521a, b, c. Devices worn by natives to protect themselves from the parasitic candirú catfish.

   a. Penistulp worn by men of the Baoró tribe, Xingu River, Amazonia, Brazil.

   b. Wuri, or pudendal, covering worn by Bakairi women, upper Xingu River.

   c. Penistulp worn by men of the Kanapó and Tapairape tribes along the Araguana River, Amazonia.

   (R. Kreuzinger, after Gudger)

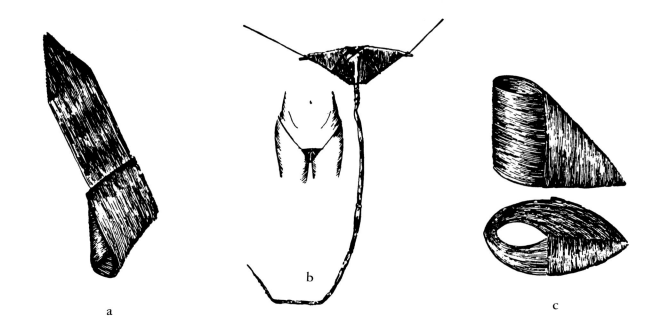

# APPENDIX I

## MAPS

## MAP I: COELENTERATE INTOXICATIONS

Map showing world distribution of reported outbreaks of coelenterate intoxications.     (L. Barlow)

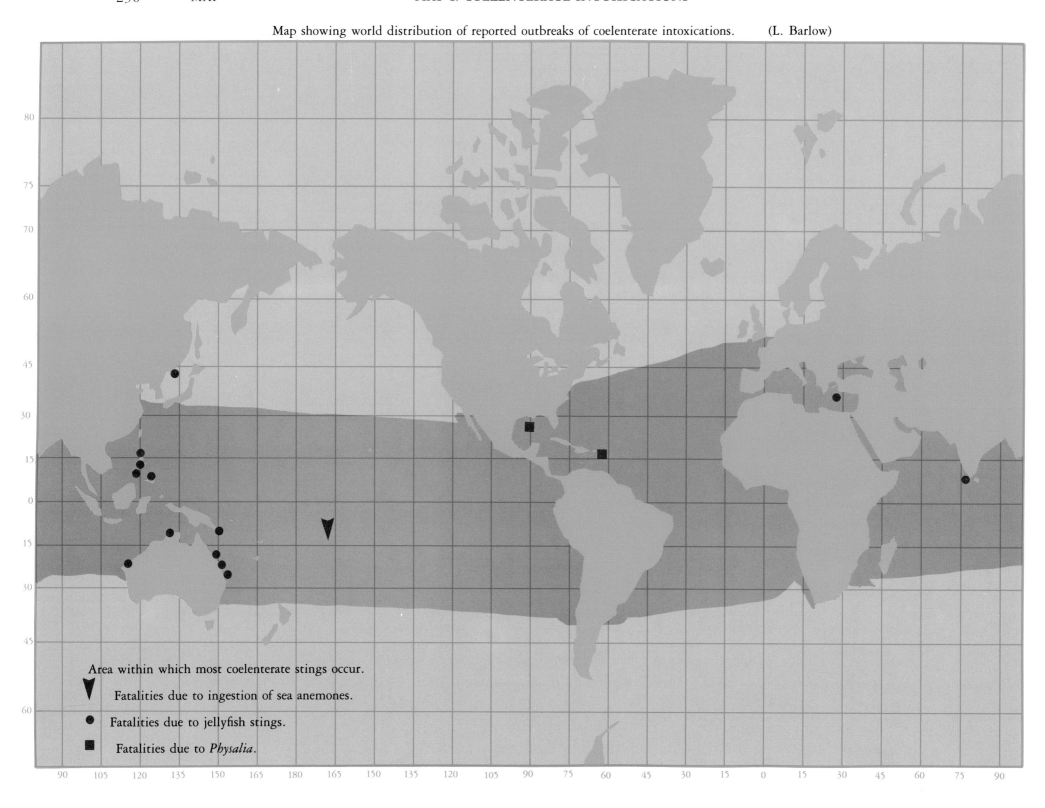

Area within which most coelenterate stings occur.

Fatalities due to ingestion of sea anemones.

Fatalities due to jellyfish stings.

Fatalities due to *Physalia*.

MAP    231

## MAP II: CONE SHELL STINGINGS

Map showing world distribution of reported cone shell stingings.    (L. Barlow)

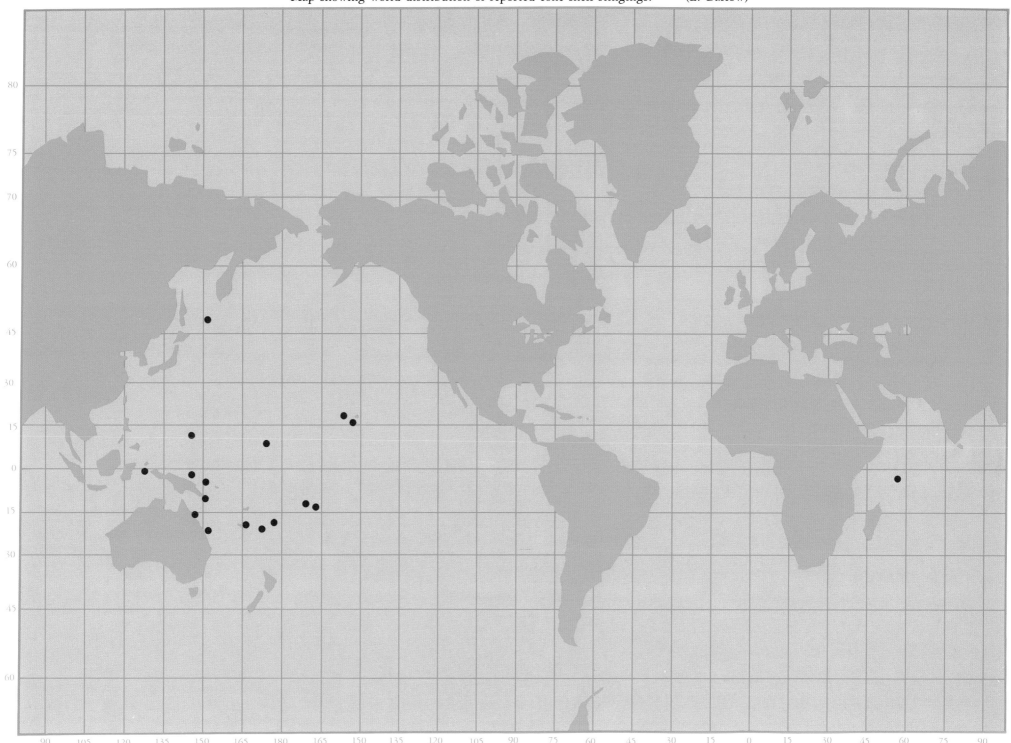

# MAP III: STINGRAYS

Map showing the approximate geographical distribution of stingrays. It will be noted that stingrays are primarily inhabitants of the warmer latitudes.

(L. Barlow)

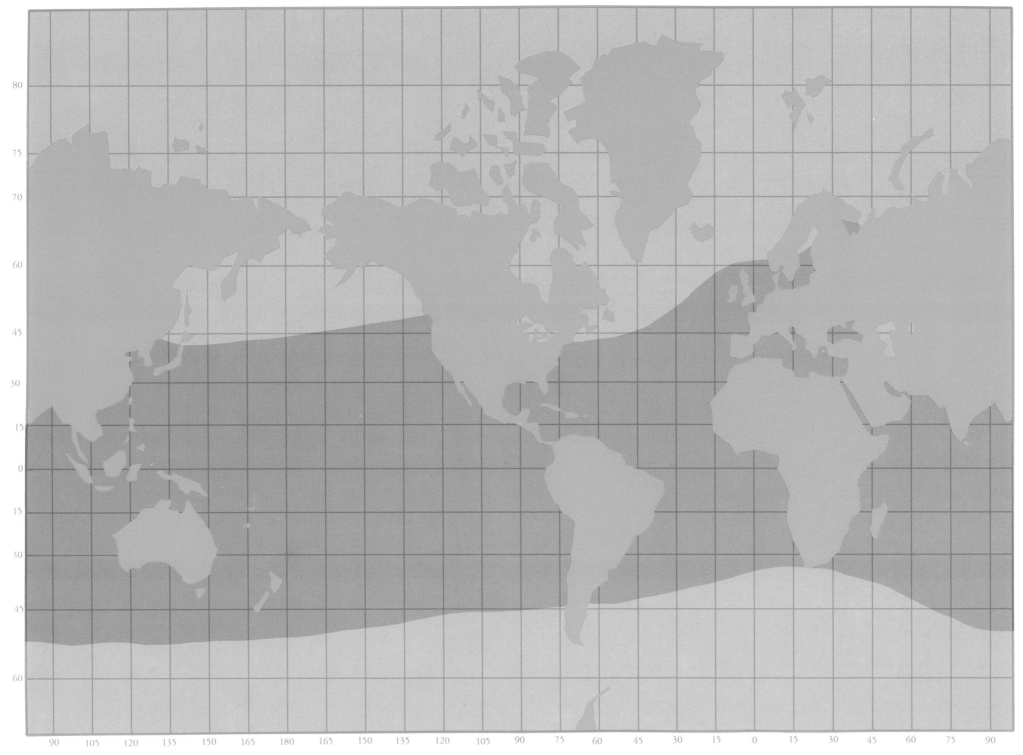

MAP 233

# MAP IV: SCORPIONFISHES

Map showing the geographical distribution of venomous scorpionfishes. The darker area indicates the distribution of the stonefish *Synanceja*.

(L. Barlow)

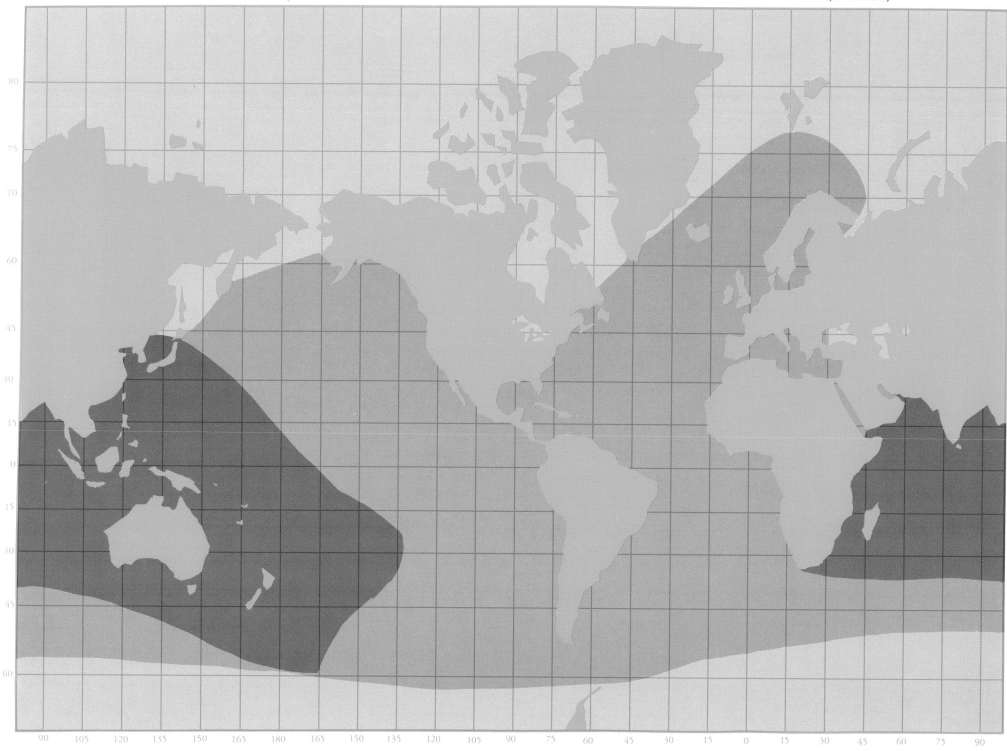

# MAP V: WEEVERFISHES

Map showing the geographical distribution of weeverfishes. *Trachinus draco* also occurs in the Black Sea.          (L. Barlow)

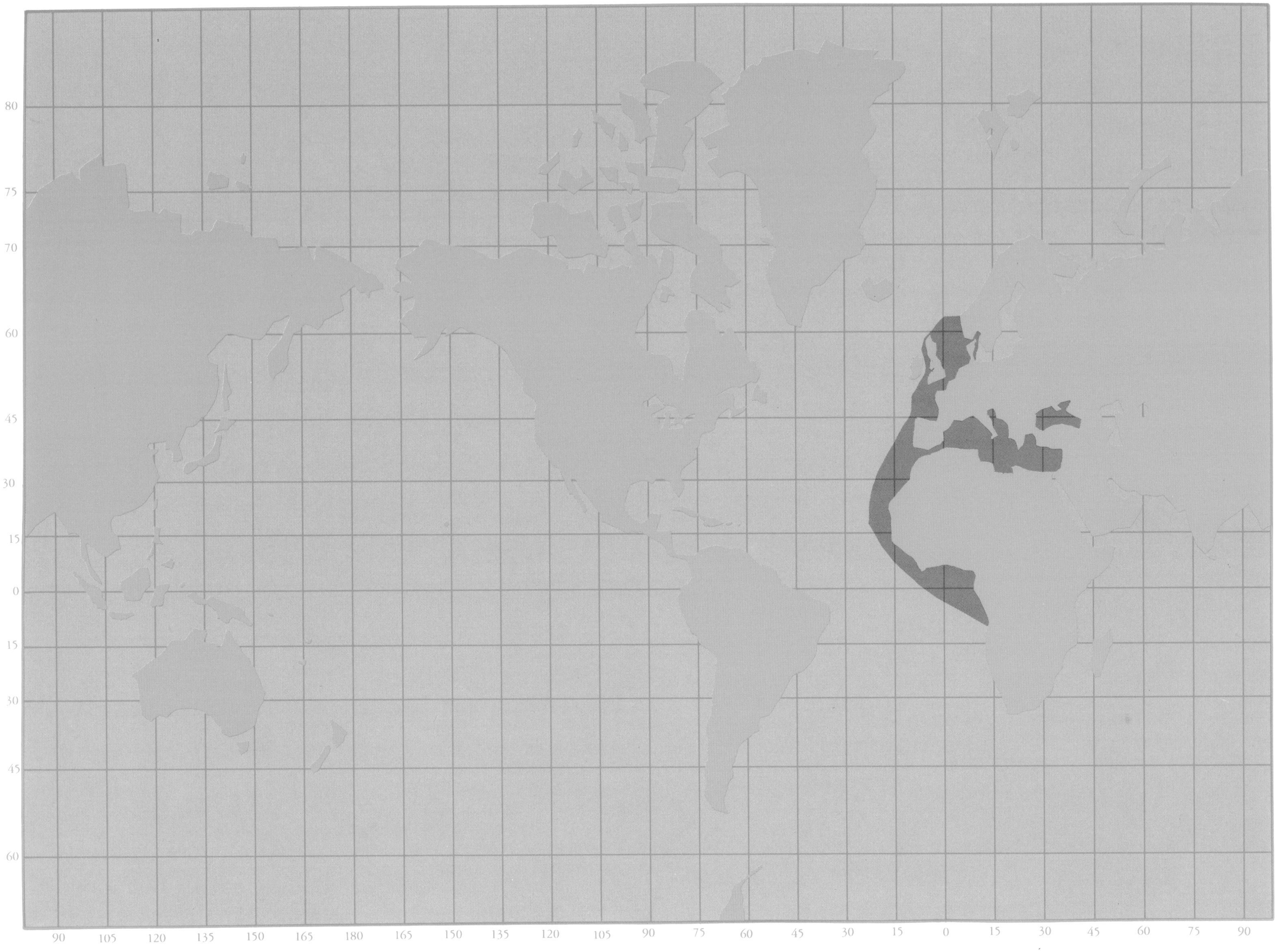

MAP        235

**MAP VI: TOADFISHES**

Map showing the geographical distribution of toadfishes.        (L. Barlow)

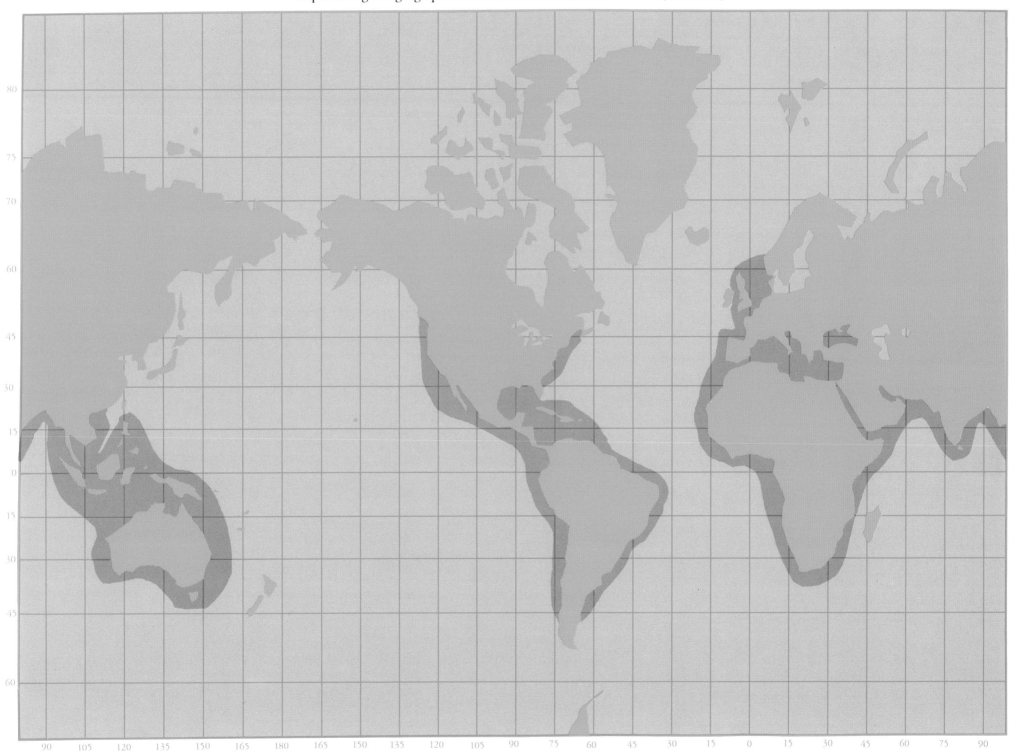

## MAP VII: SEA SNAKE SUBFAMILY *HYDROPHIINAE*

Map showing the geographical distribution of the sea snake subfamily *Hydrophiinae*.                    (L. Barlow)

MAP 237

## MAP VIII: SEA SNAKE SUBFAMILY *LATICAUDINAE* AND SEA SNAKE *PELAMIS PLATURUS*

Map showing the geographical distribution of the sea snake subfamily *Laticaudinae* and sea snake *Pelamis platurus*.     (L. Barlow)

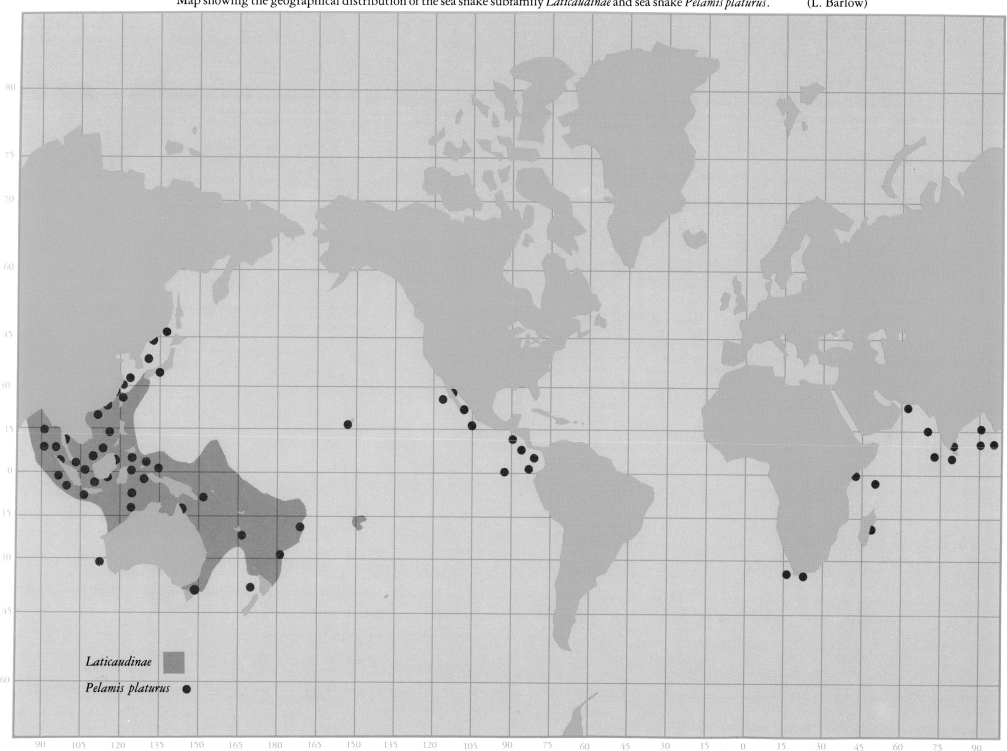

Laticaudinae
Pelamis platurus

## MAP IX: PARALYTIC SHELLFISH OUTBREAKS

Map showing world distribution of paralytic shellfish outbreaks.                    (L. Barlow)

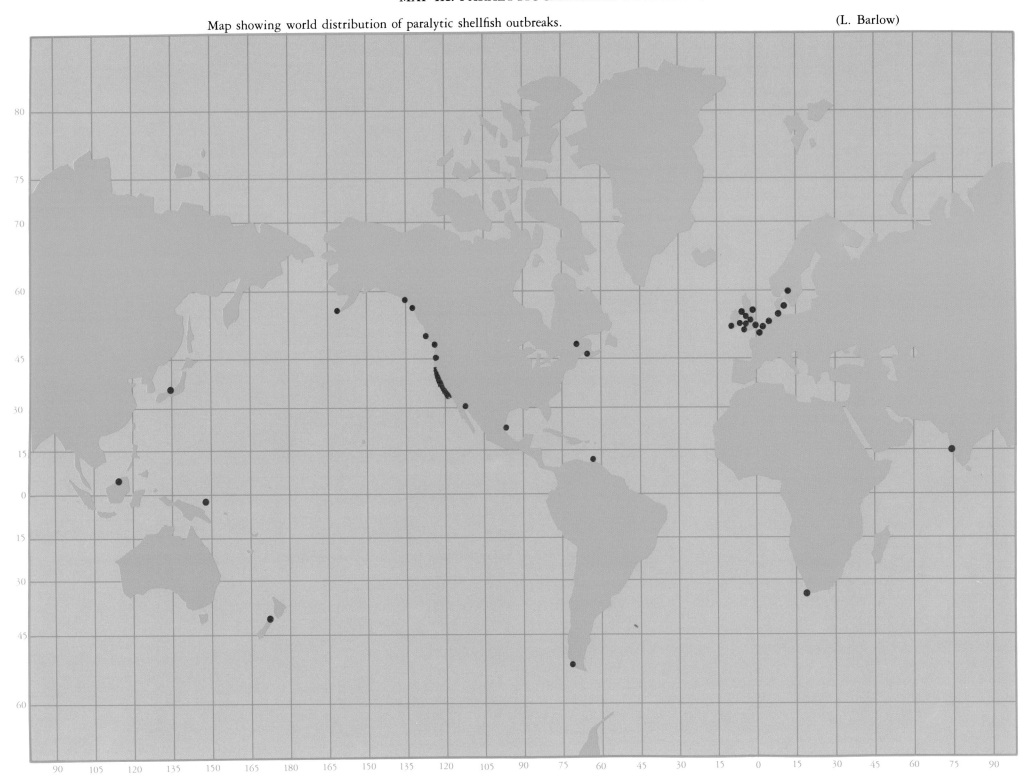

MAP    239

## MAP X: CIGUATOXIC FISHES

Map showing the approximate geographical distribution of ciguatoxic fishes. In general, ciguatoxic fishes are found in greatest abundance in subtropical-tropical insular areas of the West Indies and the Pacific and Indian oceans.        (L. Barlow)

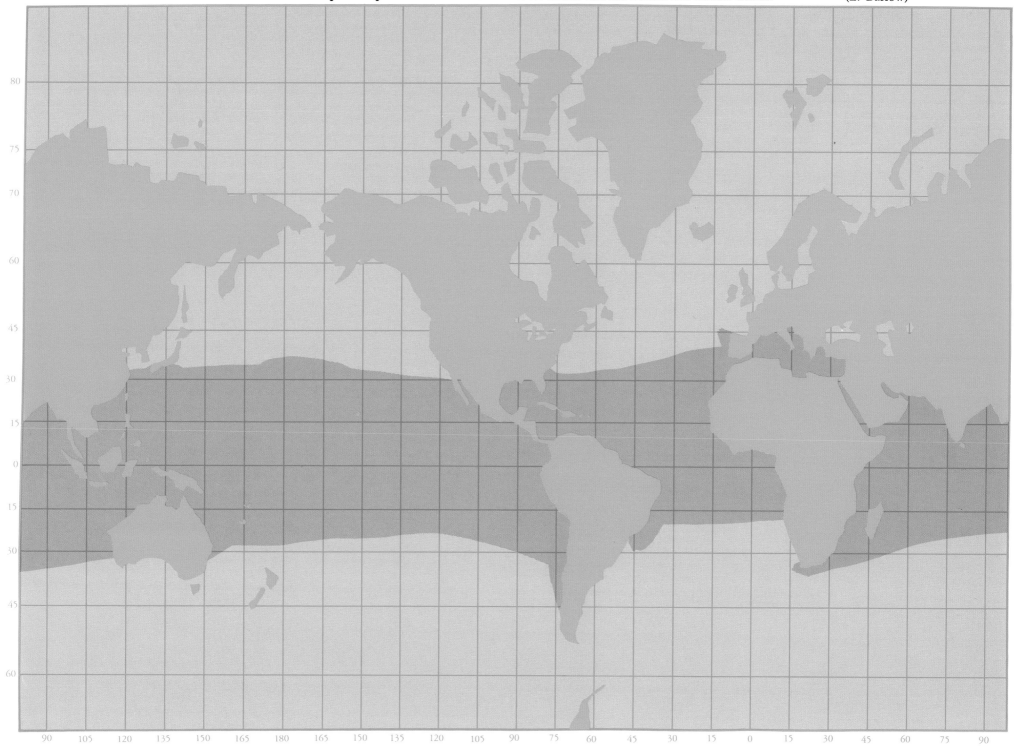

## MAP XI: TETRAODONTIFORM FISHES

Map showing the world distribution of poisonous tetraodontiform fishes.    (L. Barlow)

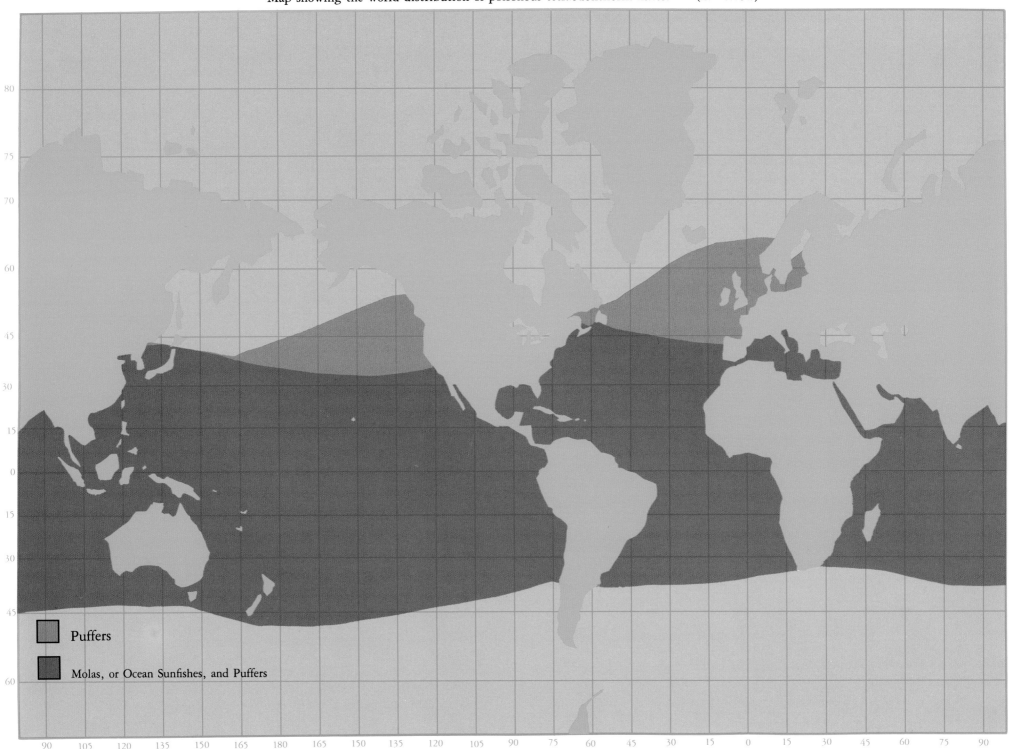

Puffers

Molas, or Ocean Sunfishes, and Puffers

# APPENDIX II

## PREVENTION, FIRST AID, AND EMERGENCY TREATMENT PROCEDURES

(in collaboration with Paul S. Auerbach, M.D.)

## WOUND-PRODUCING AQUATIC ANIMALS (Chapter II)

### SHARK ATTACKS

TREATMENT

Shark bites may consist of a single bite or of several. The wound may have jagged edges, multiple concentric linear cuts, and massive tissue loss, depending upon the nature of the bite and the type of shark. Bleeding may be extensive.

First aid begins with the rescue of the victim from the water. Most shark fatalities are the result of massive tissue loss and hemorrhage or of panic and drowning. It may be necessary to partially control the bleeding by manual compression directly over the wound while the victim is still in the water. The victim should be removed from the water as soon as possible to avoid further attack, control the bleeding, prevent shock, and diminish the effects of hypothermia. All shark bites, large or small, should be taken seriously.

Initial treatment should begin on the beach or in the rescue boat. Place the victim in a head-down position. The patient should be sent to a trauma center as soon as possible.

Contamination of the wound by various bacterial pathogens is a serious matter and must be adequately treated at the trauma center. Major pathogens such as genera *Vibrio, Erysipelothrix, Pseudomonas, Clostridium,* and numerous others must be considered. The physician should irrigate the wound with sterile saline, lactated Ringer's solution, or with nonsterile freshwater if surgical irrigation fluid is not available. If transport to a hospital is delayed for more than 12 hours, the victim should be given oral tetracycline 500 mg every four hours, or ciprofloxacin 500 mg, or trimethoprim-sulfamethoxazole 160/800 mg every 12 hours.

The control of bleeding is essential to avoid hypovolemic shock. All means available should be used to apply compression dressings. For a pressure bandage, use whatever is available: gauze, cotton, clothing, towels, sackcloth, etc. Even if a large blood vessel has been severed, bleeding can usually be controlled with direct pressure, which allows vasospasm and early clot formation. If traumatic amputation has occurred, bleeding may be profuse. If bleeding from a visible major artery or vein threatens the victim with exsanguination, the vessel may be directly ligated or a proximal arterial pressure point may be compressed. Never attempt blindly to clamp vessels, as this is rarely effective and frequently leads to inadvertent and irreparable nerve damage. The decision to ligate a large blood vessel or to apply a tourniquet is essentially one to sacrifice a limb in order to save a life. If a constriction band is used to occlude arterial blood flow, apply direct pressure to the wound simultaneously. Every ten minutes, loosen the tourniquet briefly to see if direct pressure alone will control the bleeding.

If possible, intravenous fluids should be administered to the patient en route to the hospital, particularly if transport will be prolonged or delayed. If volume must be replaced in large quantities, at least two large-bore intravenous lines should be inserted in the uninvolved extremities. Administer lactated Ringer's solution, normal saline, plasmalyte, hetastarch, hypertonic saline-dextran, or group O Rh-negative blood until type-specific or fully cross-matched blood products are available. Administer oxygen by face-mask at 5–10 liters per minute. If necessary, a three compartment MAST suit should be applied, provided there will be no excessive hemorrhage from areas not covered by the suit.

Keep the patient warm, but do not smother him in hot blankets on a hot beach under a broiling sun. Do not give the victim liquids by mouth if he has altered mental status or if it is likely that he will soon go to the operating room.

If the patient is cardiovascularly stable, naloxone-reversible narcotics may be administered in increments for pain relief. Reassure the victim frequently.

PREVENTION

There is no completely effective means of preventing shark attack other than staying out of the water. However, there are a few basic principles that if followed could be helpful. Sharks are unpredictable; therefore, when swimming in hazardous areas, precautionary measures should *always* be taken. Sharks are generally present in warm temperate and tropical seas, even though they may not be visible to the diver. If dangerous sharks are known to be in an area, stay out of the water, particularly if the water is murky.

Sharks are attracted by blood and low frequency vibrations, and they are *keenly* sensitive to distress signals such as flopping about, slapping the water, and erratic movements.

Don't turn your back on a shark if you are confronted by one. Moving in the direction of the shark rather than fleeing is frequently effective in warding off a curious shark. But this technique may not be effective if the shark means business.

Do not provoke an attack by spearing, poking, grabbing, riding, or hanging on to the tail of a shark. The skin of the shark is rough, covered with denticles similar to coarse sandpaper, and may inflict severe skin abrasions.

Treat all sharks with respect. Even small sharks can inflict serious bites. It is the teeth of the shark that count, not necessarily the shark's size.

Food and blood attract sharks. Avoid swimming in the vicinity of established garbage dumps. Sharks become very excited when blood is in the water. Do not enter or remain in the water with a bleeding wound. Women should not swim in shark-infested waters during their menstrual periods if bleeding is heavy and cannot be contained.

Refrain from swimming far from shore in deep water, deep channels, or in drop-offs likely to be inhabited by sharks. When spear fishing, do not tie the fish to your body. Dead fish should be tossed into a boat or anchored some distance from where you are diving.

Wear dark, protective clothing or swimwear. Bright, shiny objects and highly contrasting clothing tend to attract sharks (and barracuda).

Sharks will frequently circle their intended victim several times before coming in for the strike. Watch for agonistic behavior: dropping of the pectoral fins, arching of the back, and erratic movements of the body and tail. These are danger signals and mean that the shark is highly agitated and about to strike. This behavior has been commonly observed in the gray reef shark. If sharks appear to be in an agitated state, get out of the water as rapidly as possible. Use a rhythmic beat with the feet, moving steadily toward the boat or shore, keeping the shark in view. This is the time not to panic. If wearing a scuba outfit, remain submerged until reaching the boat. You are more vulnerable at the surface. If you are using scuba and unable to get out of the water immediately, it is best to move to a more protected area, with a coral reef or rock or some other immoveable object to your back, and face the aggressor.

In the event of an air or sea disaster, do not abandon your clothing when entering the water. Clothing will not only afford some protection from abrasions, but may help to preserve body heat. Try to remain as quiet as possible in order to conserve energy. Attempt to use a lifeboat or a raft when possible. Do not trail arms or legs over the side of a raft. Do not fish from a raft when sharks are nearby.

## GIANT MANTA RAY ABRASIONS

TREATMENT

Manta rays do not inflict bites. The skin of manta rays is covered by coarse dermal denticles, which can inflict a severe skin abrasion if one brushes up against them. Skin abrasions should be scrubbed thoroughly with soap and water and then irrigated vigorously with a forceful stream of freshwater or normal saline in order to remove any foreign material that might be contaminating the wound. The wound may be covered with a nonadherent dressing over an antiseptic ointment. Wounds that appear infected should be cultured and treated properly with a suitable antibiotic.

PREVENTION

Scuba divers have found it to be a challenging experience to grab on to the appendages of a manta in order to catch a ride. This is an interesting activity, but one should be equipped with gloves and protective clothing to avoid skin abrasions. In general, it is best to observe these magnificent animals from a distance and not to frighten them by rough handling.

## BARRACUDA ATTACKS

TREATMENT

Barracuda bites are rare. Barracuda wounds can be differentiated from those from a shark in that shark wounds are parabolic, curved like the shape of their jaws, whereas barracuda wounds consist of two nearly parallel rows of teeth marks. Barracuda bites should be treated in the same manner as shark bites.

Barracuda are attracted by brightly colored and shiny objects. They are always curious and at times can become very aggressive. Precautions should be taken not to attract barracuda or to arouse them unduly. They will strike a speared fish, so handle speared fish with care when in the presence of barracuda. When swimming in the company of the great barracuda, treat it with respect and caution—*it* may be the rare one that bites.

## MORAY EEL BITES

TREATMENT

Moray eels are notoriously powerful and vicious biters; however, they are usually not aggressive unless provoked. When wounded or speared, they become extremely aggressive and are capable of inflicting a severe laceration. They have narrow muscular jaws that are equipped with strong, knife-like teeth that can come down with great force. They may retain a bulldog-like grip until death. Moray eel bites should be treated in the same manner as are shark bites. The palatine mucosa of some morays is believed to produce a toxic substance. The nature of the poison is not known.

PREVENTION

Most eel bites are provoked by poking one's hand into a hole or crevice or under a rock occupied by a moray eel. Don't poke your hand into a hole without first examining it visually.

## BLUEFISH BITES

TREATMENT

The bluefish is equipped with sharp, conical canine teeth and is a vicious biter. The wounds are multiple in type and are similar to those inflicted by piranha. Although the wounds are smaller, the basic therapeutic principles apply as in treating shark bites. No lethalities have been reported, and bluefish bites are uncommon.

PREVENTION

Bluefish travel in large schools and are voracious feeders. Occasional contacts with bluefish have occurred in the surf or shallow waters. If bluefish are present in the water in large numbers, it is advisable to either get out of the water or be very cautious. Little seems to be known concerning their aggression to man.

## NEEDLEFISH ATTACKS

TREATMENT

Wounds from needlefish are usually of the puncture type. Fatalities have occurred from puncture wounds to the chest or brain. The same general principles in treating shark wounds apply to needlefish wounds.

PREVENTION

Needlefish injuries are most likely to be encountered when night-light fishing. Avoid being in the flight pattern between needlefish and the light. A person should be constantly aware of the danger from needlefish when working from a small boat in tropical waters at night.

## GIANT GROUPER BITES

TREATMENT

Giant groupers tend to be very curious and bold and are voracious feeders. There are records of divers being attacked by them. They usually do not bite, but are considered a potential hazard because of their large size, cavernous jaws, and fearless attitude. However, they do not consti-

tute a hazard in the same sense as do sharks. Wounds produced by groupers are not likely to result in massive tissue loss as in shark attacks because of the difference in their tooth structure, but grouper wounds should be treated in the same manner as shark wounds.

PREVENTION

Groupers are most likely to be encountered in large underwater caves. Be cautious when entering such areas.

## SAWFISH ATTACKS

TREATMENT

Sawfish do not bite, but they can inflict a very painful wound with the large saw-like proboscis that extends from the head. Contact with these fishes is not common and actual attacks are rare because of their bottom-feeding habits. Treat sawfish attacks following the same general principles as in treating shark wounds.

PREVENTION

Keep out of the way of the saw-like protuberance. Sawfish tend to be slow swimmers and cumbersome, but can thrash the saw-like appendage with rapidity.

## MARLIN (BILLFISH ATTACKS

TREATMENT

Attacks from billfish (marlin, swordfish) are rare, but could be lethal under certain circumstances. Small boats have been rammed by swordfish with their bills. Billfish are large, powerful fishes equipped with a formidable weapon. Their wounds are of the puncture variety and should be treated following the same therapeutic rationale as for shark bites.

PREVENTION

Contacts with billfishes generally occur when these magnificent fishes are being brought on board a boat. They must be handled with care.

## PIRAÑA BITES

TREATMENT

Piraña usually attack when blood is in the water, at which time they go into a frenzy and may become vicious biters. Wounds are multiple in nature and in the aggregate may result in considerable tissue loss. Although the bites are small, the same basic principles apply as in treating shark bites.

PREVENTION

Piraña are attracted by blood and low frequency vibrations in the water. Check with the local inhabitants as to the advisability of swimming in areas inhabited by them. Attacks have resulted from trailing one's fingers in the water while riding in a boat—a habit that should be avoided.

## SABRE-TOOTH CHARACIN BITES

TREATMENT

The sabre-tooth characin has long, fang-like teeth and is capable of inflicting painful bites. Little appears to be known concerning the nature of the bites of this fish. Follow the same therapeutic principles as in dealing with shark bites.

PREVENTION

Little is known concerning the habits of this fish. It is believed to be similar in habits to the piraña.

## TRIGGERFISH BITES

TREATMENT

Some of the larger species of triggerfishes are capable of inflicting painful bites. The treatment of triggerfish bites should follow the same general prnciples that apply in the treatment of shark bites.

PREVENTION

Divers should avoid swimming toward large triggerfishes that do not move away when approached.

## CROCODILE, ALLIGATOR, GAVIAL BITES

TREATMENT

Crocodiles and their kin usually kill their victims by drowning them. Their bites are usually serious, extensive in nature, and result in massive tissue loss. Death is usually due to drowning or massive tissue loss. Treatment is therefore seldom possible, because the victim is drowned before rescue is possible. If treatment of the wound is possible, the wound should be treated in the same manner as are shark bites. Crocodile wounds are frequently contaminated and may result in tetanus or gangrene.

PREVENTION

Check with the local inhabitants to ascertain if crocodiles, alligators, or gavials are present. Stay out of the water. Avoid swimming in murky, brackish water inlets, swamps, and river mouths inhabited by these beasts. On land, they are fast on their feet and in water are excellent swimmers. They can inflict a lehtal blow with their tails and are more dangerous than sharks.

## SEAL, SEA LION, WALRUS BITES

TREATMENT

Generally, seals and sea lions are not very aggressive, but during the breeding season, the bulls tend to become very protective and will not hesitate to attack or inflict a wound. Seals have large conical teeth and can inflict a bite similar to a dog bite. Their bites should be treated in the same manner as are shark bites.

PREVENTION

Avoid swimming in the vicinity of sea lion herds during the reproductive season.

## POLAR BEAR ATTACKS

TREATMENT

Polar bears are formidable creatures on the ice or in the water. They are true hunters, cunning and silent, and can move with considerable speed. Polar bears have been reported to hunt down a man and attack small open boats. They have large claws and can rip open a person with one swipe. They are also vicious biters. The basic therapeutic principles in dealing with shark bites also apply here.

PREVENTION

Avoid polar bears. Keep in mind that they can easily outrun you.

## KILLER WHALE BITES

TREATMENT

The crushing power of the jaws of a killer whale is immense. They are equipped with large powerful conical teeth and are capable of inflicting lethal crushing wounds. Wounds should be treated in a manner similar to shark bites.

PREVENTION

Killer whales should be treated with considerable respect in the wild, despite their playful antics in captivity. Most experts are convinced that killer whales do not hunt humans for food, but there is always the possibility of mistaken identity. Be cautious.

## GIANT TRIDACNA CLAMS

TREATMENT

Divers have reportedly become trapped in the open jaws (valves) of these giant clams and have drowned. The clams do not bite.

PREVENTION

Care should be taken when handling the open valves of these clams.

## GIANT SQUID

TREATMENT

Bites from giant squid and contact with their cutting suckers are rare in humans. Their bites should be handled following the same therapeutic principles as for shark bites.

PREVENTION

Contact with giant squid in the water is only likely to occur in deep water at night, where they are generally found, but they may come to the surface during the day to feed. Usually, they are encountered by humans only during nightlight fishing. Keep clear of their biting jaws.

# STINGING AQUATIC INVERTEBRATES (Chapter III)

## SPONGE DERMATITIS

TREATMENT

It is usually difficult to separate a reaction due to spicule irritant dermatitis from an early hypersensitivity reaction. The skin should be gently dried and a layer of adhesive tape applied to attempt to peel away any superficial spicules. An alternative method is to apply a commercial facial gel, which may be used as a "peel." Five percent acetic acid (vinegar) soaks should be applied for 15 to 30 minutes, 3 to 4 times daily. If acetic acid is not available, isopropyl alcohol (40 to 70 percent) may be substituted. The remainder of treatment is generally much the same as for severe poison ivy dermatitis. Although corticosteroid lotions may help to relieve the secondary inflammation, they appear to be of little value in the initial decontamination. Following the initial decontamination, a mild emollient cream or steroid preparation may be applied to the skin. If the allergic component is severe, particularly if there is weeping, crusting, and blister formation, systemic corticosteroids should be used. Severe itching may be controlled with an antihistamine.

PREVENTION

Avoid touching sponges with your bare hands. Divers working in tropical waters should be completely clothed with protective lightweight diving suits of some type, nylon or a light-weight neoprene suit, in order to avoid contact with stinging sponges. Most sponges are harmless, but some of them are capable of producing a painful dermatitis.

## CNIDARIAN (COELENTERATE) STINGS: Hydroids, Jellyfishes, Sea Anemones, Corals

TREATMENT

The first aid and definitive treatment of cnidarian stings have been topics of speculative and conflicting opinions and involve a wide range of detoxicants, some of which are ineffective and may even enhance envenomation. Recent clinical investigations in the United States and Australia, whose waters are inhabited by some of the world's most dangerous stingers, have provided some valuable therapeutic guidelines.

The primary objectives of first-aid measures directed at emergency detoxification for coelenterate stings are to minimize the number of nematocysts being discharged into the skin and to reduce the immediate harmful effects that follow envenomations. The severity of the sting is dependent upon the nature of the venom, the number of nematocysts, and the size and underlying health of the victim. In the case of *Physalia* species and scyphozoan jellyfishes, there may be a prolonged encounter with tentacles carrying a vast number of nematocysts. Initial contact with the tentacles may result in only a modest envenomation. However, subsequent efforts to disengage the tentacles may result in further discharge of larger numbers of nematocysts, which often worsens the envenomation. Thus, removal of the adhering tentacles must be done carefully in order to minimize the opportunity for further envenomation. *Physalia* stings can be fatal.

If a person is stung by a venomous species, the following steps should be taken:

1. If vinegar is not immediately available, immediately rinse the wound with seawater, *not* with freshwater. (Freshwater will stimulate any nematocysts that have not already discharged.) Do not attempt to remove the tentacles with abrasive techniques. If it is absolutely necessary to remove the adhering tentacles, this should be done with care, using a sharp-edged blade, shell, or stick. Avoid rubbing the skin with a towel, rag, seaweed, or a handful of sand. The palm of a rescuer's hand is usually protected from a sting, but if at all possible, a rescuer should wear hand protection. Remove the larger tentacles with forceps if possible.

2. To prevent nematocyst discharge and to detoxify the venom, it is recommended that the adherent tentacles and the stung areas be immediately treated with a substance that will prevent further nematocyst discharge. Apply a soak of acetic acid 5 percent (vinegar) or isopropyl alcohol 40 to 70 percent to the skin. There is some *in vitro* evidence that alcohol may stimulate the discharge of nematocysts. The clinical significance of these findings is as yet unclear, as most clinical experience supports the effectiveness of alcohol. Methylated spirits, such as perfume and after-shave lotion, and high proof liquor (ethanol), should never be used; in some cases, they only prolong the agony. The detoxicant should be applied continuously for at least 30 minutes or until there is marked pain relief. Other substances reputed to be effective as alternatives include dilute ammonium hydroxide, urine, sodium bicarbonate, and papain (papaya

latex or unseasoned meat tenderizer). A proprietary product known as Stingose® (an aqueous solution of aluminum sulfate 20 percent and surfactant 1.1 percent) is a less effficacious alternative. Formalin is too toxic for routine use. The pressure-immobilization technique for venom sequestration should not be used until *after* detoxication. Application of a cold pack may be useful, so long as there is no surface condensation (freshwater). A proximal venous-lymphatic constriction band should only be considered if a topical detoxicant is unavailable, the victim suffers from a severe systemic reaction, and transport to definitive care will be delayed.

Once the wound has been rinsed and soaked with acetic acid, the remaining nematocysts must be removed. The easiest way to accomplish this is to apply shaving cream or a paste of baking soda, flour, or talc and to shave the area with a razor or similar sharp-edged object. If sophisticated facilities are not available, the nematocysts may be removed by making a sand or mud paste with seawater and using this to help scrape the victim's skin with a sharp-edged shell or a piece of wood. The rescuer must take care not to become envenomed in the process; bare hands should be frequently rinsed.

The foregoing first-aid measures do not interfere with any subsequent therapeutic measures likely to be employed. Further treatment should be directed toward three objectives: (1) neutralizing the effects of the poison; (2) relieving pain; and (3) controlling systemic effects. Most coelenterate stings are relatively mild and require minimal care. Brief application to the skin injury of meat tenderizer (papain), local anesthetic creams, ointments, lotions or aerosols, and antihistamines have been used with varying degrees of success. Rare paradoxical reactions have been noted with benzocaine, which in some instances is a skin sensitizer.

The patient should be taken to a hospital

or physician's office for further systemic care. An antivenin is available from the Commonwealth Serum Laboratories, Melbourne (Australia), for use in the event of a severe sting from *Chironex fleckeri*, which can be fatal.

PREVENTION

Most coelenterate stings are encountered because of a person's failure to protect one's self when swimming or diving in areas in which dangerous coelenterate species are present. Divers should be fully covered by protective clothing, including gloves. The tentacles of some species of jellyfishes may trail as much as 15.5 meters (50 feet) or more behind the body of the animal. Dead jellyfish washed up on a beach may still be capable of inflicting severe envenomations with their tentacles. The tentacles of a jellyfish may adhere to the skin of the victim even though they are detached from the animal. These tentacles must be removed as rapidly as possible or envenomation will continue, as discussed in the treatment section. Upon being stung, the victim should get out of the water as soon as possible.

## CORAL CUTS

TREATMENT

Stony corals have calcareous outer skeletons with razor-sharp edges that are capable of inflicting nasty wounds. The severity of coral cuts is due to a combination of factors: mechanical laceration of the skin by the razor-sharp exoskeleton of the coral; envenomation by the nematocysts when inflicted by living coral; introduction of foreign material into the wound; secondary bacterial infection; and tropical climatic conditions of high temperatures and humidity.

All fresh coral cuts and abrasions should be scrubbed thoroughly with soap and water and then irrigated vigorously with a forceful stream of freshwater or normal saline in order to remove all foreign material. If stinging is a major symptom, there may be an element of envenomation from nematocysts. A *brief* rinse with acetic acid 5 percent (vinegar) or isopropyl alcohol 40 to 70 percent usually diminishes the discomfort. It may be useful to use hydrogen peroxide one half strength to bubble out small particles of "coral dust."

Once irrigated, the wound may be managed in several ways. In no case should a coral cut be sutured tightly closed, as infection will surely follow. A preferred technique is to apply sterile wet-to-dry dressings utilizing normal saline or dilute antiseptics. Dressings are changed daily. The addition of nontoxic topical water-soluble powdered antibiotics is of no proven benefit. An alternative therapy is to cover the wound with a nonadherent dressing over an antiseptic ointment. Despite the best efforts at primary irrigation and decontamination, the wound may heal slowly, with moderate to severe soft tissue inflammation and ulcer formation. All devitalized tissue should be debrided regularly utilizing sharp dissection. This should be continued until a bed of healthy granulation tissue is seen to form. Wounds that appear infected should be cultured and treated with antibiotics as previously discussed in the section on shark attacks.

## MOLLUSKS

### Cone Shell Stings

TREATMENT

Cone shell stings are potentially lethal and should be taken seriously. There is no antivenin available for cone shell stings. Incision and suction are of little value and should be avoided. A new treatment method that is gaining popularity is the pressure-immobilization technique of venom containment. If practicable by virtue

of the location of the sting, a cloth or gauze pad of approximate dimensions 6–8 centimeters (length and width) x 2–3 centimeters (thickness) should be placed directly over the sting and held firmly in place by a circumferential bandage 15–18 centimeters wide, or one that surrounds nearly the entire arm or leg, applied at lymphatic-venous occlusive pressure. The arterial circulation should not be occluded, as determined by the detection of arterial pulsations and proper capillary refill. The bandage should be released after the victim has been brought to proper medical attention and the rescuer is prepared to provide systemic support. The patient should rest as much as possible and be moved to a hospital as soon as convenient, with the involved extremity kept in a dependent (lower) position. Respiratory distress may develop, requiring advanced life support with artificial ventilation until the patient can be placed on a mechanical ventilator.

PREVENTION

Live cone shells should be handled with extreme care. Avoid coming in contact with the soft parts of the animal. Do not place a live cone in pockets of swimwear, a buoyancy compensator, or a shirt. They have been known to inflict a sting through clothing.

## OCTOPUS

TREATMENT

The Australian blue-ringed octopus, *Octopus (Hapalochlaena) maculosus,* and some related species are capable of inflicting fatal bites. There is no effective antivenin for the bite of the blue-ringed octopus. First aid at the scene might include the pressure-immobilization technique described previously, although this is as yet unproven for management of an octopus bite.

Treatment is based on the symptoms and is supportive. Prompt mechanical respiratory assistance has by far the greatest influence on the outcome. Respiratory demise should be anticipated early, and the rescuer should be prepared to provide artificial ventilation, including endotracheal intubation and the application of a mechanical ventilator. The duration of intense clinical venom effect is 4 to 10 hours, after which time the victim who has not suffered an episode of significant hypoxia will show rapid signs of improvement. Complete recovery may require 2 to 4 days.

PREVENTION

Octopuses should be handled with gloves. The small species are some of the most aggressive biters and are more dangerous than the larger species. If you are not familiar with the specimen, leave it alone, particularly when working in Australian waters.

## ECHINODERMS

### Crown-O-Thorns Starfish Stings

TREATMENT

The outer surface of the venomous starfish *Acanthaster planci* is covered by large, sharp spines that can easily penetrate through gloves or thin-soled shoes. The spines are covered by a thin skin that produces a poison. Contact with these spines can produce a painful envenomation. The spines are calcareous structures that may (rarely) break off into the wound and may be difficult to remove without surgery.

Spines are sometimes embedded and may have to be surgically removed in order to avoid the formation of a granulomatous lesion similar to that from a sea urchin puncture. The wounded area should be immersed in hot water to tolerance (113°F or 45°C) for 30 to 90 minutes or until there is significant pain relief. Take care not to scald a victim. If the spine is embedded, infiltration of the wound with 1 to 2 percent lidocaine without epinephrine may be required for pain control. The puncture wound should be irrigated and explored to remove all foreign material. If there is any question of a foreign body, a soft tissue radiograph will often identify the calcareous fractured spine. The contact dermatitis component is best treated with topical solutions, such as calamine with 0.5 percent menthol, or corticosteroid preparations. Exposure of the wound to the suction pads of a living starfish is said to be helpful in alleviating the pain; we can neither verify nor condemn this remedy.

PREVENTION

Care should be taken when handling this venomous starfish. You should wear heavy gloves. Only the soft undersurface of the animal is safe to contact with bare hands.

## SEA URCHIN STINGS

TREATMENT

Sea urchin wounds may be inflicted by their spines and in some species by their pedicellariae.

*Spines*: Some species have long, hollow, and slender spines that are dangerous to handle. The sharp tips permit ready penetration of the spines into the flesh of the victim, but they are extremely difficult to remove because of their brittleness. The spines usually break off into the wound and may require surgical removal. The spines of some sea urchins are venomous. The aboral spines of *Asthenosoma* are encased within a venom gland.

Further treatment of wounds from sea urchin spines should follow the foregoing recommended treatment for starfish wounds.

Sea urchin spines that penetrate into a joint or directly involve a neurovascular structure should be surgically removed. This should be performed in a properly-equipped operating theatre using an operating microscope. If the spine has entered into an interphalangeal joint, the finger should be splinted—until spine extraction is performed—in order to limit fragmentation and further penetration. The use of organic solvents to attempt to dissolve spines is ineffective and potentially tissue-toxic. External pounding of the skin to achieve fragmentation may prove disastrous. Because sea urchin wounds frequently become infected, antibiotic therapy may be required.

*Pedicellariae*: Pedicellarial envenomations may produce severe reactions because they involve venom more potent than that found in the spines. After the pedicellariae are removed, the wound should be bathed with acetic acid 5 percent (vinegar) or isopropyl alcohol 40 to 70 percent if the hot-water technique is not effective. Bronchospasm and other allergic reactions can usually be controlled with epinephrine and antihistamines. Unfortunately, there are no specific antivenins available for sea urchin stings. Treatment is largely symptomatic. All pedicellariae clinging to the skin must be removed as promptly as possible in order to prevent continued envenomation.

PREVENTION

Sea urchins with long needle-like spines should not be handled. Their spines can readily penetrate through gloves, sneakers, and even fins. Care should be taken when handling any of the tropical species of sea urchins without gloves because of the venomous pedicellariae. Night divers should be cautious about brushing up against sea urchins.

## WORM STINGS:

### Bristle Worms

TREATMENT

Marine polychaete worms such as genera *Hermodice, Chloeia, Eurythöe,* and others possess elongate, pungent, and chitinous bristles or setae that project from the parapodia. Some of these worms can retract or extend their setae to a remarkable degree. Their setae are believed to release a toxic substance that can produce a severe skin reaction and swelling of the affected area. The treatment of bristle worm stings is largely symptomatic. All large, visible bristles should be removed with forceps. The smaller bristles can best be removed by applying adhesive tape to the skin and peeling it off. After this maneuver, acetic acid 5 percent (vinegar), isopropyl alcohol 40 to 70 percent, dilute ammonia, or a paste of unseasoned meat tenderizer (papain) may provide some relief. If the inflammatory reaction becomes severe, the victim may benefit from topical or systemic corticosteroids. Antibiotics may be required to treat a secondary infection.

PREVENTION

Rubber or heavy gloves are necessary when handling bristle worms. The setae of these worms can readily penetrate cotton gloves.

## GLYCERA STINGS

TREATMENT

*Glycera* possess a long, tubular proboscis that can be explosively extended from the body of the worm. The end of the proboscis is equipped with four jaws to which are attached venom glands. Bites from glyceral worms can result in a severe skin reaction with swelling and pain. The use of antihistamines, steroids, and antibiotics may be required. Treatment is largely symptomatic since there is no specific antivenin.

PREVENTION

Glyceral worms should be handled only with gloves.

# STINGING AQUATIC VERTEBRATES (Chapter IV)

## VENOMOUS FISH STINGS

### TREATMENT

The treatment of venomous fish stings follows a similar mode regardless of the fish source of the envenomation.

To maximize success, treatment should be initiated as rapidly as possible. Efforts in treating venomous fish stings are directed toward achieving three objectives: (1) combating effects of the venom; (2) alleviating pain; and (3) preventing secondary infection. Pain follows the trauma produced by the fish spine(s), venom-mediated tissue effects, and the introduction of slime and other irritating foreign substances into the wound. In the case of a stingray-induced puncture, the retrorse barbs of the spines may produce severe lacerations with considerable trauma to the soft tissues, which may extend into muscle compartments, the thorax, and peritoneal cavity. Severe wounds of the extremities should be promptly irrigated with sterile saline or water, if such is available. Clean seawater may be used only as a last resort. Fish stings of the puncture-wound variety, such as those of a catfish or weever, are usually small in size, and rapid removal of the poison is therefore more difficult. It may be necessary to surgically debride the wound edges in order to apply immediate effective irrigation.

There is divided opinion as to the advisability and efficacy of using a ligature in the treatment of fish stings. Arterial-occlusive tourniquets are extremely hazardous and should be used only in instances of a potential life threat, when the rescuer is willing to sacrifice a limb in order to save a life. If used, the constriction bandage should be placed at once between the site of the sting (if it is on an extremity) and the body, as near the wound as possible. The bandage should be venous-lymphatic occlusive only, and should be released every 10 minutes for 1 to 2 minutes in order to maintain adequate circulation.

Most physicians recommend soaking the wound in nonscalding hot water for 30 to 90 minutes, or until pain is relieved. The water should be maintained at as high a temperature (113°F or 45°C) as the patient can tolerate without skin injury, and the treatment should be instituted as soon as possible. If the wound is on the face or body, hot moist compresses or irrigation with heated fluid can be employed. The heat may have an attenuating effect on the heat-labile components of the venom, as is seen with stingray venom *in vitro*. The addition of solvents, potassium permanganate, magnesium sulfate, or epsom salts to the water is of no particular benefit, and may be harmful if the additive is tissue-toxic. Recurrent pain that develops after an interval of 2 to 3 hours may respond to a repeat hot-water treatment.

Treatment at a trauma center is mandatory. Stings from the deadly stonefish, *Synanceja* species, are extremely painful and can be lethal. The Commonwealth Serum Laboratories, Melbourne, Australia, has developed an effective antivenom for stonefish stings.

### PREVENTION

Fish stings are usually encountered as a result of careless handling of the fishes that have been captured or of recklessly placing a hand or foot with disregard for a venomous fish habitat.

*Stingrays:* Probably the most common fish stings are caused by stingrays. Stingrays usually lie almost completely buried in the upper layer of a sandy or muddy bottom. They are therefore a hazard to anyone wading in water inhabited by them. The chief danger is in stepping on one that is buried. Since the body of the stingray is usually pinned down by the weight of the victim, it thereby permits the beast to make a successful strike. Pushing or shuffling one's feet along the bottom eliminates the danger and at the same time chases the stingray from its lair. It is also recommended that a stick be used to probe along the bottom in order to rid the area of hidden rays.

In general, divers should have a healthy regard for the habitat of venomous fishes. Tropical and warm temperate regions have the largest numbers of venomous fishes.

*Scorpionfish:* Zebrafish stings are usually contracted by individuals who are attracted by the slow movements and lacy-appearing fins and who attempt to pick the fish up with their hands. Most scorpionfish stings result when an individual removes the fish from a hook or net and is jabbed by the venomous spines. Stonefish are especially dangerous because of the difficulty of detecting them from their surroundings. Placing one's hands in crevices or in holes inhabited by these fishes should be done with caution. Knowledge of the habits and appearance of these fishes is most important.

*Weeverfish:* Weeverfish stings are most commonly encountered while wading or swimming along sandy coastal areas of the eastern Atlantic Ocean or Mediterranean Sea. Weevers are usually encountered partially buried in the sand or mud. Persons wading in waters where weevers abound should wear adequate footwear. Skin divers should avoid antagonizing these fishes, since they are easily provoked into stinging. A living weever should never be handled under any circumstances. Even when dead, weevers can inflict a nasty wound.

*Toadfish:* To avoid stepping on toadfish, persons wading in waters inhabited by them should take the precaution to shuffle their feet through the mud. Removal of toadfishes from hooks or nets should be done with care.

*Rabbitfish:* In handling rabbitfishes, one should be careful to avoid being jabbed with the dorsal, pelvic, or anal stings.

*Stargazers:* Stargazers should be handled with care in order to avoid being jabbed by the shoulder spines.

## SEA SNAKE BITES

TREATMENT

Sea snakes are among the world's most venomous reptiles. They produce extremely toxic venoms. Fortunately, their fangs are small and easily dislodged from the jaws. Not all sea snake bites result in envenomations, because the teeth frequently fail to penetrate the skin. Sea snake bites are sometimes difficult to detect because they usually do not elicit a localized reaction such as occurs in pit viper bites.

Sea snake envenomation is a medical emergency requiring immediate action. A delay in instituting proper medical treatment can lead to consequences far more tragic than might be incurred with an ordinary traumatic injury. The pressure immobilization technique, previously described for cone shell stings, should be applied immediately. The next step is to determine if envenomation has occurred. With any evidence of envenomation, polyvalent sea snake antivenin (Commonwealth Serum Laboratories, Melbourne, Australia) prepared from the venoms of *Enhydrina schistosa* and *Notechis scutatus* should be used. Monovalent *E. schistosa* antivenin is not yet widely available. Sea snake antivenin is specific and absolutely indicated in cases of envenomation. Supportive measures, while critical in management, are no substitute. The administration of antivenin should begin as soon as possible and is most effective if initiated within 8 hours of the bite. The minimum effective adult dosage is one ampule (1000 units), which neu-

tralizes 10 gm of *E. schistosa* venom. Three thousand to 10,000 units may be required, depending upon the severity of the envenomation. The proper administration of antivenin is described clearly on the antivenin package insert. The antivenin should be administered intravenously if possible, as the intramuscular route is less controlled and may be less effective. There is no reason to inject the antivenin into or near the bite site, and it should *never* be injected into a finger or toe.

If the clinical situation permits following a sea snake envenomation, a skin test should be performed for sensitivity to horse serum. This test should only be done after the determination to administer antivenin has been made and not to determine whether or not antivenin is to be given. The skin test is performed with an intradermal injection of 0.02 ml of a 1:10 dilution of horse serum test material in saline, with 0.02 ml of saline in the opposite extremity as a control. Erythema and pseudopodia are present in 15 to 30 minutes in a positive response. Because antivenin contains many times the protein content of horse serum used for skin testing, the use of antivenin for skin testing may increase the risk for an anaphylactic reaction. If the skin test is positive, the antivenin should be diluted in sterile water or saline to a 1:100 concentration for administration.

If hypersensitivity reactions occur, they can usually be controlled with corticosteroids, epinephrine, and antihistamines. In cases of severe hypersensitivity, an intravenous epinephrine infusion may be necessary. Emergency desensitization with graded doses of antivenin may be performed. The purification of antivenin products is an area of ongoing research that may soon yield antibody fragments of high specificity allergic potential.

Serum sickness is caused by the formation of immunoglobulin G antibodies in response to antigens present in antivenin. Symptoms are

generally present within 8 to 24 days and may be managed with the administration of corticosteroids, tapered over a 2 to 3 week course.

Supportive measures such as blood transfusions, vasoregulatory support with pressor agents, antibiotics, oxygen, and mechanical ventilation may be required. More severe reactions may be anticipated in the very young, elderly, and infirm.

PREVENTION

Although sea snakes are generally considered to be docile and at times reluctant to bite, some species are aggressive and have no biting inhibitions. It should be kept in mind that even the "harmless" snakes are fully equipped with a venom apparatus and potentially lethal poison. Sea snakes may occasionally bite a bather. It is estimated that one sea snake bite occurs per 270,000 man bathing hours in an endemic area such as Penang, Malaysia. The most dangerous areas in which to swim are river mouths. It is probable that accidents are more likely to occur in a river mouth where the sea snakes are more numerous and the water more turbid. The turbidity of the water and resulting poor visibility for the sea snake may contribute to their becoming fearless and less discriminating in their biting habits. When possible, avoid swimming in a river mouth. When wading in an area inhabited by sea snakes, shuffle your feet. This will prevent stepping on them. The majority of sea snake bites have taken place among native fishermen removing fish from their nets. A person should be extremely careful in handling a net haul containing sea snakes. It is advisable first to remove the snakes with the use of a hooked stick or a wire before attempting to handle the fish. Sea snakes are occasionally captured while fishing with a hook and line. Do not attempt to remove the hook from the mouth of the snake. Cut the line and let the snake drop into the water. Do not handle the snake.

# AQUATIC ANIMALS POISONOUS TO EAT: INVERTEBRATES (Chapter V)

## SHELLFISH POISONING

TREATMENT

There are seven clinical types of shellfish poisoning. They are distinctly different and require different treatments. All seven types may be present concurrently.

1) *Gastrointestinal type.* This type is characterized by symptoms of an ordinary gastrointestinal upset: nausea, vomiting, diarrhea, and abdominal pain. This gastrointestinal type is usually caused by bacterial contamination and may require an antibacterial agent such as trimethoprim with sulfamethoxazole. Viruses that infest shellfish do not respond to antibiotic therapy.

2) *Allergic type.* This type is characterized by symptoms of a typical allergic reaction: redness of the skin, swelling, development of hive-like rash, itching, headache, nasal congestion, dryness of the throat, swelling of the tongue, palpitations of the heart, and difficulty in breathing. These symptoms are the result of a sensitivity of the individual to shellfish. The symptoms can be relieved with the use of epinephrine and an antihistamine agent.

3) *Paralytic shellfish poisoning* (PSP). This type of shellfish poisoning is caused by a specific dinoflagellate poison that is present in the shellfish. This is a very dangerous form of poisoning and must be vigorously treated. This form of poisoning is characterized by a tingling or burning sensation of the lips, gums, tongue, and face, which gradually spreads throughout the body. Movement of muscles and breathing may become increasingly difficult. Death may ensue.

Therapy is supportive and based upon symptoms, as there is no specific antidote. If the victim is treated within the first few hours after ingestion, the stomach should be emptied with gastric lavage or emesis induced by syrup of ipecac (30 ml). Lavage with alkaline fluids, such as solution of 2 percent sodium bicarbonate or ordinary baking soda, is said to be of value, since the poison is acid-stable. Following gastric emptying and alkaline irrigation, the victim should be administered activated charcoal (50-100 gm) in a sorbitol-based solution. Magnesium-based cathartics should be avoided.

The greatest danger is respiratory paralysis, which may require advanced life support. Oxygen should be administered and mechanical ventilation introduced where appropriate. Any victim who may have ingested paralytic shellfish poison (PSP) should be rushed to an emergency facility for observation and therapy. The development of antibodies directed against PSP may in the near future allow more specific treatment.

4) *Neurotoxic shellfish poisoning* (NSP), or *Brevitoxic shellfish poisoning* (BSP). Treatment is similar to paralytic shellfish poisoning. There is no specific antidote.

5) *Diarrhetic shellfish poisoning* (DSP). Therapy is supportive; no specific antidote is available.

6) *Amnesic shellfish poisoning* (ASP). Therapy is supportive; no specific antidote is available.

7) *Venerupin shellfish poisoning* (VSP). See the next section.

PREVENTION

The extremely toxic nature of PSP cannot be overemphasized. Most areas where paralytic shellfish poisoning is likely to occur are examined by local public health authorities. When toxic shellfish are discovered, the area is placed under quarantine. One should adhere strictly to local quarantine regulations, since poisonous shellfish cannot be detected by their appearance, smell, or by discoloration of a silver object, or garlic placed in cooking water. It is only by careful scientific laboratory procedures that paralytic shellfish poison can be determined with any degree of certainty.

The digestive organs, or dark meat, gills, and, in some shellfish species, the siphon, contain the greatest concentration of the poison. The musculature or white meat may be harmless; however, it should be thoroughly washed before cooking. The broth, or bouillon, in which the shellfish is boiled is especially dangerous since the poison is water-soluble. The broth should be discarded if there is the slightest doubt. The tidal location from which the shellfish were gathered cannot be used as a criterion for whether the shellfish are safe to eat. If in doubt, throw them out or ask the local fishermen. (The fishermen's replies may be helpful, although not always accurate.)

## VENERUPIN SHELLFISH POISONING

TREATMENT

Treatment is based upon symptoms and is supportive. If the victim demonstrates gastroenteritis, he should be started on a low-protein diet and observed for signs of liver failure. If allergic symptoms are present, an antihistamine should be used.

PREVENTION

Shellfish taken in the Schizuoka and Kanagawa Prefectures, Japan, should not be eaten during the months of January through April. This form of shellfish poisoning is endemic to Japan. Toxic shellfish cannot be detected by their taste or odor, since decomposition is not a factor in the production of the poison. There are no simple tests for toxic venerupin shellfish.

## COELENTERATE POISONING

### TREATMENT

Poisoning from coelenterates are of two types, namely:

1) *Accidental swallowing of jellyfish tentacles.* If a tentacle fragment containing nematocysts is ingested (usually by curious children), an intraoral envenomation may occur. This is extremely painful and may cause rapid swelling of the lips, tongue, and soft tissues of the pharynx and hypopharynx, leading to airway obstruction. The airway should be rapidly assessed for patency, and a dangerous situation recognized by marked swelling, drooling, change in voice, difficult breathing, cyanosis, and agitation. In such case, the rapid placement of an endotracheal tube directly through the vocal cords maintains the airway and allows the victim to breathe through such an unpleasant episode. Under no circumstances should anything be given to the victim for a mouthwash or gargle unless he is alert, breathing freely, and capable of unrestricted, purposeful swallowing.

2) *Ingestion of poisonous sea anemones.* Intoxication from the ingestion of poisonous sea anemones are rare, but occasionally occur in the tropical Pacific, especially Samoa, where sea anemones are eaten by the local natives. Most poisonings occur in children who eat them raw. Cooked sea anemones are sometimes safe to eat. There is no specific antidote. Treatment is symp-

tomatic. It is important to induce vomiting as soon as possible. See also treatment section on paralytic shellfish poisoning.

### PREVENTION

The accidental ingestion of jellyfish tentacles is most likely to occur as a result of swallowing sea water in a region where there has been a recent storm. During stormy weather, jellyfish tentacles may be torn from the animal and are found floating loose in the water. Accidental swallowing of sea water may thereby result in ingestion of tentacles and cause an intraoral envenomation. One should be aware of the danger of swallowing sea water under these conditions.

Ingestion of raw tropical sea anemone species should be avoided.

## ECHINODERMS:

### Sea Cucumber Poisoning

### TREATMENT

Certain species of tropical sea cucumbers are sometimes poisonous to eat. There are no specific antidotes. Treatment is symptomatic. See also treatment section on paralytic shellfish poisoning.

### PREVENTION

Check with the local natives as to the edibility of tropical sea cucumbers.

## SEA URCHIN POISONING

### TREATMENT

Poisonings may occur from the ingestion of sea urchin eggs, especially during the repro-

ductive season of the year. The symptoms are usually those of severe gastritis. Treatment is symptomatic since there is no specific antidote. Follow the basic therapeutic principles as given for paralytic shellfish poisoning.

### PREVENTION

Check with the local inhabitants as to the edibility of sea urchin eggs.

## ARTHROPODS:

### Asiatic Horseshoe Crab Poisoning

### TREATMENT

The symptoms resemble those of paralytic shellfish poisoning. Death may ensue. Follow the same basic procedures as in paralytic shellfish poisoning therapy.

### PREVENTION

Asiatic horseshoe crabs should not be eaten, especially during the reproductive season.

## TROPICAL REEF CRAB POISONING

### TREATMENT

Violent poisonings and fatalities have been reported from the ingestion of tropical reef crabs. Tetrodotoxin is present in some of these crabs. There is no specific antivenin. Follow the same therapeutic procedures as given for puffer poisoning. (*See* pp. 254–55.)

### PREVENTION

Tropical reef crabs should not be eaten. Advice from the local inhabitants is not always reliable.

# AQUATIC ANIMALS POISONOUS TO EAT: VERTEBRATES (Chapter VI)

## FISH POISONINGS

GENERAL TREATMENT

There are several different types of fish poisonings. They are cyclostome, elasmobranch, chimaera, ciguatera, clupeoid, scombroid, hallucinogenic, tetrodotoxic, and ichthyootoxic fish poisoning. There are some general principles of treatment that are recommended for all types of fish poisonings.

With the exception of scombroid poisoning, in which the patient should be administered antihistamine drugs, there are currently few specific pharmaceutical antidotes for fish poisoning. However, a few general procedures have frequently been of value. If nausea and vomiting are not prominent features of the intoxication and the victim is suspected to have ingested a significant quantity of a dangerous toxin, the stomach should be emptied at the earliest possible moment. Gastric lavage using 2 to 3 liters of fluid in 200–300 ml aliquots through a large-bore orogastric hose is probably more efficacious than emesis induced by the ingestion of syrup of ipecac (30 ml in adults; 15 ml in children). Following gastric emptying, activated charcoal 50–100 gm in a sorbitol-based solution (cathartic) should be placed in the stomach to bind residual toxin.

The pulmonary aspiration of gastric contents is an ever-present danger. At all times, the airway should be protected to the degree dictated by the patient's respiratory status and level of consciousness. Endotracheal intubation may be necessary. Supplemental oxygen should be administered at the earliest sign of respiratory insufficiency.

Hypotension generally responds well to the judicious administration of intravenous crystalloid, such as lactated Ringer's solution.

Whenever possible, a portion of the suspected poisonous fish should be retained for analysis.

## CYCLOSTOME POISONING

TREATMENT

Symptomatic and supportive. There are no specific antidotes.

PREVENTION

Cyclostomes should not be eaten.

## ELASMOBRANCH POISONING

TREATMENT

Symptomatic and supportive. No specific antidote is available.

PREVENTION

Shark livers should not be eaten. Caution should be used in eating shark flesh of tropical species. Check with the local inhabitants.

## CHIMAERA POISONING

TREATMENT

Symptomatic and supportive. No known antidote.

PREVENTION

Do not eat chimaeras.

## CIGUATERA FISH POISONING

TREATMENT

This is one of the most common forms of fish poisoning in tropical insular areas of the world. Treatment is supportive and based upon symptoms. Gastric lavage or emesis induced with syrup of ipecac, followed by ingestion of activated charcoal in sorbitol, may be of benefit if performed within the first three hours after ingestion. Magnesium-based cathartics should be avoided. The most severe systemic effect is hypotension, which may require the administration of intravenous crystalloid for volume replacement. Some clinicians recommend the administration of calcium gluconate (1–3 gm IV over 24 hours) for the management of hypotension, although clinical hypocalcemia has not been observed. There have been clinical reports of the efficacy of a manitol infusion (0.25–1.0 gm/kg IV) to treat victims with severe cardiovascular or neurological syndromes. Bradyarrhythmias usually respond to atropine (0.5 mg IV up to 2.0 mg). Generalized itching may respond to cool showers or the administration of hydroxyzine (25 mg po q 6–8 hours). Amitriptyline (25 mg po bid) has been recommended to treat pruritis and dysesthesias.

A chronic or persistent syndrome of ciguatera poisoning, marked by paresthesia and other neurological signs of greater than 7 days' duration, may be due to the presence of prostaglandin precursors or an immune sensitization phenomenon. In such cases, beneficial drugs include acetaminophen for headache, indomethacin for arthralgias-myalgias-pruritus-temperature sensation reversal, and cyproheptadine (experimental) for pruritus. Antihistamines and corticosteroids are of little benefit. During recovery from ciguatera poisoning, the victim should avoid fish, nut products, and alcohol.

PREVENTION

One cannot detect a poisonous fish by its appearance. The University of Hawaii has developed a stick enzyme immunoassay method for the rapid detection of ciguatoxin and related poisons directly from fish tissues. This procedure simplifies the detection of ciguatoxic fish. However, at present, the most common native method is to feed a sample of the flesh of a suspect fish to a cat or a dog and observe it for a period of several hours for symptoms. The viscera, liver, and intestines of tropical marine fishes should *never* be eaten. Also, the roe of most marine fishes is potentially dangerous and in some cases may produce rapid deaths. Fishes that are unusually large for their size should be eaten with caution. This is particularly true for barracuda (*Sphyraena*), jacks (*Caranx*), and grouper (*Epinephelus*) during their reproductive seasons. Do not eat moray eels. Even some of the "safe" species may at times be violently poisonous.

If one is living under survival conditions, and questionable fishes must be eaten, it is advisable to cut the fish into thin fillets and to soak them in several changes of water—fresh or salt—for at least 30 minutes. Do not use the rinse water for cooking purposes. This serves to leach out the poison, which is somewhat water soluble. If a questionable species is cooked by boiling, the water should be discarded. It must be emphasized that ordinary cooking procedures do not destroy or significantly weaken the poison. The advice of native people on eating tropical marine fishes is sometimes conflicting and erroneous, particularly if they have not lived within a particular region over a period of time. Nevertheless, one should always check with the local natives as to the edibility of fish products in any tropical island area. Keep in mind that an edible fish in one region may be deadly poisonous in another region. Do not eat scaleless fish, such as moray eels.

## CLUPEOTOXISM

TREATMENT

Follow the same therapeutic principles as given for ciguatera fish poisoning.

PREVENTION

Same as for ciguatera fish poisoning.

## SCOMBROID FISH POISONING

TREATMENT

Treatment is directed against the histaminic effects and symptoms of allergy. In minor intoxications, intravenous diphenhydramine (25–75 mg) usually is sufficient. If there is a respiratory component, the physician should add a nebulizer bronchodilator such as albuterol or a subcutaneous injection of aqueous epinephrine 1:1000 (0.3–0.5 ml). If the combined pseudoallergic reaction and gastroenteritis result in hypotension, it may be necessary to administer intravenous fluids to support the blood pressure until the syndrome begins to abate. In refractory cases, the rescuer might administer intravenous cimetidine (300 mg) or ranitidine (50 mg), particularly if there has been a poor response to diphenhydramine.

PREVENTION

As long as properly preserved, scombroid fishes are not dangerous to eat under most circumstances. Commercially canned fish are without the slightest danger. Scombroids should be either promptly eaten soon after capture or preserved, by canning or freezing, as soon as possible. Fish left in the sun for longer than two hours should be discarded. Examine the fish before eating; if there is any evidence of staleness, such as pallor of the gills or an off-odor, discard the fish.

## HALLUCINOGENIC FISH POISONING

TREATMENT

Same as for ciguatera fish poisoning.

PREVENTION

Same as for ciguatera fish poisoning.

## PUFFER POISONING (TETRODOTOXISM)

TREATMENT

Early treatment seeks to remove the gastric-acid stable toxin, which is partially inactivated by alkaline solutions. If the victim is seen within three hours of ingestion, gastric lavage should be performed with at least one liter of 2 percent sodium bicarbonate. This is followed with activated charcoal in sorbitol solution. If the victim has difficulty swallowing or breathing, or is not alert, intragastric manipulation should be preceded by endotracheal intubation.

Supplemental oxygen and ventilatory assistance should be promptly instituted as respiratory paralysis progresses. The physician should remember that the paralyzed victim may be fully conscious and should offer the victim frequent verbal reassurances.

Hypotension induced by tetrodotoxin may require the intravenous administration of crystalloid fluid augmentation. Bradyarrhythmias generally respond to atropine (0.5mg IV up to

2.0mg). Severe heart block may require the placement of a temporary transvenous pacemaker.

While a minor intoxication may be limited to paresthesias, all victims should be observed for at least eight hours to detect deterioration, particularly respiratory failure. Under no circumstances should anyone with dysphagia be given liquids by mouth.

PREVENTION

All puffers in certain regions are poisonous, and they should not be used for food unless the individual is thoroughly familiar with their preparation as a food; even then, there is considerable risk.

## ICHTHYOOTOXISM

TREATMENT

Same as for ciguatera fish poisoning.

PREVENTION

Check with the local inhabitants.

## TURTLES

TREATMENT

There is no known antidote. Some of the recommendations presented for the treatment of fish poisoning are pertinent here.

PREVENTION

Marine turtles in the tropical Indo-Pacific region should be eaten with caution. If in doubt, a check with local native groups will determine if they are safe to eat in that locality. Turtle liver is especially dangerous to eat.

## WHALES AND DOLPHINS

TREATMENT

There is no known antidote. Treatment is supportive and based on symptoms.

PREVENTION

Check with the local inhabitants as to edibility; otherwise, don't eat.

## FURTHER READING

For further reading on the treatment of marine animal injuries, see Auerbach and Halstead (1989); Edmonds (1976, 1984); Halstead, Auerbach, and Campbell (1990); Mandojana (1987); Miller (1991); and Russell and Egen (1991).

# APPENDIX III

# GLOSSARY

The following is a list of technical terms most commonly encountered in marine biotoxicology. Definitions of many of these terms are not generally available in current dictionaries.

**ABALONE VISCERA POISON**—A form of intoxication resulting from the ingestion of the viscera of certain Japanese abalone of the mollusk family Haliotidae.

**ACTINOCONGESTIN**—A synonym of congestin, a poison obtained from the stinging tentacles of sea anemones. *See also* Congestin.

**ACTINOTOXIN**—The term applies to the crude poison obtained from alchoholic extracts of the tentacles of sea anemones.

**AMNESIC SHELLFISH POISONING (ASP)**—Poisoning caused by eating mussels and clams that have been feeding on the diatom *Nitzschia pungens*. The causative agent is domoic acid. This type of poisoning may be lethal.

**AMPHIPORINE**—The toxic substance obtained from tissue extracts prepared from the nemertean worm *Amphiporus lactifloreus* and other species. Amphiporine is said to resemble acetylcholine and nicotine in its pharmacological properties. Its chemical nature is unknown.

**APLYSIATOXIN**—The poison first derived from the nudibranch mollusk of the genus *Aplysia*, now known to contain two fractions, aplysiatoxin and debromoaplysiatoxin. Both of these toxins are known to be derived from *Lyngbya majuscula*, a blue-green alga upon which *Aplysia* feeds.

**APLYSIN**—The neurotoxin obtained from the digestive gland of the sea hare *Aplysia*.

**APPROXIMATE LETHAL DOSE (ALD)**—The approximate lethal dose required to kill a test animal. This term is generally unacceptable.

**ASARI POISON**—A synonym for venerupin shellfish poison. *See also* Venerupin.

**BATRACHOTOXIN**—A highly toxic steroidal alkaloid present in the skin of certain South American frogs of the genus *Phyllobates*.

**BIOGENESIS**—Refers to the origin of natural-occurring chemical agents in living organisms. *See also* Biosynthesis.

**BIOSYNTHESIS**—The manner in which chemical compounds are synthesized by living organisms. *See also* Biogenesis.

**BIOTOXICOLOGY**—The science of poisons produced by living organisms, their cause, effects, nature, detection, antidotes, and the treatment of intoxications produced by them. *See also* Toxinology.

**BIOTOXINS**—Poisons derived from either plants, animals, or other living organisms.

**BIOTOXICATION**—Intoxications resulting from plant or animal poisons.

**BREVITOXINS**—The term used to designate the poison derived from the dinoflagellate *Gymnodinium (Ptychodiscus) breve*. At least ten types of brevitoxin are known: Brevitoxin A has a molecular formula of $C_{49}H_{70}O_{13}$. Brevitoxin B has a molecular formula of $C_{50}H_{70}O_{14}$. Brevitoxin C has a molecular formula of $C_{49}H_{69}O_{14}$. The chemical identities of some of the brevitoxin types have not been fully elucidated. *See also* Neurotoxic Shellfish Poisoning.

**BREVITOXIN SHELLFISH POISONING**—The preferred term for poisoning caused by ingesting shellfish that have fed on the red-tide dinoflagellate *Gymnodinium breve*. *See also* Neurotoxic Shellfish Poisoning.

**CALLISTIN SHELLFISH POISONING**—A form of shellfish poisoning caused by eating the mollusk *Callistin brevisiphonata* in the vicinity of Mori, Hokkaido, Japan. The intoxication is believed to be due to choline which is present in large quantities in the ovaries of the shellfish.

**CEPHALOTOXINS**—The poisons found in the salivary glands of cephalopods. One of these toxins is believed to be an active protein (also known as Eledoisin). There is evidence that one of the toxins, maculotoxin, found in *Octopus maculosus*, is chemically identical to tetrodotoxin.

**CEREBRATULUS TOXINS**—A complex of three toxic polypeptides derived from the nemertine worm *Cerebratulus lacteus*.

**CHELONITOXIN**—The poison present in the flesh, fat, blood, and viscera of certain species of marine turtles. The poison is believed to be derived from toxic marine algae that are eaten by turtles. The term comes from *Chelonia*, the order of turtles. The chemical and pharmacological properties of the poison are unknown.

**CIGUATERA**—One of the forms of ichthyosarcotoxism caused by eating the flesh or viscera of various species of subtropical and tropical marine shore fishes. The intoxication is characterized by a gastrointestinal upset, paresthesias, reverse temperature sensation, muscular weakness, paralysis, and various other neurological distrubances. The empirical formula of ciguatoxin is $C_{60}H_{86}O_{19}$, and is 100 times more potent than tetrodotoxin.

CIGUATERA—(cont.)

This is among the most potent of marine toxins known. The complete clinical syndrome of ciguatera poisoning is now believed to be caused by a complex of poisons including ciguatoxin, maitotoxin, scaritoxin, and possibly others.

CIGUATERATOXIN—The term used to designate the poison found in ciguatoxic fishes. Ciguateratoxin is a synonym of ciguatoxin. The latter is the preferred term.

CIGUATOXIN—The term used to designate the primary poison present in ciguatoxic fishes. The molecular formula is $C_{60}H_{86}O_{19}$. See also Ciguatera, Maitoxin, Scaritoxin.

CIGUATOXICATION—A clinical designation for ciguatera poisoning.

CLUPEOID FISH POISONING—One of the principal types of ichthyosarcotoxism, which is usually caused by a clupeoid fish (generally one of the tropical herrings). Identity of the poison is unknown. See also Clupeotoxism.

CLUPEOTOXISM—The clinical designation for clupeoid poisoning. The first reference to this form of fish poisoning was in the West Indies in 1770, but the earliest case history is 1808. See also Clupeoid Fish Poisoning.

CNIDAE—A term generally used interchangeably with nematocysts.

CNIDOCIL—The trigger-like hair situated on the outer surface of the cnidoblast, which, when stimulated, discharges the contents of the nematocyst.

CNIDOBLAST—The interstitial cell from which the nematocyst develops.

CNIDOCYST—A synonym of nematocyst.

CNIDOM—The nematocyst pattern or spectrum of a particular coelenterate. The types of nematocysts present in a particular coelenterate are believed to be sufficiently specific and consistent to be of taxonomic significance.

COMPLETE LETHAL DOSE (CLD)—Complete lethal dose required to kill a test animal. This term is generally unacceptable.

CONGESTIN—A term proposed to designate a toxic substance derived from the tentacles of sea anemones. When injected into dogs, congestin causes an intense congestion of the splanchnic vessels.

CONOTOXINS—A term used to designate the venoms found in cone shells, members of the gastropod genus Conus. The term conotoxin was first described in 1978.

CRINOTOXIN—A poison produced by a specialized gland in the skin of a marine organism. Crinotoxic secretions are not associated with a venom apparatus, but are merely released into the water.

CUNEIFORM AREA—The thickened wedge-shaped area on the dorsum of the caudal appendage ventral to the proximal portion of the batoidean sting. The glandular epithelium of the cuneiform area is believed to produce venom.

CYPRININ—The toxic substance obtained from the milt of the carp Cyprinus carpio.

DEBROMOAPLYSIATOXIN—A dermonecrotic poison, which is one of two toxic fractions found in the nudibranch Aplysia, aplysiatoxin, and has also been isolated from the blue-green alga Lyngbya majuscula (syn. Microcoelus lyngbyaceus). The molecular formula is $C_{32}H_{45}Br_3O_{10}$. See also Aplysiatoxin.

DIARRHETIC SHELLFISH POISONING (DSP)—Poisoning caused by ingestion of mussels, scallops, or clams that have been feeding on the dinoflagellates Dinophysis species. The intoxication involves okadaic acid, dinophysistoxins, pectenotoxins, and yessotoxin.

DINOPHYSISTOXIN—One of the poisons produced by the dinoflagellate Dinophysis species, which causes diarrhetic shellfish poisoning. The basic molecular formula is $C_{45}H_{68}O_{12}$. See also Diarrhetic Shellfish Poisoning.

ENVENOM or ENVENOMATE—The act of stinging, or introducing a venom into an organism by means of a venom apparatus. See also Stinging.

ENVENOMATION—The poisonous effects resulting from the introduction of a venom from a venomous organism. See also Venom.

EPTATRETIN—A term proposed to designate a potent cardiostimulant obtained from the branchial heart of the Pacific hagfish Eptatretus stouti. The substance is reported to be a highly unstable aromatic amine. Its chemical structure has not been fully defined, but it is not a catecholamine or some other commonly occurring biochemical.

EQUINATOXIN—The term first proposed for a lethal poison derived from the sea anemone Actinia equina.

ERABUTOXIN—The active toxic principle obtained from the venom of the sea snake Laticauda semifasciata. The term is derived from the Japanese vernacular name of the sea snake, "erabu-umihebi."

EZOWASURE-GAI POISONING—The Japanese term for callistin shellfish poisoning caused by gastropods of the genus Callista. See also Callistin Shellfish Poisoning.

FUGAMIN—A term proposed to designate one of two crystalline substances isolated from puffer poison. The chemical nature of the substance is unknown. The term is now obsolete.

FUGU TOXIN—The Japanese term for puffer poison. See also Tetrodotoxin.

GEOGRAPHUTOXIN—The term used to designate the polypeptide poison present in Conus geographus. Thus far two fractions have been determined, geographutoxin I and II.

GLANDULAR TRIANGLE—A term proposed to designate a cross section of the ventrolateral-glandular gtooves of the stingray's sting, but which was later expanded to include cross sections of the glandular grooves of other fishes regardless of the anatomical position of the groove.

GONYAULAX POISON—The toxic principle produced by certain members of the dinoflagellate genus, *Gonyaulax*, sometimes termed paralytic shellfish poison, mussel poison, clam poison, mytilotoxin, or saxitoxin.

GONYAUTOXINS—There are about 12 derivatives of saxitoxin, the primary poison responsible for paralytic shellfish poisoning. There are about 8 sulfonated derivatives known as Gonyautoxins.

HALITOXIN—The term applied to the crude toxic aqueous extract obtained from the marine sponge *Haliclona viridis*.

HALLUCINOGENIC FISH POISONING—A form of ichthyosarcotoxism caused by eating the head or flesh of certain species of tropical marine shore fishes. Surgeonfish, chub, mullet, damsel, grouper, and goatfish have been incriminated. These fish may produce hallucinations or frightening dreams when eaten. The term "hallucinatory fishes" has been used by some authors, but "hallucinogenic" is preferred. *See also* Ichthyoallyeinotoxin.

HAPLOTOXIN—The term proposed for a potent toxin isolated from the posterior salivary glands of *Octopus (Hapalochlaena) maculosus*, which is said to differ from tetrodotoxin, which may also be present.

HOLOTHURIN—A term used to designate the toxic mixture of steroid glycosides obtained from holothurians or sea cucumbers. In some species, holothurin is found to be most concentrated in the Organs of Cuvier, but may be found in other parts of the organism as well. A, B, and C fractions of holothurin have been isolated.

HOLOTOXIN—A steroidal glycoside obtained from the sea cucumber *Stichopus japonicus*, which exhibits antifungal activity against *Trichophyton, Candida,* etc.

HYPNOTOXIN—A term proposed to designate a toxic substance obtained from the tentacles of the hydrozoan *Physalia*. The drug characteristically produces a central nervous system depression affecting both motor and sensory elements.

ICHTHYISMUS—An obsolete clinical term formerly used to designate fish poisoning. *See* Ichthyootoxism.

ICHTHYOACANTHOTOXIN—The poison secreted by the venom apparatus of fishes. Synonymous with the term "fish venom."

ICHTHYOACANTHOTOXISM—The clinical term proposed to designate an intoxication resulting from injuries produced by the stings, spines, or "teeth" of venomous fishes.

ICHTHYOALLYEINOTOXIN—The generic term to designate the poison produced by hallucinogenic fishes. The poison when ingested by humans generally produces frightening dreams. *See also* Hallucinogenic Fish Poisoning.

ICHTHYOCRINOTOXIN—The term used to designate the poison produced by a glandular secretion of fishes that is not associated with a venom apparatus. Ichthyocrinotoxic glands are generally located in the skin of the fish, and the glandular contents are released directly into the water. The secretions from these glands are toxic and usually lethal to other fishes.

ICHTHYOHEMOTOXIN—The toxic substance present in the blood of certain species of marine fishes.

ICHTHYOHEMOTOXISM—The clinical term used to designate fish poisoning caused by ingesting toxic fish blood.

ICHTHYOOTOXIN—A toxic substance derived from fish roe. This particular term is reserved for those fish poisons that appear to be limited in their anatomical distribution to the roe. This term should not be confused with ichthyosarcotoxin. Ichthyosarcotoxins may also be found in other parts of the fish as well, whereas an ichthyootoxin is limited to the roe.

ICHTHYOOTOXISM—The clinical term used to designate intoxications resulting from the ingestion of the toxic roe of fishes.

ICHTHYOSARCEPHIALTILEPSIS—The clinical term proposed for hallucinogenic (hallucinatory)

fish poisoning. The term for obvious reasons has not been generally adopted.

ICHTHYOSARCOTOXIN—The poison found in the flesh of poisonous fishes. This term does not include those poisons produced by bacterial contamination.

ICHTHYOSARCOTOXISM—A generic clinical term used to designate fish poisoning.

ICHTHYOSISMUS—An obsolete clinical term formerly used to designate fish poisoning.

ICHTHYOTOXICOLOGY—The science that treats poisons derived from fishes, their effects, nature, antidotes, and recognition.

ICHTHYOTOXICUM—A term proposed to designate the toxic substance found in eel serum. The term is now obsolete.

ICTHYOTOXIN—A general term used to designate any type of poison derived from fishes. This term has also been used to designate poisons that are toxic to fishes.

ICHTHYOTOXISM—A general term used to designate any form of intoxication produced by fish.

ICHTHYOVENIN—A toxic substance reputedly produced by a special toxigenic bacteria acting on the flesh of inadequatedly preserved scombroid fishes. Ichthyovenin is now believed to be histamine. The term ichthyovenin is now obsolete.

INTEGUMENTARY SHEATH—The integument that envelops the spine or bony portion of the venomous sting of a fish.

IRUKANDJI STINGS—A type of jellyfish sting. It is a well-defined clinical syndrome caused by the carybdeid jellyfish *Carukia barnesi*. The term "Irukandji" refers to the name of the local aboriginal tribe whose area was roughly the same as that in which the stingings have taken place, namely, the vicinity of Cairns, Queensland, Australia.

IWASHIKUJIRA LIVER POISONING—The Japanese clinical term for sei whale liver poisoning, which is caused by eating the liver of *Balaenoptera borealis*. The nature of the poison is

IWASHIKUJIRA LIVER POISONING—(cont.) unknown, but is believed to be a histamine-like substance.

LATICOTOXIN—The toxic principle obtained from the venom of the sea snake *Laticauda laticaudata*.

LETHAL DOSE$_{50}$ (LD$_{50}$)—The amount of poison required to kill 50 percent of the animals tested.

LIPOSTICHAERIN—The term proposed to replace the term "Dinogunellin" because of the revision of the generic name of the fish from *Dinogunellus* to *Stichaeus*. Lipostichaerin is said to be analogous to "lipovitellin" in hen egg yolk. Lipostichaerin has been fractionated into α-, β-, and γ-lipostichaerins. α-, β-, and γ-stichaerins represent the protein moieties of the corresponding lipostichaerins.

LOPHOTOXIN—A term used for a neuromuscular poison obtained from Pacific sea whips of the genus *Lophogoragia*.

LYNGBYATOXIN A—A toxic indole alkaloid isolated from the marine alga *Lyngbya majuscula* (syn: *Microcoleus lyngbyaceus*), which produces an inflammatory reaction. It has a molecular formula of $C_{27}H_{39}N_3O_2$. This is the third toxin isolated from *L. majuscula*.

MACULOTOXIN—A potent neurotoxin found in the posterior salivary glands of the blue-ringed octopus, *Octopus maculosus*, now considered to be identical with tetrodotoxin. *See* Tetrodotoxin.

MAITOTOXIN—The term used to designate a poison that is sometimes associated with ciguatoxin, first isolated from the Tahitian surgeonfish *Ctenochaetus striatus* from which it derives its name. This is believed to be the most potent toxin known. The mouse lethality has an LD$_{50}$ of 0.13 μ/kg. The molecular formula is $C_{160}H_{225}S_2O_{74}$.

MARINBUFAGIN—A cardiotonic steroid found in the poison from the parotid gland of the toad *Bufo marinus*.

MEDUSO-CONGESTIN—A term proposed to designate a toxic substance derived from the tentacles of the jellyfish *Rhizostoma cuvieri*. Injection of the substance into laboratory animals results in intense visceral congestion. Meduso-congestin is believed to be identical with the substance termed congestin. *See also* Congestin.

MIMI POISONING—A form of intoxication caused by the ingestion of Asiatic horseshoe crabs and their eggs.

MINIMUM LETHAL DOSE (MLD)—The smallest amount of poison required to kill a test animal.

MUREX POISON—The toxic principle found in the hypobranchial gland of the mollusk *Murex*. A synonym of murexine. *See also* Murexine.

MUREXINE—A term proposed to designate the neurotoxic principle derived from the median zone of the hypobranchial gland of *Murex* and other prosobranch mollusks. The substance has been defined chemically as β-imidazolyl-(4)-acrylcholine. The substance is believed to be the same as Dubois' purpurine. *See also* Purpurine.

MYTILOCONGESTIN—A term proposed to designate a toxic substance derived from *Mytilus edulis*. Upon injection, the substance produces congestion and hemorrhage—as does congestin. The chemical nature of the poison has not been defined.

MYTILOTOXIN—A term proposed to designate the neurotoxin derived from toxic mussels of the genus *Mytilus*. It is sometimes used interchangeably with paralytic shellfish poison, mussel poison, clam poison, or saxitoxin complex.

NEMATOCYST—One of the minute stinging capsules of coelenterates.

NEMATOCYTE—A synonym for cnidoblast.

NEMERTELLINE—A combination of two toxic substances, chemically identified as 2, 3′-bipyridal and 3″-D²″; 4″, 3-tetrapyridyl, obtained from the nemertine worm *Amphiporus angulatus*. The substance is primarily toxic to crustaceans.

NEMERTINE—A nerve stimulant extracted from the tissues of nemertean worms *Lineus lacteus* and *L. longissimus*. The chemical and pharmacological properties of nemertine are unknown.

NEOSAXITOXIN—First isolated as a minor toxic constituent from the Alaska butter clam, *Saxidomus giganteus*. It is one of the saxitoxin derivatives. *See also* Saxitoxin.

NEREISTOXIN—A neurotoxic substance first isolated from the Japanese polychaete annelid *Lumbriconereis heteropoda*. The molecular formula is $C_5H_{11}NS_2$.

NEUROTOXIC SHELLFISH POISONING (NSP)—A poison caused by ingesting shellfish that have fed on the red-tide dinoflagellate *Gymnodinium breve*. Also referred to as brevitoxin shellfish poisoning. *See also* Brevitoxin.

OKADAIC ACID—One of the primary poisons found in diarrhetic shellfish poisoning. The molecular formula is $C_{44}H_{66}O_{12}$.

OSTRACIN—The term originally proposed to designate the ichthyocrinotoxin produced by fishes of the genus *Ostracion*, but was later amended to ostracitoxin, which is the preferred designation. *See also* Ostracitoxin.

OSTRACITOXIN—The term proposed to designate the ichthyocrinotoxin produced by fishes of the genus *Ostracion*. The poison is heat-stable, non-dialyzable, hemolytic, and nonprotein in nature.

PAHUTOXIN—A poison isolated from the mucous secretions of fishes of the family Ostraciontidae, the boxfishes. *See also* Ostracitoxin.

PALYTOXIN—A potent poison isolated from the marine zoanthid *Palythoa vestitus* by Paul Scheuer at the University of Hawaii. The molecular formula is $C_{129}H_{221}N_3O_{54}$.

PARALYTIC SHELLFISH POISON (PSP)—The toxic principle found in poisonous mussels, clams, and other shellfish originally derived from toxic dinoflagellates. A term that is sometimes used interchangeably with mussel poison, clam poison, dinoflagellate poison, or saxitoxin. It is believed to have a molecular formula of $C_{10}H_{18}N_7O_8S$. *See also* other terms listed above.

PARATRYGONICA—A term applied to the clinical entity of envenomations from freshwater

PARATRYGONICA—(cont.)
stingrays. It is more generally referred to as the *paratrygonic syndrome.*

PARDAXIN—The term applied to the toxic secretion of the Red Sea Moses sole, *Pardachirus marmoratus.*

PECTENOTOXINS—A generic term that has been used to designate some of the poisons associated with diarrhetic shellfish poisoning (DSP). Named after the toxic shellfish *Patinopectin yessoensis.* The molecular formula is $C_{47}H_{70}O_{15}$. Six types of pectenotoxin are known. *See also* Diarrhetic Shellfish Poisoning, and Yessotoxin.

PELOMETOXIN—The name previously applied to the nonprotein, heat-stable, toxic compound found in scombroid fishes; also termed scombrotoxin or saurine—a histamine-like substance. Pelometoxin is seldom used. The poison is now known to be histamine.

PHYSALAEMIN—A polypeptide obtained from the South American amphibian *Physalaemus fuscumaculatus* having pharmacological properties similar to cephalotoxin.

PLOTOLYSIN—The hemotoxic fraction of the catfish poison plototoxin. *See also* Plototoxin.

PLOTOSPASMIN—The neurotoxic fraction of the catfish poison plototoxin. *See also* Plototoxin.

PLOTOTOXIN—A term proposed to designate the poison derived from the catfish *Plotosus lineatus.* The toxin is said to be comprised of a hemotoxic fraction, plotolysin, and a neurotoxic fraction, plotospasmin.

POISON—Any substance that when ingested, injected, absorbed, or applied to the body in relatively small quantities by its chemical action may cause damage to structure or disturbance of function in a biological system.

PUFFER FISH POISONING (PFP)—Poisoning due to the ingestion of pufferfish belonging to the family Tetraodontidae. The poison is involved in tetrodotoxin.

PURPURINE—A term proposed to designate the neurotoxic principle derived from the median zone of the hypobranchial or purple gland of the gastropods *Murex* and *Purpura.* The substance is believed to be an ester or a mixture of esters of choline, which has been termed "murexine." *See also* Murexine.

SAURINE POISONING—Saurine is now known to be histamine. *See* Scombroid Fish Poisoning (SFP).

SAXITOXINS—A generic term used to designate a family of toxins obtained from poisonous mussels (*Mytilus*), clams (*Saxidomus*), and plankton (*Gonyaulax*). Saxitoxin has been used interchangeably with paralytic shellfish poison or clam poison or gonyaulax poison. It is estimated that there are about 24 toxins in the saxitoxin complex. The basic saxitoxin is said to have a molecular formula of $C_{10}H_{18}N_7O_8S$.

SCARITOXIN—A poison closely related to ciguatoxin. The chemical structure is unknown. Symptoms resemble those of ciguatera fish poisoning. Intoxication results from eating parrotfish of the family Scaridae.

SCOMBROID FISH POISONING (SFP)—A form of ichthyosarcotoxism caused by the improper preservation of scombroid and other dark-meated marine fishes, which results in certain bacteria acting on histidine in the muscle of the fish converting it to histamine, and possibly other toxic substances resulting in an allergic-like reaction. *See also* Scombrotoxin.

SCOMBROTOXIN—The term used to designate the toxic substance associated with scombrotoxism. The poison, formerly designated a saurine, is now believed to be histamine, which has been potentiated by the inhibition of histamine-metabolizing enzymes.

SIGUATERA—An old misspelling of the term ciguatera. Now obsolete.

SPHEROIDINE—A term proposed to designate a toxic fraction from puffer poison. Spheroidine is believed to have the empirical formula $C_{12}H_{17}O_{13}N_3$. *See also* Tetrodotoxin.

SPINE—The bony portion of the sting exclusive of the integumentary sheath, venom gland, and other soft tissue.

STING—The osseous spine, integumentary sheath, and accompanying venom glands. The integumentary sheath generally includes the venom glands that are associated with it. This particular definition is in reference to the stings of fishes only. Generally speaking, the term "sting" refers to the complete venom apparatus of the organism.

STINGING—The act of introducing venom into the flesh of a victim by means of a venom apparatus. *See also* Envenom.

STRIATOXIN—A potent cardiotonic glycoprotein isolated from the venom of *Conus striatus.*

SUBERITIN—A term proposed to designate a toxic substance derived from the marine sponge *Suberites domunculus,* which when injected into dogs produces intestinal hemorrhages and respiratory distress. The chemical nature of the poison has not been defined.

SURUGATOXIN—A poison obtained from the Japanese ivory shell, *Babylonia japonica,* having an empircal formula of $C_{25}H_{26}BrN_5O_{13}7H_2O$; it produces mydriasis in laboratory animals. It is also toxic to humans.

SYGUATERA—One of several spellings of the term ciguatera. This term is now obsolete.

TARICHATOXIN—The potent neurotoxin that occurs in the California newt *Taricha torosa.* The term "tarichatoxin" was first applied to this newt poison, but the poison is now known to be identical to tetrodotoxin. *See also* Tetrodotoxin.

TESSULATOXIN—A protein toxin isolated from the venom of *Conus tessulatus* and found to have potent vasocontractive properties.

TETRAMINE—A term proposed for $N(CH_3)_4OH$, tetramethylammonium hydroxide, which was isolated as a toxic fraction from the sea anemone *Actinia equina.*

TETRAODONTOXIN—This term was proposed as a substitute for "tetrodotoxin" since the name

TETRAODONTOXIN—(cont.)
of the fish was "tetraodon," but the term has never found acceptance, and since tetrodotoxin is so firmly entrenched in the literature, the term tetraodontoxin has been discarded.

TETRODOTOXIN—The term proposed for the pure crystalline puffer poison. It is also called fugu or puffer toxin. Although improperly spelled, the term "tetrodotoxin" has become widely adopted and is now deeply entrenched in biotoxicological literature. It is the pure crystalline puffer poison derived originally from fish of the genus *Tetraodon*, but has since been found in a large number of other organisims including gastropods, fishes, octopuses, reef crabs, flatworms, horseshoe crabs, salamanders, frogs, algae, and bacteria. The molecular formula is $C_{11}H_{17}O_8N_3 \pm YH_2O$. *See also* Tetraodontoxin.

THALASSIN—A term proposed to designate a toxic compound derived from the tentacles of *Anemonia sulcata*. The substance when injected into dogs was found to produce allergic symptoms.

TJAKALANG POISONING—A synonym of scombroid poisoning. *See* Scombroid Fish Poisoning.

TOMEA—The Tahitian term for scombroid poisoning.

TOXICOLOGY—The science that treats of poisons (regardless of their origins), their effects, their detection, and treatment of the conditions that they produce.

TOXIGENESIS—The process of poison production. *See also* Biogenesis, and Biosynthesis.

TOXIN—Any poisonous substances of microbic, mineral, vegetable, or animal origin. There is some disagreement in the use of this term since, in the older and strictest sense, toxins are more or less unstable, do not cause symptoms of intoxication until after a period of incubation, and are antigenic. However, in modern usage the terms "toxin," "toxicology," and "toxic" have been widely adopted to designate inorganic and organic poisonous substances having a vast array of chemical and biological properties. The term toxin has also been used interchangeably with venom.

TOXINOLOGY—a term proposed by the International Society of Toxinology to designate biological poisons or biotoxins. Because of the confusion that exists between the terms "toxicology" and "toxinology," the term "biotoxicology" is recommended since it clearly designates the biological origin of the poison, whereas "toxinology" does not.

TRANSVECTOR—An organism that serves as a purveyor or transmitter of a poison that is not generated within its body but is obtained from another source. A typical example would be the mussel *Mytilus*, which serves as a transvector of paralytic shellfish poison derived from the dinoflagellate *Gonyaulax*.

TRUNCULOPURPURINE—A term used to designate the form of purpurine now called murexine, obtained from the median zone of the hypobranchial gland of *Murex trunculus*.

VENERUPIN—The toxic principle believed to be an amine found in certain Japanese pelecypods, which were formerly placed under the genus *Venerupis*. This toxin is entirely distinct from paralytic shellfish poison found in other types of bivalves. the exact chemical nature of the toxin is unknown. The poison is now believed to originate with a dinoflagellate (*Prorocentrum* sp?), which is ingested by the shellfish in a manner similar to paralytic shellfish poisoning.

VENERUPIN SHELLFISH POISONING (VSP)—An organotropic form of shellfish poisoning resulting from the ingestion of oysters (*Crassostrea gigas*) or asari (*Tapes semidecussata*) from certain areas of Japan. The exact chemical nature of the poison is unknown but is believed to be an amine. *See also* Venerupin.

VENOM—The poison secreted by a specialized venom gland of the venom apparatus of an animal. Venoms are usually a large molecular protein or are in association with a protein that may serve as a carrier; but it is becoming increasingly obvious that there may be exceptions to this generalization.

VENOM APPARATUS—The traumatogenic device, venom gland, and accessory organs directly concerned with the production and transmission of a venom.

VENOMOUS ANIMAL—An animal that is equipped with a traumatogenic device, i.e., a spine, tooth, nematocyst, etc., and a poison or venom gland, and associated accessory organs capable of introducing the venom into the flesh of the victim and thereby producing an envenomation.

WHELK POISONING—A form of intoxication resulting from the ingestion of whelks, members of the mollusk family Buccinidae. The poison is localized in the salivary gland of the mollusk, and the principal ingredient is believed to be tetramine.

YESSOTOXIN—One of the dinoflagellate poisons present in the Japanese scallop *Patinopectin yessoensis*, which causes diarrhetic shellfish poisoning. The molecular formula is $C_{55}H_{80}O_2Na_2$. *See also* Diarrhetic Shellfish Poisoning.

# APPENDIX IV

## SUGGESTED READING

AHMED, F. E.
1991 *Seafood Safety*. Institute of Medicine, National Academy of Sciences, Washington, D. C.

ANDERSON, D. M., WHITE, A. W., and D. G. BADEN, eds.
1985 *Toxic Dinoflagellates*. Elsevier Science Publishing Co., Inc. New York.

AUERBACH, P. S. and E. C. GEEHR, eds.
1989 *Management of Wilderness and Environmental Emergencies*. C. V. Mosby Co., St. Louis.

AUERBACH, P. S. and B. W. HALSTEAD
1989 "Hazardous Aquatic Life" in *Management of Wilderness and Environmental Emergencies* (P. S. Auerbach and E. C. Geehr, eds.). 2nd ed. C. V. Mosby Co., St. Louis, pp. 933–1028.

BALDRIDGE, H. D.
1974 *Shark Attack*. Berkley Publishing Corp., New York.

BROWN, T. W.
1973 *Sharks—The Search for a Repellant*. Angus and Robertson Publishers, Sydney, Australia.

CARAS, R. A.
1964 *Dangerous to Man: Wild Animals—A Definitive Study of Their Reputed Dangers to Man*. Chilton Books, Philadelphia.
1974 *Venomous Animals of the World*. Prentice-Hall, Inc. Englewood Cliffs.

CASTRO, J. I.
1983 *Sharks of North American Waters*. Texas A & M University Press, College Station.

COPPLESON, V.
1982 *Shark Attack*. Angus and Robertson Publishers, Sydney, Australia.

COVACEVICH, J., DAVIE, P., and J. PEARN, eds.
1987 *Toxic Plants and Animals: A Guide for Australia*. Queensland Museum, S. Brisbane, Australia.

DARWIN, C. R.
1945 *The Voyage of the Beagle*. Reprinted. E. P. Dutton and Co., Inc., New York.

DAVIES, D.
1964 *About Sharks and Shark Attack*. Shuter and Shooter, Pietermaritzburg, S. Africa.

DUNSON, W. A.
1975 *The Biology of Sea Snakes*. University Park Press, Baltimore.

EDMONDS, C.
1976 *Dangerous Marine Animals of the Indo-Pacific Region*. 2nd ed. Wedneil Publications, Newport, Australia.
1984 *Marine Animal Injuries to Man*. Wedneil Publications, Newport, Australia.

EIGENMANN, C. H.
1918 "The Pygidiidae, a Family of South American Catfishes," *Mem. Carn. Mus.* 7(5): 259–392.

EIGENMANN, C. H. and W. R. ALLEN
1942 *Fishes of Western South America*. The University of Kentucky, Lexington.

EVANS, H. M.
1943 *Stingfish and Seafarer*. Faber and Faber, Ltd., London.

GILBERT, P. W., ed.
1963 *Sharks and Survival*. D. C. Heath and Company, Boston.

GOPALAKRISHNAKKONE, P., and C. K. TAN, eds.
1987 *Progress in Venom and Toxin Research*. National University of Singapore, Republic of Singapore.

GRANÉLI, E., SUNDSTROM, B., EDLER, L., and D. M. ANDERSEN
1990 *Toxic Marine Phytoplankton*. Elsevier, New York.

GUDGER, E. W.
1930 "On the Alleged Penetration of the Human Urethra by an Amazonian Catfish Called Candirú," *Amer. J. Surg.* 8(1): 170–188; 8(2): 443–457.

HALL, S. and G. STRICHARTZ, eds.
1990 *Marine Toxins. Origin, Structure, and Molecular Pharmacology*. American Chemical Society, Washington, D.C.

HALSTEAD, B. W.
1965 *Poisonous and Venomous Marine Animals of the World*. U.S. Government Printing Office, Washington, D.C. vol. 1.
1967 ibid. vol. 2.
1970 ibid. vol. 3.
1978 *Poisonous and Venomous Marine Animals of the World*. rev. ed. Darwin Press, Inc., Princeton.
1980 *Dangerous Marine Animals*. Cornell Maritime Press, Centerville.
1988 *Poisonous and Venomous Marine Animals of the World*. 2nd rev. ed. Darwin Press, Inc., Princeton.

HALSTEAD, B. W., AUERBACH, P. S., and D. CAMPBELL
1990 *A Colour Atlas of Dangerous Marine Animals*. Wolfe Medical Publications Ltd., London.

HASHIMOTO, Y.
1979 *Marine Toxins and Other Bioactive Marine Metabolites*. Japan Scientific Societies Press, Tokyo, Japan.

JOBERT, C.
 1898  "Sur da Prétendue Penétration de uréthre Poissons daris l'uréthre," *Arch. Parasitologie* (Paris) 1: 493–502.

JORDAN, D. S.
 1905  *The Study of Fishes.* Henry Holt and Company, New York, vols. 1 and 2.

KEELER, R. F. and A. T. TU, eds.
 1983  *Handbook of Natural Toxins: Plants and Fungal Toxins.* Marcel Dekker, Inc., New York.

LOCICERO, V. R., ed.
 1975  *Proceedings of the First International Conference on Toxic Dinoflagellate Blooms.* Massachusetts Science and Technology Foundation, Wakefield, Mass.

MANDOJANA, R. M., ed.
 1987  *Aquatic Dermatology.* J. B. Lippincott Co., Philadelphia. 5(3): 1–173.

MILLER, D. M.
 1991  *Ciguatera Seafood Toxins.* CRC Press, Boca Raton.

MYERS, C. W. and J. W. DALY
 1976  "Dart-poison Frogs," *Bull. Amer. Mus. Nat. Hist.* 157(3): 175–262.

OHSAKA, A., HAYASHI, K., and Y. SAWAI, eds.
 1976a *Animal, Plant and Microbial Toxins: Biochemistry, Pharmacology and Immunology.* Plenum Press, New York, vol. 1.
 1976b *Animal, Plant and Microbial Toxins: Biochemistry, Pharmacology and Immunology.* Plenum Press, New York. vol. 2.

RAGELIS, E. P., ed.
 1984  *Seafood Toxins.* American Chemical Society. Washington, D.C.

RUSSELL, F. E.
 1971  *Poisonous Marine Animals.* T.F.H. Publishing, Inc. Neptune City.
 1980  *Snake Venom Poisoning.* J. B. Lippincott Co., Philadelphia.

RUSSELL, F. E. and N. B. EGEN
 1991  "Ciguatera Fishes, Ciguatoxin (CTX) and Ciguatera Poisoning," *J. Toxicol. Toxin Reviews* 10(1): 37–62.

RUSSELL, F. E., GONZALEZ, H., DOBSON, S. B., and J. A. COATS
 1984  *Bibliography of Venomous and Poisonous Marine Animals and Their Toxins.* Office of Naval Research, U. S. Government Printing Office, Washington, D.C.

SMITH, M.
 1926  *Monograph of the Sea-snakes.* British Museum, London.

SMITINAND, T. and W. R. SCHEIBLE
 1966  *Edible and Poisonous Plants and Animals of Thailand.* Joint Thai-U.S. Military Research and Development Center, Bangkok, Thailand.

SPRINGER, V. G. and J. P. GOLD
 1989  *Sharks in Question: The Smithsonian Answer Book.* Smithsonian Institution Press, Washington, D.C.

STRAUSS, R. H., ed.
 1976  *Diving Medicine.* Grune and Stratton, New York.

SUTHERLAND, S. K.
 1983  *Australian Animal Toxins: The Creatures, Their Toxins and Care of the Poisoned Patient.* Oxford University Press, Melbourne, Australia.

TAYLOR, D. L. and H. H. SELIGER, eds.
 1979  *Toxic Dinoflagellate Blooms.* Elsevier/North-Holland, New York, vol. 1.

TU, A. T.
 1977  *Venoms: Chemistry and Molecular Biology.* John Wiley & Sons, Inc., New York.

TU, A. T., ed.
 1984  *Handbook of Natural Toxins: Insect Poisons, Allergens, and Other Invertebrate Venoms.* Marcel Dekker, Inc., New York. vol. 2.
 1988  *Handbook of Natural Toxins: Marine Toxins and Venoms.* Marcel Dekker, Inc., New York. vol. 3.

WU, C. H.
 1984  "Electric Fish and the Discovery of Animal Electricity," *Am. Sci.* 72(6): 598–607.

ZAHURANEC, B. J., ed.
 1983  *Shark Repellents from the Sea: New Perspectives.* Westview Press, Inc., Boulder, Colorado.

**Further Reading**

For information on continuing research in the field of toxicology, the reader is referred to the journal *Toxicon*, published by Pergamon Press (Oxford, United Kingdom), and *The Journal of Natural Toxins*, Alaken, Inc. (Fort Collins, Colorado).